marine designs

Serving the amateur boatbuilder since 1953

Dear Friend:

If you thought the boat of your dreams was out of reach, we hope this catalog will change your mind. Every year, thousands of amateurs much like yourself build their own boats the proven GLEN-L way. Most builders *save at least 1/3* and many save 50% *or more* over the price of a factory-built boat. It's easier than you might think, and it can be a rewarding experience. Not only will you get more boat for the money, you'll have a boat that will literally be "*custom made*" to match your needs exactly.

Building your own boat gives you a pride and satisfaction unsurpassed by any other hobby. Your friends and family will truly be amazed when you tell them "I built it myself". Our approach to building your own boat offers personal and financial rewards second to none. By choosing a GLEN-L design, you'll be backed by the leader in the do-it-yourself boatbuilding field. All of our designs were prepared by our own in-house world-known Naval Architects, so you're assured of the professional results you're looking for.

Glen-L designs also come with Full Size Patterns which are a huge time saver. Most designs just come with the lines to scale and you have to redraw them to full size. We believe your time is valuable and have done this for you. Plus, Glen-L plans & patterns come with a 30-day no questions asked guarantee. We believe in our products and want you to be happy.

Once you invest in a set of plans and materials, the journey begins. At Glen-L, we don't believe anyone should "go it alone" so we have set up an online community of other builders and experts to help you along the way. The online Boatbuilder Forum is free and is the place to ask questions, read what others are doing and "talk" to builders and experts. To join in, just click on the link "Boatbuilder Forum" from our home page at www.Glen-L.com.

As you page t   , you will notice that we   space to devote to each design. The front "INFORMATION" section of the catalog is meant to answer questions about our kits and building methods that cannot be covered on each design page. We have tried to arrange boats by type, however, it will become obvious that many boats are not easy to categorize. Power boats can frequently be built with either inboard or outboard power so we have attempted to put these designs where they seemed to be most appropriate. Page through the complete catalog before selecting a design... who knows what you may find.

On each design page there is a black box that will tell you what materials the boat was designed for. Although in some cases it may be possible to build the boat using other materials, *they are only detailed for the materials listed*. We do not do custom design alterations for other materials.

If you do not see the design you are looking for, look for designs that have the hull you want. It is usually possible to alter cabins or other interior arrangements.

Please visit our website www.Glen-L.com for much more information and photos than can be shown here. We are daily adding to our site, so be sure and visit us online today!

Contents

INDEX TO DESIGNS

The letters in parentheses after the design name designate the construction material or method. Keys: A=aluminum, C=cold-molded, F=fiberglass, P=plywood, S=steel, SG= stitch-n-glue, SP=strip plank, ★=new design since previous catalog

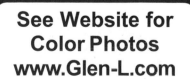

See Website for Color Photos www.Glen-L.com

3

CUSTOMER TESTIMONIALS...

These unsolicited comments were taken from letters written by GLEN-L customers.

"I wish to commend your organization for the excellent plans you provide. I have previously purchased three sets of plans from you and have found their detail and layman's terminology to be a great help...I will eagerly await your new catalog by return mail."

R.W. - IL

"...is to express my appreciation for the accuracy and completeness of the plans and patterns I purchased from you. I have had no problems with its construction in so far as the plans and details have been concerned. Incidentally, several years ago at the age of 41, I suffered a coronary heart attack...and attribute much of the success of my recovery to my boatbuilding project."

H.G.W. - Florida

(ED NOTE: Mr. W. lost his left arm at age 5, and at age 20 lost portions of three fingers of his right hand and yet was able to build a 22' cruiser.)

"I have received your two excellent books and I must confess that I didn't expect such thoroughly good work on your part. These books can really be used in any country, not just in English-spoken ones, because of the photographs and graphic explanation of the boatbuilding process."

P.J. - Yugoslavia

"It's about the sweetest sailing boat I've had the pleasure of sailing! Directions and the plans were very complete to help me with this project."

R.S. - California

"You have been a great company to work with and I have enjoyed building my boat because of your easy-to-read plans."

D.M. - Maryland

"i can't tell you how much it means to an amateur builder to have your kind of talent behind him!"

J.G. - New York

"Glen-L has shown me that there still are companies that care, and act with integrity."

P.A. - Puerto Rico

"Your plans are detailed, the directions clear and well written, and the material specifications would allow us to build from scratch without additional GLEN-L material--if we chose to do so...It's nice to run across a professional company that delivers exactly what it promises."

"The drawings are simply top notch in every respect...without a doubt this is the cornerstone of your business success...It's a pleasure doing business with a company that has pride in its work."

A.P. - Pennsylvania

"Thank you! For your efficiency, honesty and speed - you're great!" R.S. - California

"I am delighted with the way she handled in all conditions...she prompts lots of friendly, admiring questions and comments. Best wishes!"

G.R.D. - NJ

"Twenty one years ago...and it has been in the water seven months every year. This boat has given us (my family) so much pleasure all these years and is still such an eye catcher and is still in very sound shape. That is why I'm writing you after deciding to build another boat."

R.B. - Pennsylvania

"I and my friend are 15 years old and built the boat for a class project. I like the boat very much and it looks great."

J.S. - Colorodo

"I can't tell you how much it means to an amateur builder to have your kind of talent behind him!"

J.G. - New York

**For more customer testimonials, please see our website:
www.BoatDesigns.com**

QUESTIONS & ANSWERS

Q. Can I build my own boat?

A. Building your own boat is less a matter of skill than of determination. People who don't finish boats quit. Not because of difficulty, but because they don't feel like doing it any more. We have seen people with physical handicaps and with virtually no do-it-yourself skills of any kind, build our boats. You must answer whether *you* can do it. If you really *want* it, and have patience, you can build a boat using GLEN-L plans that will impress even the most critical observer.

Q. What the heck is lofting any-way?

A. Lofting is the process of drawing the hull lines full size from the designer's scale drawings. The intersections of the contours of various horizontal and vertical sections are measured from an imaginary "base line" using an architect's scale. These junctions are then laid out, point by point, in their full size. Because it is difficult to take accurate dimensions from a small drawing, it is necessary to adjust these lines to assure that they are "fair". A listing of these points is called a *table of offsets*. It takes a lot of space to loft. This, along with the difficulty, makes it a daunting task and a real drag to those builders who just want to get at the "wood". All GLEN-L designs have full size patterns... no lofting required.

Q. What tools do I need?

A. It depends on the construction method. For an absolute minimum, Stitch-N-Glue requires the least. If you had no tools, it would require only a minor investment. Other *plywood* boats can be built using ordinary hand and power tools. What is *needed* and what are desirable is not necessarily the same. You will need tools to do the following: make wide boards into straight edged narrow boards. Cut wood into irregular shapes. Bevel wood to a changing angle, drill holes, drive screws, and sand. You will need a lot of clamps. Fiberglass construction requires the same procedures with much more emphasis on sanding.

Q. How long will it take to build my boat?

A. How high is up. No one can answer this question but yourself. It all depends on your ability to do the work. A small Stitch-N-Glue boat can be done in a couple of weeks, but most boats require longer. Few builders work "straight through". Smaller plywood boats can be built in as little as a few weeks, while the very largest boats may take years to complete. Steel and aluminum construction are generally faster than wood. Fiberglass is probably somewhat faster than

plywood, with fiberglass planking being faster than sandwich core. In any case, the GLEN-L methods are specifically intended for the amateur and are designed to save time and prevent errors which can occur when using designs that are "unplanned" or intended for the professional builder.

Q. Can I modify your designs?

A. Yes. Adding special features to your boat is one of the important reasons for building your own. However, any major change which could make the safety or performance of the design questionable should be avoided. Most boats, *except* sailboats, Stitch-N-Glue boats, or boats with a sheer harpin, can be lengthened or shortened by 10%. This is done by respacing the frames a proportional amount. Changing the beam or depth is not usually advised. Please contact us if you anticipate making any major changes.

Q. Do I have to use marine plywood?

A. It depends... Domestic marine and exterior plywood use the same types of wood and glues. The important difference is in the inner plies. In marine plywood, the inner plies butt together without voids (or very small voids), and there are no open knots. Exterior plywood can have both voids between veneers and open knots. The difference between the two is structural. Marine plywood is desirable in the planking where the plywood is being bent. On flat bottom row boats, or other low speed boats, exterior plywood is frequently used. It can also be used in "flat" areas of the hull. We almost never use marine plywood for transoms, stems, floor timbers, or gussets. If you plan to build a high speed boat, we would recommend marine plywood for all planking. When using exterior plywood, we do not recommend using less than "A" or "B" faces (no open knots).

Q. Do I have to use long sheets of plywood on plywood designs?

A. NO. Although many of our plans list sheets longer than eight foot in the Bill of Materials, standard 4'x8' sheets can *always* be used. Plywood can be joined using "butt blocks" or can be "scarfed" together. Details for these methods are given in the plans. On our test models we most often use standard sheets with butt blocks.

Q. Do I have to fiberglass a ply-wood boat? If I fiberglass can I use thinner plywood?

A. NO. NO. Fiberglass is applied to the outside of the boat to protect the surface

and to substatially reduce maintenance. Although it is not necessary, as our shop foreman says, "Anyone who doesn't fiber-glass their boat is crazy". In answer to the second part, the strength in a plywood boat comes from the plywood; fiberglass adds no appreciable strength. It is simply a means of prolonging the life of your boat. Some builders have suggested decreasing the thickness of the plywood and adding additional layers of fiberglass to *cut* weight. This would almost certainly *increase* weight and *reduce* strength.

Q. I'm afraid of fiberglassing, can I really do it?

A. Yes. Fiberglassing is very easy... if you do it right. It isn't practical to try to explain fiberglassing in this small space, however, each fiberglass kit comes with a one page instruction sheet and a cut list. If you feel you want more information, we have a book and a DVD on the subject described under the BOOKS and DVD's sections of this catalog. Undoubtedly, the hardest part of fiberglassing is sanding it for painting.

Q. Will my boat look as good as one of your test models or a production boat?

A. Considering that "look good" is a matter of personal preference, you should be able to make your boat "look" better... if you are willing to spend the time. A good finish is primarily a matter of "elbow grease" and the right choices of colors and accent designs. In our catalog or in magazines, you can get ideas for color and stripes or whatever to give your boat a look that makes it unique and something you will be proud of.

Q. Why should I buy GLEN-L plans instead of someone else's?

A. Not all plans are designed by Naval Architects, or by people who have actually built boats. Many plans do not include full size patterns or instructions. Ours *are* designed by Naval Achitects with years of experience building boats and simplifying building methods so that no matter what size boat you build, it will be made as easy as is practical. *All* plans include full size patterns. With the advent of computer programs that allow "anyone to design a boat", more plans have become available from hobbyists.

Unfortunately computers do not know everything, and they don't write instructions. While there are other good plans available... from GLEN-L you *know* what you will be getting, and you will be dealing with people who are here to answer your questions.

PLANS & PATTERNS

GLEN-L has set the standard for boat plans for over half a century. All of our plans are intended for the amateur. It is not necessary that you have any experience with blueprints. Our plans are easy to read and easy to understand. You can find plans that sell for more, but they frequently offer much less. It is unlikely that you will find plan packages as complete as ours at any price.

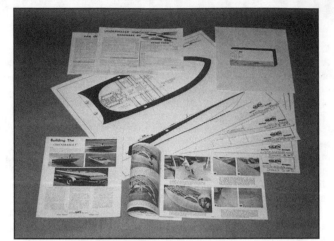

Here's a typical example of a set of PLANS for a GLEN-L design. They cover all phases of the construction of your boat. All PLANS come with FULL SIZE PATTERNS.

WHY ARE FULL SIZE PATTERNS IMPORTANT?

Most novices do not realize that with many boat plans the builder must first "loft", or actually redraw the lines of the hull to full size before he can even begin construction. Learning to loft from an often confusing list of dimensions (Table of Offsets) is a major project in itself. In addition, there are logistical problems in lofting, unless you happen to have a flat floor virtually as long as the boat to do the layout. We at GLEN-L decided many years ago that this process alone was enough to discourage most beginners, and set out to find a better way. The result was the GLEN-L FULL SIZE PATTERN system of boat building. In short, *we* do the lofting, to save you *time, effort*, and to *prevent errors*. It has taken a lot of time and experimentation to develop our pattern methods, but if you have ever tried to build a boat the "old way", we know you'll feel it was worth the effort. Full size patterns are available for every GLEN-L design. As the originator of the pattern systems, we have perfected the methods necessary to insure absolute accuracy so that your GLEN-L design can be duplicated just as the designer intended.

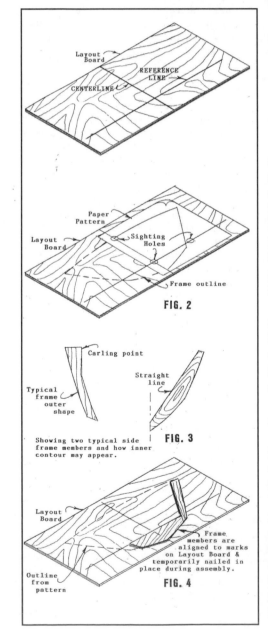

FIG. 2

FIG. 3

Showing two typical side frame members and how inner contour may appear.

FIG. 4

CABIN PATTERNS

What they are....

Full size CABIN PATTERNS are available on selected designs. While all designs with cabins *have* the necessary information and dimensions to build the cabin, the use of CABIN PATTERNS speeds up and simplifies the layout. These patterns are transferred to the wood using the same procedure as described under FULL SIZE PATTERNS.

If CABIN PATTERNS are not available for the design you are building, it is probably because the nature of the cabin structure is so basic that patterns do not offer much benefit.

CABIN PLANS

Several boats in this book have been designed without cabins and CABIN PLANS have later been added in response to builder requests. These plans contain all of the information and dimensions to build the cabin, including instructions. In many cases, the plans will be adaptable to several designs or offer cabin options for a single design. See the description on the design page for specific information.

FASTENING KITS.....

NOTE: FASTENING KITS do NOT include bolts or glue.

Don't waste time, money, and effort scrounging around for the proper marine fastenings to build your GLEN-L design. We've got them in a FASTENING KIT specifically intended for the boat you are building, at a cost that can't be beat. Due to volume purchasing, we are able to offer our FASTENING KITS at a price substantially less than local suppliers.

Most hardware stores don't even stock *silicon bronze* screws, and, of course, it's unlikely that they will even know what a *bronze annular boat nail* is. The FASTENING KIT includes *all* nails and screws in the quantity and size specified in the Bill of Materials for the GLEN-L boat you are building.

- BRONZE screws are genuine *silicon* bronze as recommended by the experts; not low-strength brass which will tend to break even in the softest woods. Our screws feature frearson heads for easy, fast machine driving.

- The nails used in our FASTENING KITS are high quality *silicon bronze annular thread boat nails*. This is the only type of nail we supply with our Kits.

- BRONZE KITS: The *ultimate* choice in quality and corrosion resistance. Use on boats that will remain in salt or brackish waters. The extra cost is usually repaid with higher resale value.

STITCH-N-GLUE KITS

A *must* for building our Stitch-N-Glue boats; much more than a fastening kit. Includes copper stitching wire, screws, bolts, and boat nail fasteners (if required), silica and microspheres fillers, fiberglass tape for inside laminates, plus POXY-SHIELD epoxy resin for gluing, making fillets, encapsulating the interior, and applying interior laminates. Each kit is specifically intended for the Stitch-N-Glue boat you are building.

For many designs there are two kits available: A and B. The A Kit is the less expensive. This kit includes the materials described above and is meant to be used in conjunction with the Fiberglass Covering Kit. Kit B is used when

you do *not* intend to fiberglass the outside. In addition to the material in the A Kit, tape and resin is supplied to tape the outside seams. *Note: It is always necessary to have fiberglass on both the inside and outside of planking junctions. Since most boats are fiberglassed, the Fiberglass Kit frequently supplies only the outside lamination. If you do not fiberglass the outside, you* must *use the B Stitch-N-Glue Kit if there are A and B options.*

Order with the fiberglass covering kit that contains material for the outside of the boat. Stitch-N-Glue Kits *do not* include plans and patterns.

Our Stitch-N-Glue 9-1/2' Glass Bottom Boat.

FIBERGLASS COVERING KITS.....

GLEN-L FIBERGLASS COVERING KITS..... WHAT THEY CONTAIN.....

Every FIBERGLASS COVERING KIT is a complete package specifically prepared for the GLEN-L design you are building, including:

- Top quality fiberglass cloth specially treated for easy wet-out, high bonding adhesion, and superior peel strength.
- POXY-SHIELD Epoxy resin specially formulated for use by amateurs in ample amounts to cover the cloth.
- Proper types and amounts of hardener to cure the resin.
- Application tools specifically for use with fiberglass and resin, including rollers, brushes, and squeegees.
- Special cutting instructions on how to utilize the materials.
- Step-by-step procedural application instructions for professional results.

Because of our bulk quantity purchasing direct from raw material suppliers, we can offer these kits at the **LOWEST PRICE**. Why waste time, money, and effort attempting to locate these special materials when we've already got them in handy kits.

ABOUT THE RESIN USED IN OUR FIBERGLASS COVERING KITS.....

Kits contain our specially formulated **POXY-SHIELD EPOXY RESIN**. You won't find these resins in any stores. **POXY-SHIELD** is formulated to our exact specifications to be easy for amateurs to achieve professional results. Because we sell in high volume, you're assured of fresh stock with a long shelf life. By dealing directly with raw material suppliers, the "middleman" is eliminated. The cost savings is passed on to you.

EPOXY RESIN: For *ultimate* strength and protection, EPOXY is unsurpassed. Bond strength is superior to polyester, yet the epoxy resin retains a flexibility not possible with other resins. Although more costly, the added cost is often recouped by higher resale value. If you want the longest life from your boat, there is no substitute for EPOXY.

UNFAMILIAR WITH FIBERGLASS WORK?

Many beginners are hesitant about working with fiberglass and resins. Actually, the work is easier than most people think. But to do the job properly does require following instructions and doing a little reading to get the most from the products while avoiding the pitfalls. That's why we offer a DVD and several texts specially prepared by our staff of Naval Architects specifically intended for the amateur. They include:

- **How to Fiberglass Boats**
- **Fiberglass Boatbuilding for Amateurs**
- **Glen-L Epoxy System Technical Manual**
- **How to Fiberglass a Boat (DVD)**

All of these texts and the DVD are described elsewhere to help you determine which is most suited to your needs.

NOTE: FIBERGLASS COVERING KITS are used only on WOOD or PLYWOOD designs; not on FIBERGLASS or STEEL designs.

SAILBOAT ACCESSORY KITS

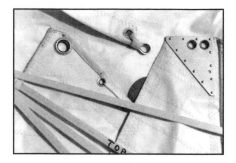

Many of our sailboat builders don't realize that we have accessories for the boat they are building. In addition to Fastening Kits and Fiberglass Covering Kits, we offer SAILS, RIGGING KITS and HARDWARE for many of our sailboat designs. Kits that save you money and eliminate the effort and time to find the right materials.

HARDWARE KITS

...Hardware kits supply the blocks, gooseneck, eye straps, cleats, gudgeons and pintles, and many other hardware items you will need to make your boat work. GLEN-L has assembled Hardware kits that offer value and convenience.

SAILS

...Our sails come in classic white dacron with hand sewn detailing that sets them off from all but the most expensive custom sails. Why spend your valuable building time shopping for a sail maker, only to pay more, when you could order your sails from the people who know the most about your boat?

RIGGING KITS

...The term rigging is often misunderstood by novice sailors. Standing rigging is what holds the spar (mast) up. Our standing rigging consists of high quality stainless steel wire rope with various stainless eyes, jaws, toggles or turnbuckles "swaged" on the ends as required by the design. Swaging is a very strong and clean method of attaching fittings to wire rope. Our Rigging Kits also include the running rigging, the finest polyester yacht braided line, used to control the sails and haul them up the mast.

It is impossible to fully explain the contents of the kits with all the variations in this small space, therefore we suggest that you refer to the website for further details. If you have any questions, give us a call.

BUILDING METHODS

PLYWOOD

For most amateurs, plywood is the material of choice. Plywood is a building material that the average do-it-yourselfer is both familiar and comfortable with. Plywood is also, pound for pound, stronger than steel. Because of its high strength to weight, plywood construction yields a boat that is much lighter and performs better than a "chopper gun" fiberglass boat. When used with the GLEN-L Fiberglass Covering Kit, plywood is as long lasting and as low in maintenance as any other material. No exotic tools are required, and with the possible exception of enough "C"-clamps, plywood boats can be built with the tools in the average home workshop. To take full advantage of the material, our PLANS and PATTERNS detail simplified construction methods geared to the abilities of the amateur. No difficult woodworking procedures, such as steam bending, are ever required, and the GLEN-L pattern system makes the difficult lofting procedure unnecessary.

Plywood is used as a "sheet" material in the majority of plywood boats, including Stitch-N-Glue. Plywood is also used in "cold-molded" construction and "multi-diagonal" planking. On each design page the method is listed under "Hull" in Characteristics.

SHEET PLYWOOD: This is the most common type of construction used by the home builder. Plywood is used in panels of one or two layers. This requires a minimum of cutting and fitting and requires much fewer frames than most "traditional"

planking methods. Stitch-N-Glue also uses sheet plywood. (see Stitch-N-Glue section).

COLD-MOLDED or MULTI-DIAGONAL: This method is utilized on round bilge hulls or hulls with compound shapes. The method involves cutting the ply-

wood into strips (widths vary depending on curve), and laying up layers at angles to each other, glued and fastened. Epoxy is the recommended adhesive.

Typically, plywood boat construction would follow these steps:

1. Layout, cut, and assemble frames.

2. Make building form, position frames on form.

3. Install "longitudinals", those long pieces that run from front to back: keel, chine, sheer, and battens.

4. "Fair" longitudinals and frames so that plywood will mate on flat surfaces where it will be glued and fastened.

5. Fit and install planking.

6. Fill screw holes, etc, and sand.

7. Fiberglass and paint.

8. Finished hull of the Glen-L Thunderbolt. Enjoy the fruit of your labor and the pride of being able to say, "I built it myself"!

STITCH-N-GLUE PLYWOOD

This *quick and easy* boatbuilding method consists of plywood planking panels cut to shape from full-size patterns which are "stitched" and "glued" together at the seams. Such a boat can be assembled in a matter of hours after cutting out the parts.

The stitching is done with short lengths of copper wire passed through small holes along seam edges. These are twisted together to hold the panels together. The glue is an epoxy putty formed in a cove-shaped fillet along the seams, usually on the inside. The stitched and glued seam is then covered with strips of resin-coated fiberglass tape inside and out.

Just about anybody can build a boat using the GLEN-L STITCH-N-GLUE system. This method eliminates many members that ordinarily require fitting, fairing, and bevelling. Thus, it's *ideal for beginners*. A hand saber saw and drill are about the only power tools required. The resulting boat is *incredibly light- weight, strong, and durable.*

Plans packages for Stitch-N-Glue designs include instructions, material layouts, and material listings. In addition, the FULL SIZE PATTERNS provided with most Stitch-N-Glue designs are precise since they're taken from the actual panels used to build our prototype boats. All patterns are reproduced either as full or symmetrical half-section patterns, and most include *all* planking members.

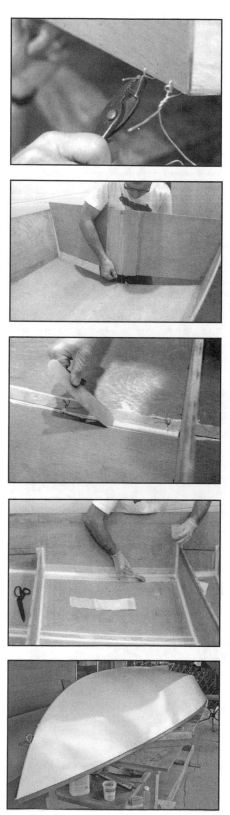

Bull's-Eye Stitch-N-Glue sailboat

FAST-G

FAST-G....**F**old **A**nd **S**titch **T**hen **G**lue. *FAST-G* was developed to make Stitch-N-Glue building of a vee bottomed boat easier. Remember when you were a kid in school? The map of the world, even though it is round, was shown flat on the pages of the geography book with various gores of cut outs. Essentially, that is what we've done. The planking is assembled flat on the ground. Then the boat is *folded* together to form the vee bottom hull. *FAST-G* PLANS and PATTERNS supply templates for all planking. Since the panels are developed for sheet material, the planking folds readily into shape without undue effort. Final stitching, filleting, and finishing is done the same as on our other Stitch-N-Glue designs.

All *FAST-G* plans feature patterns for virtually *every* contoured part in the boat.....and that's a lot of templates.

FIBERGLASS CONSTRUCTION

From time to time new boatbuilding methods are touted as a breakthrough in boat construction. We have by-passed many of these "breakthroughs" because we don't believe in experimenting with your time and money. There have been several such methods of fiberglass construction that have proven to be less than advertised or not suited to the production of one boat.

Factory made fiberglass boats utilize a female mold with laminates made of sprayed resin and chopped glass fibers or, in more expensive boats, hand laid fiberglass and resin. These methods are only suitable for volume production due to the high cost of the mold.

Our methods make it practical to produce a single boat using fiberglass materials. GLEN-L has done a great deal of research into the various options for "one-off" construction. This research has resulted in our 400 page book: FIBERGLASS BOATBUILDING FOR AMATEURS. It has also produced several designs which are detailed in our design pages.

There are two types of one-off construction detailed in our plans; sandwich core and fiberglass planking (C-FLEX). By using either of these methods you can produce a fiberglass boat that is equal to or exceeds the quality of factory-built boats. Using these materials is well within the abilities of the amateur, even those who have never built a boat before. The GLEN-L methods are especially designed with you, the amateur, in mind.

In these photographs, we use the FOAMEE to illustrate the sandwich core construction method, and the FEATHER to illustrate the C-FLEX method. These boats were designed to give you an introduction to the one-off methods.

FIBERGLASS PLANKING (C-FLEX) METHOD

Closely spaced forms and a few battens make up the male mold. The C-Flex is unrolled and cut with heavy shears.

The planking strips are laid on the form and fastened in place. The material forms easily to contoured shapes.

Fiberglass laminate is built up over the fiberglass planking to form a stiff, strong hull.

The hull is sanded and removed from the mold and the interior laminates applied.

SANDWICH CORE CONSTRUCTION METHOD

Widely spaced forms with closely spaced longitudinal battens make up the mold.

The easily shaped PVC foam is heated, bent to shape, and fastened to the mold. Balsa core does not require heating.

The outer laminate is built up over the foam, faired, and sanded.

The hull is removed from the frame and supported in a cradle. The inner laminates are then applied.

PLEASE NOTE: While we are enthusiastic about these one-off fiberglass methods, in order to be properly utilized, the boat must be specifically designed for the materials. We have designs which are specially adapted to these methods and have detailed them accordingly. We do NOT recommend building our other designs using one of these methods unless they are specifically intended for fiberglass construction. Our plans detail clearly the best method for building each particular boat. To protect your investment and have a boat you'll be proud of, avoid improvising.

BUILDING IN STEEL

ALUMINUM

Steel is an excellent boatbuilding material, proven in use worldwide. However, due to the relatively high weight compared to other boatbuilding materials, and the care required in the design stage with regard to hull development, structural integrity, stability, and balance, the plans used to build a steel boat should be intended specifically for use with this material. Using plans for a design intended for some other material and converting it to steel should not be done, at least without careful (and usually costly) redesign by a qualified naval architect. That's why GLEN-L has developed a series of low cost stock designs intended for steel construction.

For the amateur boatbuilder who has knowledge of proper weld types and welding sequences, together with the necessary electric and gas welding skills, steel is an ideal material. On a cost-per-square-foot basis, steel is probably the cheapest of all boatbuilding materials. Construction is simple when using the building methods specified in GLEN-L plans, and faster than just about any other boatbuilding material. No special shelters or structures are required, and the materials are readily available just about anywhere without special order. For strength, steel is just about tops in all respects. Repairs and modifications can be easily made anywhere in the world as long as a welding set is available.

Even if you don't know how to weld, acquiring the necessary welding skills is relatively quick and easy. Numerous welding schools and classes are available in most areas, either through public school systems or through private trade schools. As for applying these skills to steel boatbuilding, we recommend you obtain one of the several texts on the subject.

To further put steel boatbuilding within the realm of the amateur, *all* GLEN-L steel boat plans include our comprehensive STEEL BOATBUILDING MANUAL to supplement the plans and abilities of the builder. This general instruction manual discusses the various building procedures and options for setting up, proper hull assembly sequence, welding recommendations, tank construction, insulating methods and materials, joinerywork, electrical, finish-

ing, and much more. To enable the builder to fabricate many of the usual "store bought" parts, the plans are further supplemented by numerous detail sheets showing hatch construction, rail details, rudder fittings, shaft tube and stern bearings, mast steps, chainplates, deck details, cabin-hull junctions, and joinery details.

Full size patterns mean even faster construction since no lofting is necessary. For those who desire to loft their boats, however, a Table of Offsets is also provided. And of course, our comprehensive plans include all the typical information you'd expect to find in a GLEN-L plan set. They cover all aspects of the design including structural views and sections, scantlings, cabin construction, joinery arrangements, tank configurations, engine placements, rudders and underwater fittings, and spars on sailboat designs. In short, you get everything you need in the way of information to build your very own steel boat, and at a low price! That's why at GLEN-L we mean it when we say, "You get custom design quality at low stock plan prices."

TO ESTIMATE THE COST OF YOUR STEEL HULL....

The steel used is normally mild (plain low carbon) steel of welding quality, although corrosion-resistant grades, such as "Cor-Ten" (a trade name) are optional, but more expensive and hard to work. Steel is usually sold in quantity by weight. That's why for each steel design we provide an estimate of the weight of the steel hull components. Simply use this figure times the cost of steel per pound in your area to arrive at a reasonable estimate for hull material costs.

Glen-L UNION JACK, a 31' Steel Cruising Yacht

Aluminum is also a superb material for boatbuilding by the person qualified in aluminum welding. Aluminum boats using welded marine alloy construction are strong, lightweight, durable, and easy to maintain. As with steel, the designs should be specifically intended for this material.

Plans listed for aluminum construction include all the details necessary to build the boat in sheet aluminum. As with all our designs, they include FULL-SIZE PATTERNS so that no lofting is required. In addition, all aluminum designs include our comprehensive ALUMINUM BOATBUILDING GUIDE as well as a hull material listing. See our "Boatbuilding & Marine Supplies" catalog for additional publications on aluminum construction.

TO ESTIMATE THE COST OF YOUR ALUMINUM HULL....

The following can be used as a general guideline for selecting materials. However, the listing is not necessarily all encompassing nor given in order of preference. To figure hull cost, use weight of hull times cost per pound.

COMPONENTS & MATERIAL

Hull plating and decking
    5052-H32 to H36
    5086-H32, H34, H112 or H116
    5456-H116

Framing
    5052-H32 to H36
    5086-H32, H34, H112, or H116
    5050-H34 or H36
    5456-H116, 6061-T6

Extrusions
    6061-T4 or T6, 5086
    5052, 6061-T6

Piping
    6063-T6, 5456-H116

NOTES ON PRECEEDING:
When buying aluminum sheet or plate goods, the terminology "sheet" refers to material of .188" or less (nominally 3/16" or thinner), while the terminology "plate" refers to material .25" (1/4") or more.

BUILDING IN SHRINK-WRAP STEEL

This admittedly low-tech and forgiving variation on steel boatbuilding is ideal for the short-handed do-it-yourself boatbuilder who can weld, and who wants a small steel boat that will look great. While in use, the process looks much like any other steel boat in progress. But we've perfected some novel techniques making construction quicker and more accurate. At the same time our methods allow the use of thinner plates than is typical so that the work is easier and the completed boats are not too heavy. Finally, our SHRINK-WRAP methods assure super-smooth, fair surfaces virtually free of welding distortion. The need for surface fairing and filling compounds becomes largely unnecessary. As these photos show, final hull surfaces end up so fair that they might be confused with a molded fiberglass boat. SHRINK-WRAP methods are used for all our steel MINI-TUGBOAT designs: SWEET 16, GOLIATH, TITAN & FRED MURPHY. The photos below show the shrink-wrap steel boatbuilding method in progress building the FRED MURPHY design.

Fig 1 - Hull is built upside down over light frame having straight line contours between sheer and chine, and chine and keel. Round bars back up longitudinal junctions at chines and sheer.

Fig 2 - Flat bar longitudinal stiffeners are bent around and notched into frames, but not welded. Thin "door-skin" plywood is used to make templates of plating areas because they are lightweight and easy to fit with accuracy. Once cut, these are traced around over the plates which are then cut and welded in place around perimeters.

Fig 3 - Note the smooth hull surfaces. Panels are welded only around perimeters at this stage. Interior welding largely takes place after righting the hull.

Fig 4 - Righting a hull is not as difficult as many think. Most attention has to be paid to letting the hull down in the right side up position. A chain hoist, fork lift, light crane or similar means is helpful in this regard.

Fig 5 - Flat bar stiffeners previously in place are now bent to the plating from inside and lightly welded to it. Stiffeners are in turn lightly welded to the frame. But frames are NOT welded to the plating. The result is fair, smooth plating surfaces as the next photo shows.

Fig 6 - Completed FRED MURPHY - the hull is so fair you'd never guess it was a welded steel boat.

"HOW-TO" DVD's

HOW TO FIBERGLASS A BOAT DVD
1 hour 30 minute DVD   #16-100
Book/DVD Combination:#16-037

Learn how to fiberglass the easy way, by looking over the shoulder of an expert who is working on actual boats. This DVD can easily pay for itself by preventing mistakes that can waste expensive fiberglassing materials.

HOW TO FIBERGLASS A BOAT explains the process of covering a boat with fiberglass using epoxy and polyester resins, applied by both "wet" and "dry" methods. The DVD shows in a few scenes what may take pages of written text to explain. The scenes showing cloth application and smoothing out the inevitable wrinkles and air bubbles illustrate how easy the task can be when you know the "tricks". The section on making and using resin-putty will be of special interest to Stitch-N-Glue boatbuilders as will the detailed explanations and views of taping seams with standard and biaxial fiberglass.

SPECIAL PRICE
HOW TO FIBERGLASS BOATS
Book *Plus*
"HOW TO FIBERGLASS A BOAT"
DVD Combination
#16-037

STITCH AND GLUE BOATBUILDING DVD
1 hour 25 minute DVD   #16-101

The STITCH and GLUE BOATBUILDING DVD pulls the curtain and exposes the what's, why's, and how's of this novel boatbuilding method. With straight forward narration explaining the procedures, see how the average Joe or Jane can build a boat even though their abilities and tools may be limited. This is a compilation of proven methods and ideas on Stitch-N-Glue boatbuilding gleaned from building craft of various types.

The DVD starts with an explanation of Stitch-N-Glue methods and a series of completed boats in action. If the views of these beautiful boats don't start the boatbuilding urge, nothing will. After the introduction, you're taken through the processes of Stitch-N-Glue boatbuilding. Every phase of the subject is explored ...in detail.

This DVD will show that building your own boat is not a far-fetched dream, but can be a reality. STITCH AND GLUE BOATBUILDING should convince you that this method requires only rudimentary tools and skills, and that even the rankest amateur can produce a professional looking, quality boat.

BUILDING THE CONSOLE SKIFF DVD
30 minute DVD   #16-102

This DVD will take you through building the 15' 9" GLEN-L CONSOLE SKIFF from duplicating the patterns to the wood, through building the console. Each phase of building the prototype is shown and explained. See the boat planking spread on the ground, and then folded together to form the hull. See the nitty-gritty of resin putty fillet and fiberglass reinforcement application. And while you watch, listen to the detailed explanation of the little tricks that make boatbuilding with Fast-G Stitch-N-Glue methods even easier.

Includes numerous action views of the boat in the water, idling, at speed, interior views of the bright mahogany trim, attractive upholstered seats, finished console, and large walk-around cockpit. We've also included a group of action photos of a half dozen other Glen-L Stitch-N-Glue boats you can build.

This DVD is ideal for the person who contemplates building the CONSOLE SKIFF or CABIN SKIFF (the hulls are similar), but wants to know more about the construction. In fact, anyone contemplating construction of any Stitch-N-Glue boat will benefit. The person building the CONSOLE or CABIN SKIFF will find viewing the progressive building process and detailed explanation a valuable supplement to the Plans and Patterns.

Glen-L.com

15

THE ELECTRIC BOAT PART I ...an overview
45 minute DVD   **#16-105**

Did you know electric powered boats were popular in the late 1800's; that they can reach speeds in the 70 MPH bracket; that they have probably the most environmentally friendly boat propulsion system? Learn all about these craft in THE ELECTRIC BOAT-PART I, a general overview of electric boats, their propulsion systems, and how they work.

The DVD begins with a brief history of electric boats and the general hull lines of such craft and the various motors and drive systems that are used. You will be shown: How the speed is controlled using the electronic "black box" controller and a potentiometer or simple dial. How direction is controlled manually or electronically.

Basic formulas are given to find boat speed, battery duration, voltage versus amperage, along with discussions of wiring and multiple battery bank diagrams. Also covered are electrical vehicle batteries, types of cable and wires, crimping cable ring eyes, and series connections, battery chargers as well as the helm control consoles and instrumentation used on electric boats.

THE ELECTRIC BOAT PART II ...how to build three electric boats
47 minute DVD   **#16-106**

The ELECTRIC BOAT-PART II shows and describes building three electric boats using the Stitch-N-Glue method, each with a different drive system.

The first boat shown is the 15' 7" LO VOLTAGE, a striking mahogany deck launch with a central helm console, powered with a surplus golf cart motor and related parts running through the

electric drive (ED). ED uses the lower portion of an outboard motor with the electric motor to make a fully contained drive system that is an integral part of the boat and pivots for steering. The DVD illustrates how easy ED is to make and its feasibility to power most boats.

The second featured craft is the 13' 7" AMP EATER, a four place open utility launch powered with an inboard mounted 1/2 HP electric inboard motor, belt driven by a prop, with shaft running through an underwater skeg. Details on how the boat is built, the propulsion system installed, and how the electronic system controls the motor speed and direction of rotation are all shown.

The 17' POWERYAK is a two passenger kayak powered with an electric trolling motor (ETM) converted and modified, with the submerged powerhead projecting through the boat bottom and the tiller/control separated and mounted forward. Building the ETM motor mount and control bracket is shown and described in detail as is each facet of building the boat.

If you want to know more about electric boats, how to build the boat and related drives, both DVD's are a must for your DVD library.

BUILDING THE EIGHT BALL-SG DVD
30 minute DVD   **#16-104**

This DVD is the perfect companion to the EIGHT BALL-SG plans and patterns package. And, it's an ideal way to give the individual builder, or a group or organization an overview of the various steps and procedures for building this boat or any Stitch-N-Glue boat. The information to build the EIGHT BALL-SG

is all included in the Plans and Patterns, but many builders find it easier to understand when they can see our boatbuilder's hands actually doing the work. The DVD is also a good way to let distant relatives or others "in" on your project.

This step by step DVD was filmed at Glen-L and shows the actual prototype of the EIGHT BALL-SG being built by our shop foreman. See not only the steps of construction, but the boat being rigged and sailed. The EIGHT BALL-SG is the ideal beginning project and the DVD is the ideal way to get your "creative juices" flowing.

BUILDING THE SEA KAYAK DVD
30 minute DVD   **#16-103**

BUILDING THE SEA KAYAK describes how almost anyone can build their own Stitch-N-Glue touring kayak.

The DVD covers all phases of construction, making it an ideal companion to the plans and patterns.

You're taken step-by-step through the building procedure starting with the basics of how the patterns are used to duplicate the required plywood parts. Progressively, in a simple direct photo/voice combination, the viewer is led through forming the plywood panels, stitching them together, applying glue fillets and fiberglass laminates. The DVD even shows how simple it is to make your own double bladed asymmetrical paddle.

The finished boat is shown on the beach and in action from numerous angles. The graceful clean lines are apparent and gives the viewer the "itch" to start building his own SEA KAYAK.

This is an ideal DVD for the individual who wants to learn more about building the SEA KAYAK; as a "study" DVD or a building aid. It is also helpful if building the SEA KAYAK TWO, our double or two cockpit version of this design.

BOATBUILDING BOOKS

HOW TO FIBERGLASS BOATS
2nd EDITION

by Ken Hankinson
Over 100 photos and illustrations, glossary, index, 120 pages, 8 1/2"x 11", softcover. #12-437
Book/DVD Combination: #16-037

This book presents the most up-to-date and complete information available from a single source for anyone interested in covering new or used boats with a protective layer of fiberglass using either polyester or epoxy resins. This easy-to-read book takes the fear and mystery out of fiberglass work and helps the amateur avoid costly and tedious pitfalls. The clearly described methods are both simple and proven, making a first-class job possible by anyone willing to follow the easy non-technical instructions. Topics include fiberglass sheathing materials and which to use, resins, hardeners, catalysts, pigments, "wet" and "dry" application methods, tips the pros use, safety aspects, estimating materials, surface prep for both old and new boats, finishing methods, and much more! In addition to fiberglass, alternative materials such as polypropylene, Dynel, Arabol, Kevlar, and carbon fiber are covered as they apply to sheathings.

For those who are more visually oriented, see the DVD pages for information on our DVD "How to Fiberglass a Boat" or order both at a special discounted price.

BOATBUILDER'S NOTEBOOK

by Glen L. Witt
Index, hundreds of photos, drawings, and illustrations, 138 pages, 8 1/2"x11", softcover, Spiral Bound, 2008. #12-429

The information contained in this book was obtained from more than 50 years of dealing with amateur boatbuilders. What their questions were during their boatbuilding project formed the outline for this comprehensive journal. Information was also gleaned from previous GLEN-L books, our library of boating books and the notes and instructions from our design group. The text includes valuable information on how a boat is designed, boat types and shapes, plans explanation, and similar subjects to better inform the prospective builder what they will be undertaking.

The nitty gritty of boatbuilding is well covered with progressive subjects from the building form, constructing the framework, installing longitudinals, planking the boat (both sheet plywood and cold molded), decking frame and covering, plus details for virtually every phase of what a typical builder will need to do.

The general outline covers building boats in either sail or power. However, specific information on installing inboard motors, outboard motor wells, and related subjects are also detailed. And of course sailboat construction and information such as rig types, sail nomenclature, spars, rigging, centerboard and rudder construction is also covered; even a Glossary of sailboat terminology.

BOATBUILDING WITH PLYWOOD

by Glen L. Witt
Index, hundreds of photos, drawings, and illustrations, 312 pages, 8 1/2"x 11", hardcover. #12-430

This is the THIRD EDITION of the well-known text covering plywood and its use in boatbuilding, especially from the standpoint of the amateur builder. It has become the recognized standard on a subject usually covered in other books in a chapter at best. Widely used as a reference text in college level boatbuilding classes, this practical book explains the simple ways to build your own boat, taking you step-by-step from lofting to finish. You can almost build a boat by "reading" the pictures and drawings. All aspects of plywood boat construction are covered including lofting, materials to use, tools required, framing methods, covering with fiberglass using either epoxy or polyester resin, cold-molded planking, cabin joinery work, Stitch-N-Glue construction, and much more. This is a must-have book for both the beginner and accomplished boatbuilder who plans to build a boat using plywood. Numerous drawings and photos help put this building method in perspective and illustrate how almost anyone can build a plywood boat. The revised text also covers the use of epoxies for adhesives, encapsulation, and fiberglass over plywood use. The author is a practicing Naval Architect and boatbuilder who specializes in the field of amateur boatbuilding. He knows his subject because he builds boats to develop new methods; not as a professional boatbuilder repeating the same building procedure.

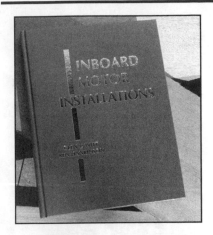

INBOARD MOTOR INSTALLATIONS

by Glen L. Witt & Ken Hankinson
Index, hundreds of photos, drawings, and illustrations, 8 1/2" x 11", hardcover. #12-431

A new revision of the original text, INBOARD MOTOR INSTALLATIONS IN SMALL BOATS. This is the only how-to book covering inboard motor installations in all types of pleasure boats, both power and sail. It is required reading for anyone installing an engine in a new boat or repowering or understanding the installation in an existing craft.

Marine engines are covered as well as converting an auto engine for marine use, with photos of the entire process for a typical automotive conversion. Also covered in detail are: matching motor and boat, installing the required hardware, aligning the motor, transmission types including v-drives, stern drives, and jet drives, exhaust systems, tanks and fuel systems, rudders and steering systems, controls and instrumentation, electrical systems, cooling systems, engine ventilation, trim-plates, and much more. Written in non-technical, easy-to-understand language so that even the novice can master this often misunderstood subject. The authors are both boat designers with many years of experience in designing and working with all sorts of powerboats and sailboat auxiliaries, and realize the problems that confront the amateur. They've written this book to enable you to do a professional installation.

FIBERGLASS BOATBUILDING FOR AMATEURS

by Ken Hankinson
Index, glossary, appendices, bibliography, supplier listing, 127 drawings, 25 charts, tables, and graphs, 400 pages, 8 1/2" x 11", softcover. #12-435

This practical how-to book is especially written for the amateur who may have little or no knowledge of fiberglass boat construction, as well as for the professional looking to expand his knowledge. It covers all aspects of the subject with emphasis on proven methods and materials. This is the most comprehensive, up-to-date book on the subject, explaining the cost differences, labor-saving methods, and how to avoid the pitfalls. By following the easy-to-read, easy-to-understand text, you'll have the knowledge to build a fiberglass boat equal or superior to one made in a factory. This book covers both female and male "one-off" methods using materials such as C-Flex, AIREX and other foam cores, end-grain balsa, and even high-tech materials such as S-Glass, KEVLAR, and carbon fiber. The chapter on the 9-STAGE vacuum bag technique alone is worth the price of the book. This huge oversize text was written by a naval architect who has specialized in the design of boats for amateurs for over 20 years. It includes numerous construction details, trouble shooting, cost comparisons, tools required, resin types, laminate configurations, how to lay up a hull, finishing methods, gel coats and paint systems; in short, dozens of chapters covering everything you'll need to know to achieve professional results for the least amount of money and effort.

HOW TO BUILD BOAT TRAILERS - 2nd Edition

by Glen L. Witt
Over 100 photos, drawings, diagrams and charts, 96 pages, 8 1/2" x 11", softcover. #12-432

Building your own boat trailer is the best way to get an exact fit to suit your boat. Even if you can't weld, you can still use this book to plan your boat trailer for local assembly by your own welder, and still save money. It covers everything, including axles, hubs, wheels, brakes, tires, springs, couplers, frame construction methods, and much more in easy-to-read non-technical language. It even covers handling, launching, retrieving, and maintenance. If you have had bad experiences with stock trailers, such as poor tracking, or beating the bottom out of your boat, solve the problem by building your own trailer the correct way as shown in this book.

BOAT TRAILER PLANS

GLEN-L BOAT TRAILER PLANS show you how to build your own boat trailer at a fraction of the cost of factory-built or so-called knockdown "kit" boat trailers. Even if you are not familiar with welding, you can have a local welder use our plans and still save plenty. These plans are custom-matched to your GLEN-L boat, but can be readily adapted to similar designs. The low price of these PLANS will be more than repaid by the elimination of costly errors common to builders who do not use plans.

Trailering your boat may be the hardest usage your boat will receive if your trailer and boat are not matched properly. The best way to as-sure a perfect combination is to build your own trailer. Each plan includes an illustrated manual detailing all aspects of the project for quick and easy assembly.

These boat trailer plans cover the latest in axles, wheels, hubs, brakes, suspension systems, tires, couplers, frame details, hull support systems, jackstands, and more. All parts and materials specified are standard items readily available anywhere. The best part of building your own trailer is that you'll get one that fits your boat exactly. See the chart below to find the recommended model to suit your needs.

VISIT OUR WEBSITE: WWW.GLEN-L.COM

TRAILER	LOAD CAPACITY	BOAT LENGTH	TYPE OF BOAT	NO. AXLES
SERIES 750/1000	750-1000 lbs	11' to 16'	Any	1
SERIES 1200/1800	1200-1800 lbs	15' to 19'	Any	1
SERIES 2300/2800	2300-2800 lbs	16' to 22'	Any	1 or 2
SERIES 2900/3800	2900-3800 lbs	17' to 23'	Any	1 or 2
SERIES 5000/6000	5000-6000 lbs	18' to 26'	Any	2 or 3
SERIES 7000/10000	7000-10000 lbs	23' to 33'	Any	2 or 3
SERIES 2000/3800-PC	2000-3800 lbs	18' to 26'	Twin Hulls/Pontoons	1 or 2
SERIES 4000/6000-PC	4000-6000 lbs	22' to 30'	Twin Hulls/Pontoons	2 or 3
CANOE/KAYAK TRAILER PLANS -	To 1000 lbs	For single or multiple canoes & kayaks		Single
HUCK FINN TRAILER PLANS -	Fits All Versions			Single or dual
SUPER HUCK TRAILER PLANS -	Fits all 8' Beam Versions			Dual or triple

DESIGN CHARACTERISTICS

CHARACTERISTICS

On each design page a list of "Characteristics" is given to describe the design. The accompanying diagrams illustrate how some of these dimensions are measured and what the various terms mean.

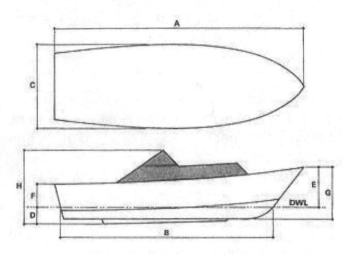

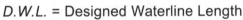

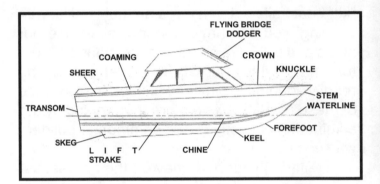

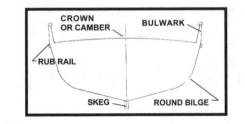

D.W.L. = Designed Waterline Length

A = *Length overall* of the boat

B = *Length waterline* is the length of the boat at the designed waterline.

C = *Beam* is the overall width of the boat.

D = *Draft* is the depth of the hull structure below the designed waterline.

E = *Freeboard forward*

F = *Freeboard aft*

G = *Hull depth* is the overall height of the hull.

H = *Height overall* is the height of the boat including cabin and windshield.

DISPLACEMENT = The theoretical designed weight of the boat plus everything aboard including passengers, gear, tanks, motors, etc. The displacement will always be more than the boat weight.

HULL WEIGHT = The bare weight of the hull only, based on materials specified.

Visit our website: www.Glen-L.com

GLOSSARY OF TERMS

AFT - Toward the stern.

ANTI-TRIP CHINE - A flared-out aft section of the side/bottom of the boat. The purpose is to prevent the hard chine of the boat from catching a wake or small wave on a sharp turn.

ASPECT RATIO - The relationship between the height of a sail and its breadth. i.e.: A sail with a height of 30' and a breadth of 20' has an aspect ratio of 3:2.

ATHWARTSHIP(S) - Across the boat.

BACKSTAY - A wire-rope from the top of the mast leading aft to prevent the mast from bending forward.

BALLAST - Weight carried low in a boat to increase stability. The lower, the greater the benefit. Ballast can be lead, iron, concrete, etc., depending on the space available. Some boats require lead (a more expensive material) because the space available will not allow sufficient lighter material to achieve the required ballast weight.

BOBSTAY - A chain, wire-rope, or rod supporting a bowsprit or boomkin against upward pull.

BOOMKIN - A spar projecting from the stern to which is attached a backstay or sheet.

BOTTOM SHAPE (As it affects performance in a planing boat.): Maximum speed will be achieved when the bottom of the boat that forms the planing surface is flat. When the planing surface is a vee, the boat will have a softer ride, but less potential speed, and will take longer to come up on a plane. A flat bottom makes a better drag boat, a deep vee will be a better rough water boat.

BOWSPRIT - A tapered pole extending forward of the bow of a sailboat to which the forestay fastens. The purpose being to increase the amount of sail area without raising the center of effort.

BREASTHOOK - A knee which mounts atop the stem, to which the sheers attach.

BRIGHT WORK - A term used to describe wood that is finished natural, using varnish or other clear coating.

BULBOUS FOREFOOT - A convex entry at the keel/stem junction (as opposed to a sharp vee) incorporated to soften the ride. When used in conjunction with a reverse curve at the chine, it usually makes sheet materials impractical requiring other planking methods in the forward section.

BULWARK - An extension of the planking above the deck to form a rail.

BULKHEAD - A vertical, athwartship partition, most often serving as a set-up member or frame.

BURGEE - A triangular shaped flag denoting the yacht club to which the owner belongs.

CAMBER - Athwartship curve of the vessel's deck or cabin top. Curve.

CARLING - A longitudinal structural member at the cockpit perimeter supporting the inboard side of the side deck. (See COAMING)

CARVEL PLANKING - Solid wood planks, butted together, fastened to the frames, with a flexible caulking between the planks. Should not be fiberglassed.

CATAMARAN - A vessel with two parallel hulls.

CENTERBOARD - A pivoting "keel" that retracts into a case inside a sailboat. Used to prevent leeway.

CENTER OF EFFORT (CE) (Sail) - The fore and aft and up and down point on a sail at which the pressure of the wind is concentrated; the geometric center of the sail. The higher the CE, the more leverage the wind has to heel the boat. When there is more than one sail, CE's will be given on the drawing for each sail plus a combined CE. On a triangle, the CE is the point at which the lines bisecting each angle cross. The location of the CE fore and aft affects the way the boat turns into the wind. (See LEE and WEATHER HELM)

CENTER OF LATERAL RESISTANCE (CLR) - The geometric center or pivot point of the underwater hull profile.

CHAINPLATE - A metal strap to which shrouds or fittings are attached.

CHINE - The junction of the side and bottom planking or the member backing this junction.

CLIPPER BOW - A bow where the stem has a forward curve and sides have a lot of flare. Also called a schooner bow.

DOUBLE CHINE - Having an additional planking junction between the chine and the sheer, giving the hull a more rounded look.

CLUB-FOOTED JIB - A jib with a boom or "club" on the foot of the sail.

COAMING - A non-structural longitudinal member at the cockpit perimeter; a decorative piece fastened to the carling, usually protruding above the side deck to prevent water from entering the cockpit.

CRUISER - (Power boat) A boat with appurtenances for living afloat. These are sleeping accommodations, cooking facilities, a toilet, some lounging space, and fuel and water tanks. The terms sedan, express, and day are loose categories meant to place emphasis on certain capabilities. A sedan cruiser has more glass and more lounging area, express is faster, and a day cruiser has minimal accommodations and is usually only practical for limited overnight stays.

DAGGERBOARD - A blade shaped centerboard that is lifted out of a case when raised. Usually only suitable for small boats.

DEAD-RISE - Looking at the hull in cross section, the angle the bottom rises from a horizontal.

DEEP VEE - A hard chine power boat having a 15 degree or more angle deadrise at the transom.

DISPLACEMENT HULL - A hull that will not greatly exceed a fixed speed. Speed potential increases with the length of the hull. Additional power will only allow a hull to maintain hull speed against a head wind or under load. (See PLANING HULL)

DORY - The traditional dory is a small, flat-bottomed fishing boat with high flaring sides, and considerable sheer. The commercial fishing dories of New England were stacked on a larger boat and transported to the Grand Banks where they were off-loaded with a fisherman, and later retrieved. The boats were noted for their seaworthiness. The term dory appears to have come from an Indian term for a dugout. Over the years the dory has evolved to encompass various types of boats, usually characterized by flat bottoms and flaring sides. Some of the improvements of previous models have made them hard to recognize as dories. The Pacific Dory has a flat bottom, flaring sides, a wide transom and is capable of planing. The following designs are classified as dories: DORY, LUCKY PIERRE, BIG/LITTLE/WEE HUNK, HUNKY DORY, ALPHA 2, JEAN PIERRE and CHUNKY DORY.

DOUBLE HEADSAIL RIG - Two sails forward of the mast as in a cutter.

DRAFT - The depth of water a boat can travel over without hitting the bottom.

FAIRING - The process of beveling the stem, chine, sheers, keel, and frames so that the planking will have flat surfaces to glue and fasten to. A fair hull is one with no dips or bumps in the longitudinal lines of the hull. Fairness is checked by sighting down the longitudinal lines.

FILLET/FILLETING - A fillet is a cove-shape made with putty on an inside corner. The term is most often used in reference to Stitch-N-Glue boat building. A fillet is made with activated epoxy resin, thickened with various fillers, to a putty consistency. The putty is "globbed" into place and smoothed with a rounded tool. (See Boatbuilding Methods: Stitch-N-Glue.)

FORETRIANGLE - The area forward of the forward mast in which sails can be set. A sail that fills that area.

FREEBOARD - The distance from the water to the sheer.

GAFF RIG See SAILBOAT RIGS

GARVEY HULL - A hard chine hull in which the chines do not join on the stem centerline. (See PLAY PEN design)

GENOA - A large, low cut, jib that overlaps the mast.

GOOSENECK - A fitting used to attach the boom to the mast and which permits the boom to pivot.

GUDGEONS AND PINTLES - Hardware used to connect an "outboard" rudder to the back of the boat. The pintle has a pin (male part), The gudgeon accepts the pintle (female part). There are different styles, sometimes with the pintle on the rudder, sometimes on the transom.

GUNKHOLING - Cruising in shoal water or overnighting in small coves.

HARD CHINE -Having a distinct bottom/side planking.

HOUND - A wraparound mast fitting used to secure the forestay and other fittings to the mast on a jibhead rig.

I/O (Inboard/outboard) - A propulsion system that uses an inboard motor, mounted at the transom, with a propeller assembly, similar to the bottom of an outboard, mounted on the outside of the transom, bolting to the motor with the transom sandwiched between. Also called a stern drive. In most designs it can be used optionally to a vee-drive, or jet drive.

JIB - A triangular sail forward of the forward mast, usually attached to the forestay.

JIBHEAD RIG - See SAILBOAT RIGS

KEEL - The junction of the bottom planking along the centerline of the boat or the inside member backing this junction aft of the stem. The term also refers to an outer longitudinal appendage on the centerline. The purpose of this member is to keep the wind from blowing the boat sideways from its forward course. The keel also serves to protect the prop on a power boat.

KEEL, FIXED - Usually associated with a sailboat, this is simply a non-retractable keel. A fixed keel trailerable boat requires a special trailer and special launch facilities.

KNOT SPEED CONVERSION - To convert to miles per hour, use the following formula: speed in mph = speed in knots divided by .87.

LAUNCH - A large, open motorboat.

LEAD - The distance between the CLR and the CE of a vessel. (Pronounced "leed".)

LEEBOARD - These are paddle-shaped boards installed on the outside of the gunwale on each side of a sailboat. The board on the "lee" side is lowered to prevent leeway. Single leeboards are used as a way of converting a non-sailing boat to sail without the necessity of cutting holes in the hull or installing permanent outside keels.

LEE HELM - A condition in which the tiller must be held toward the downwind side of a sailing vessel in order to maintain course. An undesirable condition for safety and hydrodynamic reasons. (See WEATHER HELM)

LEEWAY - To drift from course in the direction of the wind.

LIFT STRAKES - Longitudinal members running fore and aft on the outside bottom of the hull. The purpose is to stabilize and create lift on a deep vee hull when under power.

LOFTING - The process of drawing the hull lines full size from the designer's scale drawings. The intersections of the contours of various horizontal and vertical sections are measured from an imaginary base line using an architect's scale. These junctions are then laid out, point by point, in their full size. Because it is difficult to take accurate dimensions from a small drawing, it is necessary to adjust these lines to assure that they are fair. A listing of these points is called a table of offsets. It takes a lot of space to loft. This, along with the difficulty, makes it a daunting task and a real drag to those builders who just want to get at the wood. All GLEN-L designs have full size patterns... no lofting required.

LONGITUDINALS - Those hull framing members that run the length of the boat (i.e. chine, keel, sheer, battens).

LUFF - The front or leading edge of a sail.

MASTHEAD RIG - The forestay attaches to the masthead.

MIZZEN - A sail aft of the aft mast on a multi-masted boat.

MONOCOQUE - A structure in which the outer covering (planking) carries all or a major part of the stresses.

MONOHEDRON - From the Greek word hedron (a geometrical figure having any number of planes). The theoretical ideal shape for planing over the water surface is one of constant (mono) section. Thus monohedron describes a hull that has a running surface of constant section; in practice the sections may not be exactly the same.

MOTORSAILER - A combination of sailboat and motorboat; a compromise, neither the ideal sailboat or powerboat.

MOTOR WELL - When an outboard motor is mounted on the transom, a motor well is a box-like structure in front of the motor that catches water that may wash over the outboard cut-out and allows it to drain over the transom and not into the boat. When a motor is mounted in front of the transom, motor well refers to a box-like structure that surrounds a hole in the bottom of the boat. The well usually allows the motor to tilt up, frequently through a cut-out in the transom. This type of motor well allows the handling of nets or fishing lines over the transom without having to work around the motor.

MULTI-CHINE - Having one or more additional planking junctions between the chine and the sheer.

OFFSETS - Measurements supplied by a designer for the builder in order to lay down the lines of the hull. Glen-L patterns eliminate the need for a table of offsets.

OUTHAUL - The line used to pull a sail toward the end of the boom, or the grommet at the corner of the sail to which that line attaches.

P & S - Port and starboard (both sides). The port is the left side of a boat looking forward, starboard on the right.

PAINTER - A line made fast to the bow of a small boat.

PEAK - The upper aft corner of a gaff-headed sail.

PENNANT - A pointed flag.

"PINKIE" STERN - Sometimes applied to a sharp sterned skiff, but more properly to a stern projection of the gunwales to a sharp point above a narrow transom, originally to carry a coat of arms or other decoration.

PLANING HULL - A hull that lifts and skims the surface of the water causing the stern wake to break clean from the transom. In practical terms, a planing hull has a speed potential limited only by weight and power. (See DISPLACEMENT HULL)

PLANKING METHODS-WOOD

SHEET PLYWOOD - The simplest wood planking method.

STITCH-N-GLUE - Simplified sheet plywood method which eliminates the use of stems and chines, thus avoiding the "fairing" required in conventional plywood construction.

DOUBLE (MULTI-) DIAGONAL - More involved; used when compound shapes are incorporated into the hull (i.e. "bulbous forefoot", "reverse curve", "round bilge"). Uses strips of plywood or solid wood veneers laid over the hull in layers of opposite diagonals, glued together, most often with epoxy.

COLD-MOLDED - A term that can be used interchangeably with above.

STRIP - Utilizes thin strips of wood, edge glued together. One method uses the wood as a "core" with fiberglass on both sides (see STRIPPER, GLEN-L 11 designs). The more common method uses strips fitted, glued, and fastened on edge with optional fiberglass on the outside only (See WHITEHALL, HARBOR MASTER, AMIGO designs).

PRAM - A dinghy with a transom at the bow and stern.

PRISMATIC COEFFICIENT - The ratio the hull displacement bears to the displacement of a shape which is the same length as the waterline length of the boat and has the same constant cross-sectional area as the greatest cross-sectional area the hull.

QUARTERING SEAS - Waves coming toward the aft corner (quarter) of a boat.

RAKE - The fore or aft angle of the mast from perpendicular.

REEVE - To thread a line through a block, fairlead or hole of any kind.

REVERSE CURVE - The opposite of bulbous; a concavity in bottom or side. The usual purpose is to deflect spray.

RUNNING RIGGING - Sheets, halyards, topping lifts, etc. by which the sails are raised, trimmed or controlled.

SAILBOAT RIGS:

CAT RIG - Having a single mast and a single sail.

CUTTER RIG - One mast, one sail aft of mast, two or more forward. Similar to a sloop except that there are at least two triangular sails forward of the mast. The mast is stepped farther aft than a sloop, creating a larger foretriangle. Because of the large area, multiple, smaller sails, are easier to handle than one large sail. The rig allows more versatility than a single large sail but is less powerful in light airs.

GAFF RIG - Has a lower boom and an upper "mast" or boom that attaches to the mainmast. The sail is a quadrangle. This is an older style rig currently used to give a boat a traditional look. Does not come to windward as well as "modern" rigs, requires more hardware, including separate halyards, one for the main and one for the upper boom. Generally less efficient for top performance, but does have less windage aloft when sail is reduced.

JIBHEAD RIG - The forestay does not attach to the masthead but at a point lower on the mast where the top of the jib meets the mast.

KETCH RIG - Two masts, three sails. The ketch is very similar to the yawl. Both rigs have a main, foretriangle, and a mizzen. The ketch generally has its mizzenmast (aft mast) farther forward than a yawl allowing for a larger mizzen. There are various definitions of what constitutes the difference between the two rigs: A ketch's mizzen must be at least 2/3 of her main, a yawl's mizzenmast is less than half the height of her mainmast. At the extremes, these rigs are easy to distinguish but there is a mid "gray" area where identification is open to interpretation.

LATEEN RIG - One mast, one sail, two booms. (See BUCKBOARD design)

SLOOP RIG - One mast, two sails. Has a main aft of the mast and a triangular sail (jib) forward of the mast, usually attached to the forestay. A sloop is more maneuverable than a cat rig, and more versatile for reducing sail.

SPRIT RIG - A sprit is a boom that extends upward from the mast to the topmost corner of a quadrangle sail. A sprit rig allows more sail area on a short mast. (See SNEAKBOX design)

SANDWICH CORE - A one-off fiberglass construction method that uses an inner core that is temporarily fastened to a form, covered with fiberglass laminates, removed from the form, and fiberglass laminates applied to the inside. (See Building Methods/Fiberglass.)

SHAFT HORSEPOWER (SHP) - A theoretical measurement of horsepower at the propeller. If the BRAKE HORSEPOWER is known (normally the rated horsepower), for gasoline engines, multiply by .7 for the approximate constant SHP.

SHARPIE - "Sharp"-bowed, flat bottomed skiff. A term usually applied to flat bottomed sailing skiffs over 20' in length. All types of rigs were traditionally used.

SHEER - The junction of the side and deck or the member backing this junction. A boat with a "lot of sheer" is higher at the bow and stern than the center when viewed in profile; with little sheer, the sheer arc will be closer to a straight line (a sheer hog).

SHOAL - Shallow

SHP - See SHAFT HORSEPOWER

SKEG - A longitudinal appendage on a boat, on the outside, at the centerline, providing directional stability and/or protection for the prop and rudder.

SOLE - Cabin or cockpit floor

SPAR - Same as mast.

SPEED-LENGTH RATIO - A formula used to compare potential speeds of displacement or semi-displacement hulls; not used for full planing hulls. Formula: Speed in knots=1.34 x square root of the waterline length.

SPILING - A method of fitting longitudinal planking junctions.

SPONSON - A projection or addition to the side or bottom of the boat to help stabilize or provide lift. (See the TINY TITAN, SUPER SPARTAN, and PICKLEFORK.)

STEM - The junction of the planking at the forward end of a typical hull. The member to which the planking attaches at this junction.

STRIP PLANKING - A planking method that uses strips of wood installed longitudinally and edge-glued and fastened together. Planks most often are made with "bead" and "cove" edges (somewhat like male and female "ball and socket") to eliminate fitting the plank edges.

TABLOID CRUISER - A small cruiser.

TRANSOM - The member forming the aft (stern) end of the boat.

TUMBLEHOME - The top is closer to the centerline than the bottom. Can be applied to the hull or cabin.

VEE BOTTOM - Not flat athwartships. In a flat bottom boat (SISSY DO), the chines meet the keel at the bottom of the stem. In a vee bottom boat, the keel fastens to the bottom of the stem and chines at a point above this junction, the higher, the more the vee. A "flat bottom ski boat" has a vee bottom forward and is flat at the transom. (See DEEP VEE, BOTTOM SHAPE)

V-DRIVE - A gear box that reverses the direction of the drive train to allow the use of a standard prop shaft and prop with a rear mounted motor.

WATERLINE LENGTH - Significance: One of the factors used to determine the speed potential of a displacement boat. The longer, the greater the speed potential. The overall length is irrelevant; overhangs fore and aft do not increase hull speed potential.

WEATHER HELM - A condition in which the tiller must be held toward the windward side of a sailing vessel in order to maintain course. A slight amount (3 to 7 degrees) is desirable. (See LEE HELM)

WIND SPEED:

Near gale: Wind speed of 28 to 33 knots.

Gale: Wind speed of 34 to 40 knots.

Strong gale: Wind speed of 41 to 47 knots.

Storm: Wind speeds of 48 to 55 knots.

Greater wind speeds: Stay home.

YARN - Fibers that are twisted together to form a rope.

YAW - A vessel which will not hold a steady course, but swings from side to side of it, is said to yaw.

DINKY

A 7', 70LB. STITCH-N-GLUE DINGHY

BUILD IN STITCH-N-GLUE

CHARACTERISTICS

Length overall .... 7'-0"
Beam .... 46"
Depth amidship .... 14 1/2"
Hull weight (approx.)................. 70 lbs.
Average passengers 1-2
Sail area .... 34 sq. ft.
Hull type: Pram for Stitch-N-Glue sheet plywood construction.
Power: Intended for rowing, sailing or 2 HP max. outboard motor.

Our **DINKY** is a marvel in ship-to-shore dinghy design. It's also a great pram for a little fishing or sailing expedition. The kids will love it and so will you since the watertight compartments with optional flotation filling make **DINKY** virtually unsinkable.

Our Stitch-N-Glue building method makes **DINKY** incredibly *fast, easy, & cheap* to build. All it takes is *two* sheets of 1/4" x 4' x 8' standard plywood. FULL SIZE PATTERNS are provided for all the planking panels and contoured parts. Simply cut out panels, stitch together, bond in place, and you have a hull.

You can make your **DINKY** into a sailboat at any time using the simple sailing rig detailed. This includes the option of making a two-part mast and folding rudder-tiller, both of which can be stored within the **DINKY** when carrying space is at a premium. The leeboard keeps the cockpit open without leaks common with daggerboard and centerboard trunks. The completed boat is light enough to transport anywhere, and small enough to store or carry in or on almost any vehicle.

AVAILABLE FOR THIS DESIGN:
- **Plans & Patterns**
- **Stitch & Glue Kit**
- **Fiberglass Kit**
- **Hardware Kit**
- **Rigging Kit**
- **Sails**
- **Stitch & Glue DVD**
See Price List

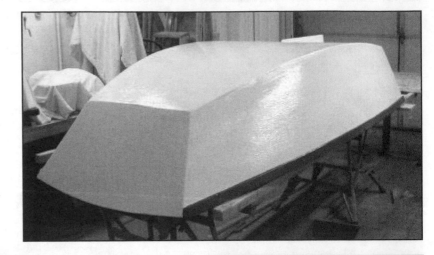

COMPLETE PLANS as dinghy with or without sail rig (single or two-part mast detailed), include **FULL SIZE PATTERNS** for the bottom and side planking, transom, bow, seats, seat uprights, skeg, bow and transom knees, tiller, rudder, mast support, and leeboard. Includes material listing and layouts, with instructions and pictorial STITCH-N-GLUE Manual.

CENTERFOLD AN 8' TAKE-APART DINGHY

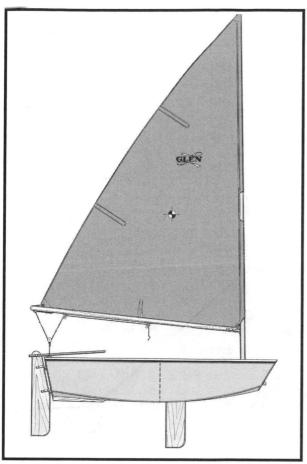

Here's the answer to the dinghy storage and portage problem - the **CENTERFOLD**! She folds or hinges right across the middle, or can be made to take apart. The two separate parts are lighter and easier to carry than a conventional dinghy. Even the mast on the sailing version can be made in two parts for easy carrying and storage. The **CENTERFOLD** is thus the *perfect* ship-to-shore dinghy for the smaller cruisers where space is at a premium. Best of all, this boat is simple, easy and inexpensive to build. No lofting, no building forms, and no frames are required.

COMPLETE PLANS include FULL SIZE PATTERNS for the sheer harpin, bow member, center frames and seat, aft and bow seats, transom and bow knees, trunk brace, rudder, tiller, and half section pattern for the mast brace. Includes instructions, Bill of Materials, and Fastening Schedule.

> **AVAILABLE FOR THIS DESIGN:**
> * **Plans & Patterns**
> * **Bronze Fastening Kit**
> * **Fiberglass Kit**
> * **Hardware & Rigging Kit**
> * **Sail**
> **See Price List**

CHARACTERISTICS

Length overall	7'-10"
Beam	48"
Hull depth	18"
Hull weight	70 lbs.
Average passengers	1-2
Sail area	39 sq. ft.

Hull type: Arc bottom pram developed for sheet plywood planking. May be taken apart or folded across the middle for storage or portage.

Power: Outboard motor to 3 HP.

EIGHT BALL
Conventional Plywood version

Over the years this boat has introduced generations to the joys of sailing, providing a "first step on to the water" for many of today's sailors.

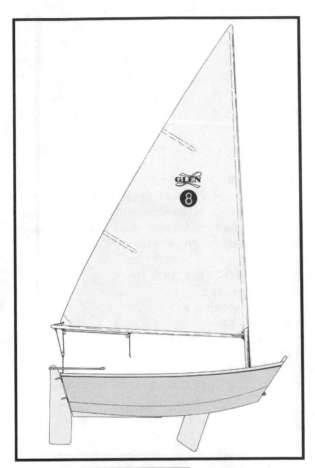

The conventionally built **EIGHT BALL** is an ideal first time project. It's also an excellent way to gain boatbuilding experience if constructing larger craft is on the agenda. No building form is required and two sheets of standard 1/4"x4'x8' plywood will plank the entire boat.

The **EIGHT BALL** is a versatile boat. Use it with oars, a small outboard, or as a sailing dinghy. The mast requires no stays and the sail is a simple sock-type which slips over the mast. An ideal project for young people *and* a boat that the whole family will enjoy. The compact size makes for easy car-topping, or it can be thrown in a van or pick-up truck. Best of all, it is an *inexpensive* way to get on the water!

The **EIGHT BALL** features a *centerboard* that pivots out of the way when not in use. However, for rowing or power, the sailing features can be eliminated.

COMPLETE PLANS include FULL SIZE PATTERNS for the centerboard, rudder, centerboard trunk, bow and stern knees, side frames, and half sections of the bow, center and stern seats, bow members, and transom. Instructions include Bill of Materials and Fastening Schedule. See PRICE LIST under EIGHT BALL.

CHARACTERISTICS
Length overall .... 7'-10"
Beam .... 52"
Hull depth .... 18"
Hull weight (approx.) .... 75 lbs.
Average passengers 1-2
Sail area .... 34 sq. ft.
Hull type: Pram with vee bottom, hard chine hull developed for sheet plywood planking.
Sail type: Cat rig with centerboard.
Power: Outboard motor to 3 HP.

AVAILABLE FOR THIS DESIGN:
- Plans & Patterns
- Bronze Fastening Kit
- Fiberglass Kit
- Hardware & Rigging Kit
- Sails
See Price List

EIGHT BALL-SG
Stitch-N-Glue version

Now you can build our most popular design, EIGHT BALL, in the original conventional method or in the Stitch-N-Glue version, designated as **EIGHT BALL-SG**. The building methods vary, but the hull is vintage EIGHT BALL!

The **EIGHT BALL-SG** features three watertight seat/compartments. Let the kids fill it full of water... it won't sink! The sailing version utilizes a daggerboard that can be removed when not sailing.

There's only so much we can say about Stitch-N-Glue before we start repeating ourselves... but if you have a minimum of tools... if you want the easiest construction method, the **SG** version is for you.

COMPLETE PLANS include FULL SIZE PATTERNS for the side and bottom planking, all uprights, transom, bow member, transom and bow knees, seats, bow cap, skeg, daggerboard and handle, case brace and cap, rudder and tiller. Includes instructions, Bill of Materials, and STITCH-N-GLUE Manual. See PRICE LIST under EIGHT BALL-SG.

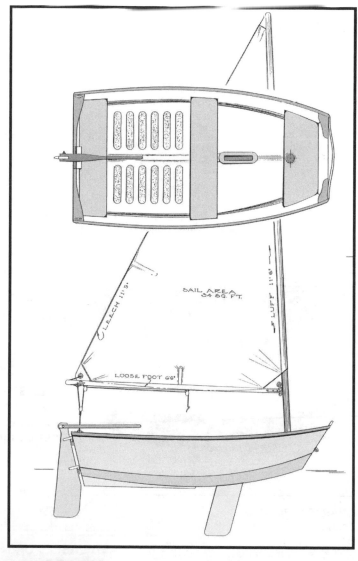

CHARACTERISTICS

Length overall	8'-1/2"
Beam	52"
Hull depth	18"
Hull weight (approx.)	85 lbs.
Average passengers	1-2
Sail area	34 sq. ft.

Hull type: Pram with vee bottom, hard chine, developed for Stitch-N-Glue, sheet plywood construction.
Sail type: Cat rig with centerboard.
Power: Outboard motor to 3 HP.

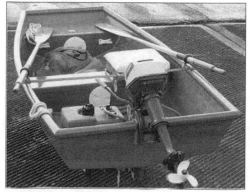

AVAILABLE FOR THIS DESIGN:
- **Plans & Patterns**
- **Stitch & Glue Kit**
- **Fiberglass Kit**
- **Hardware & Rigging Kit**
- **Sails**
- **Building the 8 Ball DVD**
See Price List

SABOTEER A 10' SAILING/ROWING PRAM

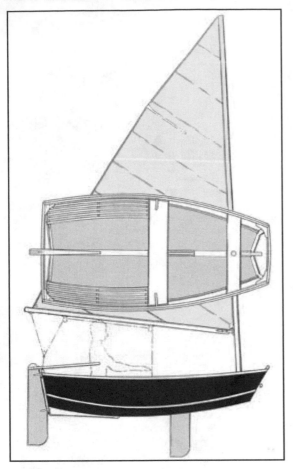

While SABOTEER is similar in hull form and type to our famous EIGHT BALL, it's much larger and an even better performer when it comes to sailing, rowing, or towing. Yet it's nearly as easy to build. Only one sheet of 1/4" x 4' x 8' and two sheets of 1/4" x 4' x 10' plywood are required (simple joining options in the plans allow 8' panels if 10' sheets not available).

SABOTEER features options such as a kick-up rudder and 2-part mast so the rig can be stowed within the boat. The free-standing low-cost wood mast is easy to make and slips readily into the sleeved sail. Or you can omit the rig and daggerboard and use as a rowboat, or hook on a small motor. The lightweight craft is easily trailed, cartopped, or carried in vans and pickups.

Construction is done over a simple jig and 3 temporary forms plus the boat's bow and stern transoms.

FULL SIZE PATTERNS are provided for 3 temporary forms plus the boat's bow and stern transoms so no lofting or layouts are required. Rudder and daggerboard patterns are also provided, plus instructions, material list, and plywood layouts.

CHARACTERISITICS

Length overall	9'7"
Beam	4'8"
Hull depth amidships	19-1/2"
Boat weight	100 lbs.
Sail area	59 sq.ft.
Average passengers	2-3

Hull type: Pram with vee bottom, hard chine hull developed for sheet plywood planking.
Sail type: Cat rig with daggerboard.
Power: Outboard motor to 3 HP.

AVAILABLE FOR THIS DESIGN:
- **Plans & Patterns**
- **Bronze Fastening Kit**
- **Fiberglass Kit**
See Price List

FOAMEE A 9' FOAM/FIBERGLASS SAILING DINGHY

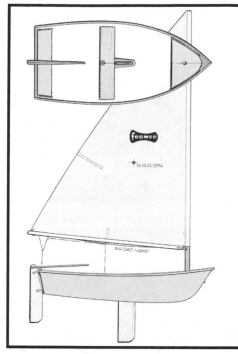

The FOAMEE uses "one-off" sandwich core construction... an excellent beginning craft for trying out this boatbuilding method.

CHARACTERISTICS

Length overall .... 9'-0"
Beam .... 4'-5"
Hull depth .... 22"
Hull weight (approx.)................. 85 lbs.
Average passengers 1-2
Sail area .... 50 sq. ft.
Hull type: Round bilge hull form designed for PVC foam or end grain balsa sandwich core construction, with fiberglass laminate each side. Suitable for cold-molded construction, but not detailed.
Sail type: Cat rig with daggerboard.
Power: Outboard motor to 3 HP.

COMPLETE PLANS include FULL SIZE PATTERNS for the stem form, transom form, form frames, daggerboard, daggerboard trunk cap, transom upright, and rudder. Includes instructions, materials and equipment listing.

NOTE: Although not detailed in the plans and pattern package, we have had several builders make this boat using the "cold-molded" wood veneer method. The hull form is well suited to cold-molded construction.

BUILD IN FIBERGLASS

The **FOAMEE** stands on its own or is an excellent ship-to-shore boat for any larger boat. The **FOAMEE** can be rowed or powered with a small outboard in addition to being a first-rate sailing trainer. The **FOAMEE** sailing dinghy uses one-off sandwich core construction with fiberglass laminates inside and out. This is an excellent beginning craft for anyone who would like to try out the method before attempting one of the larger one-off designs. One-off fiberglass construction allows boats to be built in hull forms that are not possible using sheet plywood. The finished product has the molded look that we are familiar with from fiberglass production boats, but using a method that requires no expensive female mold. Later in this book, we will introduce larger one-off projects. For more information on sandwich core construction, see the "Building Methods" section in front of this book. The pictures used to illustrate sandwich core construction are of the FOAMEE.

BUCK BOARD A 12' SAILBOARD

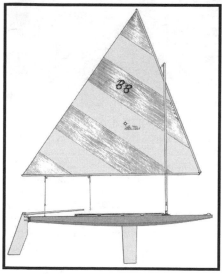

CHARACTERISTICS

Length overall .... 11'-11"
Beam .... 3'-0"
Hull weight (approx.)................. 85 lbs.
Hull depth .... 7"
Average passengers 1-2
Sail area .... 66 sq. ft.
Hull type: Sailboard developed for sheet plywood planking.
Sail type: Lateen rig with daggerboard.

The **BUCK BOARD** is simple to build, easily transportable, and a real kick to sail. Rigging is a cinch as no stays are required. Shove off from the shore, unfurl the sail, and get ready for a thrill. You'll really move out with all that sail area, but you'll be in complete control because of the simple, easy handling lateen rig.

Just about anyone can build his own **BUCK BOARD**, even the kids with a little help from pop. It's cheap and easy, too. The **BUCKBOARD** requires only two and a half sheets of 1/4" AB exterior plywood. No building form or special tools are needed and the few materials required are readily available. Step-by-step instructions carry you through the project, and the FULL SIZE PATTERNS prevent mistakes. This is an ideal summer project and a good introduction into the worlds of boatbuilding and sailing.

BUILD IN PLYWOOD

COMPLETE PLANS include FULL SIZE PATTERNS for the rudder, daggerboard, daggerboard trunk, bulkhead frames, and transom. Instructions include Bill of Materials, Fastening Schedule, and material utilization layouts.

GLEN-L 10

A 10' SAILBOAT

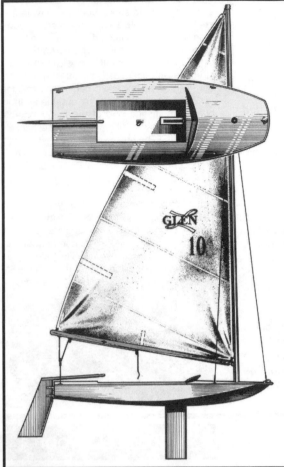

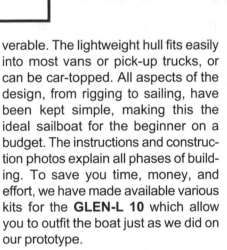

In the past...before plywood, there were a variety of different "skimmers" being built using wood planking methods. These boats were *basic* sailboats, but because of their weight (300 to 400 lbs.), they were not great performers. The **GLEN-L 10** can rightly be called a "performance boat". The instructions that come with the plans show the boat heeling over with two adults hanging out to keep the boat upright. This is possible because of the superior strength/weight properties of plywood construction.

The **GLEN-L 10** is a full fledged sailboat requiring a minimum of investment, and she's easy to build. No building form is required and all materials are used with a bare minimum of waste. Full Size Patterns make construction quick and simple, even for beginners.

The **GLEN-L 10** is very lively under sail, points well, and is highly maneu-verable. The lightweight hull fits easily into most vans or pick-up trucks, or can be car-topped. All aspects of the design, from rigging to sailing, have been kept simple, making this the ideal sailboat for the beginner on a budget. The instructions and construction photos explain all phases of building. To save you time, money, and effort, we have made available various kits for the **GLEN-L 10** which allow you to outfit the boat just as we did on our prototype.

AVAILABLE FOR THIS DESIGN:
- **Plans & Patterns**
- **Bronze Fastening Kit**
- **Fiberglass Kit**
- **Hardware Kit**
- **Rigging Kit**
- **Sail**

See Price List

CHARACTERISTICS

Length overall .... 9'-11"
Beam .... 3'-10"
Hull depth .... 12"
Hull weight (approx.) .... 88 lbs.
Cockpit size .... 2'x4'-3"
Average passengers 1-2
Sail area .... 64 sq. ft.
Hull type: Vee bottom, hard chine hull developed for sheet plywood planking.
Sail type: Cat rig with daggerboard.

COMPLETE PLANS include FULL SIZE PATTERNS for the frames, transom, stem, side planking assembly, rudder, daggerboard, daggerboard trunk, and bow piece. The instructions include Bill of Materials and Fastening Schedule.

TOPPER
A CAR-TOP SAIL OR ROWBOAT

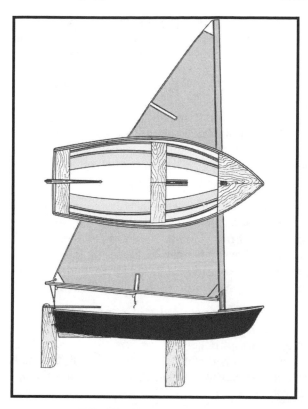

As the name implies, our **TOPPER** can be carried on top of almost any vehicle, making it easy to transport to any boating area. It's lightweight, and the free standing sail rig is easy to set up and remove. With a small outboard or oars, the **TOPPER** makes an excellent fishing boat or ship-to-shore dinghy for a larger cruising boat. Building the **TOPPER** is relatively simple, using standard 1/4"x4'x8' plywood panels. There are no permanent frames in the boat; temporary forms used during construction are later removed. The multi-chine hull features attractive lines with just a bit more fitting required than on the typical single chine hull. Plans come with full instructions as well as a material listing and fastening schedule to make it an easy and speedy project.

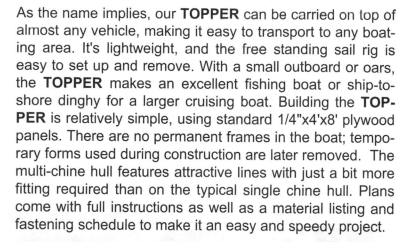

CHARACTERISTICS
Length overall .... 10'-8"
Beam .... 4'-7"
Hull depth .... 21"
Hull weight (approx.) .... 120 lbs.
Average passengers 1-2
Sail area .... 62 sq. ft.
Hull type: Multi-chine hull form developed for sheet plywood planking in 8' lengths.
Sail type: Cat rig, sock-type sail, with daggerboard.

AVAILABLE FOR THIS DESIGN:
- **Plans & Patterns**
- **Bronze Fastening Kit**
- **Fiberglass Kit**
- **Hardware & Rigging Kit**
- **Sail**

See Price List

COMPLETE PLANS include **FULL SIZE PATTERNS** for the forms, transom, stem, daggerboard trunk, breasthook, rudder, and tiller. Instructions include a Bill of Materials and Fastening Schedule.

FEATHER

AN 11' FIBERGLASS SLOOP—IDEAL FOR LEARNING THE C-FLEX METHOD

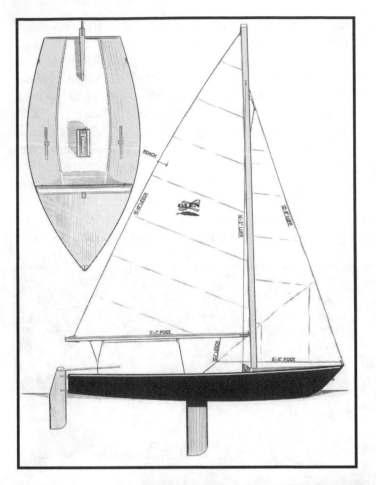

The **FEATHER** is made using C-FLEX fiberglass planking. The strips of fiberglass planking are laid around and stapled to a framework and covered with fiberglass laminate. This is one of the processes specified on larger one-off fiberglass designs. The **FEATHER** makes an excellent first project for those interested in building a larger boat using this method. Most of the form members are removed from the boat after the hull is built, leaving an all-fiberglass hull free of exposed frame members. This boat, like the FOAMEE shown previously, looks so molded that people who see it will find it hard to believe you built it.

The slippery shaped round bilge hull coupled with a generous sloop rig means that **FEATHER** is a real performer. The daggerboard trunk is formed in place to insure that it is leak-proof and offers minimal resistance. Molded-in flotation chambers make the boat unsinkable *and* form the sitting areas along each side of the cockpit.

The compact size means you can carry the boat in a station wagon, pick-up truck, or even on the car top. The detailed pictorial instructions, based on prototype testing, make construction virtually fool-proof so that it is both possible *and practical* for the homebuilder to make his own fiberglass sailboat.

COMPLETE PLANS include FULL SIZE PATTERNS for the stem and transom forms, building forms, daggerboard case form, daggerboard, rudder, instructions, materials, and equipment listing.

CHARACTERISTICS

Length overall	11'-0"
Beam	4'-6"
Hull depth	1'-9"
Hull weight (approx.)	150 lbs.
Average passengers	2-3
Sail area: Main	50 sq. ft.
Jib	30 sq. ft.
Total:	80 sq. ft.

Hull type: Round bilge hull form, designed for fiberglass planking with fiberglass laminate.

Sail type: Sloop rig with daggerboard.

Power: Outboard motor to 3 HP.

Trailer: Designed for use with GLEN-L SERIES 750/1000 boat trailer plans.

AVAILABLE FOR THIS DESIGN:
- **Plans & Patterns**
- **Hardware Kit**
- **Rigging Kit**
- **Sail**

See Price List

BULL'S-EYE AN 11' SKIFF FOR OARS, POWER, OR SAIL

A sweetheart of a boat that's easy to build. The **BULL'S-EYE** is an ideal first time boatbuilding project and a great way to get into boating.

The **BULL'S-EYE** utilizes *FAST-G* Stitch-N-Glue construction; the plywood planking is cut from standard 4' x 8' panels, assembled flat on the ground, and *folded* to form the boat. A pattern is furnished for virtually *all* contoured parts; more than 25 full-size patterns, including *planking*. Just lay the patterns over the wood, transfer to the wood, and saw to shape. No complex grids or tedious layouts from dimensions are required with GLEN-L *FAST-G* construction.

The **BULL'S-EYE** is versatile, easy to row, and adapts readily to a small outboard. Graduate to sail with the simple free sanding cat rig, or for a more lively craft, use the fully stayed sloop rig. The traditionalist may prefer the classic sprit rig with wood spars that can be carried *inside* the boat for portage.

Why delay? The water's waiting and now is the time to start... NOW!

COMPLETE PLANS include FULL SIZE PATTERNS for side/bottom planking, aft side & bottom, butt blocks, form, transom, knee, breasthook, seat end, side, & top, thwart, trunk top, bulkhead, bow

AVAILABLE FOR THIS DESIGN:
- Plans & Patterns
- Stitch & Glue Kit
- Fiberglass Kit
- Hardware Kit
- Rigging Kit
- Sails
- Fittings Kit
- Stitch & Glue DVD

See Price List

seat, rudder, tiller, daggerboard, bulkhead gusset, mast support, motorboard, seat ledge, trunk brace and skeg. Includes step-by-step photos and instructions, Bill of Materials, fastening and laminate schedule, plywood utilization and STITCH-N-GLUE MANUAL.

CHARACTERISTICS
Length overall .... 11'-0"
Beam .... 4'-5"
Hull depth .... 15"
Hull weight (approx.).............. 115 lbs.
Average passengers 2
Hull type: Sheet plywood hull for *FAST-G* Stitch-N-Glue construction with a vee bottom and rounded forward sections.
Power: Outboard motor to 3 HP.
Trailer: Designed for use with GLEN-L SERIES 750/1000 boat trailer plans.
Sail type: Three available, all with daggerboard.
Cat rig: Unstayed mast with loose footed, sock type sail . Area: 56 sq. ft.
Sloop rig: Fully stayed with a loose footed main: 49 sq. ft., jib: 25 sq. ft. Total area: 74 sq. ft.
Sprit rig: Classic unstayed, mast with sprit boom. Loose footed sail with luff laced to mast. Area: 51 sq. ft.

GLEN-L 11

WOOD/FIBERGLASS COMPOSITE WITH SLOOP OR CAT RIG

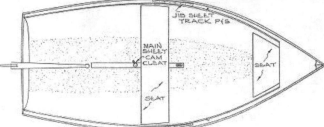

The interchangeable rig of the **GLEN-L 11** permits sailing the boat as a cat rig with single mainsail, or as a sloop rig with main and jib sails. The same spar and rigging are used in both cases. The round bottom hull construction makes light air performance especially good. This characteristic also makes rowing a pleasure if you don't want to sail. A lightweight outboard motor can be used, if you desire. The **GLEN-L 11** has beauty of line and character that will impress even those with an eye only for traditionally built boats.

However, the method of construction is far from traditional. The **GLEN-L 11** is built using the structurally sound and lightweight sandwich core principle. Inexpensive white pine boards are sawn into thin strips and bent in place over temporary forms. This is then covered with two laminations of fiber-

glass, removed from the form, and the inside is covered with fiber-glass forming a "monocoque" or one-piece hull.

After researching this method and building and designing the prototype, we tested the boat for nearly one year under all conditions. The results proved that this boat is rugged, lightweight, requires little maintenance, and that the method of construction is suitable for amateur building. The instructions provide numerous photos of the actual building methods so your **GLEN-L 11** will turn out as designed.

AVAILABLE FOR THIS DESIGN:
- **Plans & Patterns**
- **Fiberglass Kit**
- **Hardware Kit**
- **Rigging Kit**
- **Sails**

See Price List

CHARACTERISTICS

Length overall	11'-2"
Beam	4'-10"
Hull depth	22"
Draft (board down)	2'-9"
Hull weight (approx.)	190 lbs.
Average passengers	2
Sail area: Sloop rig	74 sq. ft.
Cat rig	49 sq. ft.
Hull type:	Round bilge hull form, designed for wood sandwich core and fiberglass laminates.
Sail type:	Sloop or cat rig with centerboard.
Power:	Outboard motor to 3 HP.
Trailer:	Designed for use with GLEN-L SERIES 750/1000 boat trailer plans.

COMPLETE PLANS include FULL SIZE PATTERNS for the centerboard, rudder, stem, centerboard trunk, transom, and each of the temporary building forms. Includes step-by-step written and pictorial instructions.

GLEN-L 12

A LIGHT WEIGHT 12' SLOOP

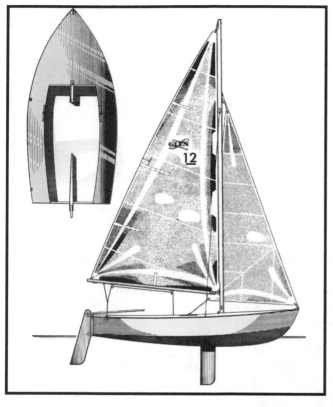

Easy and fun to build and to sail! This sums up the GLEN-L 12. It's a peppy performer, ideal for the beginner. Not too small, not too big, but stable enough for the non-sailor, and roomy enough for two adults and two kids. Yet packed with enough sail area in the sloop rig for exciting performance!

The GLEN-L 12 features simple, *low cost* construction. Only a few sheets of standard 4' x 8' plywood and some lengths of lumber are required. Our PLANS and FULL SIZE PATTERNS make the job easy even for the beginner.

You can outfit your GLEN-L 12 with our various kits. No need to waste time or effort shopping around for the right items. We've got them all *and* can deliver them directly to your door. What better way to get sailing at a fraction of the cost of factory-built boats?

COMPLETE PLANS include FULL SIZE PATTERNS for the frames, transom, stem, breasthook, deck beams, daggerboard, trunk, and rudder, instructions, Bill of Materials, and Fastening Schedule.

CHARACTERISTICS

Length overall	12'-0"
Beam	5'-3"
Hull depth	28"
Draft (board up)	7"
Draft (board down)	3'-0"
Cockpit size	7'-3"x3'-3"
Hull weight (approx.)	225 lbs.
Average passengers	2-4
Sail area:Main	60 sq. ft.
Jib	31 sq. ft.
Total:	91 sq. ft.

Hull type:Vee bottom, hard chine hull developed for sheet plywood planking.

Sail type:Jibhead sloop rig with daggerboard.

Power: Outboard motor to 3 HP.

Trailer: Designed for use with GLEN-L SERIES 750/1000 boat trailer plans.

AVAILABLE FOR THIS DESIGN:
- **Plans & Patterns**
- **Bronze Fastening Kit**
- **Fiberglass Kit**
- **Hardware Kit**
- **Rigging Kit**
- **Sails**

See Price List

GLEN-L 13

SIMPLE RIG FOR SINGLE-HANDED SAILING

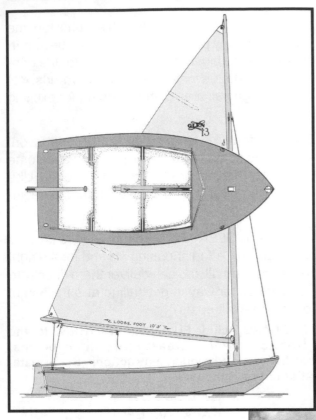

The **GLEN-L 13** is an ideal, all-around, sailing craft. The cockpit is roomy for family sailing, and yet the simple rig can be easily handled by one person. Here's a safe boat, but one which gives good performance and nimble handling. Two years were spent in the research, design, construction, and testing of the prototype to prove this design before offering it to you.

The sturdy, lightweight plywood construction makes trailering to your favorite body of water easy. A trailer designed especially for the **GLEN-L 13** is detailed right on the PLANS. The **GLEN-L 13** is a boat specifically developed with the amateur builder in mind. And the cost is low!

COMPLETE PLANS include FULL SIZE PATTERNS for the rudder, centerboard, centerboard trunk, bed logs, knees, stem breasthook, and half-section patterns for each of the frames and transom. Includes instructions, Bill of Materials, and Fastening Schedule.

CHARACTERISTICS

Length overall	12'-9"
Beam	5'-10"
Hull depth	26"
Draft (board up)	9"
Draft (board down)	3'-6"
Hull weight (approx.)	260 lbs.
Average passengers	2-4
Cockpit size	4'-8"x7'-3"
Sail area:Main	92 sq. ft.

Hull type:Vee bottom, hard chine hull developed for sheet plywood planking.

Sail type:Cat rig with centerboard.

Power: Outboard motor to 5 HP.

Trailer: Trailer plans included.

AVAILABLE FOR THIS DESIGN:
- **Plans & Patterns**
- **Bronze Fastening Kit**
- **Fiberglass Kit**
- **Hardware Kit**
- **Rigging Kit**
- **Sails**

See Price List

36

GLEN-L 14

A LIVELY 14' SLOOP

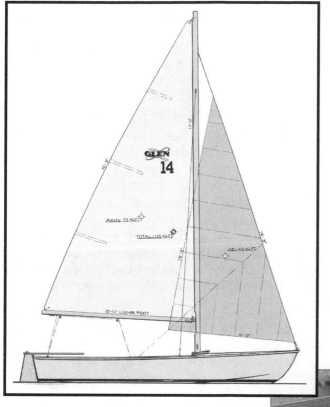

Here's a sprightly sloop that the whole family will enjoy. The broad beam not only makes the **GLEN-L 14** a safe and stable boat, but allows plenty of room for the family. Coming about is an easy process for everyone as the centerboard trunk protrudes only 10" above the cockpit sole. Although designed as a family day sailer, the **GLEN-L 14** can perform with the best of the fleet when the occasion demands.

The **GLEN-L 14** is an easy boat to build, even for the novice. Complete instructions are provided with the PLANS & FULL SIZE PATTERNS. Lightweight plywood construction keeps your costs low and makes trailering and launching a simple process.

COMPLETE PLANS include FULL SIZE PATTERNS for the centerboard, centerboard trunk, stem, rudder, breasthook, and half-section patterns for each of the frames and transom, instructions, Bill of Materials, and Fastening Schedule.

CHARACTERISTICS

Length overall	14'-0"
Beam	6'-0"
Draft (board up)	8"
Draft (board down)	3'-2"
Hull depth(approx.)	30"
Hull weight (approx.)	325 lbs.
Average passengers	2-4
Cockpit size	8'-9"x 4'-10"
Sail area:Main	73 sq. ft.
Jib	45 sq. ft.
Total	118 sq. ft.

Hull type:Vee bottom, hard chine hull developed for sheet plywood planking.

Sail type:Jibhead sloop rig with centerboard.

Power: Outboard motor to 5 HP.

Trailer: Designed for use with GLEN-L SERIES 750/1000 boat trailer plans.

AVAILABLE FOR THIS DESIGN:
- Plans & Patterns
- Bronze Fastening Kit
- Fiberglass Kit
- Hardware Kit
- Rigging Kit
- Sails

See Price List

GLEN-L 15

A ROOMY 15' FAMILY SLOOP

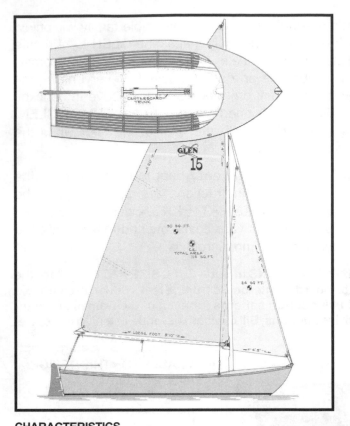

The notable feature of the **GLEN-L 15** is the big cockpit. There's over 18 lineal feet of seating and plenty of foot room. The boat is ideal for a large family, and is safe and stable. The sloop rig provides excellent performance, and if desired, the jib may be left in the bag and the boat sailed single-handed. The main sail is large enough to allow good performance by itself. The **GLEN-L 15** can perform double duty as a light fishing skiff or utility boat by using a lightweight outboard motor up to 7-1/2 horsepower.

Sailing and building your own **GLEN-L 15** is simple, even for the beginner. Our PLANS are specially intended for the amateur. You can outfit yours just as our designers intended it to be, by using our various kits. Whichever way you decide to build, you and your family will enjoy both building and sailing the **GLEN-L 15**.

COMPLETE PLANS include FULL SIZE PATTERNS for the centerboard, centerboard trunk, rudder, stem, breasthook, and half-section patterns for each of the frames and transom. Includes instructions, Bill of Materials, and Fastening Schedule.

AVAILABLE FOR THIS DESIGN:
- Plans & Patterns
- Bronze Fastening Kit
- Fiberglass Kit
- Hardware Kit
- Rigging Kit
- Sails

See Price List

CHARACTERISTICS

Length overall	15'-1"
Beam	6'-0"
Draft (board up)	7"
Draft (board down)	3'-4"
Hull depth (approx.)	24"
Hull weight	370 lbs.
Average passengers	2-5
Cockpit size	11'x4'-6"
Sail area:Main	90 sq. ft.
Jib	24 sq. ft.
Total	114 sq. ft.

Hull type:Vee bottom, hard chine hull developed for sheet plywood planking.

Sail type:Jibhead sloop rig with centerboard.

Power: Outboard motor to 7-1/2 HP.

Trailer: Designed for use with GLEN-L SERIES 750/1000 boat trailer plans.

MINUET
A 15' OVERNIGHT SLOOP

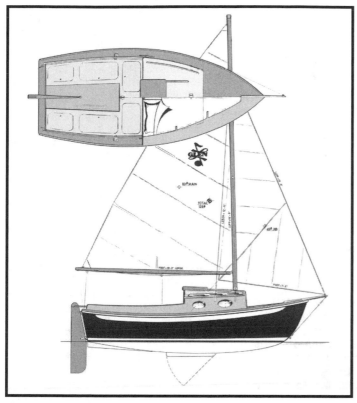

The **MINUET** captures the traditional character of many of our larger cruising designs in a size that allows trailering behind just about any vehicle, even compacts. Yet this boat has features and capabilities beyond it's diminutive 15' length. For example, the cozy cabin with nominal sitting headroom sleeps two in a 6'-4" double berth, or you can sleep under the stars in the cockpit on equally long seats. For extended camping-type cruising, there's plenty of storage space for a portable head and ice box, plus camping and cooking gear.

But don't confuse **MINUET** with less able daysailers of the same length. You'll appreciate the safety of a deep hull with self-bailing cockpit located well above the waterline, and the stiff sailing posture enhanced by a steel-plate centerboard and wide beam. The cockpit seats feature high coamings for comfort, and there's plenty of clearance so no one need duck when the boom comes across. Side decks are wide and feature toe rails and handrails for safe movement forward, even though most sail handling operations can be handled from the cockpit.

You'll be delighted with the sparkling performance of your **MINUET**. The hull features a long waterline length for maximum hull speed, and plenty of sail area in an easily handled rig. The rig is strongly stayed with upper and lower shrouds, and the centerboard allows easy beaching. If desired, a small outboard can be bracket-mounted to the transom and stored below when not needed.

Most importantly, **MINUET** is easy and inexpensive to build, even for the beginner. The sheet plywood hull requires no lofting or steam bending of members, and all plywood specified is standard 8' lengths. Our full size patterns with instructions, material listings, and fastening schedule leave virtually nothing to chance.

COMPLETE PLANS include FULL SIZE PATTERNS for the centerboard, centerboard trunk, rudder, stem, breasthook, and half-section patterns for each of the frames, transom, and cabin top beam camber, plus instructions, Bill of Materials, and Fastening Schedule.

CHARACTERISTICS

Length overall (on deck) .... 15'-0"
Length overall (with bowsprit) .... 16'-8"
Length waterline .... 13'-0"
Beam .... 6'-6"
Draft (board up) .... 1'-0"
Draft (board down) .... 2'-11"
Hull depth(approx.) .... 3'-6"
Height (board up to cabin top) ..... 4'-3"
Displacement (at D.W.L.) .... 885 lbs.
Hull weight (approx.).............. 400 lbs.
Centerboard weight (1/2" steel)120 lbs.
Cabin headroom .... 37" max.
Cockpit size .... 5'x6'-5"
Average passengers 2-4
Sleeping capacity 2
Sail area:Main .... 83 sq. ft.
            Jib .... 46 sq. ft.
            Total .... 129 sq. ft.
Hull type:Vee bottom, hard chine hull developed for sheet plywood planking.
Sail type:Jibhead sloop rig, centerboard.
Power: Outboard motor on transom bracket to 7 1/2 HP.
Trailer: Designed for use with GLEN-L SERIES 1200/1500 boat trailer plans.

LA CHATTE

A 16' SAILING CATAMARAN

CHARACTERISTICS

Length overall .... 15'-8"
Beam .... 7'-11"
Draft (boards down) .... 2'-5"
Hull depth .... 21"
Hull weight (approx.)............... 270 lbs.
Average passengers 2-4
Cockpit area .... 5'-6"x5'-4"
Sail area: Main .... 120 sq.ft.
                Jib .... 39 sq.ft.
                Total .... 159 sq.ft.
Hull type: Twin hulls each developed for plywood planking in continuous curve from keel to deck.
Sail type: Sloop rig with twin daggerboards.
Trailer: Can be used with GLEN-L SERIES 750/1000 boat trailer plans.

COMPLETE PLANS include FULL SIZE PATTERNS for the centerboard, centerboard trunk, rudder, stem, breasthook, and half-section patterns for each of the frames, transom, and cabin top beam camber, plus instructions, Bill of Materials, and Fastening Schedule.

When under sail do you want to feel the spray and wind whipping as though you are in a speed boat? Do you like the sensation of speed with only the sound of the wind and of the water being split by twin hulls? Then LA CHATTE is for you. A sloop rigged sailing cat that will really move out.

LA CHATTE is a development from the principles used on our popular L GATO. We've retained the break apart features and the construction methods. We've maintained the same principle of the lines and balance as they have been proven in practice. The results, a complete new boat with larger cockpit, more sail area and of course the sloop rig.

The construction details for building the LA CHATTE include an instruction booklet with step by step written instructions and photos. Types of glues, sizes of screws, lumber listings, itemized hardware, fastening schedule, etc., are all included in this detailed instruction booklet. The very complete plans show details on all portions of the construction. In addition to the plans, you'll also receive patterns for the contoured members of the framework--a very complete series of templates.

CHARACTERISTICS

Length overall .... 11'-11"
Beam .... 7'-10"
Draft (boards down) .... 2'-3"
Hull depth .... 20"
Hull weight (approx.)............... 220 lbs.
Average passengers 2-4
Cockpit area .... 4'x5'-3"
Sail area: .... 120 sq.ft.
Hull type: Twin hulls each developed for plywood planking in continuous curve from keel to deck.
Sail type: Cat rig with twin daggerboards.
Trailer: Can be used with GLEN-L SERIES 750/1000 boat trailer plans.

COMPLETE PLANS include FULL SIZE PATTERNS for the daggerboards, daggerboard trunks, rudders, stems, cockpit tray sides, back and splash shields, mast support beam, rudder tiller arms, and half-section patterns for each of the frame-bulkhead units and transom. Includes instructions, Bill of Materials, and Fastening Schedule.

The L GATO is a fast sailing catamaran. The rig is such that it can be handled by one man with ease. Yet, the cockpit area is large and the hull very stable so taking the kids or mate will be no problem. In addition the whole unit can be broken down for car topping or for winter storage without problem. The hull is very inexpensive to build. The novel development method enables the hull to be planked in a continuous width from keel to sheer.

The details for building the L GATO are especially complete and intended for the amateur builder with little or no previous boat building experience. The instruction booklet is a 16 page manual that carries you step by step through the building by written text and thirty photos of the boat being built as well as complete material listings. Details are also furnished on how to build the car top rack. The plans include five large scaled blue printed sheets on all phases of the construction from building form to the spar construction.

L GATO

A 12' SAILING CATAMARAN

GLEN-L 17
A 17' OVERNIGHT SLOOP

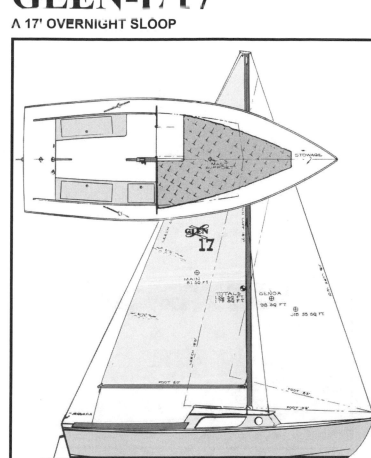

A minimum overnighter sloop rigged sail boat with generous beam...that's the **GLEN-L 17**. Sleeping facilities are provided for two with space for a portable toilet. The roomy cockpit provides plenty of space for a portable ice box and stove, with room left over for an auxiliary outboard motor and sail bin.

The **GLEN-L 17** carries a modern masthead sloop rig. The standard working sails are large enough to provide a lively boat in ordinary winds. For running or top performance, the larger genoa can be used. The rigging is such that the halyards and sheets are within handy reach of the helmsman for single-handed sailing, if desired.

The large scale plans have been especially worked out for the amateur builder and include details on building forms, spars, rigging, and step-by-step instructions with material listing.

COMPLETE PLANS include FULL-SIZE PATTERNS for the rudder, centerboard, centerboard trunk, stem, transom knee, breasthook, and half-section patterns of the frames, transom, dash, and deck beams. Includes instructions, Bill of Materials, and Fastening Schedule.

AVAILABLE FOR THIS DESIGN:
- **Study Plans**
- **Plans & Patterns**
- **Bronze Fastening Kit**
- **Fiberglass Kit**
- **Hardware Kit**
- **Rigging Kit**
- **Sails**

See Price List

CHARACTERISTICS

Length overall	17'-3"
Length waterline	15'-0"
Beam	6'-11"
Draft (board up)	1'-2"
Draft (board down)	2'-11"
Hull depth	2'-8"
Freeboard forward	2'-5"
Freeboard aft	2'-1"
Height (board up to cabin top)	4'-3"
Displacement	1287 lbs.
Hull weight (approx.)	475 lbs.
Centerboard weight (1/4" steel)	54 lbs.
Cabin headroom	3'-0"
Average passengers	2-4
Sleeping capacity	2
Cockpit size	5'x5'-6"
Sail area: Main	81 sq.ft.
Jib	55 sq.ft.
Genoa	98 sq.ft.
Total	136/179 sq.ft.

Hull type: Vee bottom hull with sheet steel centerboard, developed for 3/8" sheet plywood planking.

Sail type: Masthead sloop with centerboard.

Power: Outboard motor to 10HP.

Trailer: Designed for use with GLEN-L SERIES 1200/1800 boat trailer plans.

ALPHA-2   AN 18 1/2' *CLASSIC* SAILING DORY

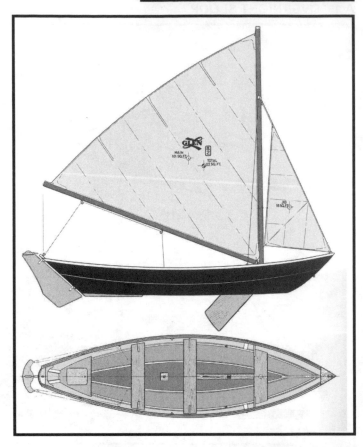

Our **ALPHA-2** is a somewhat smaller rendition of the classic "Beachcomber-Alpha" club dories of New England at the height of their popularity in the early 1900's, and akin to the famous Swampscott dories. Modified only slightly in form for adaptation to modern lightweight double-chine sheet plywood planking, the **ALPHA-2** is a close descendant of the rugged working dories well known for their seaworthiness. With easy, slimmed down lines for speed and ease of handling, our **ALPHA-2** is even faster and cheaper to build than ever before! Built over a simple temporary form, the hull has no permanent frames. Only a little over six sheets of standard sized plywood and a few board feet of lumber are required. And with our comprehensive plans featuring FULL SIZE PATTERNS, no lofting is required (although dimensions for the hull are given for those who wish to go through this excercise). Detailed instructions cover all phases of the construction making this a simple project even for the amateur.

The **ALPHA-2** features a centerboard and shallow draft rudder for easy launching and beaching. Steering is accomplished by a rudder yoke and stern sheets, however, a tiller can be fitted optionally. The **ALPHA-2** is a boat you'll be proud to own, with graceful lines that will surely turn heads wherever you choose to sail.

COMPLETE PLANS include FULL SIZE PATTERNS for the transom, stem, centerfold, centerboard trunk, rudder, rudder yoke, breasthook, and all the forms, plus instructions, bill of materials, and fastening schedule.

CHARACTERISTICS

Length overall	18'-6"
Bottom length	13'-3"
Beam	4'-11"
Draft (board up)	6 1/2"
Draft (board down)	2'-8 1/2"
Depth of board below bottom	2'-3"
Hull depth	2'-6"
Hull weight (approx.)	292 lbs.
Weight all up (approx.)	400 lbs.
Average passengers	2-4
Sail area:	Main
101 sq.ft.	Jib
16 sq.ft.	Total
117 sq.ft.	

Hull type: Double chine dory developed for 3/8" (sides), and 1/2" (bottom) sheet plywood planking.

Sail type: Sloop rig with centerboard.

Power: Sail, scull, or oars.

Trailer: Designed for use with GLEN-L SERIES 1200/1800 boat trailer plans.

AVAILABLE FOR THIS DESIGN:
- **Plans & Patterns**
- **Bronze Fastening Kit**
- **Fiberglass Kit**
- **Hardware Kit**
- **Rigging Kit**
- **Sails**

See Price List

TANGO

BUILD IN PLYWOOD

The **TANGO** design appears much larger than her handy trailerable size would indicate. Although she has plenty of traditional good looks, don't underestimate her performance ability. This is a light hull featuring a stiff, beamy, hard-chine form that can transform any breeze into brisk sailing. The jibhead rig is easy to handle while keeping a low center of effort for stability.

TANGO is a family boat meant for comfort and safety. The cockpit has plenty of depth and is self-draining, while cockpit seats are spaced for easy bracing when heeling.

The cabin has more headroom than usual for a boat this size (full sitting above the berths), with full length berths for four adults. The cockpit seats can serve double duty for sleeping under the stars; they're 6'-3" long. There are also provisions for galley gear port and starboard, as well as a portable head, and the centerboard trunk protrudes only nominally into the cabin area.

Building **TANGO** is well within the realm of the average do-it-yourselfer. No lofting or difficult woodworking operations are required. Plans cover all aspects of the project, including making your own wood spars if you wish. Building the sheet plywood hull progresses quickly and the cost is low. Our instructions, intended specifically for the amateur, will guide you through every step of the way.

CHARACTERISTICS

Length (on deck)	18'-6"
Length (with bow sprit)	20'-4"
Length waterline	16'-0"
Beam	7'-10"
Draft (board up)	1'-6"
Draft (board down)	3'-3"
Hull depth	4'-1"
Freeboard forward	3'-2"
Freeboard aft	2'-4"
Height (board up to cabin top)	5'-8"
Displacement (at D.W.L.)	1750 lbs.
Hull weight (approx.)	600 lbs.
Ballast weight (1" steel C.B.)	400 lbs.
Cabin headroom	4'-6"
Average passengers	2-4
Sleeping capacity	4
Cockpit size	5'x6'-3"
Sail area: Main	95 sq.ft.
Jib	69 sq.ft.
Genoa	104 sq.ft.
Total	164/199 sq.ft.

Hull type: Vee bottom hull with sheet steel centerboard, developed for 3/8" sheet plywood planking.

Sail type: Jibhead sloop, centerboard.

Power: Outboard motor to 10 HP mounted on outboard bracket.

Trailer: Designed for use with GLEN-L SERIES 1200/1800 boat trailer plans.

COMPLETE PLANS include FULL SIZE PATTERNS for the stem, breasthook, centerboard, centerboard trunk assembly, rudder, and half-section patterns for the transom and all frames. Includes instructions, Bill of Materials, and Fastening Schedule.

AVAILABLE FOR THIS DESIGN:
- **Study Plans**
- **Plans & Patterns**
- **Bronze Fastening Kit**
- **Fiberglass Kit**
- **Hardware Kit**
- **Rigging Kit**
- **Sails**

See Price List

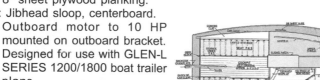

43

GLEN-L 19

A 19' TRAILERABLE OVERNIGHTER SLOOP

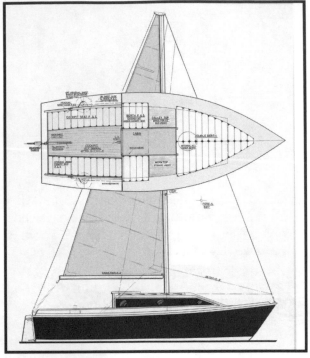

The easy-to-trailer **GLEN-L 19** features rakish styling enhanced by optional full length "black-out" side windows and long, lean lines. The beamy, hard-chine hull features a steel plate centerboard plus some internal ballast (steel pigs will suffice) and a large sail area for a combination of speed and stability. A feature that distinguishes this boat from our other designs is its lack of a centerboard trunk intruding into the cabin, thereby giving it a spaciousness seldom found in a boat of this size. The cabin has berths for four plus room for a compact galley and head, all with sitting headroom.

The **GLEN-L 19** cockpit is also generous in size, and self-draining. The easily controlled rig requires only a minimum of fittings, while lightweight, sturdy plywood construction keeps costs low. The size of the boat makes it ideal for building and storing in the average garage. Auxilliary power can be provided with a transom mounted outboard up to 10 HP.

COMPLETE PLANS include FULL SIZE PATTERNS for the stem, breasthook, centerboard trunk sides and bed logs, and half section patterns for the frames, bulkhead, transom, and deck beam. Includes Instructions, Bill of Materials, and Fastening Schedule.

CHARACTERISTICS

Length overall	19'-3"
Length waterline	16'-8"
Beam	7'-9"
Draft (board up)	1'-8"
Draft (board down)	3'-10"
Freeboard forward	2'-11"
Freeboard aft	2'-1/2"
Displacement	1900 lbs.
Hull weight (approx.)	600 lbs.
Ballast weight	400 lbs.
Average passengers	2-4
Sleeping capacity	4
Cockpit size	5'-6"x6'-0"
Sail area:Main	82 sq.ft.
Jib	83 sq.ft.
Genoa	129 sq.ft.
Total	165/211 sq.ft.

Hull type: Vee bottom hull with sheet steel centerboard and internal ballast keel, developed for 3/8" sheet plywood planking.

Sail type: Masthead centerboard sloop.

Power: Outboard motor to 10HP mounted on removable transom bracket (optional).

Trailer: Designed for use with GLEN-L SERIES 2300/2800 boat trailer plans.

AVAILABLE FOR THIS DESIGN:
- Study Plans
- Plans & Patterns
- Bronze Fastening Kit
- Fiberglass Kit
- Hardware Kit
- Rigging Kit
- Sails

See Price List

GLEN-L 21CB A 21' CENTERBOARD SLOOP

The **GLEN-L 21CB** is a centerboard sloop which means that you can sail in water a few feet deep. With the board up, the hull draws less than 10". With the board down, the boat is extremely stable due to the ballasted centerboard. A winch in the cabin on the trunk is used to raise and lower the board, or vary its position to suit sailing conditions. You can trailer the **GLEN-L 21CB** to practically anywhere a car can take it. Launching is very easy, as is handling the simple but efficient masthead rig.

The hull is a light displacement type made possible by lightweight easy-to-build plywood construction. Overnight sailing is a pleasure. There's room to sleep three, and with the hatch up, the cook can sit on the trunk and whip up a meal in the compact galley. A drop leaf table on the opposite side of the trunk can be used for dining. Plenty of space is provided under the berths and cockpit seats for storage and an ice box. The cockpit seats can be used for extra berths, if desired. All sheets lead to the helmsman in the self-draining cockpit, and rigging is simplified and inexpensive.

CHARACTERISTICS

Length overall .... 21'-3"
Length waterline .... 19'-0"
Beam .... 7'-9"
Draft (board up) .... 10"
Draft (board down) .... 4'-6"
Freeboard forward .... 2'-11"
Freeboard aft .... 2'-2"
Displacement .... 2000 lbs.
Hull weight (approx.).............. 730 lbs.
Ballast weight .... 400 lbs.
Average passengers 2-4
Sleeping capacity 3
Cockpit size .... 5'-6"x6'-0"
Sail area: Main .... 93 sq.ft.
          Jib .... 72 sq.ft.
          Genoa .... 125 sq.ft.
          Total .... 165/218 sq.ft.
Hull type: Vee bottom hull with sheet steel centerboard, developed for 3/8" sheet plywood planking.
Sail type: Masthead centerboard sloop.
Power: Outboard motor to 10HP mounted on removable transom bracket.
Trailer: Designed for use with GLEN-L SERIES 2300/2800 boat trailer plans.

AVAILABLE FOR THIS DESIGN:
- **Study Plans**
- **Plans & Patterns**
- **Bronze Fastening Kit**
- **Fiberglass Kit**
- **Hardware Kit**
- **Rigging Kit**
- **Sails**

See Price List

COMPLETE PLANS include **FULL-SIZE PATTERNS** for the stem, breasthook, centerboard, centerboard trunk, rudder, and half-section patterns for the frames and transom. **FULL-SIZE CABIN PATTERNS** for the cabin sides, windshield, knee and contoured roof beams.

45

FANCY FREE
A 21' TRAILERABLE SHARPIE

CHARACTERISTICS

Length overall (minus bowsprit) 21'-3"
Length waterline .... 19'-0"
Beam .... 7'-6"
Draft (board up) .... 8"
Draft (board down) .... 3'-3"
Freeboard forward .... 3'-0"
Freeboard aft .... 2'-1"
Displacement .... 2500 lbs.
Ballast weight .... 620 lbs.
Height to cabin top .... 4'-3"
Headroom .... 4'-0"
Sleeping capacity 2
Cockpit size .... 5'x6'
Sail area: Main .... 130 sq. ft.
            Foretriangle .... 100 sq. ft.
            Total .... 230 sq. ft.
Hull type: Flat bottom, hard chine, dory-type, centerboard hull, developed for 3/8" sheet plywood planking.
Sail type: Gaff rigged sloop.
Power: Outboard motor to 4HP, 15" nominal shaft length, mounted in well.
Trailer: Designed for use with GLEN-L SERIES 1200/1800 boat trailer plans.

COMPLETE PLANS include FULL SIZE PATTERNS for the centerboard and centerboard trunk assembly, rudder, stem, and breasthook, plus half-section patterns for each of the frames and transom, instructions, bill of materials, and fastening schedule.

AVAILABLE FOR THIS DESIGN:
- **Study Plans**
- **Plans & Patterns**
- **Bronze Fastening Kit**
- **Fiberglass Kit**
- **Hardware Kit**
- **Rigging Kit**
- **Sails**
See Price List

If you're looking for a simple, inexpensive, and compact cruising sailboat, yet one with traditional character, our **FANCY FREE** should fill the bill. The combination sharpie-dory hull of flat-bottom, hard-chine form is ideal for the beginning amateur on a budget. All frames have straight contours using standard materials. All plywood specified is standard 4' x 8' sheets. Our plans using full size patterns require no lofting. And our various accessory kits include all the hard-to-find items required to equip your very own in sailaway condition.

FANCY FREE is an ideal boat for the couple who wants to do weekend or vacation sailing along coastal waters where shoal draft is critical. Hull draft with board-up is just 8", yet the ballast gives reassuring stiffness in a breeze. The light displacement and large sail area makes this boat a surprising performer, even for the racing skipper. While not intended for long distance open ocean use, **FANCY FREE** when heeled, forms a vee at the water for a good ride with exceptional dryness.

Accommodations on **FANCY FREE** are of the "camping" type for two. There's full headroom above the berths, plus the comfort of a settee with a hinged dropleaf on the centerboard trunk. The galley area is adjacent to the hatch for standing headroom and the portable head slides out from under the bridge deck for use. A portable ice chest is also located under the bridge deck, accessible from either the cockpit or from inside the cabin. Storage spaces are located below the cockpit sides either side and below the aft deck.

Because this boat is lightweight, **FANCY FREE** is ideal for trailering and pulling up on the beach for the night. There's no need to pay for expensive mooring, slippage, or storage fees. For powering, there's a built-in outboard motor well, and some say these boats are suitable for poling or rowing as well. The cockpit is plenty roomy, yet the cockpit well is compact and self-draining for safety. The gaff sloop rig is simple to handle and requires no expensive winches or special "go-fast" fittings. Wood spars are detailed on the plans. All in all, we doubt that you'll find a more enjoyable boat to own and build considering its low cost, simplicity, and ease of maintainance.

AMIGO

A TRAILERABLE OFFSHORE CRUISER WITH A CLASSIC DESIGN

CHARACTERISTICS

Length overall (minus bowsprit) 22'-0"
Length waterline .... 19'-2"
Beam .... 8'-0"
Draft .... 3'-0"
Freeboard forward .... 4'-2"
Freeboard aft.............................. 2'-10"
Displacement .... 5100 lbs.
Ballast .... 1775 lbs.
Height to cabin top .... 8'-0"
Headroom .... 5'-10" to 6'-0"
Fuel capacity .... 13 gals.
Water capacity .... 50 gals.
Sleeping capacity 4
Sail area - Masthead rig:
    Main .... 117 sq. ft.
    Foretriangle .... 126 sq. ft.
    Total ....243 sq. ft.
Sail area - Gaff rig:
    Main .... 174 sq. ft.
    Jib .... 76 sq. ft.
    Total .... 250 sq. ft.
Hull type: Round bilge, full keel hull, designed for one-off fiberglass or strip-planked wood construction.
Sail type: Masthead or gaff sloop.
Power: Transom-mounted outboard or inboard gasoline or diesel engine, 250 lbs. max., 5 to 10 B.H.P.
Trailer: Designed for use with GLEN-L SERIES 5/0006000 boat trailer plans.

Although our **AMIGO** is compact, this pocket cruiser offers the seaworthiness, comfort, and features of much larger vessels, but at an affordable price. Not to be confused with the lighter, less-able weekender-types of similar length, this is a heavy boat capable of serious long-distance offshore and coastal cruising. Yet **AMIGO** is a boat that is easy to handle in either the masthead or gaff sloop rig, even by the singlehander. Best of all, *it's trailerable*.

A notable feature aboard **AMIGO** is the standing headroom throughout the cabin area, a remarkable feat considering the attractive and well-proportioned appearance. The fully enclosed toilet room with stall shower is formed by a series of hinged panels. These panels fold back when not needed, hiding the head from view while opening up the cabin for spaciousness. The divided cabin offers dual cabin privacy, something seldom seen on a 22' boat.

Other features include two hanging lockers, a dinette that converts to form a berth, an aft quarter berth, a 4' long galley, and

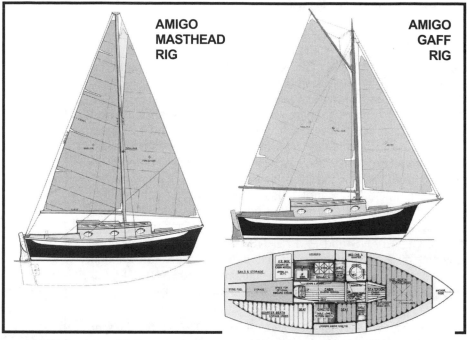

a HUGE ice box with access from the cockpit or galley. Storage space is located in every nook and cranny, including a locker at the stern for stove fuel with overboard drains for safety. The cockpit is self-draining and long enough to sleep in. For range, there is a 50 gallon fresh water capacity.

Aimed at the amateur who prides himself on quality workmanship and perseverance, building **AMIGO** will be a rewarding experience that will draw the admiration from on-lookers. Plans are available for either wood-strip or one-off fiberglass construction.

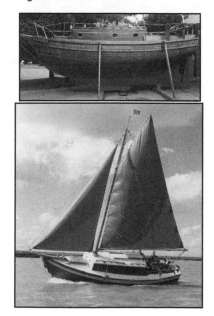

COMPLETE PLANS include FULL SIZE PATTERNS for all station, transom, and stem form contours, deck crown and cabin cambers, plus gaff and masthead rig, and inboard or outboard power options. Includes instructions, Table of Offsets, and hull materials listing. Fiberglass version includes FIBERGLASS Manual.

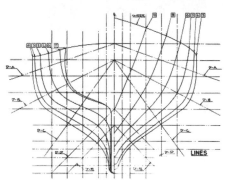

AVAILABLE FOR THIS DESIGN:
- **Study Plans**
- **Plans & Patterns**
- **Bronze Fastening Kit**
- **Fiberglass Kit**
- **Hardware Kit**
- **Rigging Kit**
- **Sails**
See Price List

GLEN-L 6.9   A 23' TRAILERABLE SLOOP

The **GLEN-L 6.9** is easy to trailer and easy to launch. The combination ballast keel and centerboard allows shoal draft maneuverability, coupled with stability and safety. Sailing vacations can be spent anywhere there is a launching ramp, and at the end of the season, simply moor your **GLEN-L 6.9** in the backyard. Accommodations include honest-sized berthing and cabin seating for four, space for a head which can be curtained off for privacy, galley facilities, and a huge hanging locker. The cockpit is roomy and comfortable, as well as being convenient for handling the rig. Power can be provided by an outboard motor hung on a transom bracket. Superior performance is assured by a generous spread of "canvas" whether using the working jib or optional Genoa. Built with "one-off" fiberglass methods and materials (either foam sandwich or fiberglass planking), the amateur can now build his own fiberglass sailboat that will equal or exceed the quality of mass-produced boats. Our PLANS and PATTERNS package shows you how, covering all aspects of the construction. Also available are various accessory kits so that building and outfitting your own **GLEN-L 6.9** will be a rewarding experience you'll be proud of.

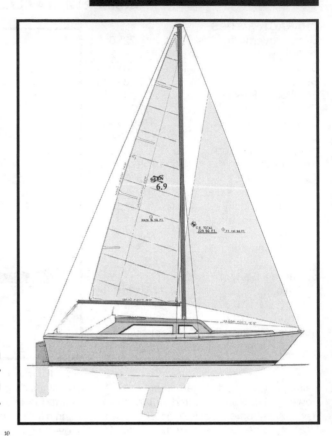

COMPLETE PLANS include FULL-SIZE PATTERNS for the stem form, keel form, centerboard, rudder, and half-section patterns for the station sections (form contours), and deck crown camber. Includes instructions, Materials listing, and GLEN-L FIBERGLASS MANUAL.

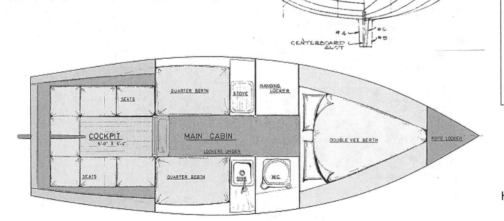

AVAILABLE FOR THIS DESIGN:
• **Study Plans**
• **Plans & Patterns**
• **Hardware Kit**
• **Rigging Kit**
• **Sails**
See Price List

CHARACTERISTICS

Length overall .... 22'-7 1/2" (6.9M)
Length waterline .... 19'-4 1/2"
Beam .... 7'-10"
Draft (board up) .... 24"
Draft (board down) .... 4'-4"
Freeboard forward .... 3'-0"
Freeboard aft .... 2'-6"
Displacement .... 3186 lbs.
Hull weight (approx.) .... 1500 lbs.
Ballast weight (with board) .... 960 lbs.

Water capacity .... 12 gals.
Height (board up to cabin top) ..... 6'-3"
Cabin headroom .... 4'-8"
Cockpit size (nominal) .... 5'x 5'-4"
Cabin size (nominal) .... 6'x 8'
Average passengers 2-4
Sleeping capacity 4
Sail area: Main .... 94 sq.ft.
          Jib .... 102 sq.ft.
          Genoa .... 190 sq.ft.
          Total .... 196/284 sq.ft.

Hull type: Round bilge hull design with combination center/ballast keel unit. Designed for "one-off" fiberglass construction using fiberglass planking laminate or PVC foam sandwich core with fiberglass laminate.
Sail type: Masthead sloop.
Power: Outboard motor to 10HP mounted on removable transom bracket (optional).
Trailer: Designed for use with GLEN-L SERIES 2300/2800 boat trailer plans.

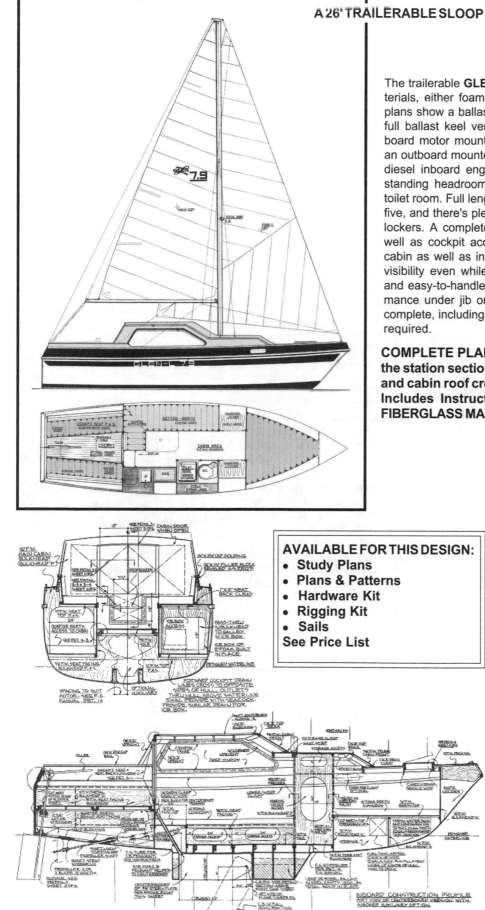

A 26' TRAILERABLE SLOOP

GLEN-L 7.9

BUILD IN FIBERGLASS

The trailerable **GLEN-L 7.9** is built with "one-off" fiberglass materials, either foam sandwich core or fiberglass planking. The plans show a ballasted centerboard version for shoal draft or a full ballast keel version. Power can be provided with an outboard motor mounted in a unique concealed transom well, or an outboard mounted on a transom bracket, or by a gasoline or diesel inboard engine. The spacious cabin area features full standing headroom, even in the optional shower area of the toilet room. Full length berths are provided for a family of four or five, and there's plenty of storage space, including *two* hanging lockers. A complete galley features an ice box with cabin, as well as cockpit access. The dining table can be used in the cabin as well as in the cockpit. The cockpit features full circle visibility even while seated, and is self-draining. The efficient and easy-to-handle rig has plenty of sail area for smart performance under jib or optional Genoa. The plans are especially complete, including full-size patterns and of course, no lofting is required.

COMPLETE PLANS include FULL SIZE PATTERNS for the station sections (form contours), floor timbers, deck and cabin roof crown cambers, and stem form contour. Includes Instructions, Bill of Materials, and GLEN-L FIBERGLASS MANUAL.

AVAILABLE FOR THIS DESIGN:
- **Study Plans**
- **Plans & Patterns**
- **Hardware Kit**
- **Rigging Kit**
- **Sails**
See Price List

CHARACTERISTICS

Length overall	25'-11 1/2" (7.9M)
Length waterline	22'-6"
Beam	7'-11 1/2"
Draft (board up CB version)	2'-6"
Draft (board down CB version)	5'-0"
Draft (fixed keel)	4'-0"
Freeboard forward	4'-1"
Freeboard aft	3'-5"
Displacement	4200 lbs.
Ballast	1200 lbs.
Fuel capacity	10 gals.
Water capacity	20 gals.
Height to cabin top (board up, CB)	8'-3"
Height to cabin top (keel version)	9'-9"
Cabin headroom	6'-2", 5'-0"
Cockpit size (nominal)	6'-6"x 5'-6"
Cabin size (nominal)	7'-0"x 16'-6"
Sleeping capacity	4-5
Sail area:Main	120 sq. ft.
Jib	137 sq. ft.
Total	257 sq. ft.
Genoa	195 sq. ft.

Hull type: Round bilge with combination centerboard/keel or fixed ballast keel. Developed for "one-off" fiberglass construction using fiberglass planking or PVC core with fiberglass laminates.

Sail type: Masthead sloop.

Power: Outboard motor to 10 HP in transom well or on transom bracket, inboard engine to 10 HP, gasoline or diesel, not to exceed 200 lbs.

Trailer: Designed for use with GLEN-L SERIES 5000/6000 boat trailer plans.

49

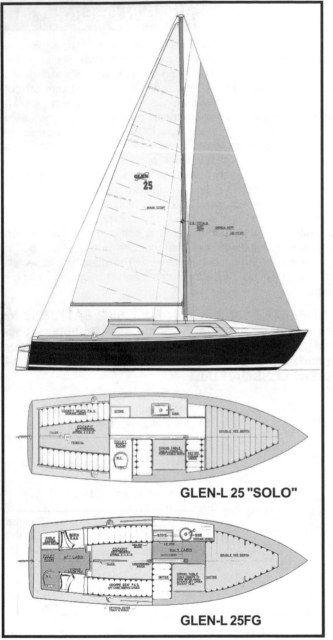

GLEN-L 25 "SOLO"

GLEN-L 25FG

You can build this 25' sloop with a single cabin aft cockpit or with a fore and aft cabin and a center cockpit. The design is available for either plywood (GLEN-L 25) or fiberglass (GLEN-L 25FG) construction. Each is an entirely separate set of plans, although the rig is the same in both cases.

The "25" is easily towed and launched because the centerboard retracts into the hull. The combination centerboard/ballast keel provides positive stability at all sailing angles, plus the ability to enter shoal waters. Handling of the simple masthead sloop rig is an easy job, as all sheets lead to the cockpit.

These popular designs have successfully cruised from the Pacific coast to Hawaii, quite an accomplishment for a boat of its size. One first-time builder entered into competition sailing with exceptional results. His trophies include one for winning first in class in the difficult and prestigious Newport, California to Ensenada, Mexico race.

PLYWOOD VERSION

The GLEN-L 25 is the plywood version, available in two cabin styles: the dual cabin DUET and the single cabin SOLO. The hull features semi-round sides and bottom, with a hard chine much less apparent than the typical plywood boat. The roundness of the hull makes it easier to drive, provides easier motion for comfort, and gives better general sailing characteristics.

The DUET features dual cabin privacy and comfortable midship cockpit. The aft cabin features two berths plus private enclosed toilet room. The forward cabin has a combination dinette/berth area. The galley is complete with standing headroom when the hatch is up.

The SOLO features a self-bailing aft cockpit. The spacious cabin has a roomy, enclosed, toilet room plus a 7' long galley area. The dinette seats four and converts to a double berth, while two can sleep in the vee berth forward. Also included is a real hanging locker and lots of storage space.

Complete PLYWOOD Plans include Full Size Patterns for the stem, breasthook, deck beams, centerboard, centerboard trunk, bed logs, ballast keel sections, and half section patterns for the frame/bulkhead members, and transom. Instructions include bill of materials and fastening schedule.

AVAILABLE FOR THE GLEN-L
25 & 25FG:
• **Study Plans**
• **Plans & Patterns**
• **Bronze Fastening Kit (PW)**
• **Fiberglass Kit (PW)**
• **Hardware Kit**
• **Rigging Kit**
• **Sails**
See Price List

CHARACTERISTICS

	PW	FG
Length overall	25'-0"	25'-0"
Length waterline	22'-3"	22'-4"
Beam	7'-11"	7'-11"
Draft (board up)	2'-1"	2'-4"
Draft (board down)	5'-0"	5'-3"
Draft (fixed keel)	N.A.	4'-0"
Freeboard forward	3'-7"	3'-6"
Freeboard aft	2'-8"	2'-7"
Displacement (at D.W.L.)	3500 lbs.	3950 lbs.
Hull weight (approx.)	1600 lbs.	1800 lbs.
Water capacity	10 gals.	20 gals.
Height (board up to cabin top)	6'-7"	6'-9"

	PW	FG
Cabin headroom (fwd)	5'-0"	5'-0"
Cabin headroom (aft)	4'-6"	4'-6"

Sail area - both:
Main	127.5 sq. ft.
Jib	117.5 sq. ft.
Genoa	167 sq. ft.
Total	245/294.5 sq. ft.

Hull type, PLYWOOD version: Combination centerboard/ballast keel for stability and ease of trailering. Hull form of semi-round bottom and sides, with soft chine between. Developed for 3/8" sheet plywood planking.

Hull type, FIBERGLASS version: Round bilge with combination centerboard/keel or fixed ballast keel. Developed for "one-off" fiberglass construction using fiberglass planking or PVC core with fiberglass laminates.

Sail type: Masthead sloop.
Power: Outboard motor to 10 HP on transom bracket.
Trailer: Designed for use with Glen-L 5000/6000 boat trailer plans.

GLEN-L 25 FG

FIBERGLASS VERSION

The GLEN-L 25FG is the one-off fiberglass version, available in two cabin configurations: the SINGLE cabin model with aft cockpit and the TWIN cabin model with aft cabin and midship cockpit. Specifically detailed for one-off fiberglass construction using fiberglass planking or PVC sandwich core. Options are given for building with two different keel configurations. One is the centerboard/ballast keel type for easy launching. The other, a fixed ballast type keel for the ultimate in stability and performance.

The SINGLE cabin features a self-bailing cockpit with plenty of room for fair weather sleeping for two. The roomy cabin offers individual berthing for five with complete accommodations for family cruising. For dining, a table hinges down in position at the settee, but is out of the way at other times.

The TWIN cabin, with self-bailing cockpit midship, provides a private aft cabin for two with head. The complete galley has standing headroom when the hatch is raised. There's storage area under all berths and a large hanging locker.

Complete FIBERGLASS Plans include Full Size Patterns for stem form contour, deck crown, ballast keel mold (for both fixed keel and centerboard versions), centerboard, centerboard trunk, and half-section patterns for all station sections (form contours). Instructions include bill of materials, fastening schedule, and the "Fiberglass Boatbuilding the Glen-L Way" manual.

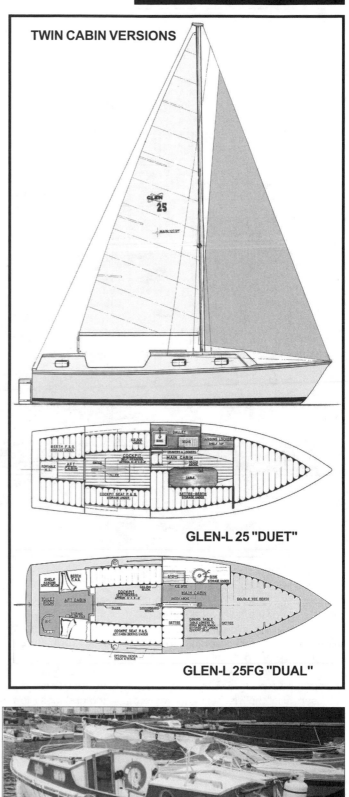

BUILD IN FIBERGLASS

TWIN CABIN VERSIONS

GLEN-L 25 "DUET"

GLEN-L 25FG "DUAL"

ENSENADA 25 A 25' TRAILERABLE PERFORMANCE-CRUISER

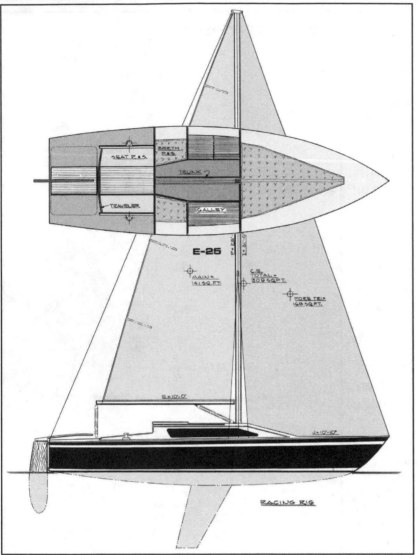

BUILD IN PLYWOOD

CHARACTERISTICS
Length overall	25'3"
Length waterline	22'3"
Beam	7'10"
Draft	2'3"/5'6"
Hull weight	1000 lbs.
Ballast weight	1200 lbs.

Sail area:
Standard Rig	287 sq.ft.
Racing Rig	309 sq.ft.

Hull type, Combination centerboard/ballast keel for stability and ease of trailering. Hull form of semi-round bottom and sides, with soft chine between. Developed for 3/8" sheet plywood planking.

Sail type: Masthead sloop.

Power: Outboard motor to 10 HP on transom bracket.

Trailer: Designed for use with Glen-L 5000/6000 boat trailer plans.

We'll talk about performance in a minute. But first, what's difficult to see here is the pleasing hull shape of this boat. Through careful design, the hull has a "rounded" form which virtually disguises it's hard-chine origins. In other words, most will be hard-pressed to believe this boat is made from sheet plywood, yet construction is easy and low in cost. The "stressed skin" hull is built over a few strength bulkheads without typical frames, all stiffened by longitudinal stringers. The result is a surprisingly stiff yet lightweight boat, and this is partly what gives the boat its performance edge.

Originally a custom design for a competitive Southern California racer/builder who had successfully raced the Glen-L 25 Solo, ENSENADA 25 is a proven performer. In its first Newport-Ensenada Race, the boat placed 2nd in PHRF "G" Class over 50 other boats, and beat the winning boats in Classes "C", "D", "E", "F", & "H" on corrected time. In addition to light weight, the hull is inherently quick with either rig option, with lots of stability due to the chined hull form and drop keel. This ballasted centerboard/keel incorporates a "high-lift" NACA foil section with a "no-drag" pennant and unique integral easy-to-make "slot sealer" device that prevents turbulence and drag around the lowered keel. Also, the efficient elliptical rudder has an integral "non-ventilation" fin.

Trailering and launching are easy, while power can be provided by a bracket-mounted outboard to 10 HP. The cabin includes four berths all 6'8" long, sitting headroom, space for a galley and head, plenty of storage, and an 8' long self-bailing cockpit, making the boat well-suited to limited cruising.

COASTER

BUILD IN PLYWOOD

A 25' TRAILERABLE DORY MOTORSAILER

Looking for a boat to cruise those favorite rivers, lakes, bays, and coastal waterways? Do you want to poke around estuaries and go gunk-holing in areas not accessible to deeper draft boats? Would you like to just run your boat up onto the beach at day's end and eliminate the cost of a mooring? Do you find the serenity and economy of sailing alluring, yet don't want to get stuck when the wind dies? At the end of your cruise, do you want to haul your boat out, trailer it home, and park it in the backyard?

Then our **COASTER** is just the design for you, it's a shallow draft trailerable motorsailer of dory that's easy and inexpensive to build. With this boat, there's no need to worry about having enough wind; just fire up the engine and you'll keep on sailing as close to the wind as necessary at speeds in the 6 to 7 knot range. And you'll do it in easy-motion comfort due to the roll-dampening effect of the sails combined with the stability imparted by the fixed ballast skeg and centerboard arrangement.

The **COASTER** hull has a fine waterline entrance with immersed forefoot that minimizes resistance and smooths the ride. A long bottom run and full lines aft dampen pitching and assure good speed. The lowered centerboard and long skeg provide weatherliness that you'll find surprising. A pronounced raised stem with ample freeboard makes this flat bottomed hull dry running even in choppy seas.

COASTER is an ideal boat for the cruising couple or small family with younger children. The U-shaped dinette forward has sitting headroom and converts to a 7' wide x 8' long berth. There's full standing headroom throughout the rest of the cabin, even in the galley and enclosable toilet room which has space for a shower. Storage space is located under all seats and berths, and a hanging locker is included. The pilothouse features plenty of windows for light, ventilation, and full-circle visibility. A raised settee for two converts to a child's berth and conceals the inboard engine below. Optionally, an outboard can be used in the cockpit just forward of the stern seat. The cockpit is approximately 34" deep making it safe for the small ones, and it's self-draining.

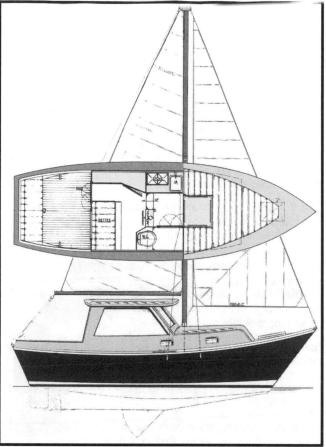

COMPLETE PLANS include instructions, Bill of Materials, Fastening Schedule, PLUS FULL SIZE PATTERNS for the stem, breasthook, centerboard, centerboard trunk, deck beams, mast step beam, cabin top beams, and half section patterns for all the frames and transom.

AVAILABLE FOR THIS DESIGN:
- **Study Plans**
- **Plans & Patterns**
- **Bronze Fastening Kit**
- **Fiberglass Kit**
- **Hardware Kit**
- **Rigging Kit**
- **Sails**

See Price List

CHARACTERISTICS

Length overall	25'-2"
Length waterline	20'-0"
Beam	8'-0"
Bottom width	6'-10"
Draft (board up)	1'-11"
Draft (board down)	4'-1"
Freeboard forward	4'-10"
Freeboard aft	3'-2"
Displacement	4900 lbs.
Ballast weight	1295 lbs.
Height (board up to cabin top)	9'-2"
Headroom (aft of windshield)	6'-2" min.
Sleeping capacity	2 adults, 2 children
Cockpit size	6'x6'-6"
Fuel capacity	20 gals.
Fresh water capacity	40 gals.
Sail area: Main	113 sq. ft.
Jib	113 sq. ft.
Total	226 sq. ft.

Hull type: Flat bottom, hard chine, dory-type, with ballast/keel and centerboard, developed for sheet plywood planking (1/2" sides, 3/4" bottom).

Ballast: Skeg-mounted lead bars plus 3/8" steel centerboard.

Sail type: Masthead rigged sloop.

Power: Inboard gasoline or diesel, or long shaft outboard in cockpit well, 6 to 16 shaft horsepower.

Trailer: Designed for use with GLEN-L Series 5000/6000 boat trailer plans.

ULTRA-PIERRE
A 26' TRADITIONAL ST. PIERRE DORY

Our trailerable Ultra-Pierre is available in either Sail or Power versions. Because beam and bottom width are wider than on other narrower St. Pierre dory plans you might see, stability is enhanced, and we can incorporate a sail option with the ability to carry a generous sloop rig. The boat also gains stability through additional internal ballast and a steel plate centerboard. This latter feature makes beaching the boat practical while simplifying trailer launching and retrieval. While wood spars are detailed, aluminum extruded types are optional.

The Power version includes several motor options. You can use a well-mounted outboard with "kick-up" ability, inboard with in-line shaft and propeller drive, or inboard with the Nova Scotia dory-type "haul-up" shaft and prop option that was once common in older types. The Sail version also includes a well-mounted outboard but without the "kick-up" feature for both performance and structural reasons. In all cases, 10 to 20 horsepower is all you need regardless of motor type.

Both versions have a self-bailing cockpit. Both also use a simple, reliable, and low-cost outboard rudder, although an inboard rudder with remote steering could be adapted if desired, and such is shown for use in the case of the inboard option.

There is full-sitting headroom above the full-length v-berth and space below for a head. Construction is sheet plywood planking over straight-contoured frames of ordinary lumber, with little additional fairing required. Plans include instructions, material list, fastening schedules, and FULL SIZE PATTERNS so no lofting is required.

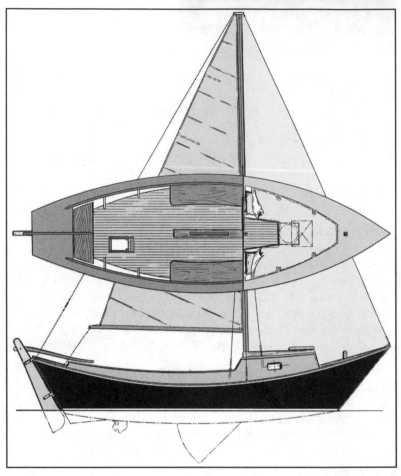

AVAILABLE FOR THIS DESIGN:
- **Study Plans**
- **Plans & Patterns**
- **Bronze Fastening Kit**
- **Fiberglass Kit**

See Price List

CHARACTERISTICS
Length overall	26'0"
Length waterline	19'11"
Beam	8'6"
Bottom width (max)	5'3"
Draft (Power Version)	1'0"
Draft (Sail Version max)	3'9"
Displacement (@ DWL)	4150 lbs.
Ballast (Sail Version)	1500 lbs.
Sail area (Sail Version)	238 sq. ft.
Fuel capacity	20-40 gals.

Hull type: Flat bottom St. Pierre type dory hull with flaring topsides, developed for sheet plywood planking.

Power: Single well-mounted outboard, conventional gasoline or diesel powered inboard, or traditional dory-type haul-up shaft inboard power with retractable shaft and propeller. Recommended horsepower from 10 to 20 depending on engine type.

Can the hull be extended or shortened? Yes. Up to 10% by re-spacing the frames from the aft end of the stem to the transom a proportional amount. We do not recommend increasing the beam.

Trailer: Designed for use with Glen-L Series 5000/6000 boat trailer plans.

See JEAN PIERRE and LUCKY PIERRE for other St. Pierre dories. JEAN PIERRE also comes with a sail option.

CHESSIE FLYER

...sing sailboat that's inexpensive and easy to build, it's ...'sharpie" type hull. Originally developed in the mid ...ter trade off Long Island Sound, where it could operate ...fety in the shoal waters, the sharpies quickly spread to ...d Florida. Our **CHESSIE FLYER** captures this tradi-...ty bowsprit and upswept "pinky" stern, the character ..., graceful sheer, and gaff ketch rig. The double ended ...to trailer and easy to launch. Even with her shallow ...file, she still offers "camping-type" accommodations ...tting headroom above the berths, standing headroom ...lley, and space for a portable head.

...ard up, the **CHESSIE FLYER** can operate in a little ...water. Auxillary power is provided by a small outboard ...vell. This is the perfect boat for "gunk-holing" or island ...is easily beached for the night to save the cost of ...While not meant for long distance open sea voyages, ...LYER is probably equal in seaworthiness to boats of ...Sufficient internal ballast plus a steel plate centerboard ...ighting moment, even when heeled to 90°. While the ...vill reduce sail and batten down her hatches in heavy ...to know that there is a high degree of safety in her ...a self-draining cockpit that's well above the waterline.

...mance? The **CHESSIE FLYER** has design characteris-...those of the "hot" ultralight displacement racing boats, ...avoids expensive winches and costly "go-fast" fittings. ...of light weight, large sail area, and a narrow double-...surprise even the most ardent racing skippers. The ...R will come into her own when reaching in a good ...ll heels, it presents a good "vee" to the water thereby ...ile tracking straight and true. The low ketch rig and flat ...ard ability in choppy headsea conditions.

...NS make this a project well suited to even the first-time ...rience. The frames feature straight bottom and side ...nking, sheathed with fiberglass for easy maintenance.

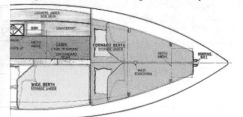

board hull with "pinkie" stern, designed for 3/8" plywood (2 layers on bottom).

Ballast: Interior ballast plus 1" plate steel centerboard.

Sail type: Gaff rigged ketch.

Power: Well mounted outboard motor to 5 HP, 15" to 20" nominal shaft.

Trailer: Designed for use with GLEN-L Series 7000/10000 boat trailer plans.

...SIZE
...for-
...ard,
...half
...ad-
...des
...Fas-
tening Schedule.

AVAILABLE FOR THIS DESIGN:
- **Study Plans**
- **Plans & Patterns**
- **Bronze Fastening Kit**
- **Fiberglass Kit**
- **Hardware Kit**
- **Rigging Kit**
- **Sails**

See Price List

JAMES COOK
A 27' TRAILERABLE CRUISING SAILBOAT

BUILD IN COLD-MOLDED WOOD OR FIBERGLASS

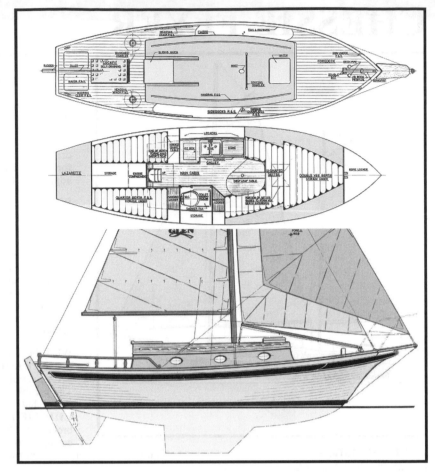

Here's a compact cruising sailboat modeled after much larger ocean going types, but with one *very* important difference: It's *trailerable*! Unlike typical trailer-sailers, our **JAMES COOK** features the safety of a fixed ballast keel. The draft is such that launching from most modern ramps or sling launching facilities is still practical, and weight is within the range of many tow vehicles. Just think of the savings in slip rental fees and the ability to cruise on distant waters often denied non-trailerable boats!

With such graceful and timeless lines together with the balanced proportions incorporated in our **JAMES COOK**, it's hard to believe that our designers could work spacious accommodations for four or more, with full 6' headroom. There's a fully enclosed centrally located head with shower, port and starboard quarter berths, a spacious U-shaped settee with drop-leaf table, and a full width vee berth forward which extends to full length when the settee back cushion is raised. Other features include a navigator's station with hinged chart table, two hanging lockers, and a complete galley with double-bowl sink, stove, and top loading ice box.

On deck, the **JAMES COOK** is much like larger ocean sailing yachts. Side decks are wide enough for easy access forward, shrouds are located inboard for sail efficiency, and there's a raised bulwark all around for safety. The cockpit well is compact for quick draining, yet deck areas are spacious for lounging. Even though our **JAMES COOK** might be called a traditional character-type boat, the hull and rig reflect many of the lastest design advances. An efficient keel "foil" and separated rudder skeg, cutaway forefoot, low wetted hull area, fine entrance angle, plenty of sail area in relation to displacement, and balanced hull lines all assure a weatherly and responsive vessel. The sail plan and mast length have been kept low for stability, and ease of trailering and launching. The **JAMES COOK** can be fitted out as either a sloop or cutter rig having a self-tacking jib. Steering is by a reliable, simple, and low cost outboard rudder and tiller. A small auxiliary motor can be installed for power, with convenient access from within the cabin.

Construction of the **JAMES COOK** is well within the abilities of most amateurs. You can build in plywood or solid wood veneers (cold-molded wood) by using the plans for the PLYWOOD VERSION. Or build the **JAMES COOK** in one-off fiberglass using PVC or balsa cores and fiberglass laminates, or fiberglass planking laminates using the FIBERGLASS VERSION plans. With either method, the cabin and deck areas use conventional lumber and plywood methods sheathed with fiberglass or equivalent materials for durability, simplicity, and low cost. Whichever method you decide on, you'll receive FULL SIZE PATTERNS so that no lofting is required. Our fully detailed plans together with voluminous instruction manuals simplify and speed your building project, and assure results you and your family will be proud of.

CHARACTERISTICS

Length (on deck minus bowsprit)	26'-11"
Length waterline	22'-0"
Beam	8'-0"
Draft (board down)	3'-9"
Freeboard forward	4'-7"
Freeboard aft	3'-4"
Displacement	5960 lbs.
Ballast weight	2250 lbs.
Headroom (nominal)	6'-0"
Height (to cabin top)	9'-0"
Sleeping capacity	4
Cockpit size	2'x3'
Fuel capacity (*)	32 gals.
Fresh water capacity (*)	30 gals.

(*) Multiple tanks allow varying balances of fuel and water to 62 gals.

Sail area:		
	Main	135 sq. ft.
	Foretriangle	182 sq. ft.
	Total	317 sq. ft.

Hull type: Round bilge hull form with fixed ballast keel. Plans available for "one-off" fiberglass using either PVC foam sandwich core or fiberglass planking with fiberglass laminates, or for cold-molded plywood construction with solid wood veneers as an alternate.

Ballast: Resin stabilized steel scrap in a welded steel shell.

Sail type: Masthead cutter (double head rig) or sloop.

Power: Outboard motor to 5HP, 15" to 20" shaft, mounted in well.

Trailer: Designed for use with GLEN-L Series 5000/6000 boat trailer plans.

COMPLETE PLANS include FULL SIZE PATTERNS for the station sections (form contours), stem form contour, balast keel unit form contours, rudder-skeg section contours, deck camber pattern, and instructions with hull material listing and GLEN-L FIBERGLASS MANUAL with fiberglass plans.

AVAILABLE FOR THIS DESIGN:
- **Study Plans**
- **Plans & Patterns**
- **Bronze Fastening Kit (WD)**
- **Fiberglass Kit (WD)**

See Price List

KODIAK

A 29' FIBERGLASS MOTORSAILER

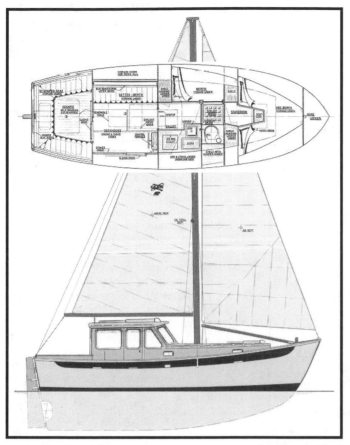

If you're disillusioned by fuel guzzeling powerboats, or tired of temperamental rule-beating sailboats, or just a lover of the sea looking for a sensible, easy to handle, economical vessel capable of cruising in just about any waters with safety, the **KODIAK** may be your boat. This motorsailer has an effective combination of power and sail to maintain speeds up to 7 knots even in rough seas over a range beyond most powerboats. Since she's not subject to the whims of the wind, you can plan your schedule more closely whether for weekend jaunts or for extended vacation voyages. Plus, you'll travel in comfort due to the motion dampening action of the sails coupled with a stiff, stable hull having a healthy percentage of ballast.

The **KODIAK** has accommodations and features that belie her modest dimensions. There are individual berths for five people in three separate cabins, two hanging lockers, an enclosed head with shower, a complete galley with a huge ice box, and an abundance of storage space for all the gear normally required for extended family cruising. Features for safety, comfort, and ease of handling have been given special consideration. For example, wide walk-around decks with protective bulwarks together with cabin top grab rails make access to any part of the vessel quick and safe, plus simplify the handling of sails, lines, and ground tackle. The simple, reliable sloop rig with self-tacking jib as well as the helm can all be controlled from either the deckhouse or from the deep, spacious, self-bailing cockpit. No expensive winches are required, and the straight leech of the sails means that troublesome sail battens are unnecessary.

The construction of the **KODIAK** is rugged and strong. The hull is intended for construction in fiberglass using the "one-off" processes, either fiberglass planking or foam sandwich core, together with fiberglass laminate. Either method is well suited to the experienced amateur or small custom yard. Balance of the structure utilizes conventional materials and fiberglass materials. Study plans are available for those who desire a more comprehensive description of the vessel as noted on this page.

CHARACTERISTICS

Length (on deck minus bowsprit) 28'-6"
Length waterline .... 25'-5"
Beam .... 9'-11"
Draft (board down) .... 4'-0"
Freeboard forward .... 5'-3"
Freeboard aft .... 3'-5"
Displacement .... 11,000 lbs.
Ballast weight .... 4200 lbs.
Headroom (nominal).................... 6'-4"
Height (to cabin top) .... 11'-2"
Sleeping capacity 5
Cockpit size (nominal) .... 5'-6"x8'-0"
Deckhouse size .... 6'-3"x6'-9"
Fuel capacity .... 60 gals.
Range (approx. power only) . 500 miles
Fresh water capacity .... 60 gals.
Sail area:Main .... 190 sq. ft.
       Jib .... 167 sq. ft.
       Foretriangle .... 194 sq. ft.
       Total .... 357/384 sq. ft.
Hull type:Full displacement round bilge hull form with maximum hull speed of 7 knots. Designed for "one-off" fiberglass construction using either PVC foam sandwich core or fiberglass planking with fiberglass laminates.

Ballast: Lead preferred, steel optional.
Sail type:Masthead sloop rig with self-tacking jib. Other head sails optional.
Power: Single diesel or gasoline engine of approx. 15 continuous HP (20 to 30 BHP), not exceeding 500 lbs. through straight shaft to max. 24" dia. propeller.

COMPLETE PLANS include FULL SIZE PATTERNS for the station sections, bulkheads, floor timber, deck crown, transom, rudder, tiller, and stem contour, including instructions, fiberglass hull material listing and GLEN-L FIBERGLASS MANUAL.

STUDY PLANS AVAILABLE

AVAILABLE FOR THIS DESIGN:
- **Study Plans**
- **Plans & Patterns**
See Price List

FRANCIS DRAKE

A 29' WORLD CRUISING SAILBOAT

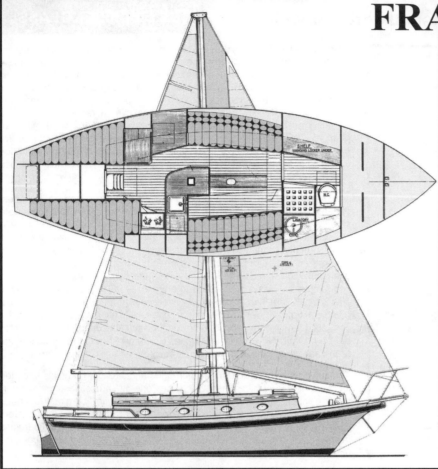

BUILD IN COLD-MOLDED WOOD OR FIBERGLASS

CHARACTERISTICS

Length (on deck minus bowsprit)	29'-0"
Length waterline	24'-0"
Beam	9'-10"
Draft	4'-6"
Freeboard forward	4'10"
Freeboard aft	3'-6"
Displacement	10,000 lbs.
Ballast weight	4,000 lbs.
Headroom (nominal)	6'-1" to 6'-4"
Height (to cabin top)	9'-10"
Sleeping capacity	4-5
Cockpit size	2'-9"x2'-5"
Fuel capacity (*)	50 gals.
Range (approx. power only)	500 mi.
Fresh water capacity (*)	80 gals.

(*) *Multiple tanks allow varying balances of fuel and water to 130 gals.*

Sail area:	Main	188 sq. ft.
	Foretriangle	275 sq. ft.
	Total	463 sq. ft.

Hull type: Round bilge hull form with fixed ballast keel. Plans available for "one-off" fiberglass using either PVC foam sandwich core or fiberglass planking with fiberglass laminates, or for cold-molded plywood construction with solid wood veneers as an alternate.

Sail type: Masthead cutter (double head rig) or sloop.

Power: Single inboard diesel or gasoline engine of approximately 10 shaft horsepower with suitable reduction gear.

Feast your eyes on our **FRANCIS DRAKE**! Here's a compact *and* economical package that offers world cruising capabilities with exceptional comfort and safety unique in this size. For the cruising couple or small family sailing on a limited budget, the **FRANCIS DRAKE** offers appealing features. Consider the fact that you can sleep 4 or 5 (including a handy double when desired), seat up to 6 for meals and conversation, and still have 2 good sea berths on either tack, plus a decent navigator's station complete with chart table, and an efficient L-shaped galley! As if this were not enough, there's a roomy toilet room-utility area forward with enclosed stall shower, head with space for a holding tank, a lavatory, a huge hanging locker, and plenty of room for sails, stores, and the anchor rode. And there's a separate oilskin locker next to the companionway, a vapor-tight locker at the transom for stove fuel, a 10 cubic foot ice box, and a centrally located engine for easy maintenance and good hull balance. Imagine all these features in a boat only 29' long!

But there's still more! On the **FRANCIS DRAKE** we've made the deck all one level with a compact watertight cockpit well and raised bulwark all around for safety. The outboard rudder and tiller are not only reliable but economical, and adapt to many self-steering systems with ease. The rig can be used as a cutter or sloop to suit a wide variety of sail combinations to match your sailing conditions exactly. The bowsprit not only adds character, but is functional as well, doing its part to make the handling of sails and ground tackle safe and easy. The hull features a long keel with cutaway forefoot for positive steering, windward ability, and quick tacking. Broad flaring topsides and trailboards forward sweeping aft to a graceful tumblehome transom will attract spectators in any port.

The FIBERGLASS VERSION utilizes either PVC foam sandwich core or fiberglass planking (C-FLEX) with fiberglass laminates over a simple male mold. The PLYWOOD VERSION, uses strips of plywood or solid wood veneer, cold-molded, protected on the outside with fiberglass. Whichever method you select, there is nothing required in the construction beyond the abilities of the amateur who is reasonably handy. Our comprehensive PLANS take you through the entire project so that you can achieve professional results you'll be proud of.

COMPLETE PLANS include FULL SIZE PATTERNS for the station sections (form contours), stem form contour, keel section contours, cabin and deck contours, table of offsets, and complete instructions with hull material listing. Fiberglass version includes GLEN-L FIBERGLASS MANUAL.

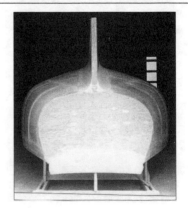

GLEN-L 30 & 30FG

30' CRUISING AUXILIARIES

Although the outboard profile and deck plan are the same for the **GLEN-L 30** and **GLEN-L 30FG**, each is a different design with a different arrangement plan and construction method. Study plans are available on both.

The **GLEN-L 30** features double diagonal plywood cold-molded planking over a series of bulkheads with longitudinals for light weight, strong hull construction. The arrangement features berths in the most comfortable portion of the boat. The settee backs form "shorty" berths ideal for the kids, with head and galley area separating the sleeping areas. It's an ideal cruising layout for families, with plenty of storage space and room below seldom found in a boat this size.

The **GLEN-L 30FG** features one-off fiberglass hull construction utilizing either fiberglass planking (C-FLEX) or foam core sandwich techniques. The arrangement offers a private stateroom forward and roomy, open cockpit aft, with plenty of storage space. The engine is located under the galley cabinet/settee for easy access. All berths are full length and spacious.

The rig on either version is identical; an easy-to-handle double headsail rig specifically intended for cruising. Long keels give protection to the underwater gear, while the shoal draft makes gunkholing practical. The cockpit is large and self-bailing and the raised deck makes for a dry boat underway.

GLEN-L 30 PLANS include Bill of Materials, Fastening Schedule, Table of Offsets, instructions, plus FULL SIZE PATTERNS for the stem, floor timbers, and contours for all structural bulkheads, transom, and deck crown. GLEN-L 30FG PLANS include material listing, instructions, GLEN-L FIBERGLASS MANUAL, and FULL SIZE PATTERNS for the stem, transom, and building form contours.

GLEN-L 30

GLEN-L 30 FG

CHARACTERISTICS-BOTH VERSIONS

Length overall	30'-0"
Length waterline	26'-0"
Beam	10'-4"
Draft	4'-6"
Freeboard forward	5'-2"
Freeboard aft	3'-4"
Displacement	11,300 lbs.
Ballast weight	4,000 lbs.(4100 lbs for FG)
Headroom (nominal)	6'+
Height (to cabin top)	9'-10"
Sleeping capacity	6
Cockpit size	6'-10"x6'+
Fuel capacity	56 gals.(50 gals.for FG)
Fresh water cap.	54 gals.(50 gals for FG)
Sail area: Main	232.5 sq. ft.
Foretriangle	266.5 sq. ft.
Total	499 sq. ft.

Hull type: GLEN-L 30 has a soft-chine (semi-round) form designed for double diagonal plywood (cold-molded) planking. GLEN-L 30FG has a round bilge hull form for one-off fiberglass using either PVC foam sandwich core or fiberglass planking with fiberglass laminates. Both versions feature fixed ballast keels.

Ballast: Lead
Sail type: Masthead double head rigged sloop.
Power: Single inboard diesel or gasoline engine of 10 to 20 SHP. GLEN-L 30 uses an engine with vee-drive, not to exceed 500 lbs. total.

AVAILABLE FOR THIS DESIGN:
- **Study Plans**
- **Plans & Patterns**
- **Bronze Fastening Kit (WD)**
- **Fiberglass Kit (WD)**
- **See Price List**

LORD NELSON

A 33' WORLD CRUISING SAILBOAT

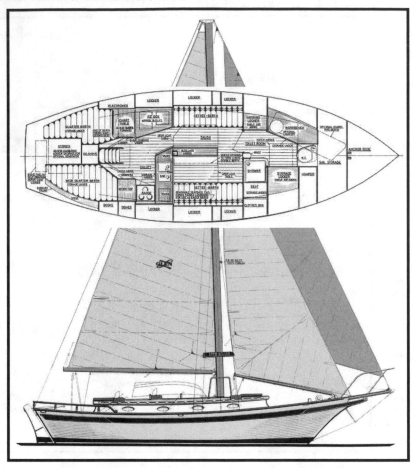

CHARACTERISTICS

Length overall (on deck) .... 33'-1"
Length overall (with bowsprit) ..... 37'-9"
Length waterline .... 26'-4"
Beam .... 11'-1"
Draft .... 5'-0"
Freeboard forward .... 5'-3"
Freeboard aft .... 3'-10"
Displacement .... 16,200 lbs.
Ballast weight .... 6,500 lbs.
Cabin headroom .... 6'-0" to 6'-5"
Sleeping capacity 4-6
Fuel capacity (*) .... 60 gals.
Range (@ 5.5 knots/power/approx.) . 600 mi.
Fresh water capacity (*) .... 110 gals.
(*) *Multiple tanks allow varying balances of fuel and water to 170 gals.*
Sail area: Main .... 298 sq. ft.
    Foretriangle .... 353 sq. ft.
    Total .... 651 sq. ft.
Hull type: Round bilge hull form with fixed ballast keel. Plans available for one-off fiberglass construction using PVC foam sandwich core or fiberglass planking with fiberglass laminates, or for molded plywood, with cold-molded veneers as an alternate.
Ballast: Lead, iron, or steel scrap.
Sail type: Masthead cutter (double-head rig) or sloop.
Power: Single inboard diesel or gasoline engine of 10 to 20 SHP with suitable reduction gear.

Our **LORD NELSON** captures the character of traditional sailboats, combines an efficient hull/rig combination, and tops it off with a modern layout to come up with a new approach for todays long distance sailor. Features abound! Settees seat six, yet convert to single berths by removing the seat backs which then form leeboards. One settee even forms a double berth when at anchor. While only intended for a crew of four, the double and a pipe berth forward means that six can be accommodated if need be. For comfort, this arrangement means *two* leeward berths on either tack! The engine is right in the middle of the boat for stability and balance. Just lift off the dinette table "console", and the engine is fully accessible. The toilet room is also a utility/storage area with workbench, shower with seat, and storage spaces.

The L-shaped galley has a double sink, trash bin, gimballed range with oven, worktop, 15 cubic foot ice box, and lots of drawers and lockers. There's a large chart table that slides forward for berth access, an oilskin locker by the ladder, and even space for a generator if desired. The cockpit well is compact for safety, yet there is plenty of room for all the crew in this area. A separate vapor-tight locker is provided for the stove fuel aft. The deck is all one level with wide side decks, raised bulwark, lots of safety rails, deck vents, and a place for a dinghy on the cabin top. The sweeping

trailboards accent a practical bowsprit which simplifies mooring and anchoring. The cutter rig gives a generous spread of sail for excellent performance, and allows a wide variety of headsails and sail combinations suitable to any weather condition. A self-tacking jib is perfect for a short handed crew. Plenty of fuel and water capacity is available for long range capability, even when under power alone.

You can build your own **LORD NELSON** in one of two versions. With the ONE-OFF FIBERGLASS VERSION, you'll be using either PVC foam sandwich core or fiberglass planking (C-FLEX). With the PLYWOOD VERSION, you can use plywood triple diagonally planked or solid wood veneer cold-molded construction. Whichever you choose, you'll probably save enough over the project to make that voyage of your dreams a reality. We feel that anyone with average do-it-yourself abilities and at least one smaller boat to his credit can build his own **LORD NELSON**, and with professional results!

AVAILABLE FOR THIS DESIGN:
- **Study Plans**
- **Plans & Patterns**
- **Fiberglass Kit (WD)**
See Price List

COMPLETE PLANS include FULL SIZE PATTERNS for the station sections (form contours), structural bulkheads, stem form, transom contour, keel and floor timber contours, cabin and deck beam contours, plus hull material listing, and complete instructions. FIBERGLASS version includes GLEN-L FIBERGLASS MANUAL.

AURORA
A 31' CRUISING CUTTER

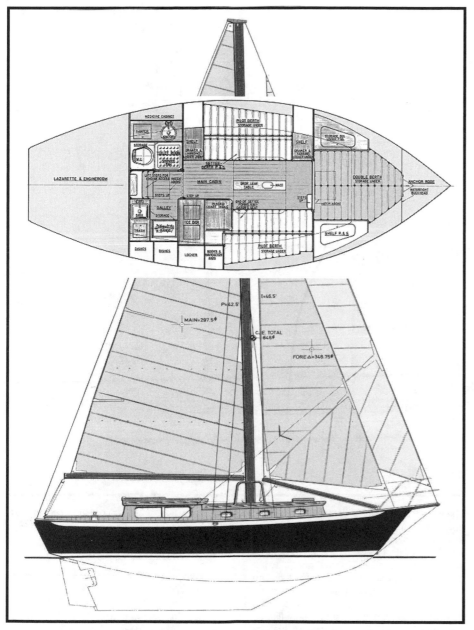

CHARACTERISTICS

Length overall (on deck)	31'-0"
Length overall (with bowsprit)	33'-0"
Length waterline	25'-0"
Beam	12'-0"
Draft	5'-0"
Freeboard forward	4'-10"
Freeboard aft	3'-7"
Displacement	16,800 lbs.
Ballast weight	6,000 lbs.
Steel components (est)	6,600 lbs.
Cabin headroom	6'-2" to 6'-4"
Sleeping capacity	6
Fuel capacity	85 gals.
Fresh water capacity	130 gals.
Sail area:Main	297 sq. ft.
Foretriangle	349 sq. ft.
Total	646 sq. ft.

Hull type:Multi-chine sheet steel hull with full length internal ballast keel.

Sail type:Masthead cutter rig with bowsprit and club-footed jib.

Ballast: Concrete and scrap steel.

Construction: Welded steel hull, keel, and deck with concrete and scrap steel ballast. Cabin superstructure, cockpit, and interior of lumber and plywood with exterior surfaces sheathed in fiberglass or equivalent.

Power: Single inboard diesel engine of 25-30 SHP with v-drive.

COMPLETE PLANS include FULL SIZE PATTERNS for the station frames, beam cambers, and stem contour, plus steel detail sheets, STEEL BOATBUILDING GUIDE, and Table of Offsets.

NOTE: Steel boat designs are intended for amateur or professional builders who have knowledge of welding practices and skills. See front section of catalog for more information about steel boat designs.

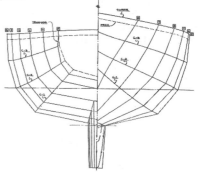

The all-steel **AURORA** hull packs an amazing amount of accommodations in it's modest length. This is a boat that will go just about anywhere and has the displacement necessary for all the gear one would like on a long voyage. The layout features berths for six, a complete head and galley, plenty of hanging space and storage lockers, and a main cabin that will handle the whole crew for dining and socializing. We've even worked in a nice navigator's station with hinged chart table and space for related gear.

To make long range cruising practical, there's plenty of fuel and water capacity from the built-in integral tanks. For safety, the hull features a long keel with internal ballast in the form of a concrete/scrap steel mix for low cost. The chain locker and cabin area are separated by a steel watertight bulkhead. The engine is located aft (preferably a diesel), connected by a v-drive. Access is convenient through the cockpit hatches or from inside through the removable ladder.

The **AURORA** features a multi-chine hull for ease and speed of construction, well within the abilities of the amateur. Our FULL SIZE PATTERNS further simplify the construction; a Table of Offsets is provided for those who want to do their own lofting. Numerous detail sheets together with comprehensive plans, complete with our construction manual, take the guesswork out of the project and let you build a super-strong boat for far less than you would imagine. If you would like more information on this design, send for our STUDY PLANS.

AQUARIAN

BUILD IN STEEL

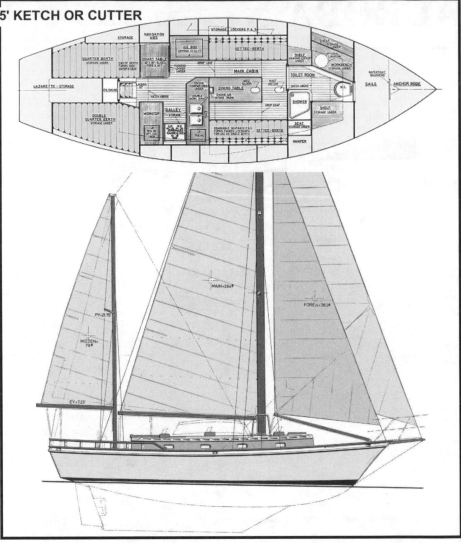

CHARACTERISTICS

Length overall (on deck) .... 35'-0"
Length overall (with bowsprit) ..... 38'-3"
Length waterline .... 28'-4"
Beam .... 12'-0"
Draft .... 5'-0"
Freeboard forward .... 4'-11"
Freeboard aft .... 3'-8"
Displacement .... 20,200 lbs.
Ballast weight .... 7,000 lbs.
Wt of steel components (est)8,000 lbs.
Cabin headroom .... 6'-2" to 6'-4"
Sleeping capacity 5
Fuel capacity .... 70 gals.
Fresh water capacity .... 160 gals.
Sail area: *Cutter*
  Main ....333 sq. ft.
  Foretriangle ....414 sq. ft.
  Total ....747 sq. ft.
Sail area: *Ketch*
  Main ....294 sq. ft.
  Foretriangle ....360 sq. ft.
  Mizzen ....79 sq. ft.
  Total ....733 sq. ft.
Hull type:Multi-chine sheet steel hull with full length internal ballast keel.
Ballast: Concrete and scrap steel.
Sail type:Masthead cutter or ketch rig with bowsprit and club-footed jib.
Power: Single inboard diesel engine of 30-35 SHP with reduction gear to suit.
Construction: Welded steel hull, keel, deck and cockpit with concrete and scrap steel ballast. Cabin superstructure, cockpit, and interior of lumber and plywood with exterior surfaces sheathed in fiberglass or equivalent.

COMPLETE PLANS include FULL SIZE PATTERNS for the station frames, beam cambers, and stem contour, plus steel detail sheets, STEEL BOATBUILDING GUIDE, and Table of Offsets.

The **AQUARIAN** layout is based on one of our most popular and successful ocean cruising designs, and features steel construction for the hull, keel, deck and cockpit. Available in either a ketch or cutter rig, in masthead form, with a self-tending jib and bowsprit. The multi-chine hull form has a long keel for safety and a steady helm while internal ballast is a mix of concrete and steel scrap for low cost. The compact cockpit well, wide side decks, and raised bulwark are perfect for the long distance boat; with room to carry a dinghy on the housetop.

The interior arrangement of the **AQUARIAN** is noteworthy for its practicality at sea. The forward area has been devoted to utility, with a complete toilet room which includes a separate stall shower. There's also a work-bench, storage cabinets, and a sail bin. The settees in the main cabin also form berths and feature removable padded seat backs which convert to padded leeboards when flipped over. Most noteworthy, however, is the engine located right in the middle of the boat where it is readily accessible, and contributes to the balance and stability of the boat. The galley, located in the most favorable area of the hull, is an efficient U-shape with a roomy ice box opposite. Port and starboard quarter berths, plus a complete navigator's station to port, complete the aft portion of the cabin.

The **AQUARIAN** is meant for long distance worldwide cruising. Generous tanks for fuel, oil, water, and waste are built integrally with the hull. A watertight steel bulkhead is fitted between the forepeak and the cabin for safety. Plenty of opening ports, water trap vents, and hatches assure a fresh flow of air throughout. Building your own **AQUARIAN** is greatly simplified by use of the FULL SIZE PATTERNS, however, for those who want to loft the lines, we include a Table of Offsets.

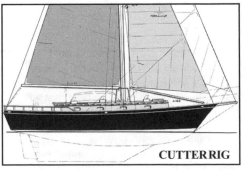

CUTTER RIG

AVAILABLE FOR THIS DESIGN:
- **Study Plans**
- **Plans & Patterns**
  See Price List

STEELAWAY

A 35' COASTAL CRUISING SAILBOAT

BUILD IN STEEL

CHARACTERISTICS

Length overall (on deck) .... 35'-0"
Length overall (with bowsprit) ..... 38'-3"
Length waterline .... 28'-4"
Beam .... 12'-0"
Draft .... 5'-0"
Freeboard forward .... 4'-11"
Freeboard aft .... 3'-8"
Displacement .... 20,200 lbs.
Ballast weight .... 7,000 lbs.
Wt. of steel components (est.) 8,000 lbs.
Cabin headroom .... 6'-3" to 6'-5"
Sleeping capacity 5
Fuel capacity .... 120 gals.
Fresh water capacity .... 170 gals.
Sail area: Main .... 333 sq. ft.
       Foretriangle .... 414 sq. ft.
       Total .... 747 sq. ft.
Hull type: Multi-chine sheet steel hull with full length internal ballast keel.
Sail type: Masthead cutter rig with bowsprit and club-footed jib.
Power: Single inboard diesel engine of 30-35 SHP with reduction gear to suit.
Ballast: Concrete and scrap steel.
Construction: Welded steel hull, keel, deck, and cockpit with concrete and scrap steel ballast. Cabin superstructure, cockpit, and interior of lumber and plywood with exterior surfaces sheathed in fiberglass or equivalent.

COMPLETE PLANS include FULL SIZE PATTERNS for station frames, beam cambers, and stern contour, plus steel detail sheets, STEEL BOATBUILDING GUIDE, and Table of Offsets.

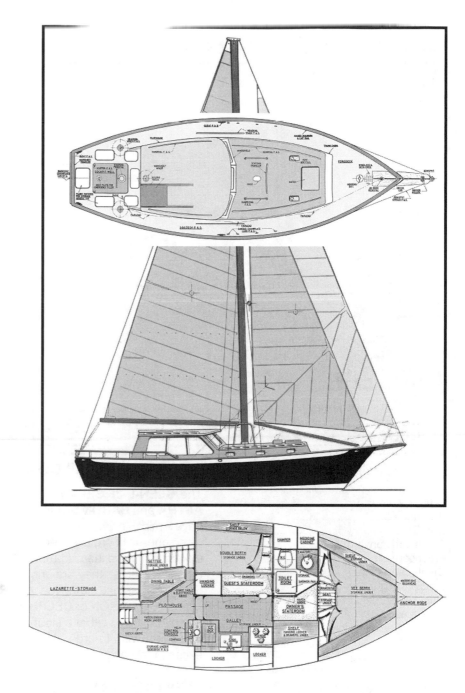

The **STEELAWAY** features an all-steel hull, long protective keel, and an easily handled cutter rig with self-tending jib ideal for safe and simple coastal cruising. Whether in fair weather or foul, dual control stations allow your voyage to continue uninterrupted. The multi-chine hull features an attractive flare forward combined with a graceful clipper bow for excellent seagoing ability. Wide walkaround decks, a raised bulwark, compact cockpit, and spacious deck areas inspire confidence in rough going. The handy bowsprit not only spreads the rig out for plenty of sail area, but allows the use of dual anchors.

Accommodations aboard the **STEELAWAY** are luxurious, comfortable, and offer a high degree of privacy. Three cabins can sleep up to five, while the two staterooms each have private access to the complete toilet room. The fully equipped galley is handy to the dining area, which is raised so that everyone can see out while seated. The cabin trunk forms a large chart table in the deckhouse opposite the inside helm. Large tanks for fuel oil, water, and waste make long distance cruises possible. All tanks are integral with the hull and the chain locker is separated from the cabin by a watertight steel bulkhead.

Power for the **STEELAWAY** is provided by a single engine under the deckhouse, preferably a diesel, driving through an inline shaft for reliability. Access is generously available from the deckhouse through large hatches. There's also plenty of storage throughout the vessel. Full size patterns mean that no lofting is required unless the builder wants to use the Table of Offsets provided in the plans. The lumber and plywood construction used for the cabin and interior keeps the project well within the abilities and budget of the average amateur. If you would like additional information, STUDY PLANS are available.

GLEN-L 36 SERIES

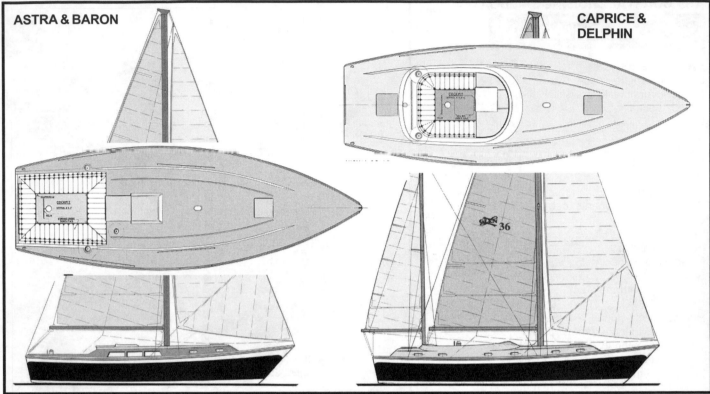

ASTRA & BARON

CAPRICE & DELPHIN

CHARACTERISTICS

Length overall .... 36'-0"
Length waterline .... 30'-0"
Beam .... 12'-1"
Draft .... 5'-0"
Freeboard forward .... 5'-4"
Freeboard aft .... 3'-9"
Displacement .... 16,500 lbs.
Ballast weight .... 6500 lbs.
Main cabin headroom .... 6'-5" nom.
Fuel capacity .... 40 gals.
Fresh water capacity .... 110 gals.
Sleeping capacity 7-8
Sail areas - Sloop:Main .... 327 sq.ft.
          Foretriangle 384 sq.ft.
          Total .... 711 sq.ft.
     Ketch:Main .... 284 sq.ft.
          Foretriangle 337 sq.ft.
          Total .... 705 sq.ft.
Hull type:Round bilge hull form with fixed ballast keel. Plans available for one-off fiberglass construction using either PVC foam sandwich core or fiberglass planking with fiberglass laminates, or for molded plywood construction.
Sail type:Masthead rig in sloop or ketch configurations.
Power: Single inboard of 20 to 30 shaft horsepower.

36' CRUISING SAILBOATS

The **GLEN-L 36 SERIES** consists of two different accommodation plans. The **ASTRA** and **BARON** feature an aft cockpit layout, the **CAPRICE** and **DELPHIN** have a midship cockpit with private aft cabin. The **GLEN-L 36 SERIES** can be built using one-off fiberglass methods or plywood construction using multiple layers of diagonal strips in the cold-molded method. However, the proper set of plans must be purchased as they are specifically detailed for only one method. For one-off fiberglass, select either the **ASTRA** or **CAPRICE**; for plywood construction, choose the **BARON** or **DELPHIN**. Whichever set of plans you purchase, the boat can be built with either a sloop or a ketch rig. Since our catalog space is limited, you might wish to order the Study Plan for a more detailed description of this exceptional design.

GLEN-L 36 ASTRA   (fiberglass)
GLEN-L 36 BARON   (plywood)

The **GLEN-L 36 ASTRA & BARON** have what is often termed as the conventional layout for sailboats this size. However, on closer examination one will see a spaciousness that is very unconventional. Because the **GLEN-L 36 SERIES** answers to no fickle racing rule compromises, there's plenty of beam throughout, enough in fact to provide truly usable pilot berths both port and starboard. Add to this a large drop leaf table, with comfortable settees on each side, and there's plenty of room for lounging, additional berthing, or an all hands banquet.

The cook and navigator have been given special attention on the **ASTRA** & **BARON**. Placed out of the traffic flow, the well-equipped U-shaped galley will bring out the gourmet in the cook. Plenty of perishables can be stored in the huge top-loading ice chest. The double bowl sink is located near the centerline for positive draining on both tacks and there is space for a gimbaled range with oven. The navigator's station is directly adjacent to the companionway along with a roomy foul weather gear locker. There is room to spread out the largest chart plus navigation gear and electronics. The quarter berth can serve as a single while underway or a double while at anchor, and provides a comfortable seat for the navigator.

GLEN-L 36 Astra & Baron

GLEN-L 36 Caprice & Delphin

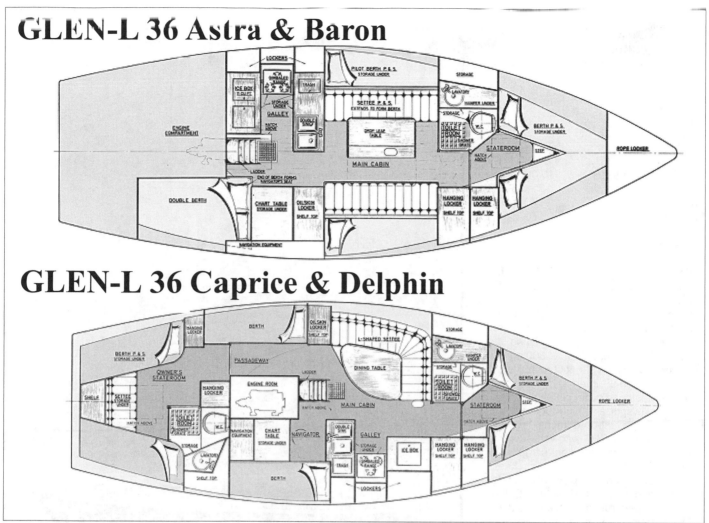

Astra & Baron continued...

The forward stateroom provides privacy for two. Double hanging lockers are immediately aft, together with the spacious toilet room, complete with shower. Cockpit and deck spaces aboard the vessel offer plenty of room for safety and easy handling of the rig and vessel. Side decks average 22" wide, while the cockpit has plenty of seating for lounging and entertaining. There's storage below for all sorts of sails and gear. If you look at all the **ASTRA** and **BARON** have to offer, you'll soon see just how unconventional these vessels are.

GLEN-L 36 CAPRICE (fiberglass)
GLEN-L 36 DELPHIN (plywood)

The **GLEN-L 36 CAPRICE & DELPHIN** feature a midship cockpit layout, unusual in a 36' boat. Whether your cruising requirements involve family, friends, or even charter use, this layout offers privacy not available in a conventional layout. Most notable is the private aft stateroom, accessible to the rest of the boat via an interior passageway. Two spacious in-

dividual berths with settee between assure comfort, while the roomy enclosed toilet room, with shower, is directly adjacent for convenience and privacy. Ample storage space is provided by a hanging locker and bureau in addition to cabinets under the berths.

Crew efficiency and comfort for extended cruises have been provided for. Quarter berths are located on each side of the boat; one for the navigator and another for the off-watch. Both are adjacent to the companionway and a foul weather gear locker. The navigator's station has a large chart table plus space for navigation gear. Careful thought has been given to the galley area and it's location. The efficient "everything-within-reach" galley provides a double-bowl sink, gimbaled range, and large top loading ice box. The location is out of traffic and away from the ladder, but immediately opposite the comfortable L-shaped dining area as well as the navigator's station. Double hanging lockers with a second toilet/shower room serve the rest of the crew. A private double stateroom forward completes the layout.

Unlike other midship cockpit boats in this size, the **CAPRICE** and **DELPHIN** do not sacrifice cockpit comfort or deck space to accommodations. With its wide beam, a cockpit over 6' in length and width is possible with room for side decks nearly 2' wide. A handy bin below the cockpit sole is reserved for sails; ample motor access is provided from the passageway. For cruising privacy in a 36' boat, the **CAPRICE** or **DELPHIN** are hard to beat.

COMPLETE PLANS include FULL SIZE PATTERNS for the stem, breasthook, and half sections for the frames and transom. Includes instructions, Bill of Materials, and Fastening Schedule.

AVAILABLE FOR THIS SERIES:
- **Study Plans**
- **Plans & Patterns**
- **Fiberglass Kit (WD)**
See Price List

SPIRIT

CHARACTERISTICS

Length overall (on deck) .... 39'-2"
Length waterline .... 31'-8"
Beam .... 12'-0"
Draft .... 5'-0"
Freeboard forward .... 4'-11"
Freeboard aft .... 3'-8"
Displacement .... 22,625 lbs.
Ballast weigth .... 7,500 lbs.
Wt. of steel parts (est.) .... 10,000 lbs.
Cabin headroom .... 6'-3" to 6'-6"
Fuel capacity .... 70 gals.
Fresh water capacity .... 170 gals.
Sleeping capacity 6

Sail area: *Cutter*
   Main ....362 sq. ft.
   Foretriangle .... 429 sq. ft.
   Total .... 791 sq. ft.
Ketch
   Main .... 334 sq. ft.
   Foretriangle .... 392 sq. ft.
   Mizzen .... 74 sq. ft.
   Total .... 800 sq. ft.

Hull type: Multi-chine sheet steel hull with full length internal ballast keel.

Sail type: Masthead cutter or ketch rig with bowsprit and club-footed jib.

Power: Single inboard diesel engine of 35-40 SHP with vee-drive.

Ballast: Concrete and steel scrap

Construction: Welded steel hull, keel, deck and cockpit with concrete and scrap steel ballast. Cabin superstructure, cockpit, and interior of lumber and plywood with exterior surfaces sheathed in fiberglass or equivalent.

COMPLETE PLANS include FULL SIZE PATTERNS for the station frames, beam cambers, and stem contour, plus steel detail sheets, STEEL BOATBUILDING GUIDE, and Table of Offsets.

Our **SPIRIT** features an all-steel hull with a high degree of performance and ease of handling ideal for long range cruising. Generous sail areas are incorporated into either a ketch or cutter rig of masthead type, both with self-tending jib. Fuel oil, water, and waste tanks are integral with the hull and ballast is located internally in the form of a low-cost mix of concrete and scrap steel. Cabin, cockpit, and interior construction is of wood and plywood for lightweight and simplicity. Wide sidedecks, raised bulwarks, an all-inboard rig, and "T" shaped cockpit insure a vessel that is safe and easy to handle.

The **SPIRIT** has spacious accommodations with a workable arrangement well suited to lengthy voyaging. The navigator's

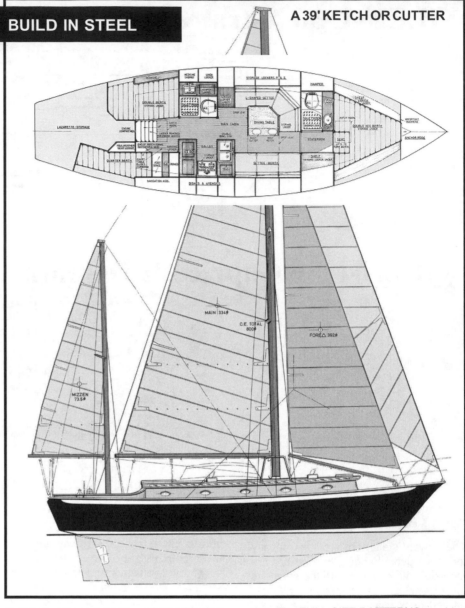

station has its own berth, a chart table that slides out of the way for berth access, foul weather gear locker, and space for electronics. A double berth is located opposite plus a hanging locker under the chart table, and a complete toilet room forward, convenient to the main living spaces. The galley is a roomy "U"-shape with double-bowl sink, trash receptacle, big ice box, and gimbal-mounted range with oven. The main cabin area features a big drop-leaf table flanked with settees that can handle the entire crew for dining or conversation. Up forward is a private stateroom with double berth, roomy hanging locker, a convertible seat, and another complete toilet room adjacent. The chain locker in the forepeak is separated from the cabin by a steel watertight bulkhead.

The **SPIRIT** hull is a multi-chine configuration for simplicity and speed of construc-

tion. The FULL SIZE PATTERNS provided with the plans simplify the construction since no lofting is necessary unless desired by the builder (a Table of Offsets is also included). The keel is a full-length type for directional stability and safety, yet the forefoot is cutaway for quick tacking. Such a configuration also protects the underwater gear and simplified haul-outs. Power is provided by a single engine (preferably a diesel) located aft and connected by a vee-drive. STUDY PLANS describing this design in much more detail are available separately.

YANKEE STAR

A 40' DOUBLE CABIN, AFT COCKPIT SAILBOAT

CHARACTERISTICS

Length overall (minus bowsprit) .	40'-0"
Length overall (with bowsprit)	43'-0"
Length waterline	31'-8"
Beam	12'-1"
Draft	5'-7"
Freeboard forward	5'-4"
Freeboard aft	3'-9"
Displacement	18,500 lbs.
Ballast weight	6,955 lbs.
Cabin headroom	6'-1" to 6'-6"
Sleeping capacity	8
Fuel capacity	60 gals.
Holding tank capacity	gals.
Fresh water capacity	110 gals.

Sail area: *Ketch*

Main	290 sq. ft.
Foretriangle	365.5 sq. ft.
Mizzen	93.5 sq. ft.
Total	749 sq. ft.

Sail area: *Cutter*

Main	340 sq. ft.
Foretriangle	409 sq. ft.
Total	749 sq. ft.

Hull type: Round bilge hull with fixed ballast keel and separate rudder/skeg.

Ballast: Lead, iron, or steel.

Sail type: Masthead ketch or cutter with bowsprit and club-footed jib.

Power: Single inboard diesel engine of 25 to 35 SHP with suitable reduction gear.

COMPLETE PLANS include FULL SIZE PATTERNS for the station sections and bulkheads (form contours), stem form contour, deck and cabin cambers, and cabin form contours, plus hull material listing, and complete instructions.

It's hard to find a yacht in this size range that combines the romance and character of traditional yachts, plus state of the art high-performance of offshore racing yachts, with the beauty of our **YANKEE STAR**. While every boat owner should love the appearance of his vessel, he will also love how this boat performs. A modern hull form of moderate displacement, plenty of sail in either a handy ketch or cutter rig, plus a divided "fin" keel and skeg mounted rudder with cutaway forefoot will let you point, reach, and run with the best of the fleet. Just watch the heads turn when you pull up to the mooring and bask in the comments when guests come aboard!

Here's a layout that offers more than just promises of privacy. The **YANKEE STAR** features double staterooms about as far separated in the vessel as possible, and each has its own complete adjoining toilet room with shower. Dual cabin entrances are the key to this innovative layout, allowing direct access from the cockpit to the owner's stateroom aft,

or to the galley/main cabin area when the owner wants privacy. The aft toilet room, galley, and navigation areas form a neat and functional nucleus right in the middle of the boat. The main cabin seats six or more for dining and sleeps up to four additional guests in comfort for a total of 8 people.

The cockpit area blends crew comfort with safe and easy handling of the vessel by virtue of its T shape. It's small in volume but large in deck area, and watertight to the rest of the vessel in the interest of safety. Wide sidedecks flush with the cockpit seats make forward passages safe in just about any weather, and the bowsprit makes dual anchor handling convenient and simple. Storage spaces are found not only in the cockpit area, but throughout the vessel, with hanging lockers in each stateroom plus an oilskin locker in the aft stateroom adjacent to the companionway.

YANKEE STAR is constructed by tried and proven methods found on many of our other designs. These include the cold-molded di-

agonal plywood or wood veneer methods, as well as the one-off fiberglass methods using materials like PVC foam or balsa sandwich core, or C-FLEX fiberglass planking. Power is provided by a single engine using a straight shaft configuration conveniently located between the aft stateroom and the galley in a sound and heat insulated compartment. Since there's so much more that we would like you to know about the **YANKEE STAR**, we suggest that you order our STUDY PLAN brochure

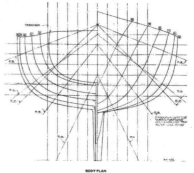

BUILD IN COLD-MOLDED WOOD OR FIBERGLASS

CHARACTERISTICS

Length overall .... 43'-11"
Length waterline .... 35'-10"
Beam .... 14'-1 1/2"
Draft (Keel version) .... 6'-0"
Draft (C.B. version-board up) .... 4'-6"
Draft (C.B. version-board down) .. 9'-9"
Freeboard forward .... 6'-0"
Freeboard aft .... 5'-1"
Displacement .... 30,000 lbs.
Ballast weight .... 10,800 lbs.
Cabin headroom .... 6'-2" to 6'-7"
Sleeping capacity 8
Fuel capacity .... 190 gals.
Fresh water capacity .... 200 gals.
Sail areas: *Sloop*
  Main .... 479 sq. ft.
  Foretriangle .... 486 sq. ft.
  Total .... 965 sq. ft.
Sail areas: *Ketch*
  Main .... 372 sq. ft.
  Foretriangle .... 446 sq. ft.
  Mizzen .... 147 sq. ft.
  Total .... 965 sq. ft.
Hull type: Round bilge hull form with fixed ballast keel.
Sail type: Masthead rig in sloop or ketch configurations.
Ballast: Lead, iron, or steel.
Power: Single inboard diesel or gasoline engine of 30 to 50 SHP with suitable reduction gear.

COMPLETE PLANS include FULL SIZE PATTERNS for all station sections (form contours), stem contour, and deck camber. Includes Material Listing and Instructions, including ketch or sloop options and *four* underbody configurations.

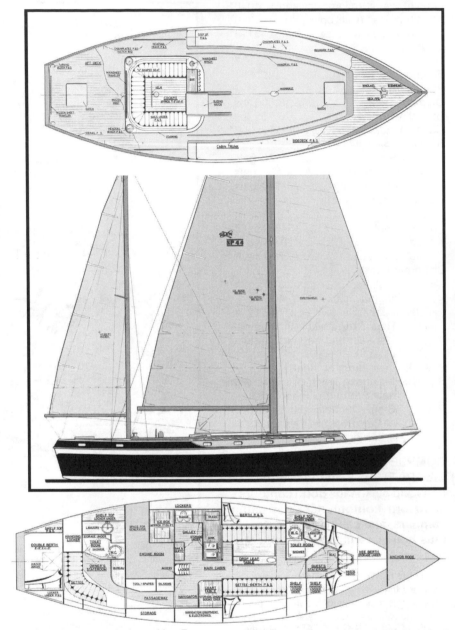

Imagine what it would be like to sail the waters of the world in your own **STARPATH 44**. There are accommodations for eight in three-cabin privacy, plus the luxury of a separate aft cabin especially for the lucky owner of this spacious vessel. Two toilet rooms complete with showers have private access from all cabins. All this privacy and there's still plenty of room for all to congregate either in the main cabin for dining or conversation, or in the sunny and dry midship cockpit. Please note the special consideration given to both the cook and the navigator. That 14'+ beam has really been put to good use, making the **STARPATH 44** an ideal boat for family cruising or charter use.

Our **STARPATH 44** was designed with performance, safety, and ease of operation paramount. Side decks are a nominal 22" wide with hefty bulwark and inboard shrouds for safe trips forward. All sheets are quickly accessible from the cockpit. The propeller is well protected from damage as is the rudder. Four scuppers assure fast drainage of the cockpit and it's watertight to the rest of the vessel. The efficient sloop or ketch rigs offer a wide array of possible sails, and a double headsail (cutter) rig could be readily adapted. The **STARPATH 44** is a stiff boat, but with a gentle motion, well suited to passage making. Smooth flowing hull lines not "bent" to conform to racing rules provide easy movement under sail or power.

Our **STARPATH 44** can be built in one-off fiberglass using either PVC foam or C-FLEX fiberglass planking, or in cold-molded wood construction using diagonal layers of plywood or veneers. The plans cover a total of four underwater configurations to suit exactly your type of sailing: the performance version with a deep keel and separate skeg/rudder, a shoal draft version with centerboard, offering a separate keel and skeg/rudder, a cruiser version with a long deep keel, and a cruising version with centerboard and shoal draft having a long keel. Whichever version you choose, you'll be able to build your own **STARPATH 44** for a fraction of the cost of comparable stock boats.

RELIANT

CHARACTERISTICS

Length overall (on deck) .... 49'-0"
Length overall (with bowsprit) .... 56'-0"
Length waterline .... 40'-0"
Beam .... 14'-4"
Draft .... 6'-6"
Freeboard forward .... 6'-11"
Freeboard aft .... 4'-6"
Displacement .... 34,500 lbs.
Ballast weight .... 12,400 lbs.
Cabin headroom .... 6'-4" to 6'-7"
Sleeping capacity 8-10
Fuel capacity .... 150 gals.
Fresh water capacity .... 220 gals.
Sail area: Main .... 442 sq. ft.
       Foretriangle .... 550 sq. ft.
       Mizzen .... 174 sq. ft.
       Total .... 1166 sq. ft.
Hull type: Round bilge hull form with fixed ballast keel. Optional separate keel and rudder/skeg configuration, or single long keel.
Power: Single inboard diesel or gasoline engine of 40 to 70 HP with vee-drive of suitable reduction.
Ballast: Steel or iron.
Construction: Plans available for "one-off" fiberglass using either PVC foam sandwich core or fiberglass planking with fiberglass laminates, and for wood diagonal cold-molded construction, using plywood or veneers.

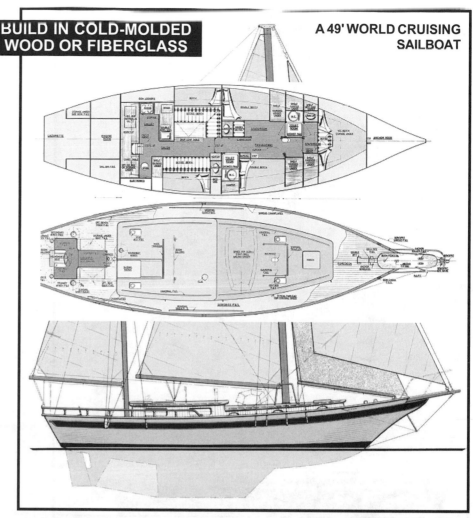

COMPLETE PLANS include FULL SIZE PATTERNS for the station sections and bulkheads (form contours), stem form contour, deck and cabin cambers, plus hull material listing, instructions and details for both PERFORMANCE and CRUISER options. The plans for the cold-molded version include the hardcover book BOATBUILDING WITH PLYWOOD while those for the fiberglass version include the GLEN-L FIBERGLASS MANUAL.

Our **RELIANT** design embodies the heritage of the sea in its graceful traditional appearance. From the raking clipper bow and sweeping bowsprit, to the graceful sheer, capped off aft with taffrails and turned stanchions, it's apparent that this boat is meant to sail anywhere in the world. The **RELIANT** offers superlative accommodations with unmatched privacy. Yet the interior is spacious, light, and airy with every feature oriented towards safety, comfort, and efficient operation.

Consider the cockpit as an example. Winches fall ready at hand and are at waist level. The helmsman has a separate seat directly behind the wheel, or he can stand on either side. Being on the same level as the deck, the cockpit seats are ideal for lounging. Yet, the cockpit is compact for safety. Side decks are wide and protected by a bulwark all around. The bowsprit makes anchoring and mooring a pleasure. There's room to carry a 10' dinghy as well.

Berths are provided for four or five couples, and the toilet rooms are strategically located so that no crew member needs to intrude on another's privacy to reach one of them. There are two heads, two showers, three lavato-

ries, three hanging lockers, an oilskin locker, a superb navigators station aft, and an efficient U-shaped galley with every convenience. Dining is possible for a large group, and a fireplace-heater centrally located will take the chill off when needed.

You can build your own **RELIANT** in either wood, using diagonal plywood or solid wood veneers, or in one-off fiberglass using C-FLEX fiberglass planking or PVC foam sandwich core. Either method is well within the realm of the experienced amateur or small professional yard. Either set of plans provides two underbody options; the PERFORMANCE option having a separate ballast keel with rudder/skeg aft, and the CRUISER option having a single long keel fairing into the rudder aft. If you need more information, a STUDY PLAN brochure is available.

LODESTAR A 55' COASTAL CRUISER

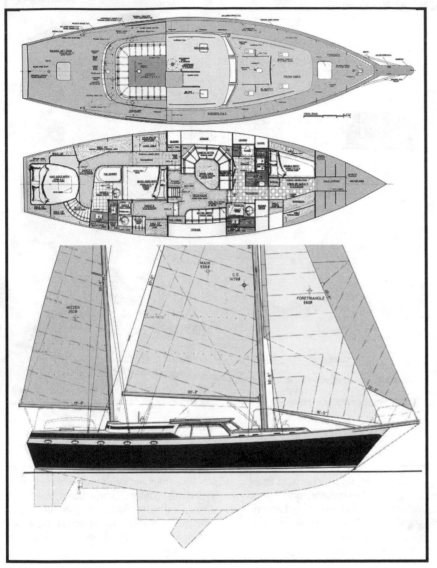

CHARACTERISTICS

Length overall (on deck) .... 55'-0"
Length overall (with bowsprit) .. 58'-11"
Length waterline .... 45'-0"
Beam .... 15'-7"
Draft (keel version) .... 7'-0"
Draft (C.B. version-board up) .... 5'-8"
Draft (C.B. version-board down) 11'-3"
Freeboard forward .... 6'-10"
Freeboard aft .... 5'-10"
Displacement .... 57,350 lbs.
Ballast weight .... 17,200 lbs.
Wt steel components .... (est.)25,000 lbs.
Cabin headroom .... 6'-5" to 6'-9"
Sleeping capacity 6-7
Fresh water capacity .... 640 gals.
Holding tank capacity .... 490 gals.
Fuel capacity .... 430 gals.
Sail area:Main .... 559 sq. ft.
          Foretriangle .... 660 sq. ft.
          Mizzen .... 260 sq. ft.
          Total .... 1,479 sq. ft.
Hull type:Multi-chine sheet steel, inter-
          nally ballasted hull, with
          separate keel and skeg-
          mounted rudder.
Sail type:Masthead ketch double headsail
          rig with club-footed jib.
Power: Single inboard diesel engine
          of approximately 75 SHP.
Ballast: Concrete and scrap steel.

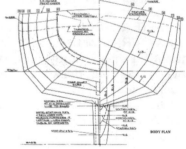

The **LODESTAR** design features all-steel construction of the hull, keel, deck, and cabin, welded together for incredible strength. The multi-chined hull form is easy and fast to build. Through careful hull design, we've moderated the chines into rounder, more attractive softer lines, making a lean hull that offers sparkling performance, considering its size and weight.

While the **LODESTAR** has the strength to sail in virtually any sea, the emphasis has been placed on cruising of the "island hopping" or touring type (we've given a centerboard option if shoal draft is necessary). Instead of cramming in numerous berths, we've kept the accommodations to three couples, plus space for an extra "stowaway" if necessary, all with luxury, sound control, and privacy paramount. Each double stateroom adjoins, or is ad-

jacent to its own complete toilet room (the owner has a tub/shower). Yet each cabin is individually accessible without crossing another.

The forepeak has been devoted to utilitarian duties instead of fitting less-than-usable vee-berths here which are so common in other boats. The galley will be the chef's delight, with plenty of work room and space for all appliances, including a washer and dryer opposite. The galley is located out of traffic, yet convenient to the deckhouse. The dinette is nearly 8' long and is raised so that everyone can see out while seated. An inside helm is optional in the deckhouse, primarily for use under power in foul weather. A large chart table is adjacent to the cockpit as well as the owner's stateroom.

Topside, the cockpit is spacious, yet well-protected, and the raised aft deck can

accommodate two dinghies, if desired. The side decks are nearly 2' wide and protected by a raised bulwark. The double headed ketch rig with club-footed jib is easy to handle and offers a wide array of sail combinations. Since this is a large design and there is so much to tell about it, we suggest purchasing the STUDY PLANS if more information is desired.

COMPLETE PLANS include FULL SIZE PATTERNS for all station frames, keel sections for both Keel and Centerboard versions, and stem contour. Includes all construction plans for both KEEL & CENTERBOARD versions, Table of Offsets, steel detail sheets, and STEEL BOATBUILDING GUIDE.

RC MODEL X-1

BUILD IN STITCH-N-GLUE PLYWOOD

CHARACTERISTICS
Length overall .... 40"
Beam .... 16"
Height overall .... 10"
Hull weight .... 4 lbs. 12 oz.
Displacement (test model) 7 lbs. 1 oz.
Hull type: Model cabin cruiser with vee bottom for radio control. Made from sheet plywood. Power: Electric motor

Model boat building is fun and very instructive if you intend building a full size craft. The RC MODEL X-1 uses the same principals of FAST-G (Fold And Stitch Then Glue) stitch and glue building method, only on a smaller scale. Not only will you learn but enjoy the building of a usable model boat.

A full size pattern is given for virtually every part in the boat. And, inexpensive door skin (1/8" thick) is used for most parts. Just duplicate the patterns to the plywood, saw them out with a jig, saber, or band saw, drill for the stitch holes, and the boat is ready to assemble, fast and simple.

The drawing and instructions are abetted with a series of captioned photos taken during the prototype building. You can almost build the boat by looking at the photos.

The boat is intended for an electric inline inboard motor with speed and forward, neutral and reverse, radio controlled. The

rudder is also remote controlled to enable right or left turns to be made, just like a full size one. The entire system is explained and detailed. Plus, we call out the parts used on the prototype and where they can be obtained for those new to the world of radio controlled model boats.

This is an excellent project for kids. Maybe with help from, mom, dad, or gramps. But of course kids come in all ages from toddlers to senior citizens. This is a project with universal appeal. Start building now. Fun is waiting, don't let it slide by.

COMPLETE PLANS and FULL SIZE PATTERNS contain Instructions that include a Bill of Materials, Laminate Schedule, 2 Plansheets and a Pattern Sheet that contains patterns for virtually every contoured part. Also included are photographs of building the prototype arranged in sequential format.

PADDLEBOARD

BUILD IN PLYWOOD

PLANS include FULL SIZE PATTERNS for frames, transom, bow piece, instructions, Bill of Materials & Fastening Schedule.

SUMMER FUN!

Our **PADDLEBOARD** is more than a toy. It's an ideal piece of excercise equipment to strengthen the upper body. Lay on your stomach and with strong, steady strokes, move across the water... stop and listen to the birds and the waves against the hull. The **PADDLEBOARD** is a non-boring way to get your excercise. It goes without saying that the kids will love it; playing "King of the Hill" or

tight rope walking, and of course, falling off.

The construction is simple, with a few lengths of lumber, one or two sheets of plywood, a little time, and you have healthful summer fun for the family.

CHARACTERISTICS

	8' Version	12' Version
Length overall	7'-10"	11'-9"
Width (max.)	1'-10"	1'-10"
Depth (max.)	6"	6"
Weight (approx.)	40 lbs.	60 lbs.
Capacity (approx.)	200 lbs.	300 lbs.

SCULLING SKIFF

A RECREATIONAL ROWING SHELL

CHARACTERISTICS
Length overall .... 17'-2"
Beam .... 27 1/2"
Depth amidships .... 10"
Passengers 1
Weight less seat (approx.) .... 40 lbs.
Hull type: Vee-bottom hull for 4mm sheet plywood Stitch and Glue construction.
Power: High performance spoon-shaped sculling oars, with riggers and sliding seat.
Trailer: Designed for use with Canoe/Kayak boat trailer plans.

Rowing or sculling is a fun and invigorating way to get in shape. The feeling of gliding over the water at a high rate of speed with nothing more than people power is indescribable. The problem is that most craft suited to this sport are expensive and, in the past, trying to build your own was not easy.

Our Stitch-N-Glue method changes all of that. Just about anyone can build our **SCULLING SKIFF** quickly, easily, and with only a minumum of tools. Two sheets of 4mm x 4' x 8' plywood plank the entire boat. When these thin panels are used, the finished weight will be comparable to costly production jobs. In fact, the original prototype hull weighed only 39 lbs. ... incredible for a 17' boat.

Although you can equip your **SCULLING SKIFF** with a production sliding seat/sculling assembly, our plans include complete details and Full Size Patterns to build your own sliding seat and riggers from readily available materials. There's no reason to deny yourself any longer. You can now have your own high-performance, high-tech **SCULLING SKIFF** with just a few days of fun and not even miss the money it takes.

AVAILABLE FOR THIS DESIGN:
- **Plans & Patterns**
- **Stitch & Glue Kit**
- **Fiberglass Kit**
- **Stitch & Glue DVD**

See Price List

COMPLETE PLANS include FULL SIZE PATTERNS for the bottom, sides, butt blocks, forward and aft frames and deck beams, and decking. Includes material listing and layouts, with instructions and STITCH-N-GLUE manual, plus patterns for making your own riggers and sliding seat assembly.

SLIDING SEAT

Build your own sliding seat rowing rig. It's easy and fun with Full Size Patterns and simple step-by-step instructions. Built of wood and other readily obtainable materials, the unit weighs only 19 lbs. Designed to be independent of the hull; lift it out as a unit for transporting. Clog spacing and angle are fully adjustable and the seat rolls with nylon sheave wheels on an aluminum rod track. (NOTE: These Plans & Patterns are included with the SCULLING SKIFF.)

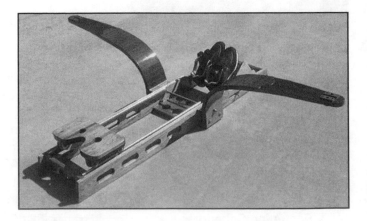

ROB ROY

BUILD IN STITCH-N-GLUE PLYWOOD

Our **ROB ROY** is truly a unique step forward in canoe design and construction, made possible by our Fast-G Stitch-N-Glue boatbuilding system coupled with advanced plywood development techniques. The result is a hull form shaped at the ends like the swift, agile, and quiet running round bottom canoes, with the stability and load carrying ability of a vee-bottom chined hull amidship.

The graceful styling of our symmetrically ended **ROB ROY** belies its ease and speed of construction. Full size patterns are provided for all parts, no lofting! No lay-outs! No scaling of plans required! Only 2 sheets of standard size 4mm (5/32") or 5mm (3/16") plywood are required - that's what makes **ROB ROY** so light (don't attempt to use 1/4" thick plywood; it's too stiff).

Simply transfer the patterns to the plywood, cut out, stitch, and glue to shape. Viola!...you'll have a fast, agile, super-light yet super-strong, stable canoe for a minimum investment in money, time, and ef-

fort. No building jig or forms are required! It's fast, fun, and easy. Best of all, your **ROB ROY**, with its clean, smooth interior and classic appearance, will turn heads wherever you go. Handling with either one or two aboard is positive, and even though the hull is unsinkable, the optional built-in flotation chambers will give added peace of mind.

CHARACTERISTICS
Length overall .... 14'-5"
Beam .... 29"
Depth amidships (approx.) .... 11"
Depth max. (approx.) .... 18"
Weight (varies with plywood used) 30-43 lbs.
Hull type: Combination single chine/round bottom hull with symmetrical ends for Stitch-N-Glue sheet plywood construction.
Trailer: Designed for use with Canoe/Kayak boat trailer plans.

COMPLETE PLANS include FULL SIZE PATTERNS for the side-bottom planking, butt blocks, frame, breasthooks, thwart, and flotation chamber bulkheads. Includes material listing and layouts, with instructions and STITCH-N-GLUE MANUAL.

AVAILABLE FOR THIS DESIGN:
- **Plans & Patterns**
- **Stitch & Glue Kit**
- **Fiberglass Kit**
- **Stitch & Glue DVD**
See Price List

MAKE YOUR OWN OARS & PADDLES

gency use in any small boat); general purpose rowing oar; and super-lightweight, spoon blade, recreational rowing or sculling oar.

Making your own oars or paddles is easier and faster than you think when you use our **OARS & PADDLES PLANS AND PATTERNS**. Anyone with a few basic woodworking skills and tools can do it with professional results. We provide all the details, instructions, and Full Size Patterns. No layouts or scaling is necessary. Just transfer the patterns to the stock, cut to shape, and fair to the noted contours. One plan set details four oar and paddle types: Simple double bladed kayak paddle; single blade canoe paddle (also great for emer-

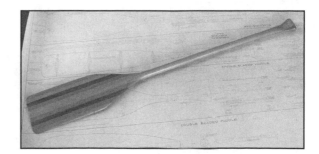

KAYAK A 17' TOURING KAYAK

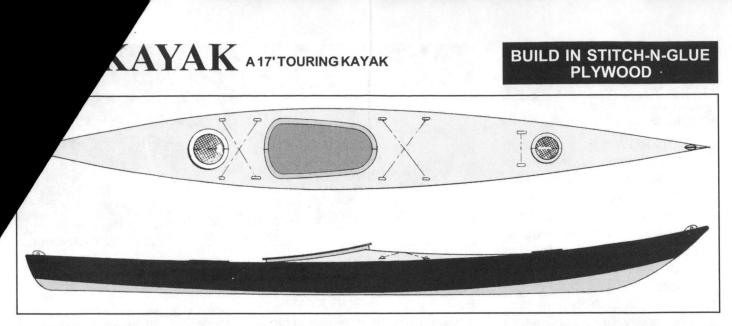

A **SEA KAYAK**, or touring kayak, provides another world of boating. This is a craft that will glide across the early morning calm and yet, when properly handled, is capable of performing well in diverse cruising conditions. Equipped with a spray skirt, the paddler remains dry.

The **SEA KAYAK** is easy to build with the simplified Stitch-N-Glue plywood building method. Virtually every part in the boat is furnished as a full size Pattern. And yes!...that does mean all planking and decking is patterned. No need to loft or enlarge from dimensional layouts with the Glen-L full pattern system. It takes only three sheets of 4mm or 1/4"x4'x8' plywood to build the entire boat. Duplicate the pattern contours to the plywood, saw to shape with a saber saw, drill for stitch holes, wire stitch the parts together, fillet and fiberglass tape the seams...and you have the boat. Truly a boat that can be built by almost anyone. For additional information on Stitch-N-Glue construction, see the front of the catalog. The plans for building your own Stitch-N-Glue paddle are included in the Plans & Pattern package.

CHARACTERISTICS
Length overall .... 17'-0"
Beam .... 24"
Midship hull depth .... 9 1/2"
Midship depth to deck .... 13 1/2"
Passengers 1
Hull weight .... 40-70 lbs
Hull type: Single chine hull, developed for 4mm or 1/4" sheet plywood, Stitch-N-Glue construction.
Trailer: Designed for use with Canoe/ Kayak boat trailer plans.

AVAILABLE FOR THIS DESIGN:
- **Study Plans**
- **Plans & Patterns**
- **Stitch & Glue Kit**
- **Fiberglass Kit**
- **Sea Kayak DVD**
See Price List

COMPLETE PLANS include **FULL SIZE PATTERNS** for the side-bottom planking, bulkheads, stern and bow breasthook, decking, form, and cockpit coaming. Includes material listing, plywood utilization details, Laminate Schedule, STITCH-N-GLUE manual, and complete building instructions with SEA KAYAK PICTORIAL. In addition, there are plans for building your own double blade cupped paddle.

DEVELOPMENT OF THE SEA KAYAK
The SEA KAYAK was developed through hours and hours of hands-on work by our experienced designers and builders. Our STITCH-N-GLUE designs are not simply plotted on paper; they are developed with hand in hand co-operation between designers and builders to assure a finished hull that can not only be easily built by almost anyone, but is a delight on the water. Our designs are not dictated by computer, but designed by builders for builders. The SEA KAYAKS, like all of our designs, are developed for the maximum use of materials, with the least waste.

SEA KAYAK TWO

A 19' TOURING KAYAK FOR TWO

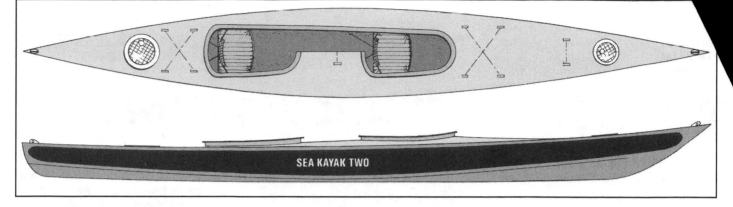

SEA KAYAK TWO

The **SEA KAYAK TWO** is built by the GLEN-L simplified Stitch-N-Glue construction method. This composite system utilizes sheet plywood planking bent to form the hull, and seams wire stitched, glued, and fiberglass laminated. This quick and easy building method is extremely strong and lightweight. No complicated dimensional layouts are required. Each part is furnished as a pattern or contained in the Wood Parts Kit.

Start now! Have fun...build your own **SEA KAYAK TWO** and experience the enjoyment of a high performance touring kayak.

The **SEA KAYAK TWO** is a touring kayak for two paddlers. There is a choice of two separate cockpits or one large cockpit. With the latter, a solo paddler's weight and position can be centered, or twin paddlers of diverse weight can adjust their positions to provide the best hull balance.

Watertight bulkheads at the bow and stern provide positive buoyancy even if the hull is flooded; an important consideration for extended touring. There is plenty of space for stowage both under and atop the deck. A gross weight of 600 lbs. will only sink the boat 6" in the water. This provides plenty of reserve buoyancy; another safety feature. Details are provided for making your own spray skirts for the dual cockpit version to keep the paddlers dry in most any condition.

CHARACTERISTICS

Length overall .... 19'-9"
Beam .... 30"
Midship hull depth .... 12"
Passengers 1-2
Hull weight .... 50-70 lbs
Hull type: Single chine hull, developed for 4mm or 1/4" sheet plywood, Stitch-N-Glue construction.
Trailer: Designed for use with Canoe/ Kayak boat trailer plans.

COMPLETE PLANS include **FULL SIZE PATTERNS** for the side-bottom planking, bulkheads, stern and bow breasthook, decking, form, and cockpit coaming. Includes material listing, plywood utilization details, Laminate Schedule, STITCH-N-GLUE manual, and complete building instructions with **SEA KAYAK PICTORIAL**. In addition, there are plans for building your own double blade cupped paddle.

AVAILABLE FOR THIS DESIGN:
- **Plans & Patterns**
- **Stitch & Glue Kit**
- **Fiberglass Kit**
- **Sea Kayak DVD**
See Price List

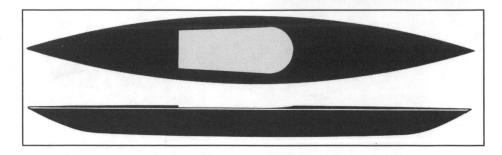

	13'	15'
......	13'-4"	15'-4"
....	2'-4"	2'-4"
....	12 3/4"	12 3/4"
(approx.)	58 lbs.	69 lbs.
...ge passengers 1		1-2

...ll type: Double ended flat bottom kayak developed for sheet plywood planking.

Trailer: Designed for use with Canoe/Kayak boat trailer plans.

Our **KAYAK** lets you shoot through the rapids or slither over shoal waters as a one person performance craft...or with two aboard enjoy exploring or just have fun on the water with a friend. The plans include details for building one or two passenger cockpit options in 13' or 15' lengths. This inexpensive kayak uses only four standard 4' x 8' plywood panels, and our construction method, designed for the amateur with little or no experience, makes building fast &

easy! Step-by-step instructions have illustrations showing construction as well as a material listing and fastening schedule. No layouts or lofting are required. The plans include details to build your own paddle.

AVAILABLE FOR THIS DESIGN:
- **Plans & Patterns**
- **Bronze Fastening Kit**
- **Fiberglass Kit**
See Price List

COMPLETE PLANS include FULL SIZE PATTERNS for stems, forms, and deck beams and includes instructions, fastening schedule, and bill of materials.

CAN-YAK   **A 12' OR 14' CANOE/KAYAK**

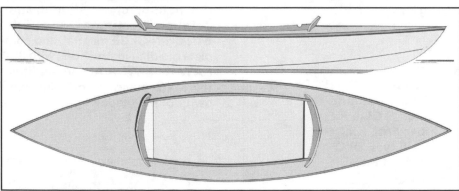

CHARACTERISTICS	12'	14'
Length overall	12'-0"	14'-0"
Beam	2'-8"	2'-8"
Depth amidships	14"	14"
Weight (approx.)	68 lbs.	78 lbs.

Hull type: Double-ender canoe-kayak designed for sheet plywood planking.

Trailer: Designed for use with Canoe/Kayak boat trailer plans.

COMPLETE PLANS include FULL SIZE PATTERNS for the frames, stems, and knees. Includes scaled layouts for planking and decking, instructions, and bill of materials.

CAN-YAK...a combination of canoe and kayak retaining the virtues of each. Whisk along the edge of that slowly winding stream...ease along the shore of a lake and explore the hidden coves...creep out on the marsh in the early morning waiting for the first flight of birds. Yes, you can do all of these with the **CAN-YAK**. It's light enough to carry and can be car topped with ease. This multi-purpose boat can provide you with a means of escape, or the kids can have a barrel of fun paddling around in protected water. Enjoy cruising around the lake at dusk, sneaking up on those big mouth bass in your own **CAN-YAK**.

CAN-YAK is intended for either one or two people paddling with double ended or single blade paddles. This double ended, shallow draft craft will move easily and silently through the water. The construction is simple and the hull is inexpensive to build. Three sheets of 4' x 8' plywood will suffice for all planking, decking and floorboards.

AVAILABLE FOR THIS DESIGN:
- **Plans & Patterns**
- **Bronze Fastening Kit**
- **Fiberglass Kit**
See Price List

STRIPPER
A 16' OR 17' STRIP PLANKED CANOE

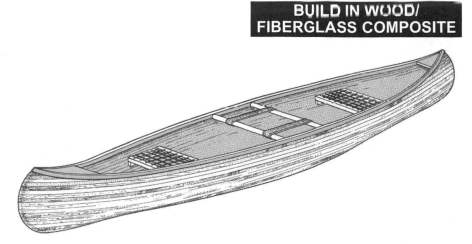

CHARACTERISTICS

	16'	17'
Length overall	16'	17'
Beam	34"	34"
Depth amidships	13"	13"

Will support 600 lbs. gross weight with 6" draft. Will submerge approx. 1" for each additional 145 lbs.

Weight (approx.) .... 50 lbs.* 60 lbs.*

Hull type: Double-ended, round bilge canoe designed for wood strip planking.

Trailer: Designed for use with Canoe/ Kayak boat trailer plans.

* Will vary with type of lumber used.

STRIPPER is a ribless canoe made from narrow wood strips, covered with fiberglass inside and out. The composite construction produces high strength with low weight while displaying the natural beauty of the wood.

This is the type of craft that brings out the ooh's and aah's from observers. Natural wood provides a warmth and richness to the sleek lines of the canoe. Yes, these craft are labor intensive, but the building method requires more patience than skill. The material required for building is relatively inexpensive in comparison to the worth of the finished craft.

The **STRIPPER** can be built 16' or 17' long. Both sizes are detailed in the plans and instructions. Full size patterns are provided for all forms and watertight bulkheads. All aspects of construction are detailed, from the simple building jig through the planking process. Instructions supplement the plans with step-by-step descriptions and a Bill of Materials.

AVAILABLE FOR THIS DESIGN:
- Plans & Patterns
- Fiberglass Kit

See Price List

COMPLETE PLANS include FULL SIZE PATTERNS for the seven frame forms, bow and stern stem forms, and complete plans, instructions, and bill of materials.

PIROGUE
A 13' CAJUN CANOE

CHARACTERISTICS

Length overall .... 13-2"
Beam .... 35"
Depth amidships (approx.) .... 11"
Passengers 1-2
Weight (approx.) .... 59 lbs.
Hull type: Flat bottom with symmetrical ends for Stitch-N-Glue sheet plywood construction.
Power: For use with a single or double paddle, small 1-2 hp outboard optional but not detailed.
Trailer: Designed for use with Canoe/ Kayak boat trailer plans.

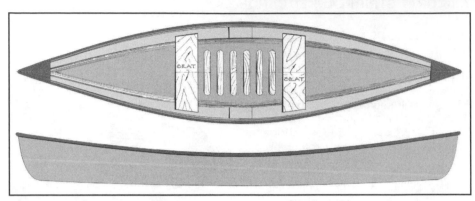

COMPLETE PLANS include FULL SIZE PATTERNS for the bottom and side planking, butt blocks, seat uprights, seats, and breasthooks. Includes material listing and layouts, with instructions and STITCH-N-GLUE manual.

The **PIROGUE** is a Cajun canoe, a type of boat popular in the marshes and bayous of the South. These flat-bottomed hulls have shallow draft and a minimal beam, and can be easily poled or paddled with either single or double blade paddles. The **PIROGUE** will slip into areas that are inaccessible to other craft. Best of all, this little craft is very easy and inexpensive to build, requiring only two sheets of 1/4" plywood.

Full Size Patterns are supplied for every part, even showing stitching holes where required. Stitch-N-Glue construction puts building this boat within the range of virtually everyone...So start building now! You'll be amazed at how fast your boat will take shape.

AVAILABLE FOR THIS DESIGN:
- **Plans & Patterns**
- **Stitch & Glue Kit**
- **Fiberglass Kit**
- **Stitch & Glue DVD**
See Price List

HURON

BUILD IN PLYWOOD

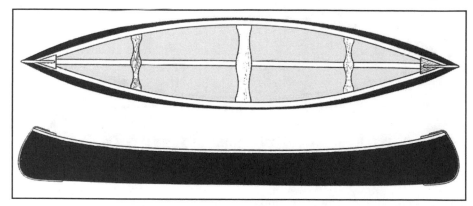

CHARACTERISTICS	13'	15'
Length overall	12'-9"	15'-0"
Beam	3'-0"	3'-0"
Depth amidships	13 1/2"	13 1/2"
Depth at bows	19 1/2"	19 1/2"
Weight (approx.)	79 lbs.	95 lbs.

Hull type: Double-ended, multi-chine canoe designed for sheet plywood planking.

Trailer: Designed for use with Canoe/Kayak boat trailer plans.

At last....a true canoe that can be built with standard size sheets of plywood using the multi-chine principle. You have a choice of two sizes (13' and 15') both fully detailed on the plans.

The construction method is simple and unique, with the canoe being built over temporary forms. After the boat is planked, these forms are removed leaving a clean interior and a hull that is light weight but still very strong.

How does this multi-chine canoe compare to the conventional round bilge type? Very well indeed! In the water the difference is not readily discernible, and performance is excellent. Truly, this is a canoe that incorporates what most builders want: Simplicity of construction and fine performance, all at a low cost.

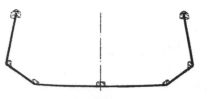

COMPLETE PLANS include **FULL SIZE PATTERNS** for stems and half section patterns of the forms. Includes instructions, fastening schedule, and bill of materials.

AVAILABLE FOR THIS DESIGN:
- **Plans & Patterns**
- **Bronze Fastening Kit**
- **Fiberglass Kit**
See Price List

CHIPPEWA

13', 15', & 17' CANOE

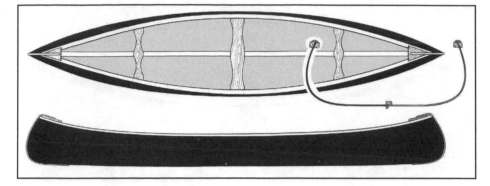

CHARACTERISTICS

	13'	15'	17'
Length overall	12'-9"	15'-0"	17'-0"
Beam	3'-0" all models		
Depth amidships	13 1/2" all models		
Depth at bow	19 1/2" all models		
Weight (approx.)	73 lbs.	87 lbs.	100 lbs.

Hull type: Typical round bottom canoe for two laminations of 1/8" plywood or 3/32" wood veneer, or one-off C-FLEX fiberglass.

Trailer: Designed for use with Canoe/Kayak boat trailer plans.

The American Indian Chippewa tribe was known as master canoe builders. Their construction methods and craftsmanship resulted in canoes with performance second to none. We've retained the quality and performance factors of these famous canoe makers, but modernized the construction to adapt to current day materials and amateur boatbuilding methods.

You can build your own CHIPPEWA canoe using either the fiberglass planking method (C-FLEX), or by using a series of thin wood veneers laid diagonally athwartship in multiple layers. Each construction method is fully detailed on the plans with specific step-by-step instructions. You have your choice of building in three different lengths: 13', 15', or 17'. All details necessary for building any of these lengths are covered in one set of low cost plans, patterns, and instructions.

The full size patterns included with the plans package an assure accurate framework for building your CHIPPEWA. The frames are temporary forms over which the hull is built, and do not remain in the finished canoe.

AVAILABLE FOR THIS DESIGN:
- **Plans & Patterns**
- **Fiberglass Kit (WD)**
See Price List

COMPLETE PLANS include FULL SIZE PATTERNS for stems and forms and includes instructions and bill of materials.

FIFE

EASY-TO-ROW, EASY-TO-TRANSPORT 12' ROWING BOAT

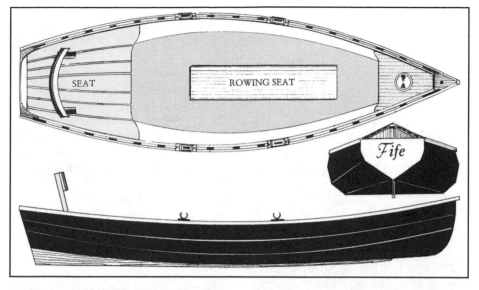

BUILD IN STITCH-N PLYWOOD

CHARACTERISTICS

Length overall .... 12'-0"
Beam .... 3'-8"
Depth amidships (approx.) .... 13"
Depth at bow .... 19 1/2"
Weight (approx) .... 100 lbs.
Hull type: Flat bottom with fore and aft rocker, multi-chine sides, designed for Stitch-n-Glue construction.
Power: Oars or small trolling motor.

COMPLETE PLANS include FULL SIZE PATTERNS for the side and bottom planking, bulkheads, seat tops, breasthook, form, and skeg. Includes material listing and layouts, with instructions and STITCH-N-GLUE manual.

The design criteria for the 12' **FIFE** was that it could be carried, easily rowed, carry three people, and be stable. FIFE is lightweight (the test model weighed only 98 lbs. including fiberglass), with a wide bottom for stability and to maximize bouyancy. The hull depth was kept to 13" to minimize windage. The rounded sides and tumblehome make this a very stiff boat even using light weight 4mm material on the sides.

Most small boats designed for serious rowing tend to feel "tippy". The wide bottom on the **FIFE** makes her remarkably stable. People who normally feel unconfortable in small boats will find **FIFE** comforting. The skeg allows her to row true even with an inexperienced oarsman. Her ample watertight storage under the fore and aft seats provide room for extra clothing or picnic supplies.

The waterline is at 3" with a 130 lb. load; 3 1/2" with 190 lbs., 5" with 395 lbs., 6" with 540 lbs. Plenty of capacity for you, a friend, and a hefty picnic basket.

With two sets of movable oar lock sockets, the rower's seat allows the oarsman to change position with different passenger weights or when a passenger sits in the comfortable stern seat.

Viewed from aft, she has a traditional "wine glass" stern. The lines guarantee that anywhere **FIFE** goes, she will get many more than a second glance.

Performance report: An inexperienced oarsman rowed one passenger around the harbor for over 2 1/2 hours without fatigue. There seemed to be little additional effort required with two passengers. With two passengers, the oarsman used the aft oar locks, allowing the forward passenter to sit on the front of the rower's seat and face forward.

VHITEHALL

A 17' TRADITIONAL ROWING CRAFT

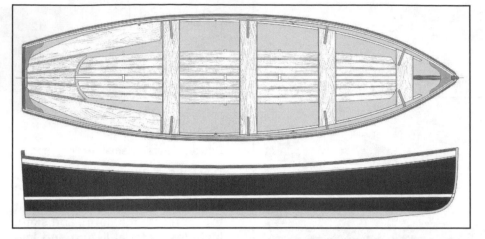

These boats have been reported to be this country's first mass-produced boat. While not a distinct American innovation, the "Whitehall" evolved and was refined from various predecessors, rather than being created by actual design. Noted for rowing easily and swiftly in both smooth and rough waters, they also have a reputation as safe, dry boats with ample load carrying ability. Having a shapely "wine glass" or heart shaped transom, the waterline form is actually a double ender with a dead-straight keel and pronounced forefoot that provides excellent directional control.

The original craft were built using wood lapstrake or carvel planking, best suited to skilled craftsmen. Our **WHITEHALL**-Wood version features a modern, yet proven, form of wood strip planking, edge glued and nailed together to form a strong stress skin hull. The Fiberglass version uses C-FLEX fiberglass planking and fiberglass laminate one-off construction. (See "Boatbuilding Methods/Fiberglass" for further information on this method.) Whether building in wood or fiberglass, the boat exhibits ample natural wood members to capture the beauty, character, and romance of their forebearers.

With our updated building methods, there are no permanent frames, no steam bending or caulking of seams, and no difficult "spiling" (fitting of planks). Full size patterns eliminate the task of lofting, even though a Table of Offsets is provided for those who want to perform this exercise.

CHARACTERISTICS

Length overall	16'-11"
Beam	4'-6"
Hull depth forward	2'-6"
Depth amidships	1'-10"
Hull depth aft	2'-2"
Weight (approx.)	350 lbs.*
Passengers	2-6

Hull type: Traditional round bilge Whitehall rowing hull for wood or fiberglass construction. WOOD version features glued and edge-nailed "bead and cove" strip planking (no plywood is used in this version). FIBERGLASS version features single skin "one-off" fiberglass planking (C-FLEX). Hull is built upside-down over temporary form members in both cases.

Power: Oars, 8' to 9' long, one to three oarsmen.

Trailer: Designed for use with Glen-L Series 1200/1800 boat trailer plans.

* Will vary with type of lumber used.

COMPLETE PLANS include FULL SIZE PATTERNS for the station forms, keel bevels, transom, transom knee, stem form, and breasthook, plus complete plans, instructions, bill of materials, and table of offsets (though not needed if you use the patterns). Add FIBERGLASS MANUAL for fiberglass version.

IMP

BUILD IN PLYWOOD

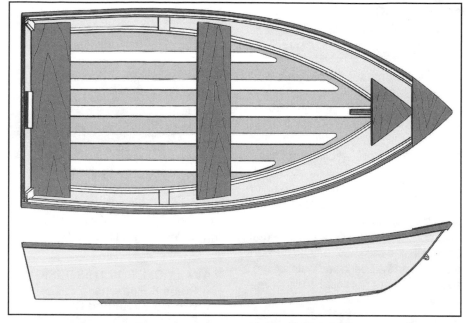

The **IMP** is a diminutive craft that wears many hats. As a ship-to-shore dinghy, you can easily tow or stow the craft on board a larger cruiser. For fishing, the flat bottom gives excellent stability with shallow draft for getting into those out of the way fishing spots. It is easily car topped or carried in the back of a pickup for transport to the water. The lightweight **IMP** is easy to row and will really scoot with an outboard motor up to 5 HP.

The **IMP** is not only a handy size, but is inexpensive to build as well. The planking is 1/4" x 4' x 8' AB exterior or marine plywood. You can plank the whole boat with two and a half sheets...with material left over. The hull is built bottom side up, over building forms that are later discarded; a simple method of construction with a resultant frame-free interior. This straight forward construction makes it possible for the average handyman to build the hull in a weekend.

COMPLETE PLANS include FULL SIZE PATTERNS for stem, transom, knee, seat brace, and building forms, including instructions and material list.

AVAILABLE FOR THIS DESIGN:
- **Plans & Patterns**
- **Bronze Fastening Kit**
- **Fiberglass Kit**
See Price List

CHARACTERISTICS

Length overall .... 9'-9"
Beam .... 4'-5"
Depth amidship .... 1'-3"
Average passengers 1-3
Hull weight (approx.).............. 105 lbs.
Hull type: Flat bottomed, developed for sheet plywood planking. A single sheet of plywood on the bottom.
Power: Oars or outboard motor to 5 HP.
Trailer: Designed for use with GLEN-L SERIES 750/1000 boat trailer plans.

SISSY DO
A 13' FLAT BOTTOM ROWBOAT

BUILD IN PLYWOOD

The multi-purpose **SISSY DO** isn't fancy or streamlined, just a sturdy, basic boat that gets the job done. After twenty years, the prototype is still going. For fly casting, the flat bottom offers more stability than common production hulls. As for riding ability, it will bring you back on any type of water a boat of this size and power should be out in. A local entrepreneur built a fleet of **SISSY DO**'s as rental boats at a beachside pier. You can draw it up on the beach and walk ashore, something that's not so easy with a vee bottom hull.

The **SISSY DO** is inexpensive and easy to build. A couple of fellows working on a long weekend should be able to slap her together without problem. The plans and patterns are especially complete with step-by-step building photos of exactly how the original was built, including written text and material list.

AVAILABLE FOR THIS DESIGN:
- **Plans & Patterns**
- **Bronze Fastening Kit**
- **Fiberglass Kit**
See Price List

CHARACTERISTICS

Length overall .... 13'-3"
Beam .... 5'-3"
Hull depth .... 1'-8"
Hull weight (approx.).............. 175 lbs.
Average passengers 2-4
Hull type:Flat bottomed, developed for sheet plywood. Single sheet chine to chine.
Power: Oars or outboard motor to 10 HP.
Trailer: Designed for use with GLEN-L SERIES 750/1000 boat trailer plans.

COMPLETE PLANS include FULL SIZE PATTERNS for the stem, knee, and half-section patterns of the transom and frames. Includes instructions and material list.

MR. JOHN   A 12' OR 14' JOHN BOAT

MR. JOHN is the type of boat known by various names such as john, jon, or joe boat; punt, garvey, scow, or bateau... different words with the same meaning. A simple boat at its best for fishing along streams, a bayou, or a lake. Power it with a small outboard, row it, pole it, or scull it as suits your fancy.

MR. JOHN can be built in either 11'-9" or 13'-7" versions. Details for building both are shown in the plans. The plans are particularly simple with concise instructions. Included are layouts for cutting the plywood components, fastening schedule, material listing, and of course the step-by-step procedures for building the boat. And *most important*...the cost to build has been kept to a minimum by the careful selection of stock sizes of material and the complete use of all plywood panels.

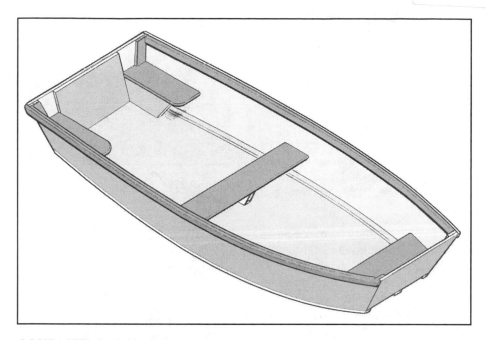

COMPLETE PLANS include FULL SIZE PATTERNS for the bow piece, transom, and each of the frames, including instructions and material list.

CHARACTERISTICS

Length overall .... 11'-9" or 13'-7"
Beam .... 4'-4"
Hull depth .... 1'-5"
Hull weight (approx.)........... 12' model 145 lbs.

14' model 165 lbs.

Average passengers 2-4
Hull type: Flat bottomed scow type, developed for sheet plywood.
Power: Oars or outboard motor to 20 HP
Trailer: Designed for use with GLEN-L SERIES 750/1000 boat trailer plans.

AVAILABLE FOR THIS DESIGN:
- **Plans & Patterns**
- **Bronze Fastening Kit**
- **Fiberglass Kit**
See Price List

ROWME

A 12' ROWBOAT

BUILD IN STITCH-N-GLUE PLYWOOD

Want a boat, but don't have the time to build...want it *now*? Then this simple Stitch-N-Glue rowboat is for you. It's *fast, easy*, and *fun* to build. Almost anyone can do it. Just trace the patterns on the plywood, cut the pieces out with a sabre saw, then Stitch-N-Glue together. Presto! You'll have a boat in a matter of days; not weeks or months.

Yet here's a boat that will provide years of service. The sturdy hull features a 3/8" bottom and 1/4" sides; and only two 4' x 8' sheets of each size are required. **ROWME** is an ideal fishing skiff. The stable, flat bottom rowboat can also be powered by a small outboard, plus there are three built-in flotation chambers for safety (flotation filling optional). So why not build your own...like *now*?

CHARACTERISTICS

Length overall .... 12'-2"
Beam .... 4'-11"
Hull depth .... 1'-6"
Hull weight (approx.) .... 145 lbs.
Average passengers 2-4
Hull type: Flat bottomed for Stitch-N-Glue sheet plywood construction.
Power: Oars or outboard motor to 5HP.
Trailer: Designed for use with GLEN-L SERIES 750/1000 boat trailer plans.

AVAILABLE FOR THIS DESIGN:
- **Plans & Patterns**
- **Stitch & Glue Kit**
- **Fiberglass Kit**
- **Stitch & Glue DVD**

See Price List

COMPLETE PLANS include **FULL SIZE PATTERNS for the bottom, sides, transom, seats, seat uprights, transom knee, and breasthook.** Includes material listing and layouts, plus instructions and STITCH-N-GLUE Manual.

POWER-ROW SKIFFS
RUGGED FLAT-BOTTOM SKIFFS FOR ROW OR POWER

CHARACTERISTICS

MODEL(*)	11½'-NB	11½'-SB	13½'-NB	13½'-SB	13½'-WB	15½'-SB	15½'-WB
Length overall	11'5"	11'5"	13'4"	13'4"	13'4"	15'4"	15'4"
Bottom length	9'8"	9'8"	11'4"	11'4"	11'4"	13'4"	13'4"
Beam overall	4'5"	4'11"	4'7"	5'1"	5'7"	5'1"	5'7"
Bottom width (nominal)	3'	3-1/2'	3'	3-1/2'	4'	3-1/2'	4'
Hull depth (maximum)	2'1"	2'1"	2'3"	2'3"	2'3"	2'3"	2'3"
Hull weight (approx.)	140 lbs.	150 lbs.	165 lbs.	175 lbs.	185 lbs.	200 lbs.	220 lbs.
Average passengers	1-2	2	2-3	3	3-4	4	5
Horsepower range	2-5	3-8	3-6	3-10	3-15	4-15	4-20

Trailer:Designed for use with GLEN-L SERIES 750/1000 boat trailer plans.
(*) NB = Narrow width bottom
SB = Standard width bottom
WB = Wide width bottom

It takes only a little time, money, and effort to build one of these rugged - yet simple - flat bottom skiffs. Every model includes details for two bottom profile shapes. Use the ROW OPTION with rockered bottom profile if you favor easy rowing or smaller motors and lower speeds under power. Or use the POWER OPTION with straight, flat bottom aft if you'll be rowing less or want more speed and power.

Three nominal lengths and bottom widths are available. NB models can be car-topped, carried in many station wagons or pick-up trucks, and are easier to row. SB models offer a good balance of easy rowing or powering, spaciousness, and stability. WB models offer the ultimate in room, stability, and speed under power, yet are still practical to row.

All models show built-in buoyancy chambers (3) and optional aft thwart (if omitted, the aft buoyancy chambers form side seats instead). All models feature low-resistance straight-steering, dry-running hull shapes of ample depth for security. Yet the nicely flared topsides with fine dory-type V-bow entries slice through a chop with little loss of headway in a breeze.

Plans include instructions with material listings and fastening schedule. Simple joining methods detailed on the plans allow you to use 8' plywood throughout with either exterior or marine grade panels (full-length panels are optional). Con-struction takes place over three temporary forms set up on a simple building base for accuracy. The few internal members can largely be pre-beveled to eliminate most fairing. Only minimal power hand tools are required (saber saw, variable-speed drill), plus some hand tools so that anyone can do it, even first-timers!

Plans include FULL SIZE PATTERNS for temporary frames, transom, and stem, instructions, material listings, and fastening schedule.

DORY A 16' ROWING DORY

Our **DORY** is ideal for launching or landing through the surf in coastal areas, or for rowing across any reasonable size body of water. The relatively narrow bottom makes rowing easy, while the wide flaring sides make the boat dry and increases the reserve bouyancy.

The dory-type boat has been in existence for hundreds of years. Fishermen the world over have used dories in all weather conditions. Our modern **DORY** is much lighter in weight and virtually leakproof in contrast to the craft of yesteryear. The lightweight but durable plywood hull adds a new dimension to the classic dory.

The construction has purposely been kept simple. The boat is built bottom side up, with simple molds made from scrap material. These molds are discarded when the boat is finished, leaving a "stress-skin, monocoque" boat. This method not only simplifies construction, but provides a smooth uncluttered interior. The construction of the **DORY** should be within the realm of almost any handyperson...and it won't take long to put together.

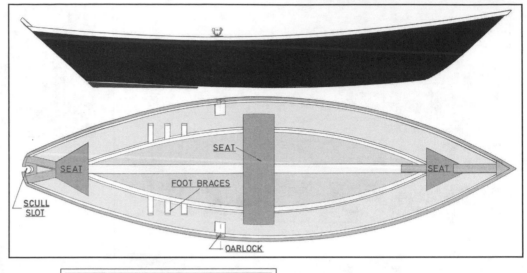

AVAILABLE FOR THIS DESIGN:
- **Plans & Patterns**
- **Bronze Fastening Kit**
- **Fiberglass Kit**
See Price List

COMPLETE PLANS include FULL SIZE PATTERNS for the building forms, transom, and stem. Including instructions and material list.

CHARACTERISTICS
Length overall .... 15'-6"
Beam .... 4'-7"
Hull depth .... 1'-7"
Hull weight (approx.) .... 200 lbs.
Average passengers 1-3
Hull type: Flat bottomed dory-type hull developed for sheet plywood.
Power: Oars or sculling.
Trailer: Designed for use with GLEN-L SERIES 750/1000 boat trailer plans.

PEDAL-IT

A 9' TUNNEL-TYPE PEDAL BOAT

CHARACTERISTICS

Length overall .... 9'-4"
Beam .... 4'-6"
Hull depth .... 13"
Total weight (test model) .... 164 lbs.
Displacement at 6" waterline . 308 lbs.
Bridge deck size .... 4' x 4'-6"
Average passengers 1
Hull type: Two vee bottom pontoons or tunnel hulls connected by a bridge deck. Hulls are developed for sheet plywood with Stitch and glue construction.
Power: Bicycle pedals, sprocket, and chain driving a stern mounted paddlewheel.
Can the hull be extended or shortened? No. We also do not recommend increasing the beam.
Trailer: Designed for use with Glen-L Series 750/1000 boat trailer plans.

COMPLETE PLANS include FULL SIZE PATTERNS for the hull sides, bottom, and tunnel sides, paddlewheel, transom, bulkheads, template, spray shroud, seat and back.

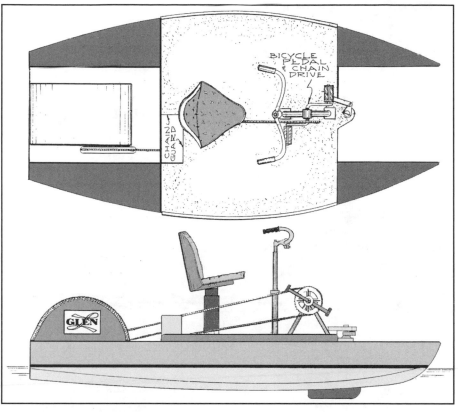

Want a watercraft that's different? ...why not PEDAL-IT! Sit in a comfortable, fully adjustable seat and pump the pedals just as you would on a bicycle. Chain and sprockets transfer the pedal motion to the paddlewheel at the stern. Want to go backwards? Crank the pedals in reverse and it's done. Go left or right by turning the bicycle type handlebars that are connected to the rudder. The essence of simplicity, and it's FUN!

This is an ideal craft for pond or small lake fishing. You sit on an elevated seat with a full view of that rocky bottom or fallen tree where the lunkers hide and you can pedal quietly to the ideal spot for the catch. But this is also a fun boat. It's fun to pedal quietly along the shore and observe Mother Nature. Or, lend it (just try and get it back) to the kids and watch the fun as they churn up the water.

PEDAL-IT is easy and inexpensive to build. The propulsion system is derived from a used bicycle, readily available at yard sales. The twin hulls are built by the fast and easy stitch and glue method with full size patterns furnished for virtually every contoured part in the boat. Parts cut from the patterns are bent around two bulkheads, stitched together, and joints bonded with fillets and fiberglass laminations. No building form is required. You'll be surprised how quickly the hull takes shape and what an excellent first time project this would make.

The detailed plans include complete progressive instructions with Bill of Materials, what fasteners to use at each junction, and the proper seam bonding laminates. In addition, GLEN-L has available a Stitch and

Glue Kit that contains everything needed to assemble the cut out wooden parts, and a Fiberglass Covering Kit to properly encase the hulls with this durable sheathing.

AVAILABLE FOR THIS DESIGN:
- **Plans & Patterns**
- **Stitch & Glue Kit**
- **Fiberglass Kit**
- **Stitch & Glue DVD**
See Price List

DUCK BOAT & DUCK BOAT TOO

A 14' DUCK BOAT FOR PADDLE

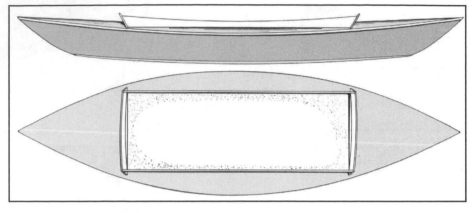

A 12' DUCK BOAT FOR POWER

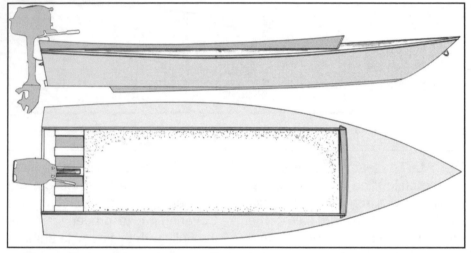

COMPLETE PLANS include FULL SIZE PATTERNS for the frames (forms), stem and transom. Includes instructions, Bill of Materials and Fastening Schedule for building either DUCK BOAT or DUCK BOAT TOO.

BUILD IN PLYWOOD

The double ended **DUCK BOAT** has a raised forefoot to enable the shallow draft flat bottom to slither over sand bars and shallow spots. The pointed prow parts the reeds and tules to allow hunting or fishing in hard-to-reach areas and easy to camouflage with reeds or grass due to the low silouette.

The **DUCK BOAT TOO** is similar, but has provisions for a small outboard motor. It's an ideal craft for reaching the isolated tule patch or fishing hole far from the launch site.

CHARACTERISTICS	DUCK BOAT	DUCK BOAT TOO
Length overall	14'-0"	12'-4"
Beam	3'-11"	3'-11"
Hull depth	13"	13"
Hull weight-approx.	96 lbs.	88 lbs.
Average passengers	1-2	1-2
Cockpit size	2'-6"x7'	2'-6"x8'-6"

Hull type:**DUCK BOAT** is a double ender with flat bottom, intended for use with paddles, and developed for sheet plywood planking.
DUCK BOAT TOO is a flat bottom skiff for sheet plywood planking for outboard motors to 7 1/2 HP.

Trailer: Designed for use with GLEN-L SERIES 750/1000 boat trailer plans.

AVAILABLE FOR THIS DESIGN:
- **Plans & Patterns**
- **Bronze Fastening Kit**
- **Fiberglass Kit**
See Price List

SNEAK BOX A SAIL OR POWER DUCK BOAT

CHARACTERISTICS

Length overall .... 12'-5"
Beam .... 4'-6"
Hull depth .... 14"
Average passengers 1-2
Hull weight (approx.) .... 115 lbs.
Sail area .... 51 sq. ft.
Hull type:Vee-bottom, hard chine, developed for sheet ply-
        wood planking.
Sail type:Sprit rig with unstayed mast and daggerboard.
Power: Oars or outboard motor to 5 HP.
Trailer: Designed for use with GLEN-L SERIES 750/1000
        boat trailer plans.

Our **SNEAK BOX** is an updated and improved rendition of the Barnegat Bay sneak box. The most important difference in our version is the inexpensive materials used and the ease with which it's built. Light weight also makes the **SNEAK BOX** an excellent recreational sailboat for those members of the family who don't hunt... a good argument to use when trying to sell the project to the family.

Only five sheets of 4' x 8' plywood are required to plank the hull, and no building form or jig is required. Unlike the old solid wood versions, the **SNEAK BOX** weighs a mere 115 lbs.

COMPLETE PLANS include FULL SIZE PATTERNS for the side planking, bowpiece, transom, frames, tiller, rudder, skeg, daggerboard trunk, knees, and motor brackets. Includes instructions, Bill of Materials, and Fastening Schedule.

AVAILABLE FOR THIS DESIGN:
- **Plans & Patterns**
- **Bronze Fastening Kit**
- **Fiberglass Kit**
- **Sail**
See Price List

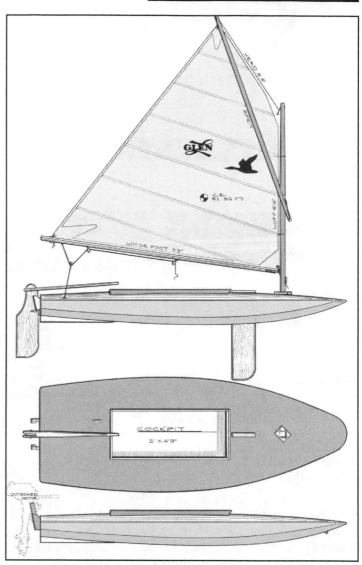

SCULL BOAT A 15' SCULLING DUCK BOAT

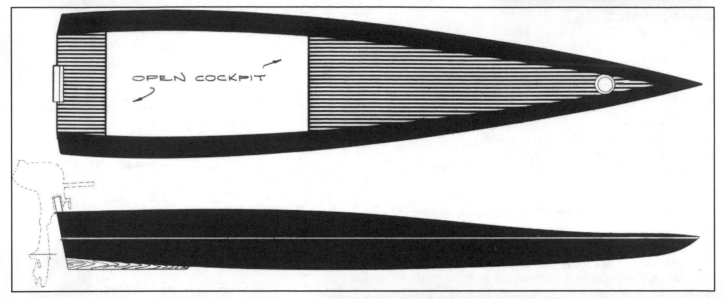

OPEN COCKPIT

CHARACTERISTICS

Length overall .... 15'-4"
Beam .... 3'-6"
Depth amidship .... 16"
Average passengers 1
Cockpit size .... 28" x 58"
Hull weight (approx.)............... 170 lbs.
Hull type: Flat bottomed with flaring sides, developed for sheet plywood planking.
Power: Single sculling oar through transom. Outboard motor to 5 HP.
Trailer: Designed for use with GLEN-L Canoe/Kayak boat trailer plans.

With our **SCULL BOAT**, you can slither through the water like a gator, sneaking up on waterfowl while not disturbing the solitude of the pond. The sculler lays on his back facing either forward or aft, with the sculling oar worked through a watertight sleeve through the transom. An optional outboard can be used where longer distances must be travelled. Because it sits so low in the water, it's easy to camouflage. The **SCULL BOAT** is easy and inexpensive to build, even for most beginners. There's no building form required and standard 4' x 8' sheets of plywood are used. Our plans include step-by-step instructions plus full size patterns.

> **AVAILABLE FOR THIS DESIGN:**
> - **Plans & Patterns**
> - **Bronze Fastening Kit**
> - **Fiberglass Kit**
> **See Price List**

COMPLETE PLANS include **FULL SIZE PATTERNS** for the frames, stem, transom, breasthook, and long beams. Includes instructions, Bill of Materials, and Fastening Schedule.

HONKER A 15' DUCK BOAT

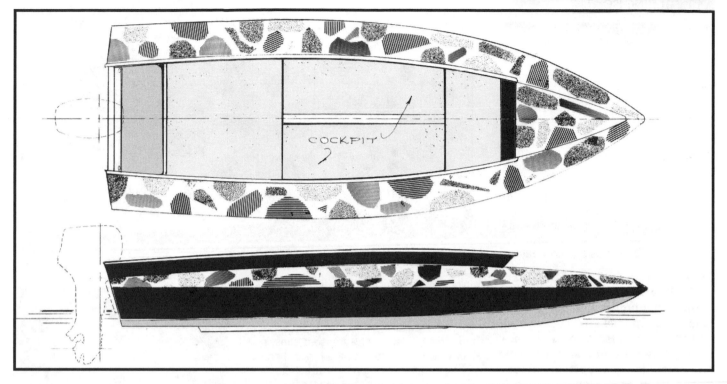

CHARACTERISTICS

Length overall .... 15'-0"
Beam .... 5'-4"
Hull depth .... 25"
Hull weight .... 350 lbs.
Displacement at 5" waterline . 760 lbs.
Required to raise waterline 1" 320 lbs
Cockpit size (nominal) .... 3' x 9'-2"
Passengers (normal) 2
Hull type: Vee bottom, hard chine hull developed for sheet plywood.
Power: Single outboard motor, short or long shaft to 25 hp.
Can the hull be extended or shortened? No. We also do not recommend increasing the beam.
Trailer: Designed for use with GLEN-L Series 750/1000 trailer.

The GLEN-L series of duck boats have been very popular. BUT, they couldn't carry hunters, dog, decoys and gear on longer trips. Now there's HONKER, larger in all ways.

The silhouette has been kept low with sloping side decks for placing comouflage that will blend into the surroundings. She has a slight vee in the bottom to part and cushion the waves, but not enough to create instability at rest; this is a solid in-water gunning platform.

And, with the flaring sides, stability is further increased and adds additional buoyancy when the hull is carrying a load. This is a boat for the serious hunter. But of course, it'll be at home for fishing or similar water sports.

HONKER is solidly built from sheet plywood with a full 3/4" bottom, it's tough. Standard lumber and 4' x 8' sheets of plywood are used and building is well within the realm of the average handy person. And the GLEN-L plans and patterns make the task even easier for the neophyte. The hull is conventional

COMPLETE PLANS include FULL SIZE PATTERNS for stem, knee, upper and lower harpin, bow piece, and half sections of each frame, and transom. Plus detailed instructions, Bill of Materials, Fastening Schedule, and Build ityourself the GLEN-L Way pictorial manual.

in construction with sawn frames with 1/4" sheet plywood sides and decks and a doubled 3/8" bottom.

The flights will be coming in. Don't miss out, start building your own HONKER and lead the action.and have fun building a practical, usable duck boat; the kind you've always wanted.

AVAILABLE FOR THIS DESIGN:
- **Plans & Patterns**
- **Bronze Fastening Kit**
- **Fiberglass Kit**
See Price List

FOLD UP
A 10' FOLDING BOAT

BUILD IN PLYWOOD

CHARACTERISTICS

Length overall .... 10' 1"
Beam .... 52"
Midships hull depth .... 16"
Weight of test model .... 105 lbs.
Folded size, two packages:
.... 10' 3" x 20" x 6" and 7' x 25" x 4"
 Average Passengers 1-2
Hull type: Flat bottom, garvey style. Folds
         Into a flat package.
Power: Oars, electric motor or outboard
         motors to 2 hp.
Can the hull be extended or shortened?
         No. We also do not recom-
         mend increasing the beam.

COMPLETE PLANS and FULL SIZE PATTERNS include large scale plans with numerous enlarged details, sequential Instructions that include a Bill of Materials and Fastening Schedule. Full size patterns are given for the bottom, sides, floor, frame, frame seat, transom seat, uprights, bow, and oarlock brace.

FOLD UP is easily transported on car top, inside an SUV or wagon type vehicle, or pick up truck. It weighs only 105 lbs. or split it into two packages of 39 and 66 lbs.

But, does it take a long time to assemble? Is it seaworthy? As a test, we unfolded the package in 12 minutes without rushing. And yes, it's seaworthy. Obviously, it's a small boat, not intended for open sea or rough waters, and no, it won't fold up when in use.

Essentially, **FOLD UP** is made from sheet plywood hinged at the seams with a flex-

ible material similar to that used on inflatable boats. The sides and two bottom halves un-fold from a flat package to a fully shaped boat. A frame spreads the boat at the center, the transom slips in place, while a bow caps the forward end of the craft. The members are held in place primarily with barrel bolts, a simple, strong fastening method.

The **FOLD UP** is simple to build; a pattern is furnished for every contoured part in the boat including planking. Standard lengths of plywood are used and the barrel bolts, hinges, etc. are readily available at a local hardware store or home center. Everything used on the prototype is listed. Instructions carry you through the construction in a step by step manner and include how to obtain the parts from the noted material, a full Bill of Materials, and the quantity, size and number of fasteners required at junctions.

Add a little effort, and you too can build your own novel and attractive FOLD-UP.

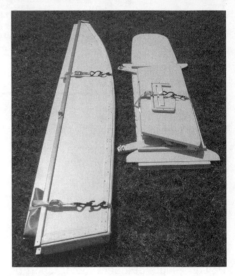

FOLD UP FASTENING KIT PLUS

All of the bronze screws required to build the boat are furnished, all in the right sizes and quantities. Not only the fasteners to build the boat, but also the fiberglass and POXY-SHIELD epoxy resin with hardener to butt join and tape the side and bottom junction. Additive to thicken the resin for gluing or filling screw holes plus sealant to bond the seam material to the hull are all a part of this KIT PLUS. Get the right stuff to do the job all in one package.

> **AVAILABLE FOR THIS DESIGN:**
> - **Plans & Patterns**
> - **Fastening Kit Plus**
> **See Price List**

GLASS BOTTOM

A 9' FLAT BOTTOM ROUND BOW GARVEY

BUILD IN STITCH-N-GLUE PLYWOOD

CHARACTERISTICS

Length overall .... 9' 6"
Beam .... 4' 6"
Hull depth .... 18"
Hull weight .... 140 lbs.
Average Passengers 1-3
Hull type: Flat bottom, rounded bow garvey style developed for sheet plywood.
Power: Outboard motors to 2 hp
Trailer: Designed for use with GLEN-L Series 750/1000 trailer..
Can the hull be extended or shortened? No. We also do not recommend increasing the beam.

COMPLETE PLANS and FULL SIZE PATTERNS include large scale plans with numerous enlarged details, sequential Instructions that include a Bill of Materials and Fastening Schedule. Full size patterns are given for the transom, bottom, bow planking, form, bow gusset, knees, and bench seat sides.

Haven't you been in a boat and wondered what was in the water beneath? A glass window in your boat bottom will open up a new world of underwater exploration. But if you just want a roomy, simple to build, stable craft for fun on the water, the window can be eliminated.

This is a BIG little boat. Less than 10' in length but with the rounded bow, the available inside space is greatly increased. That rounded bow enhances the appearance, yet is simple to build using Stitch-N-Glue building methods. Plus the flat bottom gives a very stable

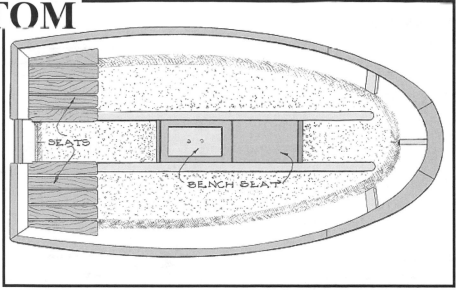

platform for viewing the depths, fishing, or just plain boating enjoyment.

The craft is equally adapted to a small outboard motor as well as rowing. The bench seat has proven to be ideal to allow the person rowing to shift their weight to better balance the boat. The seat also covers the bottom viewing window, with a part of the seat top removable; when inverted it provides a viewer or "canopy" to eliminate reflective light from interfering with a clear view through the glass.

The GLASS BOTTOM is built by the Stitch-N-Glue building method proven to be the easiest way to build a boat, and time required to accomplish the task is far less than conventional methods. And, it's fun to see a boat formed so quickly. We help you along making building within the realm of most handy people. The instructions take the builder through the construction in step by step fashion. And boating "words" are defined, You are assisted in many

ways to make the task understandable, easy and fun. You get a full Bill of Material that describes precisely what type and sizes of lumber and plywood is used. We even provide scaled layouts that illustrate how the plywood is obtained from the stock 4' x 8' panels noted. A Fastening Schedule lists the number, type, and size of fastener to use at each joint. Plus the full size patterns that are part of the plan and pattern package virtually eliminate guess work and complicated layouts.

AVAILABLE FOR THIS DESIGN:
- Plans & Patterns
- Stitch & Glue Kit
- Fiberglass Kit
- Stitch & Glue DVD
See Price List

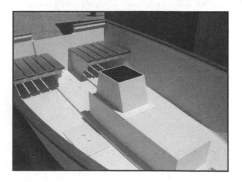

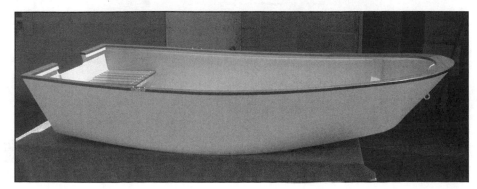

DRIFT PRAM AN 8' or 10 MINI-DRIFTBOAT

Characteristics	8'	10'
Length overall	7'9"	9'7"
Beam	54" or 60"	62"
Bottom width (max.)	41" or 47"	48"
Hull depth	15"-16"	17"-18"
Weight (approx. lbs.)	80-90	110
Average passengers	1-2	1-3

Trailer: Designed for use with GLEN-L Series 750/1000 trailer..

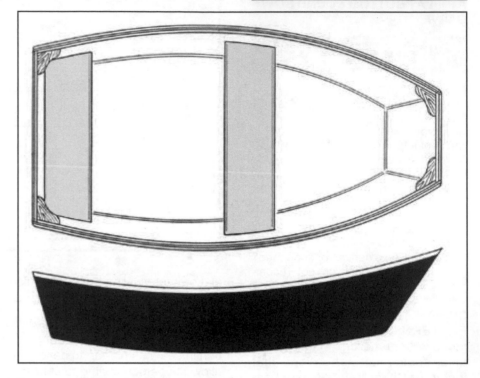

Two of our easiest and quickest designs to build, DRIFT PRAMS let you reach fishing holes bigger boats must pass by. While functionally similar to larger driftboats, they're equally suited to lakes, bays, and other protected waters. And don't rule them out as a ship-to-shore dinghy. Their wide, flat bottoms give amazing stability, while shoal draft, built-in rocker, and light weight mean instant response to oar inputs. Our 8' MODEL can be built in variable widths; 4-1/2' or 5', so it can fit most vans, pickups, or car tops. While usually single-handed, an extra passenger can be accommodated. Our 10' MODEL is nearly as easy to transport, but more closely matches the performance of true driftboats - it can easily accommodate two fishermen.

By virtue of STITCH-&-GLUE construction, weight and cost are bare-bones yet maintenance and deterioration are virtually eliminated. There are no frames, but strength is superior. The two seats stiffen the hull and form built-in flo-

tation chambers. No jig, special tools, or fastenings are used for hull assembly. FULL SIZE PATTERNS are provided for all hull components (see photos). Plans also include complete INSTRUCTIONS & MATERIAL UTILIZATION LAYOUTS. Hull panels are wire-tied together and joints bonded with epoxy filler and fiberglass tapes. Exterior hull surfaces are coated with epoxy

and fiberglass for abrasion resistance and minimum maintenance. Most can assemble in a weekend or two.

The 8' MODEL uses 3 sheets of 1/4" x 4' x 8' plywood. The 10' MODEL the same plus one 3/8"x 4' x 8'. A few sticks of lumber are added for gunnels and corner knees plus ordinary copper wire for stitching.

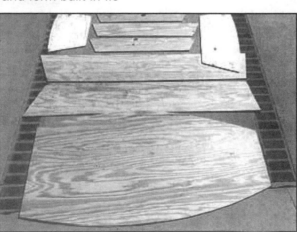

DRIFTER

A 14', 16', OR 18' DRIFTBOAT

CHARACTERISTICS

	14'	16'	18'
Length overall	14'-1"	16'-1"	18'-7"
Bottom length	11'-8"	13'-8"	15'-8"
Beam	6'-5"	6'-5"	6'-10"
Bottom width	4'-0"	4'-0"	4'-0"
Hull depth overall	3'-4"	3'-4"	3'-10"
Hull depth amidship	2'-0"	2'-0"	2'-4"
Transom width	1'-9"	1'-9"	2'-0"
Weight (approx.)	265 lbs.	300 lbs.	385 lbs.
Average passengers	3	4	5

Power: Oars or outboard motor to 10 HP for an approximate speed of 10 knots.

Trailer: Designed for use with GLEN-L Series 750/1000 trailer.

COMPLETE PLANS include FULL SIZE PATTERNS for the transom, stem, breasthook, transom knee, and building forms, including instructions, Bill of Materials, and Fastening Schedule.

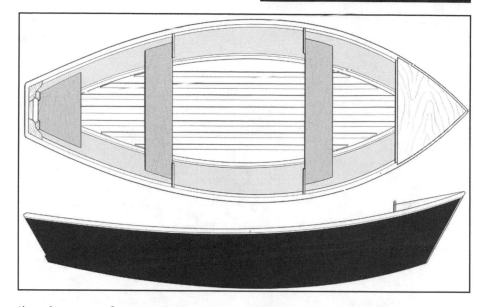

Our **DRIFTER** is a unique kind of dory better known as a "driftboat". This type of craft has evolved over the years in the Pacific Northwest and Canada for use on both wild and docile rivers. There's no reason why our **DRIFTER** won't prove just as suitable on the rivers in your part of the world. The high projecting prow and pronounced rocker make these boats ideal for any fast moving river as well as running through the surf. There's plenty of room for campers or anglers and their gear, plus watertight compartments fore and aft for stowing water sensitive items.

You can build your own **DRIFTER** in 14', 16', or 18' sizes. Construc-

tion is easy, fast, and inexpensive, even for the beginner. No special woods or tricky methods are necessary.

The **DRIFTER** can be powered with a small transom-mounted outboard motor. But remember, these boats have a limited top speed, so don't overpower. When properly used, your **DRIFTER** will

move with ease and economy, and take the rough stuff to boot!

```
AVAILABLE FOR THIS DESIGN:
● Plans & Patterns
● Bronze Fastening Kit
● Fiberglass Kit
See Price List
```

McDRIFT   A 14' OR 16' ALUMINUM DRIFTBOAT

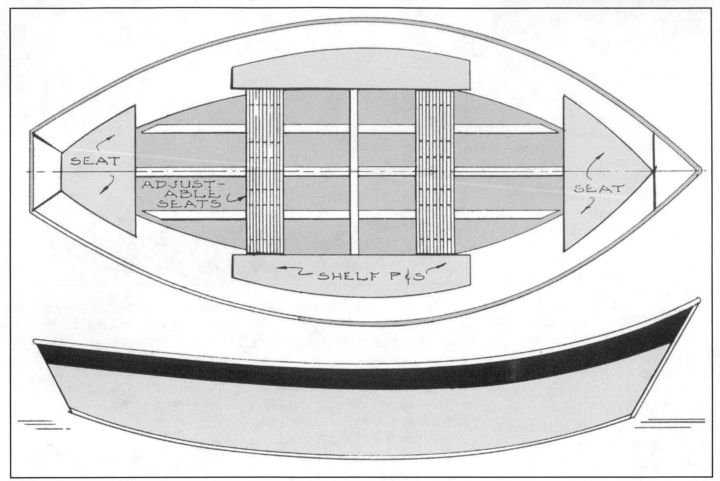

CHARACTERISTICS

	14'	16'
Length overall	14' 3"	16' 6"
Bottom length	12' 2"	13' 10"
Beam	6' 5"	6' 7"
Bottom Width	48"	48"
Midships hull depth	24"	27"
Weight (approx)	235 lbs.	255 lbs.
Average Passengers	3	4

Hull type: Flat bottom developed for welded sheet aluminum planking.
Power: Long shaft outboard to 10 HP.
Trailer: Designed for use with GLEN-L Series 750/1000 trailer.

The **McDRIFT** is a McKenzie-type drift boat designed for welded aluminum, available in 14' or 16' lengths. They are of monocoque construction where the outer covering skin carries a major part of the stresses, eliminating most internal framework. This simplifies the construction and makes for a lighter hull.

To make the construction easier, full dimensional layouts are provided for the side and bottom sheeting. No need to cut and fit the aluminum covering. The computer developed panels provide accurate contours that are quickly and easily reproduced directly to the aluminum. Plus, the layouts simplify the construction, eliminating numerous temporary forms that shape the hull to further make building quicker and easier.

The detailed plans for **McDRIFT** are available for building in 14' or 16' lengths. Standard aluminum extrusions are used in the construction, flat bars, angles, or channel sections in the noted alloys are readily available and eliminate the need for custom bending

or forming. All seams are joined by welding to make the stress skin hull extremely rugged to take it in most any conditions.

Build your own drift boat, have fun and enjoy the resultant project with the pride of accomplishment that follows building your own boat.

PLANS and FULL SIZE PATTERNS for welded aluminum include full size half section patterns of the transom and building form plus dimensional layouts for the bottom and sides. Includes "Aluminum Boatbuilding Guide", instructions, and bill of materials.

DRIFTBOATS

rugged McKenzie/Rogue-type fishing dories for whitewater rivers

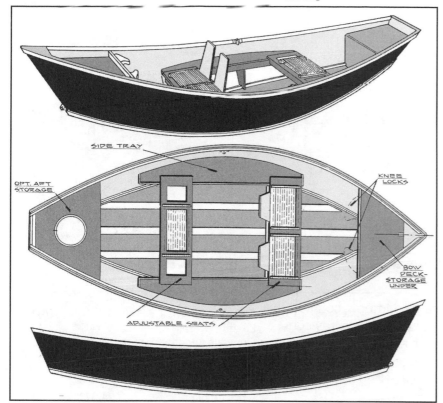

SIDE TRAY
OPT. AFT STORAGE
KNEE LOCKS
BOW DECK STORAGE UNDER
ADJUSTABLE SEATS

All plans include FULL SIZE PATTERNS for hull-forming backbone members (*) - NO LOFTING OR LAYOUTS REQUIRED! In addition, we include easy-to-follow instructions especially for beginners, material listings, and fastening schedules - NOTHING IS LEFT TO CHANCE!

Although construction time will vary depending on a builder's tools, experience and conditions, reports over the years indicate that 100 man-hours is a reasonable "ball-park" approximation of required building time for most.

CHARACTERISTICS

Abbreviations listed below: STD = Standard Bottom & Sides; STD/HS = Standard Bottom & Hi Sides; WB/STD= Wide Bottom & Standard Sides; WB/HS = Wide Bottom & Hi Sides

	12' STD	14' STD	14' STD/HS	14' WB/STD	14' WB/HS	16' STD	16' STD/HS	16' WB/STD	16' WB/HS
Length overall	12'1"	14'4"	14'6"	14'4"	14'6"	16'2"	16'4"	16'2"	16'4"
Nominal gunwale length	13-1/2'	15-1/2'	16'	16'	16'	17-1/2'	17-1/2'	18'	18'
Bottom length	10'2"	12'3"	12'3"	12'3"	12'3"	14'1"	14'1"	14'1"	14'1"
Beam overall	6'1"	6'1"	6'4"	6'7"	6'10"	6'1"	6'4"	6'7"	6'10"
Bottom width	49"	49"	49"	55"	55"	49"	49"	55"	55"
Side height	24-1/2"	24-1/2"	27-1/2"	24-1/2"	27-1/2"	24-1/2"	27-1/2"	24-1/2"	27-1/2"
Stem height	28"	31"	33"	31"	33"	31"	33"	31"	33"
Transom height	14"	19"	21"	19"	21"	19"	21"	19"	21"
Weight (hull-approx.)	150 lbs	210 lbs.	225 lbs.	230 lbs	240 lbs	235 lbs.	250 lbs.	255 lbs.	265 lbs.
Average passengers	1-2	3	3	3-4	3-4	3	3	3-4	3-4
Normal load cap.	650 lbs.	800 lbs.	850 lbs.	850 lbs.	900 lbs.	1000 lbs.	1100 lbs.	1100 lbs.	1200 lbs.

Trailer: All versions designed for use with GLEN-L Series 750/1000 trailer.

Our driftboat designs are the most-advanced available, yet specially intended for first-timers. They feature frame-free hulls (no ribs!) based on modern stress-skin engineering principles for faster, easier construction and reduced weight. Yet with our integral side trays, bow, and stern compartments with decks, strength and stiffness are superior! Special chine and gunnel designs are rugged, strong, and durable, yet simple to build. And the resulting clean interiors of our boats mean less maintenance, fewer casting snags, and a neater, longer-lasting boat.

Features and performance of our driftboats match or exceed those of production boats. Our hulls are designed for quick response to oar inputs, have exceptional stability, are dry running, and come in a wide variety of sizes to suit most any river fishing or whitewater river-running condition. Plans show adjustable, removable seats for perfect load balance, side trays, knee locks, and the option of an outboard motor up to 10 HP.

Plans detail easy ways to join standard 8' long panels to form side and bottom panels. Or you can plank with full-length panels where these may be available. You can use either a good grade of Exterior or full Marine grade plywood panels in any case & save big $$$! All plans also include FULL SIZE PATTERNS for hull-forming backbone members (*) - NO LOFTING OR LAYOUTS REQUIRED! In addition, we include easy-to-follow instructions especially for beginners, material listings, and fastening schedules - NOTHING IS LEFT TO CHANCE!

(*)For temporary frames, transom, stem, breasthook, rail braces, and knee locks.

AVAILABLE FOR THIS DESIGN:
- **Plans & Patterns**
- **Bronze Fastening Kit**
- **Fiberglass Kit**

See Price List

POWER-DRIFTER

A 15' OR 16' POWERED DRIFTBOAT

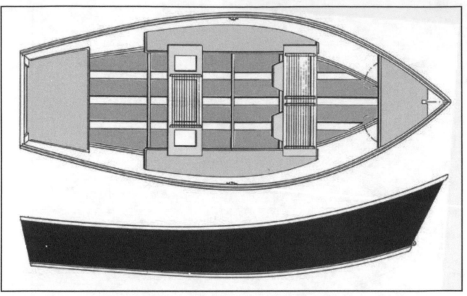

Our Power Drifter is just like our regular driftboats up forward. But back aft, we've straightened out the bottom and widened the stern so you can power upstream more efficiently in milder rivers where ordinary driftboats under power often can't overcome the current. The result is a handier boat because you can take out upstream where you put in.

Yet you still get all the features of our regular driftboats such as adjustable seating, side trays, watertight bow and stern compartments, good rowing maneuverability, and easy construction just like our regular driftboats that are especially intended for amateur builders who have never built a boat before.

And if you are not a drift fisherman, these boats still make sense for many other types of fishing. Their dory-skiff hull shape makes them stable, roomy, and easy to row or power. And they are more capable than many other rowing skiffs when it comes to rough water use or the ability to run up onto a beach.

Plan options include building in either length. Power comes from either a 15" or 20" shaft outboard. Plans include material listing and fastening schedule plus FULL SIZE PATTERNS for the temporary frames, transom, stem, breasthook, rail braces, and knee locks.

Once the temporary framework is set up, plywood planking panels are simply leaned against the forming members, marked to contour, cut to shape, then fastened and glued into position. Our special "stress-skin" design with integral stern and bow compartments plus seat/side tray configuration assure a stiff, strong hull that's lightweight and easier to use and maintain.

AVAILABLE FOR THIS DESIGN:
- **Plans & Patterns**
- **Bronze Fastening Kit**
- **Fiberglass Kit**
See Price List

CHARACTERISTICS	15'	16-1/2'
Length overall	14'9"	16'7"
Gunwale length (nominal)	15'8"	17'6"
Bottom length	12'11"	14'10"
Beam overall	6'1"	6'1"
Bottom width	49"	49"
Side height	24-1/2"	24-1/2"
Stem height	28"	28"
Transom height	20"	20"
Transom width	38"	38"
Hull weight (approx.)	270 lbs	300 lbs.
Average passengers	3	3
Maximum horsepower	15	20

Trailer: Designed for use with GLEN-L Series 750/1000 trailer.

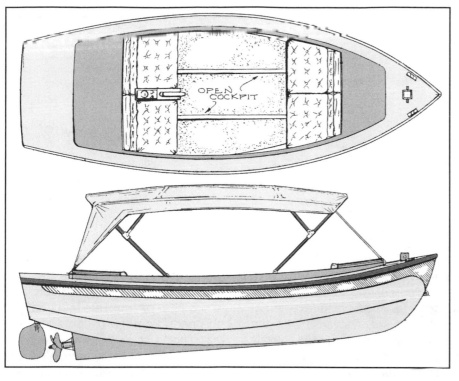

AMP EATER

A 13' ELECTRIC BOAT

BUILD IN STITCH-N-GLUE PLYWOOD

CHARACTERISTICS

Length overall .... 13' 4"
Beam .... 5' 2"
Midship hull depth .... 24"
Bare hull weight, no deck ...... 165 lbs.
Hull draft .... 10"
Displacement .... 1012 lbs.
Cockpit size (approx.) .... 3 1/2' x 7'
Average Passengers 2-4
Hull type: Vee bottom, developed for sheet plywood planking, assembled by the Stitch-N-Glue method.
Power: Electric DC motor 1/2 to 1 HP operating on deep cycle batteries connected in series to develop 24-36 volts. Utilizes a belt driven propeller shaft.
Trailer: Designed for use with GLEN-L SERIES 1200/1800 boat trailer plans.

COMPLETE PLANS include FULL SIZE PATTERNS for side and bottom planking, transom, form, breasthook, skeg, bulkheads, deck and cowl beams, thrust blocking, rudder base, floorboard, tiller, and carling. Includes instructions, Bill of Materials, Plywood Layouts, Fastening and Laminate Schedules, and Stitch-N-Glue Manual.

AVAILABLE FOR THIS DESIGN:
- Plans & Patterns
- Stitch & Glue Kit
- Fiberglass Kit
- Stitch & Glue DVD
- Electric Boat DVD's

See Price List

The **AMP EATER** features an efficient hull form that moves through the water with minimal wake. With the whisper quiet, environmentally friendly, electric motor propulsion system, the hull slicing through the water is almost the only sound.

You sit in a people friendly cockpit with the helmsperson in command in the aft seat handling the boat with a fore and aft moving tiller. The hull is very responsive; a slight movement of the tiller controls the rudder positively making turning in tight quarters quick and easy. Speed is varied by turning a small dial, while forward, neutral or reverse is operated through a fingertip actuated toggle switch. Operating the electric boat is about as easy as flicking a switch to turn on a light.

A 1/2 HP DC electric motor running on 24 volts provides a speed of about 5-1/2 mph. At cruising speed, the boat will run 8-10 hours before battery recharging is necessary. The motor drives the propeller shaft through two vee belts, reducing the propeller rpm to an efficient level.

Special EV (electric vehicle) batteries drive the motor and provide long range and durability. Four of these six volt EV batteries connected in series provide the 24 volts required.

The **AMP EATER** hull is built by the Stitch-N-Glue method with patterns furnished for virtually every contoured part of the hull. Each patterned part was drawn directly from the one used in building the prototype to assure accuracy. The instructions are based on the actual building of the boat using the running commentary and video as guides to describe the exact building procedures. The results, a complete plan and pattern package specially prepared and packaged to make building your **AMP EATER** easier and quicker. Plus, through judicious planning and adjustments, the entire hull can be built from four sheets of 1/4" x 4' x 8' plywood.

POWERYAK

A 17' ELECTRIC POWERED KAYAK

BUILD IN STITCH-N-GLUE PLYWOOD

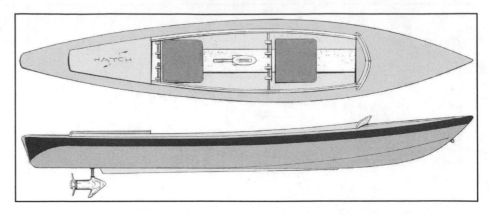

CHARACTERISTICS

Length overall .... 16'-10"
Beam .... 37"
Hull Draft at 500 lbs .... 3 1/2"
Midship hull depth .... 14"
Hull weight (approx.).............. 110 lbs.
Cockpit size (approx.) .... 2' x 7'-6"
Average passengers .... 1 or 2
Hull type: Hard chine vee bottom hull developed for 1/4" sheet plywood planking assembled by the Stitch-N-Glue method.
Power: Electric trolling motor (ETM) modified to mount inside the boat, operating on deep cycle storage batteries of 12 to 24 Volts.
Trailer: Designed for use with GLEN-L SERIES Canoe/kayak trailer plans.

COMPLETE PLANS include FULL SIZE PATTERNS for bottom and side planking, transom, form, breasthook, deck beams, longitudinals, seat brackets, coamings, and spray shield. Includes Instructions, Bill of Materials, Fastening and Laminate Schedules, Plywood Layouts, and STITCH-N-GLUE MANUAL. PLUS full details, patterns and instructions, for converting and building the mount and bracket for a typical electric trolling motor.

KAYAKS ARE FUN! They're sleek, graceful, manueverable, quiet, environmentally friendly, lightweight and transportable, *but*, even the staunchest supporter will admit that getting back to home base after a long day of paddling can be a chore (Translation: helluva lotta work). Do it the easy way, come back with power. Or for those not inclined to paddle propulsion, kayaking can still be fun with the **POWERYAK**.

The **POWERYAK** runs on a battery powered DC electric trolling motor (ETM). They're inexpensive and cost a fraction of what a fuel burning outboard does. But this isn't the unsightly looking gadget seen hanging over the side of a fishing boat. The underwater motor with projecting shaft and housing is entirely concealed under a removable hatch. The controls, steering, speed and forward, nuetral, and reverse are located forward, convenient for the helmsperson. When moving silently through the water without paddling, viewers are fascinated... what makes it go? The hull hardly ripples the water; it's quiet, almost eerie for a boat. Conversation is held with normal voice or even a whisper... you are a part of nature.

The **POWERYAK** is more comfortable than the typical kayak. There are real seats with adjustable locations; the forward seat allows the passenger to face forward or aft in a friendlier position. Shifting the seat position also helps to distribute the weight for proper hull trim whether there are one or two passengers.

The hull has a little more beam and depth than most kayaks to provide better stability and a drier ride. A generous vee bottom and flare forward provides the ability to slither through the chop or into the wind with comfort. This kayak can be paddled, but when you want a rest, flick on the power and sit back and relax.

The **POWERYAK** is built by the proven GLEN-L Stitch-N-Glue method that makes building easier and quicker than conventional methods. Full sized patterns are furnished for virtually every part in the boat including the planking, and only four sheets of standard size 4' x 8' (1/4" or 4mm) are required. Cut the parts from the patterns, drill the stitch holes, wire the planking together around a single cross form, glue/fillet the seams, remove the stitches, reinforce the junctions with fiberglass laminates, and the hull is formed. No complicated building jigs are required; the patterned plywood sides and bottom are bent around a single temporary form. Procedural instructions plus the GLEN-L Stitch-N-Glue Manual describe each step with photos, drawings, and text.

Build a powered kayak, amaze your friends and learn what real FUN really means.

ETM MOUNT & BRACKET

PLANS FOR CONVERTING AN ELECTRIC TROLLING MOTOR TO INBOARD USE

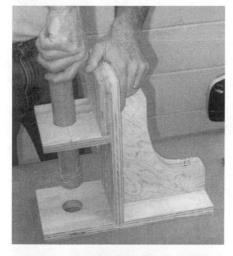

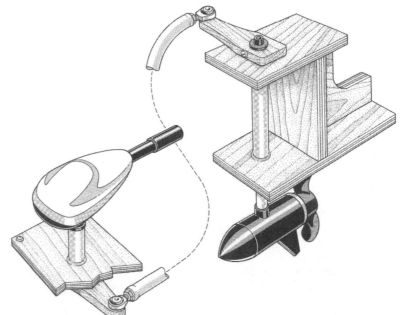

These Plans and Patterns are included with the POWERYAK plans package. However, they can be ordered separately to convert an ETM (electric trolling motor) to an inboard position projecting through the boat bottom with the controls mounted at a more convenient forward position.

The **ETM MOUNT & BRACKET** details using a typical transom mount electric trolling motor of 30 plus lbs. thrust and converting it to an inboard position. The control portion of the motor is moved forward, or to any convenient location, and mounted on a bracket. The shaft and trolling motor is located in the aft section of the hull, mounted on a motor bracket with the underwater motor suspended on a shaft that rotates in a tube. The lower unit projects through the boat bottom and pivots for steering; a rudder is not required. The drive has been designed to be built by the average handyman with nothing more than average tools........no machining or welding.

Plans are complete with drawings and instruction for building the motor mount, tube, bracket, and connecting links. Patterns are included for most of the parts as the bracket and mount are drawn full size.

POWERYAK plans and patterns include the ETM MOUNT & BRACKET plans and patterns.

The POWERYAK was designed and built especially to accommodate the **ETM** and acted as a testing boat.

LO VOLTAGE A 15 1/2' ELECTRIC LAUNCH

CHARACTERISTICS

Length overall .... 15'-7"
Beam .... 6'-0"
Hull draft at 940 lbs .... 5"
Hull weight (approx.).............. 250 lbs.
Cockpit size .... 5' max x 10'
Average passengers 2-5
Hull type: Multi-chine hull developed for sheet plywood planking, assembled by the Stitch-N-Glue method.
Power: Electric DC motor commonly used in such industrial applications as golf carts. The motor operates on deep cycle storage batteries connected in a series to provide 24-36 volts.
Propulsion: Two systems can be used. (1) The ELECTRIC DRIVE, described elsewhere on this page, utilizes the lower unit of an outboard motor coupled to an electric motor. (2) A conventional propeller and shaft, sported by a strut, is coupled to the electric motor.
Trailer: Designed for use with GLEN-L SERIES 1200/1800 boat trailer plans.

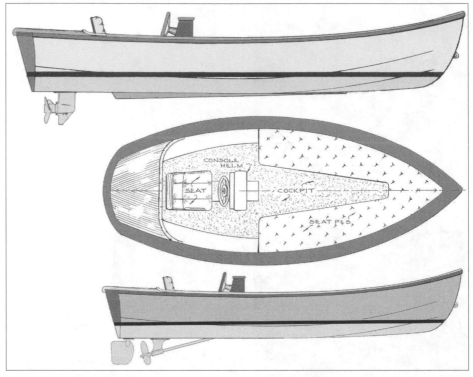

The **LO VOLTAGE** electric powered launch provides quiet, peaceful, tranquil boating. The hull glides silently through the water, and is environmentally friendly and accepted by nature. The silent propulsion method allows conversation at normal levels, and the passengers are in a friendly grouping with the helmsperson.

LO VOLTAGE is powered by an electric golf cart DC motor readily available from golf courses or related suppliers new, re-built, or used. They provide adequate power to drive the hull at 4-6 MPH for about 5 hours before recharge, although speed and voltage used can vary the running time considerably. The batteries are readily "re-fueled" by a charger connected to standard 110-120 volt AC household current.

The **LO VOLTAGE** is easy to build, as full size patterns are furnished for virtually every part in the boat including the planking. It's simple: cut the parts from the patterns, drill the stitch holes, wire the planking together, glue-fillet the seams, reinforce the seams with fiberglass laminates, and the hull is formed.

Best of all, you can build with readily available materials, only six 1/4" x 4' x 8' plywood panels are used for the hull and interior panels.

There are two different sets of plans available for the **LO VOLTAGE** as described on this page.

COMPLETE PLANS include FULL SIZE PATTERNS for all planking, transom, form, knee, floorboards, seat sides and ends, bulkhead, breasthook, seat top, and deck beams. Includes instructions, Bill of Materials, Fastening & Laminate Schedule, Stitch-N-Glue Manual, and Plywood Layouts, *plus the following*.

ELECTRIC DRIVE PROPULSION: **Includes full details, patterns and instructions for building the ELECTRIC DRIVE.**

CONVENTIONAL PROP SHAFT: **Includes motor beds and full details and instructions for coupling the electric motor to a conventional prop shaft.**

AVAILABLE FOR THIS DESIGN:
• **Plans & Patterns**
• **Stitch & Glue Kit**
• **Fiberglass Kit**
• **Stitch & Glue DVD**
• **Electric Boat DVD's†**
See Price List

GLEN-L ELECTRIC DRIVE "ED"

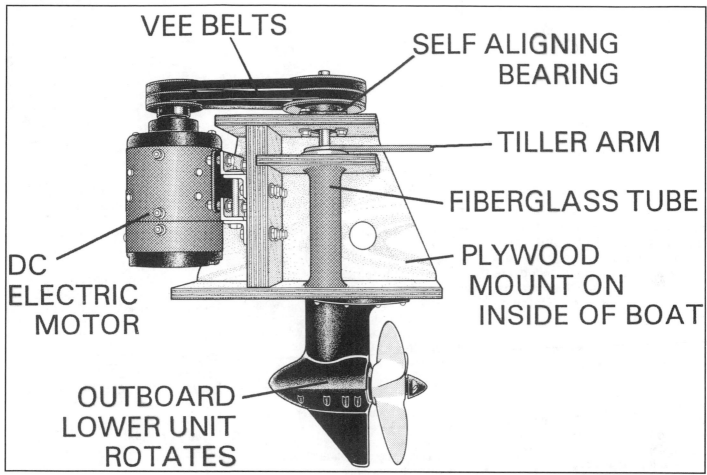

VEE BELTS

SELF ALIGNING BEARING

TILLER ARM

FIBERGLASS TUBE

DC ELECTRIC MOTOR

PLYWOOD MOUNT ON INSIDE OF BOAT

OUTBOARD LOWER UNIT ROTATES

The **ELECTRIC DRIVE** plans and patterns are included with the LO VOLTAGE plans for the Electric Drive version. However, plans and patterns are available separately as the drive can also be used on other boats to approximately 20' with a relatively flat bottom near the transom.

The novel **ELECTRIC DRIVE** utilizes a portion of the lower unit of a used outboard motor with other readily available components, mounted on a special wooden motor mount. The drive has been designed to be built by the average handyman with machining and welding held to a minimum. The lower unit projects through the boat bottom and pivots for

steering; a rudder is not required. The electric DC motor is attached to the mount and drives the prop through vee belts.

The Plans are complete with instructions for building the drive, mounting the motor, and pertinent

details. Patterns are included for most of the metal parts and the plywood motor mount sides.

Remember: The LO VOLTAGE plans and patterns INCLUDE the ELECTRIC DRIVE plans and patterns.

KE-PAU

A 6' PADDLE WHEEL BOAT FOR KIDS

BUILD IN PLYWOOD

CHARACTERISTICS

Length overall .... 70"
Beam .... 31 1/2"
Hull depth .... 9"
Hull weight .... approx. 35 lbs.
Finished weight .... approx. 42 lbs.
Passengers .... 1 or 2 children
Hull type: Scow-type for sheet plywood.
Power: Hand cranked paddle wheels.

COMPLETE PLANS plus FULL SIZE PATTERNS for side planking, curved chine, bearing base, knee, paddlewheel disc and pad, paddles, and half section of the spray shroud. Also included are complete step by step Instructions, Bill of Materials, and Fastening Schedule.

It's a boat for kids; not big kids but children kids. The type that enjoy fun on the water. Are there any that don't? Kids will enjoy propelling the boat themselves and the splash of the paddlewheels. Put one at each crank and watch the merry-go-round fun that is created when they don't synchronize the paddle wheel turning. And it's one the adults can't practically ride in; it's too small. Sorry pop this one is not for you*.

This is a simple boat to build. It's flat bottomed with vertical sides. This eliminates any fairing or shaping. A project the kids can help with. Of course helped and supervised by mom or pop, grandma or grandpa; even great grandparents.

The hull requires a single sheet of 1/4" x 4' x 8' plywood and we illustrate how the parts are obtained with virtually no waste. Information is provided to build a "cheapy" that will last until the kids grow up or a boat that can be handed down to the younger fry. Building is fun and watching the kids enjoy the results will make the adult "helper's" day ...and many more to come.

* When we subjected the Ke-Pau to the "family test", we found out what we should have known... adults, yes and one dad of over 200 pounds decided this was for BIG kids too. They paddled all over the small pond; one got out, another got in. This is a fun boat for kids of all ages, but let's be practical... not 200 pounders.

PADDLE-WHEELER

A 7-1/2' PADDLE WHEEL BOAT

CHARACTERISTICS

Length overall .... 7' 8""
Beam .... 4'
Hull Depth .... 15"
Width with paddlewheels .... 5' 3"
Hull weight (approx.) .... 95 lbs.
Typical passengers 1- 3
Hull type:Pram dinghy for Stitch-N-Glue plywood.
Power: Hand cranked side paddle wheels.
Trailer: Designed for SERIES 750/ 1000 trailer plans.

COMPLETE PLANS include FULL SIZE PATTERNS for side planking, paddlewheel disc and pad, paddles, crank, bow, transom and half section patterns of the bottom planking and building form. Also included are complete step-by-step Instructions, Bill of Materials, Laminating and Fastening Schedules.

A while back we did a little paddlewheel boat for kids, "KE-PAU" (previous page). The boat was built and we found out a very important factor. Most of the "kids" were rather large. No, let's be honest; they were full grown adults, some more than 200 lbs....and they were having FUN, **BIG** FUN. Thus the idea came up for a similar "Big" kid's paddleboat and **PADDLE-WHEELER** was born.

This boat is a modified pram type. It has the deck outline of a pram but the bottom forward comes to a point. This feature provides extra room and improves efficiency. The twin paddlewheels make the craft exceptionally maneuverable. Spinning in a circle or stopping on the proverbial dime is easy and quick. The hull moves easily through the water with little effort in turning the paddlewheels. No loud motor noise; just the chunk chunk of the rotating paddles.

The boat is easy to build with Stitch-N-Glue construction. A full

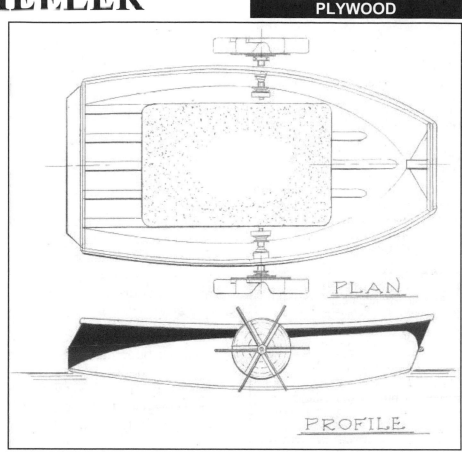

PLAN

PROFILE

size pattern is given for the sides and one in half section for the bottom: no complicated layouts required. Of course many other full patterns are given, even for the paddlewheels. And there isn't any special hardware required for these wheels. A full listing of the parts is given and their sources, even down to the nuts and bolts. However, most parts are readily available in neighborhood locales.

The hull requires only two sheets of standard ¼" x 4' x 8' plywood. And a Plywood Layout illustrates how the parts are laid out on the plywood with virtually no waste.

Comment: We do not mean to infer that this craft is only for adult big kids. This is really for kids of most any size and weight. Even for people who are not kids but would still like to be one!

The above photos are an example of big "kids" enjoying the Ke-Pau, so we decided to build a larger version of this fun little boat to accommodate more weight and provide more comfort... build your own Paddle-Wheeler today!

107

KIDYAK — A 9' KID SIZED KAYAK

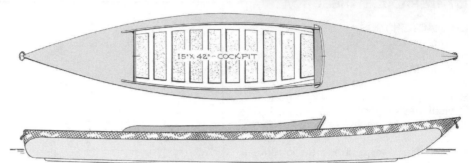

15" X 42" COCKPIT

CHARACTERISTICS

Length overall .... 9'-0"
Beam .... 22"
Hull depth midship .... 9"
Average passengers 1-2
Hull weight (approx.)................. 20 lbs.
Hull type: Flat bottom kayak for Stitch-N-Glue sheet plywood construction.

COMPLETE PLANS include FULL SIZE PATTERNS for bottom, sides, fore and aft bulkheads, decking, coamings, cockpit front, paddle, and Plywood Layout. Plus instructions, Bill of Materials, and Laminate Schedule.

The **KIDYAK** is a 9' kid's kayak. It's compact and light, about 20 lbs. It'll sink in the water 3" when the gross weight with boat is about 100 lbs., and it's safe; two watertight compartments provide plenty of flotation.

The **KIDYAK** is easy and inexpensive to build, and requires only a single panel of plywood. Inexpensive 1/8" luan "door skin" plywood was used on the prototype, although 1/4" fir is optional.

Building is quick and easy with the Stitch-N-Glue building method, and the GLEN-L full sized patterns are furnished for *every* part in the boat. Plus, patterns and instructions are furnished for making your own double bladed paddle.

Why wait? Start now and give your special kid a fun boat of their own.

KID-ROW — A 6' KID SIZED ROWBOAT

CHARACTERISTICS

Length overall .... 6'-1"
Beam .... 28-3/4"
Hull depth midship .... 9-1/2"
Average passengers 1
Hull weight (approx.)................. 15 lbs.
Hull type: Flat bottomed kids rowboat for Stitch-N-Glue sheet plywood construction. At a gross weight of 89 lbs. the hull will have 3" of draft.

The **KID-ROW** is only 6' long, but a bundle of fun for lighter and smaller kids. An ideal craft for swimming pool, pond, or similar protected water. Watch how fast they develop rowing skills, and in a project *they* can help build. Sanding edges and slapping on some paint can be done by even the youngest.

The **KID-ROW** has three watertight compartments that will keep the boat afloat even when flooded with water. (From the voice of experience: kids seem to love filling a boat with water!)

Only a single sheet of plywood is required; inexpensive 1/8" luan "door skin" plywood was used on the prototype. With a full size pattern for every part in the boat, and using the GLEN-L simplified Stitch-N-Glue method, building is quick and easy. Details are furnished for building your own oars and oarlocks from readily available materials.

Make your favorite youngster the envy of their peers, and become their special favorite person... GUARANTEED!
COMPLETE PLANS include FULL SIZE PATTERNS for the bottom, sides, transom, seats, seat uprights, knees, breasthook, floor strips, oars, and Plywood Layout. Plus instructions, Bill of Materials, and Laminate Schedule.

TUBBY TUG
A 9' TUGBOAT FOR KIDS OF ALL AGES

CHARACTERISTICS

Length overall .... 9'-0"
Beam .... 4'-8"
Hull weight approx. .... 175 lbs.
Hull depth midship .... 20"
Hull depth aft .... 28"
Cabin headroom...................... 3'-10"
Height overall .... 4'-1"
Displacement at 4" waterline 520 lbs.
Average passengers 2-3
Hull type: Flat bottom with sides and bottom developed for Stitch-N-Glue sheet plywood con-struction.
Power: Outboard to 5 HP.
Trailer: Designed for use with GLEN-L SERIES 750/1000 boat trailer plans.

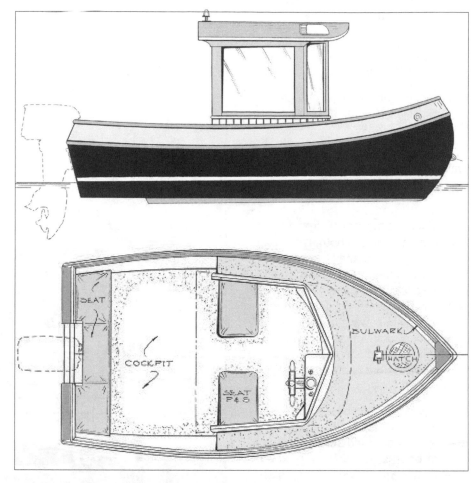

We've been amazed at the attention this little boat receives whenever we take her out. For children, a ride in the **TUBBY TUG** is more than a boat ride, it's an *event.* They become tugboat captains or explorers, chugging out into an imaginary world full of danger or adventure. Even though this boat was designed with children in mind, we expected that adults just might want to take her out once in a while. We've found, however, that once dad gets in, it's hard to get him out. So if you're looking for a boat for "kids" of *all* ages, take a close look at the **TUBBY TUG.**

For safety, the **TUBBY TUG** has four watertight compartments that provide flotation even if the boat is filled with water. The wide beam and generous hull depth provides more stability than most small boats.

The hull is built from standard 8' sheets of plywood by the Stitch-N-Glue construction method, described in detail in the front of this catalog. With patterns for virtually every part of the hull, including planking and decking, the hull takes shape quickly, *and* building is a FUN project.

TUBBY TUG can be built with the cabin as shown or the roof and window portions eliminated. Build it either way, but be ready for the attention you'll get trailering, launching, or underway.

AVAILABLE FOR THIS DESIGN:
- **Plans & Patterns**
- **Stitch & Glue Kit**
- **Fiberglass Kit**
- **Stitch & Glue DVD**
See Price List

COMPLETE PLANS include **FULL SIZE PATTERNS** for bottom, sides, bulwark, transom, fore and aft and seat bulkheads, foredeck, knees, breasthook, cabin arc, windshield frame, cabin ledge, cabin crown, and Plywood Layout. Plus instructions, Bill of Materials, and Laminate Schedule.

AIRBOAT A 12' 9" SWAMP BOAT

CHARACTERISTICS

Length overall .... 12'-9"
Beam .... 7'-0"
Hull depth .... 14"
Hull weight (approx.).............. 265 lbs.
Average passengers 1-2
Hull type: Flat bottom scow developed for sheet plywood planking.
Power: Volkswagen (VW Beetle), air cooled engine, driving an airplane-type propeller.
Trailer: Designed for use with GLEN-L SERIES 750/1000 boat trailer plans.

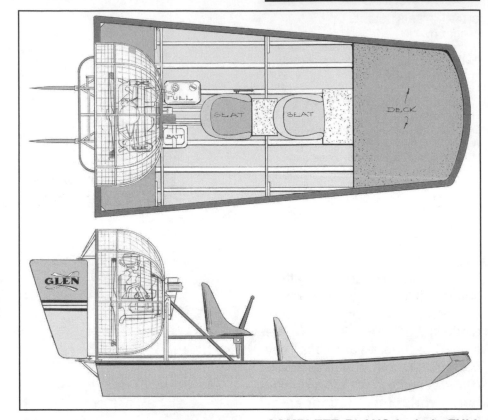

AIRBOAT is a mixture of airplane and boat with the thrills of both. It's a boat powered by an airplane-type propeller with above-the-water rudders that is capable of skimming over a few inches of water and vegetation. If you need to go through shallow water to get to the best fishing, or if you simply want the excitement of exploring new and usually inaccessible waterways, then *airboating* is for *you*.

Our **AIRBOAT** is simple to build; no complicated building form, difficult curves, or compound bends. This flat bottom boat is made from inexpensive, lightweight plywood using standard 4' x 8' sheets. Patterns are given for all framing members to make building easier and eliminate possible errors. Complete material listing and step-by-step instructions take you through building the hull *and* explain in detail all of the engine components from motor stand to guard, through steering and controls. Readily obtainable materials are used throughout the construction; materials should be available at your local lumber and hardware store, with the exception of the motor. Plenty of VW aircooled "Beetle" engines are available and they make an ideal, simply modified, powerplant for the **AIRBOAT**.

COMPLETE PLANS include FULL SIZE PATTERNS for the rudder, rudder sections, long beam, sawn chine & upright, bulwark knee, and half-section patterns for each of the frames, transom, and four bow pieces. Includes step-by-step instructions, Bill of Materials, and Fastening Schedule. *In addition, complete details are provided on motor mount, guard, steering assembly, with materials list and text on the "HOW TO" of the propulsion system plus FULL SIZE PATTERNS for steering stick, rudder arms, bell crank, and engine mount bracket.*

AVAILABLE FOR THIS DESIGN:
- **Plans & Patterns**
- **Bronze Fastening Kit**
- **Fiberglass Kit**
See Price List

110

POWER SKIFF 12 & 14

A 12' OR 14' STITCH-N-GLUE POWER SKIFF

CHARACTERISTICS

	12'	14'
Length overall	11'-5"	13'-5"
Beam	5'-0"	5'-0"
Depth forward (approx.)	2'-3"	2'-3"
Depth aft	1'-4"	1'-4"
Hull weight (approx.)	110 lbs.	125 lbs.
Average passengers	1-3	2-4

Hull type: Arc bottom, hard chine hull in mid-to-aft areas with rounded side/bottom vee'd sections forward. For sheet plywood Stitch-N-Glue construction.

Power: Single short shaft motor to 15 HP.

Trailer: Designed for use with GLEN-L SERIES 750/1000 boat trailer plans.

A quantum leap ahead in truly *simplified* boat construction... that's our **POWER SKIFF**. It's all made possible by our revolutionary *FAST-G* Stitch-N-Glue building system, using an advanced approach to plywood planking development. The result is an incredibly lightweight, frameless craft, that's strong, able, and pleasing to the eye.

Best of all, the **POWER SKIFF** won't send you to the poor house. All it takes to complete the 12' model is three sheets of 1/4"x4'x8' plywood and a half panel of 3/4". Assembly is *quick & easy*--just cut out the plywood parts after transferring them from the patterns, stitch up and glue the seams, and you have a hull. No lofting, no layouts, no building jigs required.

The **POWER SKIFF**'s unique *FAST-G* hull design features a hard chine, arc bottom aft for agility, stability, and speed. Chines fade out forward for rounded side/bottom sections which form an easy riding convex vee entrance. Built-in flotation chambers and the naturally bouyant wood hull gives piece of mind. Although engines up to 15 HP can be used, a 5 HP engine gives ample performance. If you want a boat pronto, without much effort, especially for the amateur, our **POWER SKIFF** is taylor-made for you.

AVAILABLE FOR THIS DESIGN:
- **Plans & Patterns**
- **Stitch & Glue Kit**
- **Fiberglass Kit**
- **Stitch & Glue DVD**

See Price List

COMPLETE PLANS include FULL SIZE PATTERNS for the side-bottom planking, aft side and bottom planking, butt blocks, aft bulkhead and seat, transom, transom and stern knees, seat ledge and brace, center seat, breasthook, form, keel, and keel strip. Includes material listings and layouts, with instructions and STITCH-N-GLUE manual.

PEE WEE
AN 8' MINI-RUNABOUT

BUILD IN PLYWOOD

The **PEE WEE** is small in size, small in cost, but BIG in fun. While not intended for hulking 200 pounders, it's great for the younger set or feather-weight adults. A tiny outboard motor will really make it scoot, and yet it's safe when used within its capabilities.

The **PEE WEE** is inexpensive to build. Only two sheets of 4' x 8' plywood are required for the planking, while the decking and interior will consume most of another. A few "sticks" of lumber and a handful of fastenings are just about all that's required to complete the project. Dad will be the "hero" of the kids when he builds them a **PEE WEE**. In fact, they can build their own with a little supervision.

```
AVAILABLE FOR THIS DESIGN:
• Plans & Patterns
• Bronze Fastening Kit
• Fiberglass Kit
See Price List
```

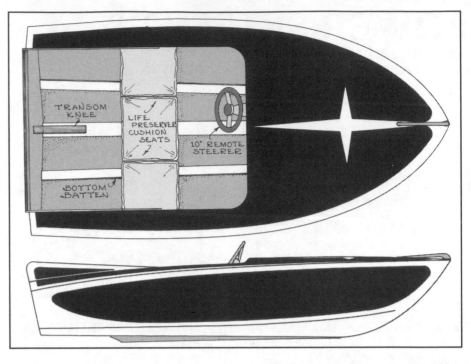

CHARACTERISTICS
Length overall .... 7'-6"
Beam .... 4'-0"
Hull depth .... 21"
Average passengers 1
Hull weight (approx.) .... 50 lbs.
Hull type: Vee bottom hard chine hull developed for sheet plywood planking.
Power: Outboard motor to 5 HP.

COMPLETE PLANS include **FULL SIZE PATTERNS for the stem, transom knee, and half section patterns for the frames and transom.** Includes instructions, Bill of Materials, and Fastening Schedule.

XP-8   AN 8' OR 9' MONOPLANE SPEEDSTER

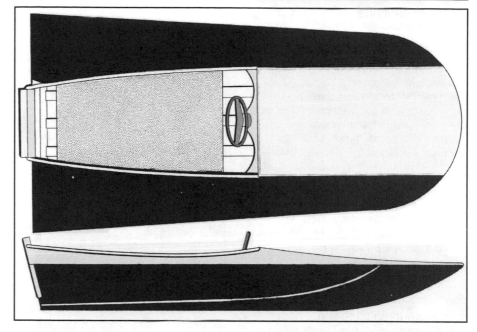

The **XP-8** is a high speed monoplane-type hull intended for the best possible speed with the least amount of power. Since speed is the purpose, the cockpit is intended to seat only the person driving the boat. Also, since speed is a function of weight, both the boat and the driver should be as lightweight as possible. As with any small boat intended for high speed, don't use the **XP-8** in rough unprotected waters.

The **XP-8** can be built in either 8' or 9' lengths from the same PLANS and FULL SIZE PATTERNS. The larger version provides greater carrying capacity. Either hull is simple to construct. No building forms are required... the plans are especially complete... the instructions include actual photos of the construction of the original prototype... in short, nothing is left to chance. Add it all up and you will find the **XP-8** the ideal craft for the beginner who wants an exciting little boat.

AVAILABLE FOR THIS DESIGN:
- **Plans & Patterns**
- **Bronze Fastening Kit**
- **Fiberglass Kit**
  See Price List

CHARACTERISTICS

Length overall .... 8'-3" or 9'-3"
Beam .... 4'-0"
Hull depth .... 14 "
Average passengers 1
Hull weight (approx.) .... 90 lbs.
Hull type: Vee bottom monohydroplane developed for sheet plywood planking.
Power: Outboard motor to 5 HP.

COMPLETE PLANS include FULL SIZE PATTERNS for all frames, transom, bowpiece, deck pad, transom knee, stem, dash board, and transom cap. Includes instructions, Bill of Materials, and Fastening Schedule.

PICKLEFORK

A 9' HYDROPLANE

CHARACTERISTICS

Length overall ....9'-6"
Beam ....5'-3"
Hull depth.......................................14"
Average passengers 1
Hull weight (approx.) .... 90 lbs.
Hull type:Picklefork-type three-point hy-
droplane developed for sheet
plywood planking.
Power: Outboard motor to 80 lbs.
Trailer: Designed for use with GLEN-L
SERIES 750/1000 boat trailer
plans.

Our **PICKLEFORK** is a three-point hydroplane *super-simplified* for the first time builder. It resembles the racing pickleforks found on the competition circuits, but in a more compact form. While not meant as a competition hydro, many will no doubt be built in groups for match racing. The reputation for speed of the larger types is well known, and our **PICKLEFORK** will offer equal thrills, but with far less power and expense.

The **PICKLEFORK** plans can't be beat for ease of construction. Perspective drawings, step-by-step construction photos of the original testing prototype, and easy-to-read instructions insure *sure-fire* success even for the beginner. But we've gone several steps farther! Each part in the entire boat is either a full size pattern or a simple rectangular shape, all keyed for *easy assembly*. A layout of materials shows how to make each part in order to use a bare minimum of materials. No building form, "jig", or elaborate set-up procedures are required! The entire boat can be put together on a work bench or on the floor.

AVAILABLE FOR THIS DESIGN:
- **Plans & Patterns**
- **Bronze Fastening Kit**
- **Fiberglass Kit**
See Price List

Unusually **COMPLETE PLANS** in booklet form include dozens of step-by-step construction photos and pictorial drawings. Easy-to-read instructions include Material listing, Fastening Schedule, and numbered parts listing keyed to the patterns or kits. PATTERNS are *full size* for *every contoured part*, including all frames, transom, stems, knees, bowpiece, dash beam, coamings, and every contoured planking panel. Includes a scaled plywood layout.

TINY TITAN & SUPER SPARTAN

8' AND 10' HYDROPLANES

BUILD IN PLYWOOD

CHARACTERISTICS	TINY TITAN	SUPER SPARTAN
Length overall	8'-2"	10'-2"
Beam	4'-5"	5'-0"
Hull depth	12"	12"
Hull weight (approx.)	65 lbs.	100 lbs.
Average passengers	1	1

Hull type: Three-point hydroplane developed for sheet plywood planking.

Power: Short shaft motor up to 20 HP (TINY TITAN), 35 HP (SUPER SPARTAN).

Trailer: Designed for use with GLEN-L SERIES 750/1000 trailer plans.

For straight-out speed on the water, not much can match a three-point hydro. The two sponsons or "runners" provide stability at high speeds while air rushing under the tunnel provides lift and a cushion of air. Little, if any, of the aft end of the boat is in the water. At speed the boat will ride on the two sponsons and the propeller.

Our **TINY TITAN** is an 8' mini version of competition boats that will provide excitement with low powered motors. Our **SUPER SPARTAN** is a larger version ideal for "big kids" (adults, that is), capable of handling bigger loads and motors. Either boat is *very* easy and quick to build. Neither boat requires a building form. Building your own would save you big bucks if it weren't for the fact that you probably couldn't find a ready-made if you tried.

These "thrill" boats should *only* be used in smooth or protected waters, free from wind and chop. *Always* wear a safety helmet and life jacket and keep weight to a minimum for optimum performance and safety. Either boat will make an excellent beginning project, even for youths to build on their own, or with a little help from Mom or Dad.

AVAILABLE FOR THIS DESIGN:
- Plans & Patterns
- Bronze Fastening Kit
- Fiberglass Kit
- See Price List

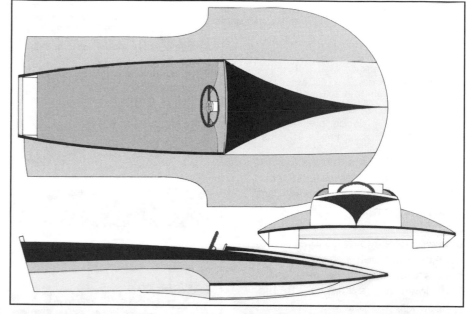

Although PLANS are different for each design and listed separately on the price list, the following will be included in both. COMPLETE PLANS include FULL SIZE PATTERNS for the runner chines, bowpiece, dash beam, coaming, side planking, and half-section patterns for the transom and each frame. Includes instructions, Bill of Materials, and Fastening Schedule.

NC 0957 CU

TUNNEL-MITE A 10' TUNNEL HULL

CHARACTERISTICS

Length overall .... 10'-0"
Beam .... 4'-10"
Hull depth.................................. 20"
Hull weight (approx.) .... 120 lbs.
Average passengers 1
Hull type: Tunnel hull with full length twin sponsons, developed for sheet plywood planking.
Power: Outboard motor to 100 lbs.

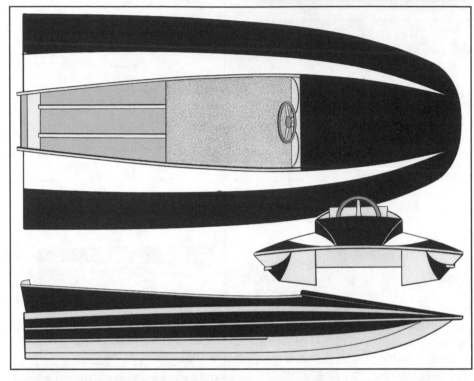

TUNNEL-MITE is a compact replica of those exciting competition racing boats, cleaning up the "silverware" on the world's racing circuit. The high speed hull rides as if on rails due to the twin, full length sponsons. The air cushion effect between the twin hulls makes for a smooth ride, besides cutting down on resistance, so high speeds are possible with low horsepower motors.

Building and driving the **TUNNEL-MITE** is great fun for all members of the family. The lightweight and compact hull is easy to carry, whether it be on the car roof, in the family van, or in a pickup truck. The rakish appearance enhances the illusion of speed, but this boat is plenty safe, even for the younger set, when operated on protected waters and powered as recommended.

Construction is simple and straight forward. No building form or jig is required, and the plans with patterns leave nothing to chance. So for fun and thrills, start building your own **TUNNEL-MITE** today.

AVAILABLE FOR THIS DESIGN:
- **Plans & Patterns**
- **Bronze Fastening Kit**
- **Fiberglass Kit**
See Price List

COMPLETE PLANS include **FULL SIZE PATTERNS** for tunnel side planking, coamings, frames, transom, motor-board, dash board, bowpiece, runner stem, and transom blocking. Includes step-by-step instructions, Bill of Materials, and Fastening Schedule.

MINIMAXED
AN 8' MINI-SPEEDSTER

CHARACTERISTICS

Length overall ....8'-0"
Beam ....4'-0"
Hull depth................................ 7 1/2"
Cockpit size ....5'-6" x 32"
Hull weight (approx.) .... 70 lbs.
Average passengers 1
Hull type: Arc bottom, hard chine hull developed for sheet plywood.
Power: Single short shaft outboard motor to 5 HP.
Can the hull be extended or shortened? No. We also do not recommend increasing the beam.
Trailer: Designed for use with Glen-L Series 750/1000 boat trailer plans.

COMPLETE PLANS include FULL SIZE PATTERNS for transom, bulkhead, longitudinals, sides, bottom, deck, motor board, knee, coaming, and steering wheel mount, PLUS detailed drawings, Instructions, Bill of Materials, Fastening Schedule, and Stitch-N-Glue Manual.

MINIMAXED is a fun boat. It's not intended for rough water and will be wet in a chop. But it's a boat kids love, yes "kids" of all ages enjoy it. This isn't our opinion, written to enhance the boat; it's a fact reported by many builders.

This is a safe boat. There are watertight (foam filled optional) compartments that will support several hundred pounds even with the cockpit full of water. And with a beam half the length, the boat is exceptionally stable.

Simplicity of building and a lot of boat for the buck were undoubtedly major attractions for the original and this holds true today. We've simplified it even further and utilized modern composites and materials unheard of in the sixties. Full size patterns are furnished for virtually every part in the boat that isn't a straight member; this includes bottom, sides, and deck.

No complicated building form is required. The hull is formed by patterned framing members that are

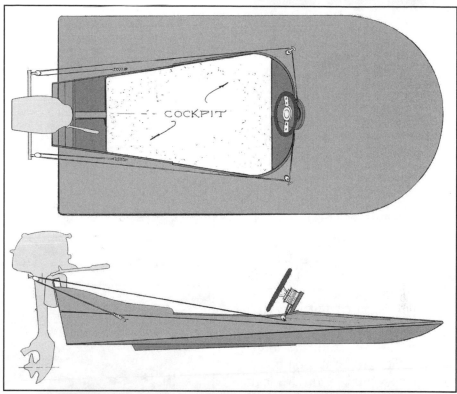

an integral part of the boat. The construction takes advantage of Stitch-n-Glue construction to eliminate shaping, beveling, and fitting many components. The main part of the building is conventional plywood construction as was the original.

The MINIMAXED requires only three sheets of standard 1/4" x 4' x 8' plywood plus a few solid lumber strips. Use the full size patterns,

duplicate them to the wood with transfer paper and you're on your way. An ideal father and son or daughter project with the reward of lots of fun when the project is completed.

AVAILABLE FOR THIS DESIGN:
- **Plans & Patterns**
- **Stitch & Glue Kit**
- **Fiberglass Kit**
- **Stitch & Glue DVD**
See Price List

TNT

AN 11' RUNABOUT

BUILD IN PLYWOOD

CHARACTERISTICS

Length overall .... 11'-0"
Beam ....5'-0"
Hull depth......................................16"
Hull weight (approx.) .... 125 lbs.
Average passengers 1-2
Hull type: Vee bottom with flaring sides to act as anti-trip chines, developed for sheet plywood planking.
Power: Outboard motor to 15 HP.
Trailer: Designed for use with GLEN-L SERIES 750/1000 boat trailer plans.

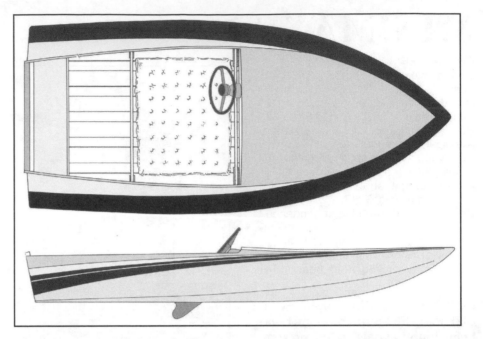

TNT is a well known explosive. It's often said that dynamite comes in small packages. This defines our "TINY 'N TERRIFIC", or **TNT** also. The styling of this sleek little runabout is based on the larger ski-type inboard boats so popular for high speed use. Our **TNT** is an explosive bundle that'll "blast off" the local hot rodders with a lot more power in their rigs than will be required in the **TNT**.

Two other outstanding features about the **TNT**... it's *simple* and it's *easy* to build. Our PLANS really make the job easy with step-by-step instructions covering all aspects of construction. You can plank the entire boat, including side decks, with just two sheets of 1/4" x 4' x 8' plywood. Any way you slice it, careful design has hacked costs down by judicious use of materials.

COMPLETE PLANS include FULL SIZE PATTERNS for the stem, breasthook, transom knee, and half-section patterns for the transom and frames. Includes step-by-step instructions, Bill of Materials, and Fastening Schedule.

AVAILABLE FOR THIS DESIGN:
- Plans & Patterns
- Bronze Fastening Kit
- Fiberglass Kit
See Price List

BULLET
AN 11 OR 12' MINI SKI BOAT

CHARACTERISTICS

Length overall	11'3" or 12'1"
Beam	5'6"
Depth (max.)	1'8"
Weight (approx.)	140 lbs.
Power (11'3"/12'1")	35/40 HP
Trailer:	Designed for use with GLEN-L SERIES 750/1000 boat trailer plans.

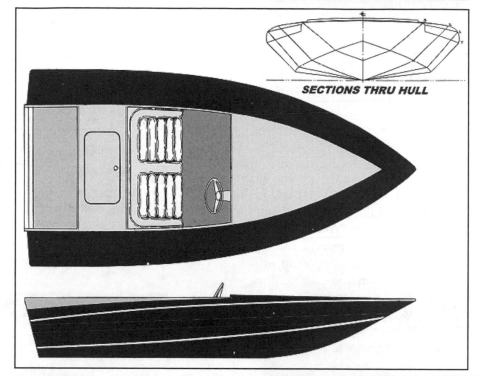

SECTIONS THRU HULL

It's shaped like a bullet and goes like a bullet - that's why we call it BULLET. The beamy, flashy hull is much like larger ski boats, and features enough vee and hull depth for ride comfort and security. What's more, you can really tow a skier, and there's real seats for 2 - no need to kneel on bent knees as in some lesser boats this size.

First, the hull has enough depth and "v" in the bottom to insure security and ride comfort. Power comes from a long (20") or short (15") shaft outboard.

Construction is low cost, quick, and easy 1/4" sheet plywood planking over a few sawn frames. Built upside down over frames and stringers, the resulting hull can endure the rough stuff. For the 11'3" model, 1/4" planking is done with one each 4' x 10' and 4' x 12' panels, although options are given for joining standard 8' panels, and this applies to the longer version also. Power can be a long or short shaft outboard.

Plans include details for both length options, full size patterns for the frame members, instruc-

tions, fastening schedule, and material listing. No lofting or layouts required. Bullet makes a great father-son project, that when complete can be enjoyed by the entire family. However, because of the size and performance potential, adult supervision is recommended if the boat will be operated by young people.

AVAILABLE FOR THIS DESIGN:
- **Plans & Patterns**
- **Bronze Fastening Kit**
- **Fiberglass Kit**
- See Price List

WILD THING
A 10' PERSONAL WATERCRAFT

CHARACTERISTICS

Length overall .... 10-2"
Beam ....5'-2"
Hull weight (approx.) .... 100 lbs.
Average passengers 1-2
Hull type:Vee-arc bottom for Stitch-N-Glue *FAST-G* sheet plywood construction.
Power: Outboard motor to 20 HP.
Trailer: Designed for use with GLEN-L SERIES 750/1000 boat trailer plans.

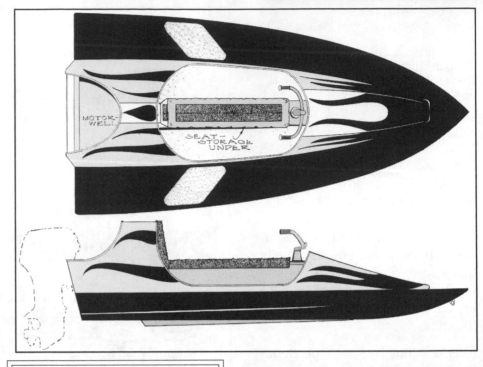

Have fun on the water like you've never imagined. **WILD THING** is wild, WILD, **WILD**, and yet safe, and above all, *fun.* You're seated much as you would be on a motorcycle. But unlike a bike, there are no wheelies when you give her the throttle. You're up and on a plane quicker than you can say **WILD THING**! Skimming over the top of the water will give you a thrill you'll never forget.

The boat is easily built by the Stitch-N-Glue *FAST-G* method. The plywood is cut to shape using the furnished patterns, the parts are assembled flat, then folded together to form the hull; no fixtures, building jig, or form required. Building is quick and simple, well within the abilities of almost anyone. Plus this little speedster is inexpensive to build from standard 1/4" x 4' x 8' plywood.

Almost every contoured part is furnished as a pattern in the complete PLANS & PATTERN package, along with material utilization and material listing, laminate schedule, and of course, fully detailed plans and instructions.

AVAILABLE FOR THIS DESIGN:
- **Study Plans**
- **Plans & Patterns**
- **Stitch & Glue Kit**
- **Fiberglass Kit**
- **Stitch & Glue DVD**

See Price List

COMPLETE PLANS include **FULL SIZE PATTERNS** for forward planking, side planking, bottom planking, butt blocks, knees, breasthook, motorwell sides, cowl end, cowl covering, and half section patterns for transom, frames, cowl frames, and seat back. Also included are Laminate and Fastening Schedules, Plywood Layouts, Bill of Materials, step-by-step instructions (written and pictorial), complete plans, and the **GLEN-L STITCH-N-GLUE** manual.

CLASS J

CHARACTERISTICS

Length overall ....9'-0"
Beam ....4'-5"
Depth amidships .... 12 1/4"
Hull weight (approx.) .... 85 lbs.
Power: Outboard motor to 7.5 HP
Hull type: High speed monoplane bottom with wide, flaring, anti-trip chine sides. Canted decks combined with wedge-shaped platforms minimize frontal resistance. All surfaces are developed for sheet plywood planking.
Structure: Strong sawn frames with double gusseted junctions, longitudinal battens with vertical uprights for bottom stiffness, and coaming-knee transom bracing combine to form a sturdy, but lightweight hull that is easy to build.
Trailer: Designed for use with GLEN-L SERIES 750/1000 boat trailer plans.

> Note: The CLASS J text below describes speeds achieved in class racing. These classes are no longer sanctioned by the APBA.
> CLASS J: over 7.5 cu.in. maximum
> These were not "stock" motors. The HP limit listed above is for pleasure use.

Small in size, but *big* on thrills, "J" class boats are capable of straightaway speeds of 35 MPH. In a small boat like this, such speeds can provide all the excitement of much higher speeds in larger craft. With a hull weight of about 85 lbs., our **CLASS J** runabout is easy to car-top to the local pond. Note that the beam is carried to its widest point at the transom to provide reserve buoyancy for safety in starting and for quicker acceleration. Wide, flaring sides prevent tripping on the wake of another boat in fast turns for that extra degree of safety so important in a class of racing where many young people are involved. And for real fun for kids and adults, this mini-speedboat is an ideal pleasure boat that offers safety and thrills at a reasonable price. Construction using our PLANS & FULL SIZE PATTERNS is well within the abilities of most first-time builders.

AVAILABLE FOR THIS DESIGN:
- **Plans & Patterns**
- **Bronze Fastening Kit**
- **Fiberglass Kit**
  See Price List

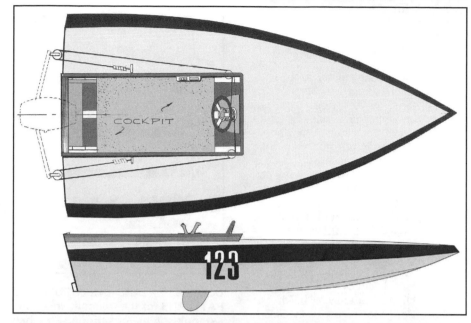

COMPLETE PLANS include FULL SIZE PATTERNS for the transom knee, breasthook, stem, coamings, and half section patterns for each frame and the transom. Includes instructions with Bill of Materials and Fastening Schedule.

CLASS A-B

CHARACTERISTICS

Length overall .... 10'-6"
Beam .... 4'-1/2"
Depth amidships .... 13 1/2"
Hull weight (approx.) .... 110 lbs.
Power: Outboard motor to 10 HP
Hull type: High speed monoplane bottom with wide, flaring, anti-trip chine sides. Canted decks combined with wedge-shaped platforms minimize frontal resistance. All surfaces are developed for sheet plywood planking.
Structure: Strong sawn frames with double gusseted junctions, longitudinal battens with vertical uprights for bottom stiffness, and coaming-knee transom bracing combine to form a sturdy, but lightweight hull that is easy to build.
Trailer: Designed for use with GLEN-L SERIES 750/1000 boat trailer plans.

Note: The CLASS A-B text below describes speeds achieved in class racing. These classes are no longer sanctioned by the APBA.
CLASS A: over 7.5 cu.in.- 15 cu.in.
CLASS B: over 15 cu.in - 20 cu.in.
These were not "stock" motors. The HP limit listed above is for pleasure use.

If you're ready to step up in size in class racing, then consider our **CLASS A-B** racing runabout. It's not a toy, but a full-fledged racing boat. Speed potentials are fantastic! Straightaway runs in excess of 60 MPH have been attained in Class "A", and over 70 MPH in Class "B"! Obviously such speeds are attained with the most finely tuned motor and boat combination. But the "A" and "B" classes do provide unlimited thrills on the racing circuit for those willing to optimize their racing machine. Our **CLASS A-B** racing runabout has all the requirements to make you a winner. Full length, flaring sides and cutaway bow prevent tripping on those fast, tight turns. Our designers took great care to reduce frontal area for minimum wind resistance, together with just the proper amount of wetted surface for maximum speeds with safety. Construction is simple, but lightweight and strong. When using our PLANS & PATTERNS, getting into the winners' circle will be easier when building your **CLASS A-B** runabout the GLEN-L way.

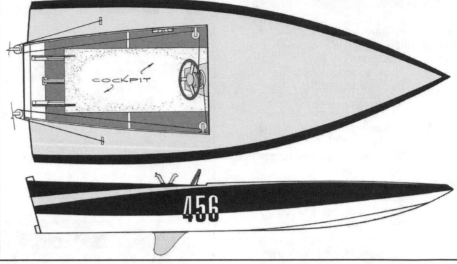

COMPLETE PLANS include FULL SIZE PATTERNS for the transom knee, breasthook, stem, coamings, and half section patterns for each frame and the transom. Includes instructions with Bill of Materials and Fastening Schedule.

AVAILABLE FOR THIS DESIGN:
• **Plans & Patterns**
• **Bronze Fastening Kit**
• **Fiberglass Kit**
See Price List

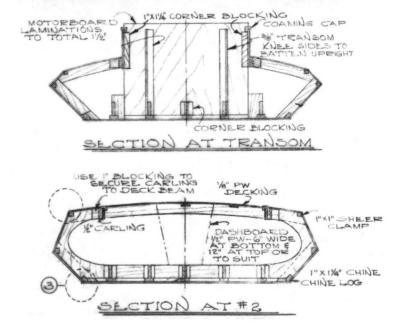

SECTION AT TRANSOM

SECTION AT #2

CLASS C-D

CHARACTERISTICS

Length overall .... 13'-2"
Beam .... 5'-2"
Depth amidships .... 16"
Hull weight (approx.) .... 135 lbs.
Power: Outboard motor to 40 HP.
Hull type: High speed monoplane bottom with wide, flaring, anti-trip chine sides. Canted decks combined with wedge-shaped platforms minimize frontal resistance. All surfaces are developed for sheet plywood planking.
Structure: Strong sawn frames with double gusseted junctions, longitudinal battens with vertical uprights for bottom stiffness, and coaming-knee transom bracing combine to form a sturdy, but lightweight hull that is easy to build.
Trailer: Designed for use with GLEN-L SERIES 750/1000 boat trailer plans.

Note: The CLASS C-D text below describes speeds achieved in class racing. These classes are no longer sanctioned by the APBA.
CLASS C: over 20 cu.in.- 30 cu.in.
CLASS D: over 36 cu.in - 40 cu.in.
These were not "stock" motors. The HP limit listed above is for pleasure use.

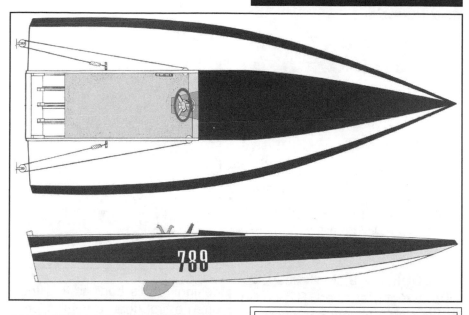

COMPLETE PLANS include FULL SIZE PATTERNS for the transom knee, breasthook, stem, coamings, and half section patterns for each frame and the transom. Includes instructions with Bill of Materials and Fastening Schedule.

AVAILABLE FOR THIS DESIGN:
• **Plans & Patterns**
• **Bronze Fastening Kit**
• **Fiberglass Kit**
See Price List

This is the largest and potentially the fastest of our CLASS runabout group. The "C-D" class attained straightaway speeds of more than 65 MPH in "C" class, and more than 75 MPH in "D" class. Our **CLASS C-D** runabout has the potential to be a winner for the person who has the patience and will take the time to turn out a well-built boat and equip it with a properly tuned motor. Winning races requires the utmost care in preparing the entire outfit. While all racing boats are potentially hazardous, we've taken special care to make our **CLASS C-D** runabout a safe as well as a competitive boat. Minimal frontal area reduces any tendency to become airborne or "kite", and full length, flaring sides make sharp turns safer and faster. Like the other boats in our CLASS series, we've kept the construction simple and basic. Our PLANS & PATTERN construction methods allow you to hold accuracy to the highest degree, so critical in building a "winning" boat.

SQUIRT

A 10' RUNABOUT

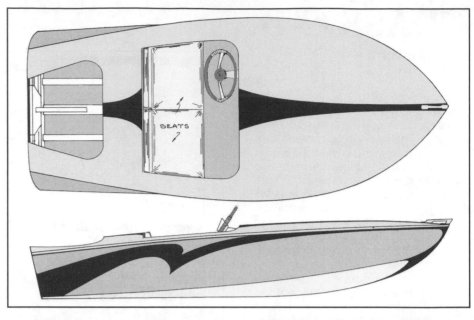

BUILD IN PLYWOOD

CHARACTERISTICS

Length overall .... 10'-0"
Beam ....4'-4"
Hull depth .... 20"
Hull weight (approx.) .... 120 lbs.
Average passengers 1-2
Hull type:Vee bottom, hard chine hull, developed for sheet plywood planking.
Power: Outboard motor to 10 HP.
Trailer: Designed for use with GLEN-L SERIES 750/1000 boat trailer plans.

The **SQUIRT** is a small runabout for the young at heart. But don't let her size fool you; she offers a lot in her short length. This little boat will move out quicker with less horsepower than the average production boat because of the lightweight construction. Traveling at even modest speed in a boat of this size can be a thrilling experience. Since the motor is normally the major expense on a small boat, her "thrill without horsepower" makes **SQUIRT** an ideal boat for the builder on a budget. The combination of smaller horsepower requirement and generous freeboard, makes this a good boat for the younger set.

We have taken special care in

designing this boat as it is most often a first boat. Construction is kept simple. As economy is always of prime importance on a small boat, the cost is kept to a minimum by the judicious use of materials.

If you want the utmost in performance with a minimum of cost and power, this little speedster may well be your best choice.

COMPLETE PLANS include FULL SIZE PATTERNS for the stem, breasthook, and half sections for the frames and transom. Includes instructions, Bill of Materials, and Fastening Schedule.

AVAILABLE FOR THIS DESIGN:
- **Plans & Patterns**
- **Bronze Fastening Kit**
- **Fiberglass Kit**
  See Price List

FLYING SAUCER

CLASSICALLY STYLED 12'
RUNABOUT

BUILD IN PLYWOOD

CHARACTERISTICS
Length overall .... 12'-3"
Beam ....5'-9"
Hull depth .... 27"
Hull weight (approx.) .... 190 lbs.
Average passengers 2-4
Hull type: Vee bottom, hard chine hull, developed for sheet plywood planking.
Power: Outboard motor to 25 HP.
Trailer: Designed for use with GLEN-L SERIES 750/1000 boat trailer plans.

Our classic design **FLYING SAUCER** is the ideal combination of utility and speed in a small boat. Going like a bomb, or carrying a whale of a passenger load is no problem for this little boat.

The **FLYING SAUCER** can also be built as an open boat for fishing; as such, she is an ideal cartop boat, easy to get to your favorite fishing spot with a minimum of hassle. The generous beam offers plenty of room for gear and load carrying.

The layout shown offers the styling of the traditional two-cockpit runabout, a look that is unique in a boat of this size. You can have your own classic runabout without all of the expense of a full-size antique. Picture yourself behind the wheel, in the center of her mahogany deck. She's a boat that

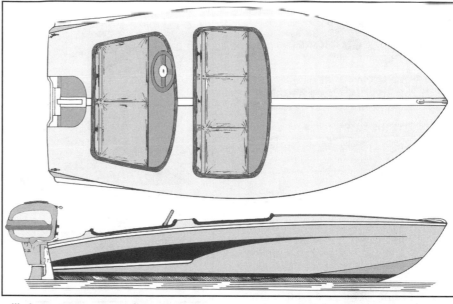

will draw stares even from the owners of the real thing.

COMPLETE PLANS include FULL SIZE PATTERNS for the stem, breasthook, and half sections for the frames and transom. Includes instructions, Bill of Materials, and Fastening Schedule.

AVAILABLE FOR THIS DESIGN:
- **Plans & Patterns**
- **Bronze Fastening Kit**
- **Fiberglass Kit**
See Price List

BINGO

A CLASSY 13' OUTBOARD RUNABOUT

BUILD IN *FAST-G* STITCH-N-GLUE

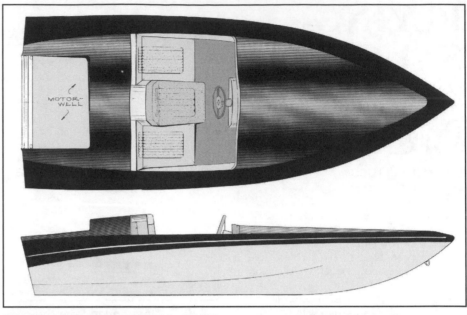

CHARACTERISTICS

Length overall .... 12'-8"
Beam .... 5'-0"
Depth amidship .... 24"
Hull weight (approx.) .... 240 lbs.
Average passengers 2-3
Hull type: Stitch-N-Glue *FAST-G* construction with sheet plywood developed to assemble flat and fold to form a 12° vee bottom with built-in chine lift strakes and spray deflector.
Power: Long shaft outboard motors to 40 HP (short shaft optional).
Trailer: Designed for use with GLEN-L SERIES 750/1000 boat trailer plans.

BINGO! You're a winner in this classy runabout where the driver is *it*! And why not? You sit in a luxurious "throne" slightly forward of passengers for a clear view over the long, lean cowl-deck. And you're in command of a sleek, *fast*, crowd-appealing runabout.

The sweeping deck lines with rounded cowl-like foredeck and raised, arced, aft deck impresses viewers that this boat is something special... *and* it is! The 12° vee bottom cushions the ride, while built-in spray deflector/lift strakes stabilize and provide a level, dry ride. The **BINGO** provides performance, and is a joy to see and be in.

COMPLETE PLANS include FULL SIZE PATTERNS (more than 25) for side/bottom planking, butt blocks, aft side, aft bottom, breasthook, bow piece, transom knee, 5 deck beams, side decking, aft deck, and half section patterns for foredeck, transom, and form, dashboard, and 5 different patterns for seat assembly. Also included are large-scale drawings, instructions, Bill of Materials, Fastening and Laminate Schedule GLEN-L STITCH-N-GLUE manual, and BINGO pictorial with more than 30 captioned photos of building the prototype.

BINGO is built by the GLEN-L, *FAST-G*, Stitch-N-Glue building method for simplicity and light weight. Constructed from standard 1/4" x 4' x 8' plywood, with patterns provided for almost *every* contoured part--it's hard to go wrong. Transfer the pattern contours to the wood, cut out, **F**old **A**nd **S**titch, **T**hen **G**lue (*FAST-G*), and **BINGO!**, the boat is formed. An excellent first boatbuilding project for almost anyone.

DYNO MITE & DYNO JET 11' DEEP VEE RUNABOUTS

BUILD IN STITCH-N-GLUE PLYWOOD

CHARACTERISTICS for both versions
Length overall .... 11'-1"
Beam .... 5'-6"
Hull depth .... 18"
Depth to coaming .... 24"
Typical passengers 1-2
Hull weight (approx.) .... 125 lbs.
Hull type: Vee bottom hull developed for sheet plywood and Stitch and Glue construction with built in chine flats.
Power: Outboards to 25 HP.
Can the hull be extended or shortened? No. We also do not recommend increasing the beam.
Trailer: Designed for use with Glen-L Series 750/1000 boat trailer plans.

COMPLETE PLANS plus FULL SIZE PATTERNS for the breasthook, transom, hull sides, bottom, butt blocks, form, transom knee, deck beams and gussets. Plus, a full set of Instructions with Plywood Layout, Bill of Materials, and Fastening and Laminate Schedules.

Dyno Mite is intended for a short or long shaft transom mounted outboard motor set in a self bailing motorwell. The Dyno Jet utilizes the popular jet pump powering system. There are plenty of "jet skis" that have suffered hull damage but the propulsion system is still in good shape. Most can be obtained very reasonably and are readily available. The hulls feature a generous 12 degree vee bottom with built in chine flats, a.k.a. spray rails, deflectors, or lift strakes. Interior longitudinal reinforcement is added after the hull is formed and consists of wide plywood laminations topped with vertical members. They're easy to spring in place, no shaping required and it's a proven strong system that reinforces the monocoque hull structure. And standard 4' x 8' plywood panels are used throughout; only three panels of 1/4" x 4' x 8' plywood will plank the entire boat.

Dyno Mite & Dyno Jet are easy to build, thanks to the simplified Stitch and Glue building method. Full size patterns are furnished for virtually ev-

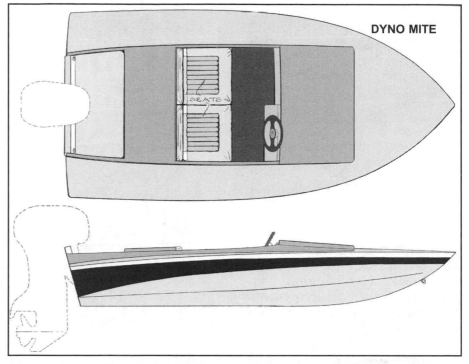

DYNO MITE

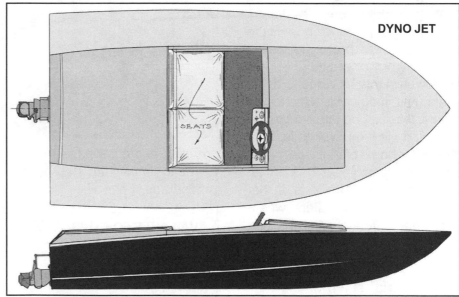

DYNO JET

ery contoured part in the boat including the bottom and side planking. The patterned parts are duplicated to the plywood panels, cut to shape, bent around a single form, stitched together, and joints bonded with fillets and fiberglass laminations. The pre-cut plywood planking forms the hull shape automatically without fairing or shaping. You'll be surprised how quickly the hull takes shape. The construction is not complex and this is an excellent first time boatbuilding project.

AVAILABLE FOR THIS DESIGN:
• Plans & Patterns
• Stitch & Glue Kit
• Fiberglass Kit
• Stitch & Glue DVD
See Price List

TUFFY

A 13' RUNABOUT

BUILD IN PLYWOOD

CHARACTERISTICS

Length overall .... 13'-1"
Beam ....6'-0"
Hull depth .... 27"
Hull weight (approx.) .... 350 lbs.
Average passengers 1-4
Hull type: Vee bottom hard chine hull developed for sheet plywood planking.
Power: Outboard motor to 40 HP.
Trailer: Designed for use with GLEN-L SERIES 750/1000 boat trailer plans.

COMPLETE PLANS include FULL SIZE PATTERNS for the stem, breasthook, chine blocking, transom knee, and half-section patterns for each of the frames and transom. Includes instructions, Bill of Materials, and Fastening Schedule.

TUFFY! A ruff and tuff runabout that is an amateur builder's dream. This high performance boat is the result of several prototype testing models which handled a variety of power-plants in virtually every maneuver imaginable. She towed skiers, was flipped into tight turns, and made to jump wakes just like the larger boats of this type. Naturally, any small boat has limitations, and the **TUFFY** is at her best in protected waters where the speed potential can be used.

When using the PLANS & PATTERNS, the **TUFFY** is an easy boat to build, even for the rank amateur. The instructions for this boat contain more than 50 con-

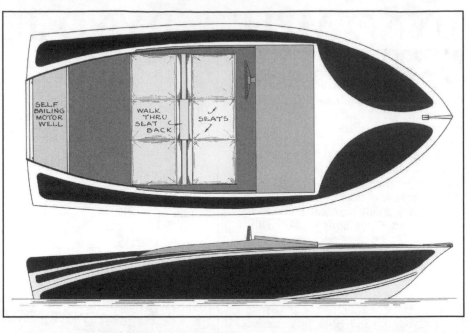

struction photographs of the prototype to amplify the step-by-step procedures.

AVAILABLE FOR THIS DESIGN:
- **Plans & Patterns**
- **Bronze Fastening Kit**
- **Fiberglass Kit**
See Price List

UTILITY

AN 11' UTILITY CRAFT

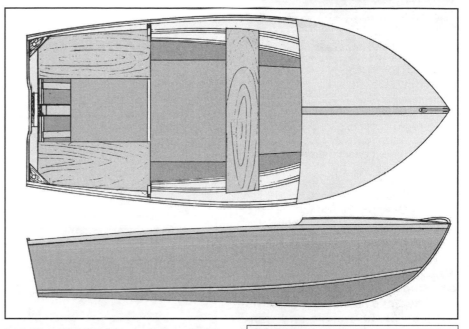

CHARACTERISTICS

Length overall .... 11'-0"
Beam .... 5'-0"
Hull depth................................ 26"
Hull weight (approx.) .... 140 lbs.
Average passengers 1-3
Hull type: Vee bottom hard chine hull developed for sheet plywood planking.
Power: Outboard motor to 10 HP
Trailer: Designed for use with GLEN-L SERIES 750/1000 boat trailer plans.

COMPLETE PLANS include FULL SIZE PATTERNS for the stem, breasthook, and half-section patterns for each of the frames and transom. Includes instructions, Bill of Materials, and Fastening Schedule.

The **UTILITY** is a practical boat ideal for fishing or water sport use. The lightweight hull is easily transported and can be car-topped. The generous beam provides plenty of room for gear or passengers. This feature also gives the boat exceptional stability. Combine this with a good "vee" and the flaring topsides, and you have the ideal modern utility boat.

The construction of the **UTILITY** is ideal for the amateur. It's easy and inexpensive to build. Three 4' x 8' sheets of 1/4" plywood will plank the entire boat. The forward part of the bottom is put on in a single sheet, slit up forward to form the vee portion. This method eliminates a joint along the keel giving a smooth, leakproof hull. The PLANS cover all aspects of the construction are designed with the amateur in mind.

AVAILABLE FOR THIS DESIGN:
- **Plans & Patterns**
- **Bronze Fastening Kit**
- **Fiberglass Kit**
See Price List

FISHERMAN

A 13' UTILITY CRAFT

BUILD IN PLYWOOD

CHARACTERISTICS

Length overall .... 13'-0"
Beam .... 5'-9"
Hull depth .... 27"
Hull weight (approx.) .... 275 lbs.
Average passengers 1-4
Hull type: Vee bottom hard chine hull developed for sheet plywood planking.
Power: Outboard motor to 45 HP
Trailer: Designed for use with GLEN-L SERIES 750/1000 boat trailer plans.

COMPLETE PLANS include FULL SIZE PATTERNS for the stem, breasthook, chine blocking, transom knee, and half-section patterns for each of the frames and transom. Includes instructions, Bill of Materials, and Fastening Schedule.

The **FISHERMAN** is a practical, rugged, and easily maintained boat for the fisherman and water sports enthusiast. A generous vee in the bottom provides a soft ride, while the flare in the sides runs clear to the transom for a dry ride and large cockpit area. The forefoot and skeg assures excellent directional control for trolling and dockside handling in a breeze.

The construction of the **FISHERMAN** is well within the realm of the first-time builder, and the cost to build fits into a tight budget. For a good all-around utility craft with style, the **FISHERMAN** is hard to beat.

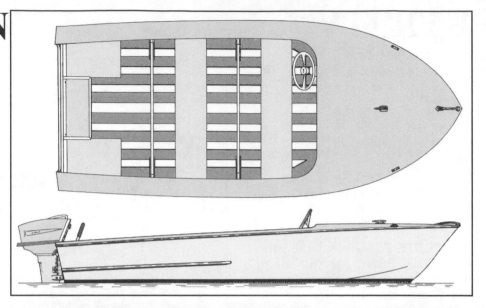

ZIP

A 14' CLASSIC STYLE RUNABOUT

BUILD IN PLYWOOD

CHARACTERISTICS

Length overall .... 14'-4"
Beam .... 5'-9"
Hull depth .... 27"
Hull weight (approx.) .... 375 lbs.
Average passengers 1-4
Hull type: Vee bottom hard chine hull developed for sheet plywood planking.
Power: Outboard motor to 40 HP.
Trailer: Designed for use with GLEN-L SERIES 750/1000 boat trailer plans.

COMPLETE PLANS include FULL SIZE PATTERNS for the stem, breasthook, transom knee, and half-section patterns for each of the frames and transom. Includes instructions, Bill of Materials, and Fastening Schedule.

ZIP is a high speed, deluxe sport runabout in the classic style. She furnishes all of the flashing speed, thrills, and performance that one could hope for. Ideally suited for towing water skiers or showing the local lads a clean pair of heels. **ZIP** can also be finished as a utility with a large open cockpit for fishing or general use. With her flaring sides, she is very dry. The bottom design allows for quick starts and excellent performance, with a generous vee forward to cushion the ride. A roomy 5'-9" beam assures stability.

AVAILABLE FOR THIS DESIGN:
- **Plans & Patterns**
- **Bronze Fastening Kit**
- **Fiberglass Kit**
- **See Price List**

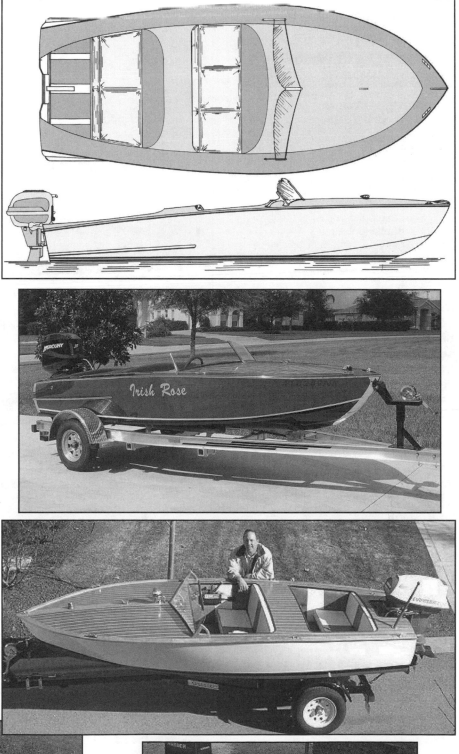

NIMROD

A 15' UTILITY CRAFT

BUILD IN PLYWOOD

CHARACTERISTICS

Length overall .... 15'-0"
Beam ....6'-0"
Hull depth .... 33"
Hull weight (approx.) .... 400 lbs.
Average passengers 1-4
Sleeping capacity 2
Hull type: Vee bottom hard chine hull developed for sheet plywood planking.
Power: Outboard motor to 60 HP.
Trailer: Designed for use with GLEN-L SERIES 750/1000 boat trailer plans.

COMPLETE PLANS include FULL SIZE PATTERNS for the stem, breasthook, transom knee, and half-section patterns for each of the frames and transom. Includes instructions, Bill of Materials, and Fastening Schedule.

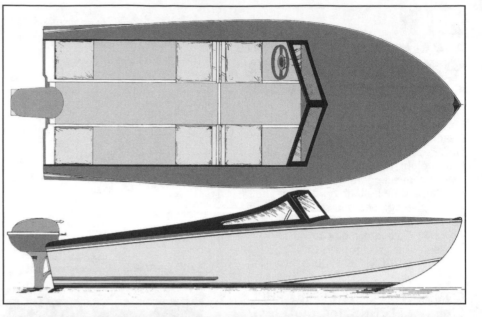

AVAILABLE FOR THIS DESIGN:
- **Plans & Patterns**
- **Bronze Fastening Kit**
- **Fiberglass Kit**
  See Price List

NIMROD is a comfortable boat. A generous vee forward cushions the shock in choppy water, and the lifted chines and relieved forefoot insures a dry, safe boat at speed. The 6' beam provides exceptional stability and load capacity. Her clean and graceful lines belie her versatility.

NIMROD has bunks for two that are formed when the seats fold forward and a portion of the cockpit floor raises. These bunks then extend under the forward decking for comfortable and roomy accommodations. Seats face both fore and aft; the roomy 4 1/2' x 9' cockpit offers room to fill the needs of fishermen, campers, water skiers or those who just want to be out on the water.

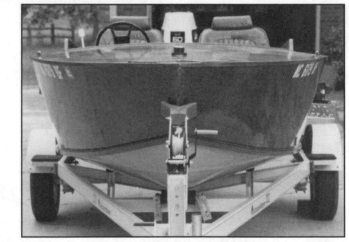

CELERITY
A 14 1/2' RUNABOUT

BUILD IN PLYWOOD

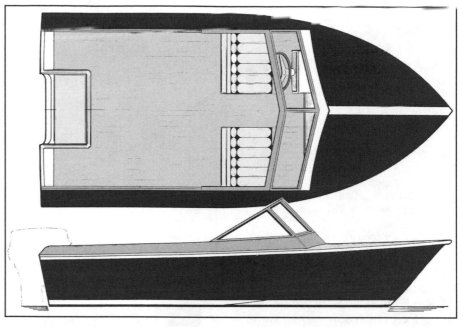

CHARACTERISTICS
Length overall .... 14'-6"
Beam .... 6'-9"
Hull depth .... 36"
Hull draft .... 9 "
Hull weight (approx.) .... 600 lbs.
Height overall ....4'-4"
Average passengers 2-3
Cockpit size .... 9'-3"x 5'-6"
Hull type: Full length 16° minimum deep
vee with bulbous forefoot, radiused keel section, and lift strakes, developed for sheet plywood planking.
Power: Single long shaft (20") outboard to 75 HP. Minimum motor recommended is 20 HP.
Trailer: Designed for use with GLEN-L SERIES 750/1000 boat trailer plans.

COMPLETE PLANS include FULL SIZE PATTERNS for the stem, breasthook, transom knee, deck beams, and half-section patterns for each of the frames and transom. Includes instructions, Bill of Materials, and Fastening Schedule.

CELERITY means swift and agile, and that's what she is. But this compact runabout is much more. Unlike the typical lightweight, skimpily built boats commonly found in this size range, **CELERITY** rides and handles like much larger boats. It has a full length deep-vee hull with a minimum 16° vee at the transom, plus a radiused keel section for a soft ride. Lift strakes assure quick acceleration and deflect spray for a dry ride. The wide beam with full length flaring topsides allows a large, stable, and deep cockpit, well suited to the fisherman or sports oriented family.

The construction of **CELERITY** is husky for durability and strength. No difficult construction procedures are necessary, and all plywood can be standard 4' x 8' sheets for economy. Our FULL SIZE PATTERNS make construction well suited to the first time builder. Instructions provided with the plans assure professional results you will be proud of.

CELERITY can be powered with a single outboard motor of at least 20 HP for optimum minimal performance. Optionally, twin motors can be used as long as power recommendations are not exceeded. While seating is shown, the builder can vary this to suit, arranging the roomy cockpit by his needs, either adding or deleting seating as desired. In short, this is a versatile, yet compact, inexpensive boat to build or own.

AVAILABLE FOR THIS DESIGN:
- **Plans & Patterns**
- **Bronze Fastening Kit**
- **Fiberglass Kit**
See Price List

SKI TOW

A 15' SKI BOAT

BUILD IN PLYWOOD

CHARACTERISTICS
Length overall .... 14'-8"
Beam ....6'-6"
Hull depth.....................................32"
Hull weight (approx.) .... 400 lbs.
Average passengers 1-4
Hull type: Vee bottom hard chine hull developed for sheet plywood planking.
Power: Outboard motor to 70 HP.
Trailer: Designed for use with GLEN-L SERIES 750/1000 boat trailer plans.

COMPLETE PLANS include FULL SIZE PATTERNS for the stem, breasthook, transom knee, chine blocking, and half-section patterns for each of the frames and transom. Includes instructions, Bill of Materials, and Fastening Schedule.

The **SKI TOW** is an outboard runabout intended for water skiing. The cockpit is very roomy with plenty of room for ski equipment or fishing gear. The boarding ladder at the transom allows the fallen skier to climb back into the boat without a lot of unnecessary bruises. The rear seat can be reversed to face aft to allow a comfortable position for the ski observer or for fishing. The forward seats may be made with the split back walk-through as shown, or as separate seats. Due to the seat construction method, the seats are not a structural part of the boat, they can be removed or altered to suit. With the seats re-

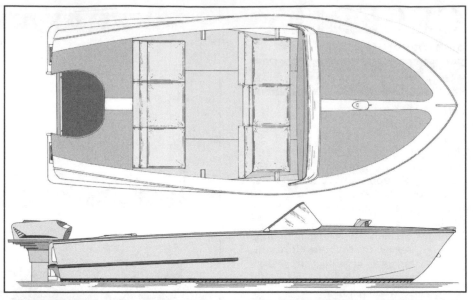

moved, a flat area 5' wide and 8' long is available for sleeping bags.

AVAILABLE FOR THIS DESIGN:
- **Plans & Patterns**
- **Bronze Fastening Kit**
- **Fiberglass Kit**
See Price List

REBEL

A 15' SKI BOAT

BUILD IN PLYWOOD

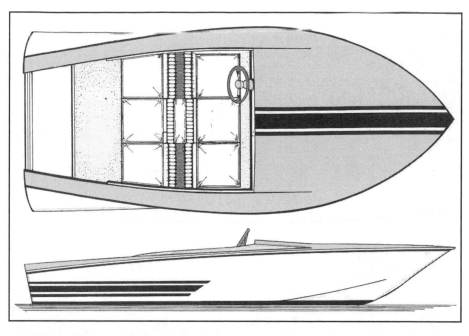

CHARACTERISTICS

Length overall .... 14'-10"
Beam ....6'-4"
Hull depth....................................25"
Hull weight (approx.) .... 400 lbs.
Average passengers 1-4
Hull type: Vee bottom with anti-trip chine developed for sheet plywood planking.
Power: Outboard motor to 80 HP.
Trailer: Designed for use with GLEN-L SERIES 750/1000 boat trailer plans.

COMPLETE PLANS include FULL SIZE PATTERNS for the stem, breasthook, transom knee, chine blocking, and half-section patterns for each of the frames and transom. Includes instructions, Bill of Materials, and Fastening Schedule.

AVAILABLE FOR THIS DESIGN:
- **Plans & Patterns**
- **Bronze Fastening Kit**
- **Fiberglass Kit**
See Price List

The **REBEL** is a pocket size ski boat for the person with limited storage space or a small tow vehicle. Since most serious water skiers or fast boat enthusiasts do not care for windshields, a cowl-type of forward deck is used. If the builder desires a windshield, there is one detailed in the plans.

The **REBEL** is intended for high speed with safety. The extra wide beam at the transom supports larger and more powerful outboard motors. The flaring, anti-trip chines provide a safety factor in turning, and smother much of the spray at the transom. Start building your own **REBEL** today.

SCOOTER

A 16' SHALLOW WATER "FLATS" BOAT

BUILD IN PLYWOOD

CHARACTERISTICS

Length overall .... 15'-9"*
Beam.. 6'-10"
Draft at 1000 lbs, gross weight ... 4"
Hull depth...................................... 12"
Hull weight (approx.) .... 600 lbs.
Average passengers 3-4
Hull type: Shoal draft semi-tunnel hull developed for sheet plywood planking.
Power: Outboard motor to 120 HP.
Trailer: Designed for use with GLEN-L SERIES 1200/1800 boat trailer plans.

Length can be extended to 17'-7" by respacing the frames. A modification sheet is included.

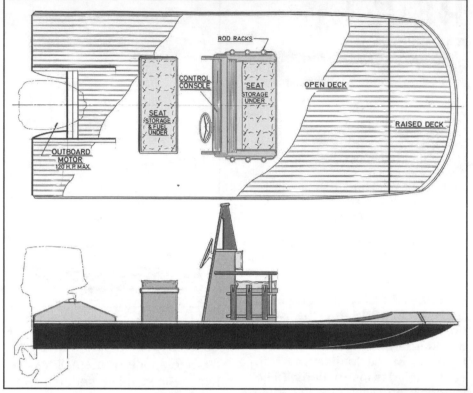

SCOOTER... "a lean, mean fishin' machine" intended for scooting over knee-deep, protected waters that other boats simply can't get into. While not a hull for deep, open water, it's the *ideal* boat for fishing the shallow flats and other skinny backwaters common to the Gulf states. Imagine a hull draft of only 4" with 1000 lbs. gross load that will take an additional 400 lbs. of load before sinking another inch.

Underway, **SCOOTER**'s through-tunnel hull enables the engine to be raised to decrease motor draft. In Texas where they are common, these boats are frequently equipped with hydraulic lifters for the motor. The boats are usually taken several miles out into the Gulf where the fisherman either fishes from the boat, or dons waders and fishes on foot in the shallow water.

The tunnel reduces wetted surface for high speeds with economy, while adding directional stability and control at the same time. A minor vee forward knifes the water for a better ride. With plenty of power capability, you'll get to where the big ones are biting in short order.

Building the **SCOOTER** is easy. No building form is required and all planking is done with standard 4' x 8' sheets of plywood to keep costs low. Simplified methods, together with clear, detailed plans covering all aspects of the boat including the console, make this an ideal project for the amateur. So why pay BIG bucks for a ready-made when you can build your own, customized to your own needs, for much less?

COMPLETE PLANS include FULL SIZE PATTERNS for the bow piece, motorboard, motorboard brace, tunnel side curved members, transom, half-section patterns for frames, tunnel side planking forward contour, and sawn forward chine. Includes instructions, Bill of Materials, and Fastening Schedule.

AVAILABLE FOR THIS DESIGN:
- **Plans & Patterns**
- **Bronze Fastening Kit**
- **Fiberglass Kit**
See Price List

PLAY PEN

A 15' SPORT CRAFT

BUILD IN PLYWOOD

CHARACTERISTICS

Length overall .... 15'-5"
Beam... 6'-11"
Hull depth................................... 26"
Hull weight (approx.) .... 550 lbs.
Average passengers 1-4
Cockpit size (approx.)....... 5'-6"x 12'
Hull type: Garvey-type with vee bottom developed for sheet plywood planking. This hull cannot be extended.
Power: Single or twin outboard motors to 75 HP, or inboard/ outboard drives to 400 lbs.
Note: *Although an inboard/outboard can be used, it must be of low silouette or it will project above the deck line.*
Trailer: Designed for use with GLEN-L SERIES 750/1000 boat trailer plans.

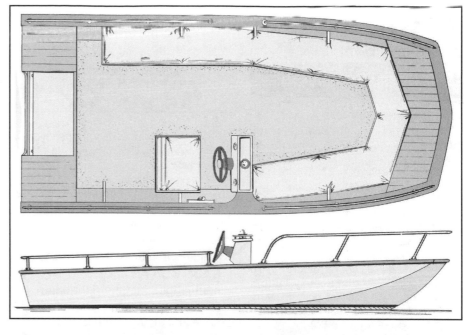

What's your choice? Fishing, scuba diving, water skiing, or just plain fun on the water? The **PLAY PEN** is at home in any type of boating recreation where a large, *very* large, open cockpit is required. And doesn't everyone want more space in their boat? With the **PLAY PEN** you have just what the name implies, a large open area for all types of boating fun and water play.

The **PLAY PEN** carries an exceptionally wide beam. An extremely generous flare is carried all the way to the transom to make a conventional beam at the waterline, yet provides almost immediate reserve buoyancy for heavy loads. The bottom lines extend from a slight vee at the transom to a generous vee bottom at the garvey bow.

The method of construction utilizes a sawn harpin and chine member. With these members sawn to shape, the normal bending of the longitudinals is eliminated. In fact, the sheer and bow member are one piece, extending completely around the boat for extra ridgidity. The construction allows considerable latitude with the interior layout. The seats aft of the helm may be completely eliminated if preferred. All of the seats may be utilized for storage, providing room to carry all types of boating and recreational gear.

AVAILABLE FOR THIS DESIGN:
- **Plans & Patterns**
- **Bronze Fastening Kit**
- **Fiberglass Kit**
  See Price List

COMPLETE PLANS include FULL SIZE PATTERNS for the transom knee, stem, buttock stems, harpin-sheer, and bow piece, with half-section patterns for the frames and transom. Includes instructions, Bill of Materials, and Fastening Schedule.

BASS BOAT

A 15' BASS BOAT

BUILD IN PLYWOOD

CHARACTERISTICS

Length overall .... 15'-5"
Beam ....5'-4"
Hull depth......................................26"
Hull weight (approx.) .... 425 lbs.
Average passengers 1-3
Cockpit size (approx.)............4' x 11'
Cockpit depth maximum ....18"
Hull type:Garvey-type with vee bottom developed for sheet plywood planking.
Power: Single outboard motors to 70 HP. Electric trolling motors may be used at bow or stern. Inboard/outboard drives may be used up to 400 lbs.
Note: Although an inboard/outboard can be used, it must be of low silouette or it will project above the deck line.
Trailer: Designed for use with GLEN-L SERIES 750/1000 boat trailer plans.

Check over the deck layout of the **BASS BOAT** and you'll see that this one has just about everything imaginable for the ultimate bass fishing boat. Maybe you don't want all of these gadgets, or maybe you even have some to add that we haven't thought of... that's the beauty of building your own. You can make it the way *you* want it, not the way some plastic boat manufacturer thinks you want it. The coins you save by building your own will buy a lot of fancy fishing gear.

The hull of the **BASS BOAT** can handle short or long shaft outboards up to 70 horsepower. The lean width is in response to the requirement specified by fishing writers, that it be able to get into those tight areas among the stumps and reeds, where the big one lies waiting. At full bore, the boat rides easy and flat, with plenty of stability at rest for steady casting. The control console can be omitted, and the popular stick steering control substituted, if you desire.

The lightweight, strong, plywood construction makes it possible for just about anybody to make his own **BASS**

BOAT using our comprehensive easy-to-understand PLANS and FULL SIZE PATTERNS.

A "real" bass fisherman is dedicated to his sport, and he's got to have the best equipment and boat. What better way to get the perfect boat than building it yourself? That's what the **BASS BOAT** is all about! It's just the right length, just the right beam, just the right depth, and if you build it... it'll have just the right fisherman.

COMPLETE PLANS include FULL SIZE PATTERNS for the transom knee, stem, bow piece, frames, and transom. Includes instructions, Bill of Materials, and Fastening Schedule.

AVAILABLE FOR THIS DESIGN:
- **Plans & Patterns**
- **Bronze Fastening Kit**
- **Fiberglass Kit**
See Price List

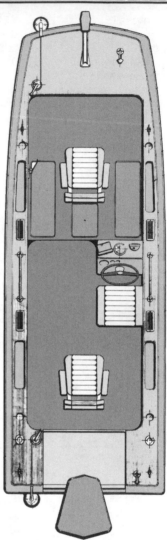

MALAHINI

A *CLASSIC* 16' RUNABOUT

BUILD IN PLYWOOD

CHARACTERISTICS

Length overall .... 15'-11"
Beam .... 6'-7"
Hull depth .... 31"
Hull weight (approx.) .... 475 lbs.
Average passengers 1-4
Hull type: Vee bottom hard chine hull developed for sheet plywood planking.
Power: Outboard motor to 85 HP.
Trailer: Designed for use with GLEN-L SERIES 1200/1800 boat trailer plans.

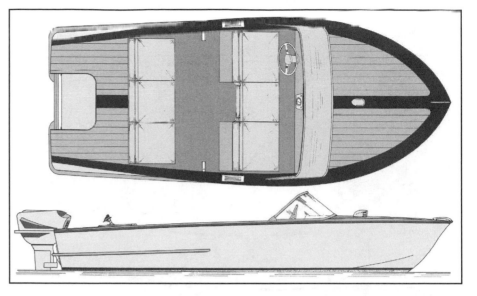

COMPLETE PLANS include FULL SIZE PATTERNS for the stem, breasthook, transom knee, chine blocking, and half-section patterns for each of the frames and transom. Includes instructions, Bill of Materials, and Fastening Schedule.

If you are looking for a boat that has the classic lines of the "woodys" of the past, the **MALAHINI** may be the boat for you. Finish her in natural mahogany plywood or paint the hull and put on a mahogany deck. Make her as plain or as fancy as you want.

The generous size of the **MALAHINI** cockpit and the modular seats that have proven so popular in our other designs, make almost any interior arrangement possible. The seats may be removed to provide a flat area 9' long and up to 5'-9" in width for sleeping or carrying camping gear. The seats can also be placed back-to-back for trolling or for the observer when pulling a water skier.

The generous vee in the forefoot and the wide beam of the **MALAHINI** make for a dry, safe, boat. The construction is rugged and intended to take it. The self-bailing well prevents any sudden wave or back wash from entering the boat. All of the construction details have been prepared for the amateur builder. Step-by-step instructions, plus photos, make it possible to have your own collector's boat at a price you can afford.

AVAILABLE FOR THIS DESIGN:
- Plans & Patterns
- Bronze Fastening Kit
- Fiberglass Kit
See Price List

JIMBO A 16' GARVEY HULL

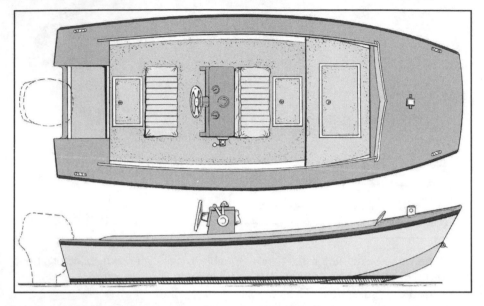

STITCH-N-GLUE PLYWOOD or WELDED ALUMINUM

CHARACTERISTICS

	S&G	Aluminum
Length overall	15'-9"	15'-9"
Beam	6'-8"	6'-9"
Draft@890 lbs. disp.	6"	7"
Hull depth midship	27"	27"
Hull/deck wt (approx.)	450 lbs.	575 lbs.
Average passengers:	2-4	2-4
Cockpit size	5' x 10'	5' x 10'

Hull type: Garvey shaped, vee bottom, developed for Stitch-N-Glue sheet plywood or welded aluminum construction.

Power: Single long shaft outboard motor to 85 HP maximum, 50 HP is more than adequate for most uses. Lightweight inboard/outboard optional but not detailed.

Trailer: Designed for use with GLEN-L SERIES 1200/1800 boat trailer.

ALUMINUM: COMPLETE PLANS include instructions, bill of materials, "Aluminum Boatbuilding Guide", full dimensional planking layouts and PATTERNS for the transom, bow, building forms, knees, gussets, motorwell sides, and deck beam crown.

PLYWOOD: COMPLETE PLANS include instructions, fastening schedule, Bill of Materials, "Stitch-N-Glue Manual", plywood utilization drawings, full dimensional planking layouts, and PATTERNS for transom, bow, form, deck crown, and knee.

A garvey hull with a squared transom bow provides more room than conventional hulls and yet, with JIMBO, a generous vee is incorporated. These are rugged craft, excellent as work boats or for the fisherman who wants a boat for fishing, not spit and polish. Sure this type of hull can be as nice appearing as one would wish, but this is a boat to use, not to pamper.

The large cockpit with raised sole forward is left open with an optional center console (fully detailed) so you can add bench seats or fishing chairs. There is lots of space under the cockpit area for storage, plus the flat floor has no frame or bulkhead protrusions.

JIMBO in ALUMINUM or JIMBO in WOOD share the same hull, but the plans and patterns are separate; these are not plans with one material then converted for another. Each version is intended for building in the material designated; WOOD/PLYWOOD or ALUMINUM.

The ALUMINUM version features sheet welded stock incorporating a chine spray rail and rugged pipe sheer bumper. The sides are 1/8" and the bottom 3/16" thick with four longitudinal reinforcing beams for extra strength. The hull is built right side up in a simple cradle building form. The side and bottom are fully dimensioned so the usual cut and fit, cut and fit, ad nauseum is eliminated. Cut out the parts, put them in the simple building form, and start welding.

The WOOD version utilizes sheet plywood planking built by the simple Stitch-N-Glue method. The sides and bottom are fully dimensioned. Lay out the side and bottom on the plywood, saw to shape, wrap the planking around the single building form, hold the seams together with wire stitches, follow with fillets (glue), and reinforce with fiberglass laminates. Vertical full length longitudinal members are added to further reinforce the monocoque hull.

With either version you get a complete set of plans and patterns especially intended for the amateur builder with little or no previous experience.

> ### AVAILABLE FOR THIS DESIGN:
> - Plans & Patterns
> - Stitch & Glue Kit
> - Fiberglass Kit
> - Stitch & Glue DVD
>
> See Price List

BRAVADO
A 17' DEEP VEE OVERNIGHTER

BUILD IN PLYWOOD

CHARACTERISTICS

Length overall .... 17'-0"
Beam .... 7'-6"
Draft .... 11"
Hull depth .... 3'-9"
Hull weight (approx.) .... 900 lbs.
Headroom (nominal) .... 3'-0"
Height overall .... 5'-5"
Cockpit size .... 8'x 6'-6"
Sleeping capacity 2

Hull type: Full length deep vee hull with lift strakes, developed for sheet plywood planking.

Power: Single or twin outboard motors to 135 HP total. Single stern mounted inboard to 650 lbs. connected to an outdrive.

Trailer: Designed for use with GLEN-L SERIES 2300/2800 boat trailer plans.

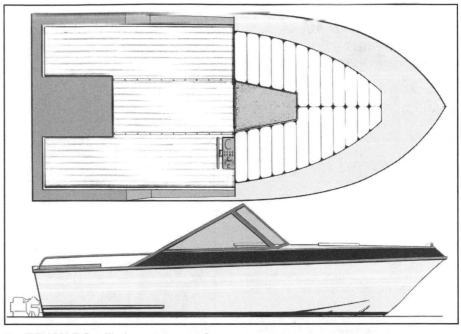

GLEN-L takes pride in the **BRAVADO**, designed to meet the demands of those who desire a deep vee hull in this size. The underbody of the **BRAVADO** incorporates a bulbous keel section for soft entry and easy steering characteristics. At the chine in the aft sections, a reverse curve has been added for spray deflection and stability. Lift strakes are designed into the hull for quick planing, fuel economy, and directional stability.

The best part of this hull is that it is easily built with sheet plywood, one of the strongest materials per pound known today. What this all means is that now the amateur builder can enjoy the benefits of the deep vee hull coupled with contemporary styling, all at a fraction of the cost of a comparable production boat. What's more,

the **BRAVADO** will sleep two people in full length berths, plus there's plenty of room for fishing and water sports in the cockpit.

AVAILABLE FOR THIS DESIGN:
- **Plans & Patterns**
- **Bronze Fastening Kit**
- **Fiberglass Kit**
See Price List

COMPLETE PLANS include **FULL SIZE PATTERNS** for stem, upper and lower breasthooks, and half-section patterns for the frames and transom. Includes instructions, Bill of Materials, and Fastening Schedule.

GERONIMO

A 16' RUNABOUT

BUILD IN PLYWOOD

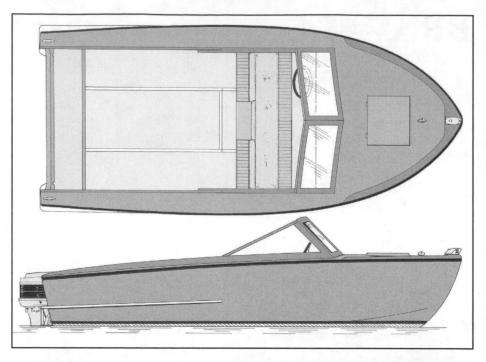

CHARACTERISTICS

Length overall .... 16'-1"
Beam .... 7'-0"
Hull depth .... 38"
Hull weight (approx.) .... 600 lbs.
Average passengers 1-4
Cockpit size .... 5'x 9'-4"
Hull type: Vee bottom hard chine hull developed for sheet plywood planking.
Power: Single or twin outboard motors to 100 HP. Inboard, stern mounted motor connected to stern drive or vee-drive, to 500 lbs. maximum.
Trailer: Designed for use with GLEN-L SERIES 1200/1800 boat trailer plans.

COMPLETE PLANS include FULL SIZE PATTERNS for the stem, breasthook, transom knee, chine blocking, and half-section patterns for each of the frames and transom. Includes instructions, Bill of Materials, and Fastening Schedule.

AVAILABLE FOR THIS DESIGN:
- **Plans & Patterns**
- **Bronze Fastening Kit**
- **Fiberglass Kit**
See Price List

GERONIMO is a husky, open cockpit runabout, that is extremely versatile. You can mount back-to-back seats and use her for fishing or water skiing. With the removable seat shifted aside, you have a flat floor in the cockpit of more that 5' x 9' in size. This provides plenty of room for sleeping bags or scuba diving gear. The deep hull and wide beam make for a safe craft for friends or family. The bottom is fast enough to hold almost any reasonable power, yet the vee at the forefoot is generous to cushion the ride.

The **GERONIMO** can be powered with various outboards, either singles or twins. The instructions cover two types of motor wells. One for single motors provides generous stowage space at the transom. The other for single or twin motors provides a wide open area for ready access to the motor or motors. Both types incorporate a self-bailing motor well that will automatically drain any water coming over the motor cut out. Optional power can be the inboard-outboard type of drive, or an inboard stern mounted motor connected to a v-drive.

TUNNEL KING A 16' TUNNEL HULL

CHARACTERISTICS

Length overall .... 16'-0"
Beam .... 7'-6"
Hull depth .... 31"
Hull weight (approx.) .... 375 lbs.
Average passengers 1-4
Hull type: Tunnel hull with full length sponsons, developed for sheet plywood planking.
Power: Outboard motor to 140 HP.
Trailer: Designed for use with GLEN-L SERIES 1200/1800 boat trailer plans.

COMPLETE PLANS include FULL SIZE PATTERNS for the motorboard, dashboard, bow piece, runner stem, tunnel side planking, and half-section patterns for each of the frames and transom. Includes instructions, Bill of Materials, and Fastening Schedule.

TUNNEL KING offers the high performance potential of the popular racing tunnel hulls in a model designed for multi-passenger use. Unlike competition models which carry only a single driver, this version can handle a driver *plus* three passengers! Naturally, the fewer the passengers, the better the performance, but even with four aboard, you'll be amazed by the rock steady ride due to the air cushion effect created by the full length twin sponsons. Maneuvering your TUNNEL KING is a new sensation if you are used to conventional boats. The boat tracks straight as an arrow, but when put into a turn, the hull remains flat and level responding quickly and positively to your action on the helm.

TUNNEL KING can be powered with moderate to high horsepower single outboards. Because all passengers sit

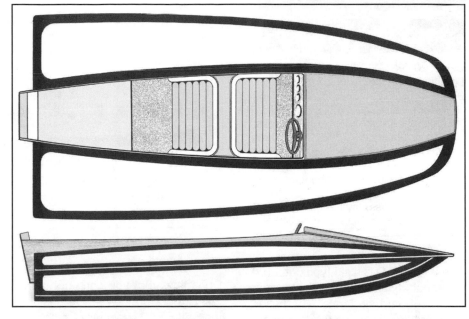

well inboard, the stability of the **TUNNEL KING** is remarkable. Just like other tunnel boats, the **TUNNEL KING** is safe and secure when operated in moderate weather conditions on protected waters. Building your own is easy when you use our PLANS and FULL SIZE PATTERNS.

AVAILABLE FOR THIS DESIGN:
- Plans & Patterns
- Bronze Fastening Kit
- Fiberglass Kit
See Price List

STILETTO

A 16' SKI BOAT

BUILD IN PLYWOOD

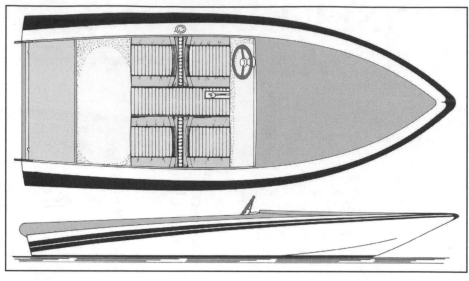

CHARACTERISTICS

Length overall .... 16'-0"
Beam .... 6'-6"
Hull depth..................................... 26"
Hull weight (approx.) .... 440 lbs.
Average passengers 1-4
Hull type:Vee bottom with sides flaring out to form anti-trip chines. Developed for sheet plywood planking.
Power: Outboard motor to 100 HP.
Trailer: Designed for use with GLEN-L SERIES 1200/1800 boat trailer plans.

The **STILETTO** is a ski-type outboard runabout styled like the popular high speed inboard ski boats. The hull is designed for high powered motors with safety in mind. The sides flare out to provide additional buoyancy at the transom as well as acting as safety anti-trip chines in faster turns. Just sit in the comfortable bucket seat, and when the skier gives thumbs up, you'll be able to pick him off the beach like few outboards can.

Don't think that you can't get results just like our prototype. We designed the **STILETTO** especially for the amateur, to be a great looking ski boat that you'll be proud of. Your **STILETTO** will really make heads turn, and you'll have a hard time convincing your friends that you didn't buy your boat from a factory.

AVAILABLE FOR THIS DESIGN:
- **Plans & Patterns**
- **Bronze Fastening Kit**
- **Fiberglass Kit**
See Price List

COMPLETE PLANS include **FULL SIZE PATTERNS** for the stem, breasthook, transom knee, and half-section patterns for each of the frames and transom. Includes instructions, Bill of Materials, and Fastening Schedule.

OUTRAGE

A 16' DEEP VEE SKI BOAT

BUILD IN PLYWOOD

CHARACTERISTICS

Length overall .... 16'-5"
Beam .... 7'-0"
Hull depth .... 26"
Hull weight (approx.) .... 450 lbs.
Average passengers 1-4
Hull type: Full length deep vee with 12° deadrise, lift strakes, and flaring topsides. Developed for sheet plywood planking.
Power: Outboard motor to 125 HP.
Trailer: Designed for use with GLEN-L SERIES 1200/1800 boat trailer plans.

COMPLETE PLANS include FULL SIZE PATTERNS for the stem, breasthook, transom knee, and half-section patterns for each of the frames and transom. Includes instructions, Bill of Materials, and Fastening Schedule.

Tired of having to cut your day on the water short because a little wind blows up a chop? Are you fed up with getting kicked around in the other fellow's wake? Do you want speed and guts for towing skiers, but demand a soft ride? Then grab onto our **OUTRAGE!** This one really digs in, whether it's a hard turn, quartering a wake, or just blasting through.

The deep hull of the **OUTRAGE** features lift strakes for fast acceleration, great directional stability, and a really dry ride. With a power capability up to 125 HP, you can take on any water ski situation with ease. The cockpit is plenty roomy, and can handle up to four. The handy walk-through coupled with high-rise coamings makes this a safe boat even with the kids along. Plus, the motor well is self-draining.

So, if you want the crowd following you (on a tow rope, that is), get yourself into an **OUTRAGE**. Build it yourself, save some dough, and have a ball!

AVAILABLE FOR THIS DESIGN:
- **Plans & Patterns**
- **Bronze Fastening Kit**
- **Fiberglass Kit**
  See Price List

CONSOLE SKIFF

A 15' 9" OPEN SKIFF WITH CENTER CONSOLE

CHARACTERISTICS

Length overall .... 15'-9"
Beam .... 6'-3"
Hull depth.................................... 25"
Hull weight (approx.) .... 350 lbs.
Average passengers 1-4
Hull type: Sheet plywood hull developed for *FAST-G* Stitch-N-Glue construction.
Power: Outboard motor to 40 HP.
Trailer: Designed for use with GLEN-L SERIES 1200/1800 boat trailer plans.

COMPLETE PLANS include FULL SIZE PATTERNS for all planking, butt blocks, building form, transom, knee, breasthook, fore and aft longitudinal beams, partial bulkhead, aft bulkhead, cockpit sole, foredeck, sidedeck, forward bulkhead, plywood layouts, and dimensional console drawings. Includes instructions, Bill of Materials, Fastening Schedule, and STITCH-N-GLUE Manual.

CONSOLE PATTERNS: Although the PLANS include all dimensions for the console and bench, the CONSOLE PATTERNS for console side, windshield bracket, and plywood layout will greatly simplify building.

RAISED BULWARK PATTERNS increase the freeboard to that of the CABIN SKIFF. Drawings and instructions are included.

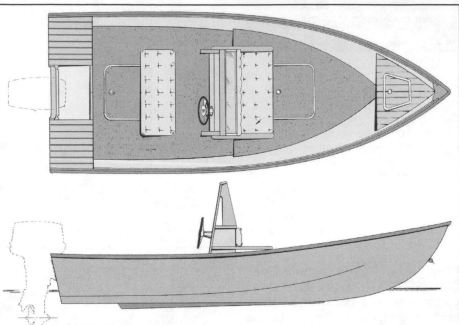

The **CONSOLE SKIFF** offers a *large* open cockpit with center console that's easy to build with the *FAST-G* Stitch-N-Glue construction method. Virtually every contoured part is furnished as a pattern. No need to use a bunch of dimensions to obtain planking and other parts. They're *all* furnished as FULL SIZE PATTERNS. Special layouts illustrate how the parts are obtained from standard 4' x 8' plywood panels with virtually *no* waste. We've done everything possible to make this design simple and inexpensive to construct.

But performance hasn't been short changed. The side/bottom forms a smooth entry with generous vee to provide a smooth ride. The skiff type hull is recognized as an excellent general use type. If a boat for fishing, skiing, just lazin' around, or having fun on the water is what you need, look no further. The **CONSOLE SKIFF** is for *you*!

AVAILABLE FOR THIS DESIGN:
• Plans & Patterns
• Stitch & Glue Kit
• Fiberglass Kit
• Stitch & Glue DVD
See Price List

POWER CATS

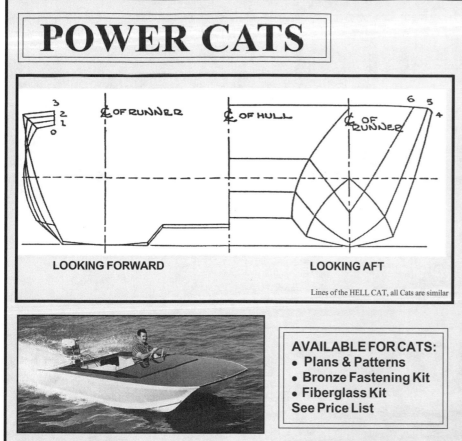

LOOKING FORWARD   LOOKING AFT

Lines of the HELL CAT, all Cats are similar

A WORD ABOUT "CATS"...

Our POWER CATAMARANS are hard to beat for speed with comfort. In a rough water chop, the air-cushion between the hulls really smooths out the ride. These boats carry heavier loads than other boats and are very stable, making them ideal family boats for fishing, skiing, or cruising. They turn flat with virtually no banking, and will handle more power than other boats in the same length. For ultimate performance, twin motors are recommended. The cockpit offers exceptional space that you must see to believe. All of our cats are extremely strong and designed for rugged use. Take a close look at the photos and drawings. These are truly unique boats; once you have one you will use it as a standard for ride and room that most other boats will not measure up to.

All models include COMPLETE PLANS plus FULL SIZE PATTERNS for the stems, bowpiece, transom knee, and half-section patterns for each of the frame/bulkheads and transom. Includes instructions, Bill of Materials, and Fastening Schedule.

AVAILABLE FOR CATS:
- Plans & Patterns
- Bronze Fastening Kit
- Fiberglass Kit
See Price List

JET CAT
A 14' POWER CATAMARAN

CHARACTERISTICS
Length overall .... 14'-2"
Beam .... 6'-10"
Hull depth .... 28"
Hull weight (approx.) .... 450 lbs.
Average passengers 1-4
Cockpit size .... 5'-2"x5'-11"
Hull type: Twin hulls developed for sheet plywood planking.
Power: Twin outboard motors to 90 HP total.
Trailer: Designed for use with GLEN-L SERIES 750/1000 boat trailer plans.

Considering its modest size, the **JET CAT** offers exceptional speed potential and comfort in a chop. The cockpit layout can be varied to suit the builder, and if desired a windshield could be added. Like all of our cats, the **JET CAT** offers space that has to be experienced to be believed. With a little effort, even the beginner can build this surprisingly big, little boat.

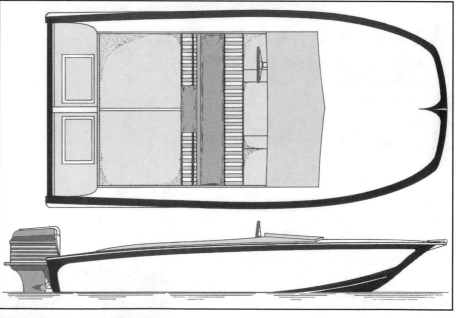

147

HELL CAT

A 16' POWER CATAMARAN

CHARACTERISTICS

Length overall .... 15'-11"
Beam .... 7'-11"
Hull depth .... 31"
Hull weight (approx.) .... 700 lbs.
Average passengers 4-6
Cockpit size .... 6'-5"x6'-9"
Hull type: Twin hulls developed for sheet plywood planking.
Power: Twin outboard motors to 100 HP total.
Trailer: Designed for use with GLEN-L SERIES 1200/1800 boat trailer plans.

The **HELL CAT** features a very large cockpit with plenty of room to haul diving gear, passengers, etc. As with all the cats the optimum word is comfort with the space to spread out, and a ride that cannot be compared to any other type of boat you may have ridden in. The tough structure, proven in prototype testing, is built to take it. Using our complete PLANS and PATTERNS will allow you to build your own **HELL CAT** just the way it was designed.

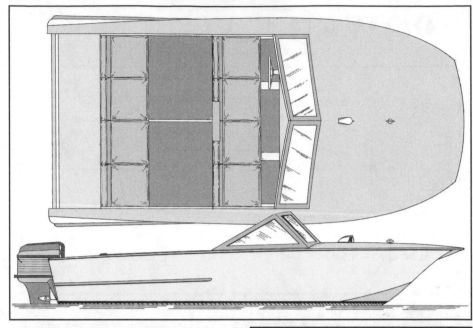

AQUA CAT

AN 18' POWER CATAMARAN OVERNIGHTER

CHARACTERISTICS

Length overall .... 18'-2"
Beam .... 8'-0"
Hull depth .... 33"
Hull weight (approx.) .... 850 lbs.
Average passengers 1-4
Height overall .... 5'-5"
Cockpit size .... 6'-5"x5'-1"
Sleeping capacity 2
Hull type: Twin hulls developed for sheet plywood planking.
Power: Twin outboard motors to 110 HP total.
Trailer: Designed for use with GLEN-L SERIES 2300/2800 boat trailer plans.

The **AQUA CAT** offers everything that the other cats offer... and more. Here, the wide beam of the boat provides room for a generous double bunk, plus room for a head and galley, making it ideal for cruising with the family. If you desire a very large open boat for diving or fishing, or for taking the gang sight seeing, the cabin can be omitted to make one huge cockpit nearly 11' long. Whichever way you build her, the **AQUA CAT** will stop them in their tracks, whether on the trailer or on the water.

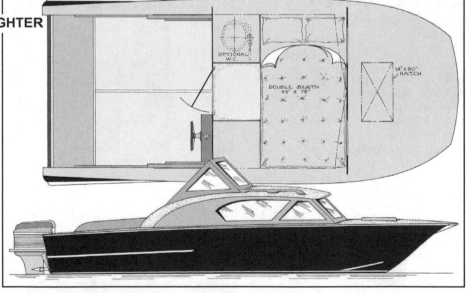

WILDCAT E-X-T SPORT &

CHARACTERISTICS - SPORT
Length overall .... 22'0" (*)
Beam .... 8'6"
Draft (hull) .... 13"
Hull depth max. .... 4'4"
Displacement .... 4500 lbs.
Boat weight (dry, approx. Ply or Alum)
.... 2200 lbs.
Fuel capacity .... 90 gals.
Cockpit length .... 14'8"
Cockpit width .... 7'6"
Cockpit depth .... 24"-27"
Recommended total HP:
(Twin 25" Extra Long Shaft Outbd)
.... 90-230
Trailer: Designed for use with GLEN-L
SERIES 2000/2800PC boat
trailer plans.

CHARACTERISTICS - CUDDY
Length overall .... 24'0"
Beam .... 8'6"
Draft (hull) .... 13"
Hull depth max. .... 4'4"
Displacement .... 5000 lbs.
Boat weight (dry, approx. Ply or Alum)
.... 2500 lbs.
Fuel capacity .... 100 gals.
Cockpit length .... 13'2"
Cockpit width .... 7'6"
Cockpit depth .... 24"-27"
Recommended total horsepower:
(Twin 25" Extra Long Shaft Outboards)
.... 100-260
Trailer: Designed for use with GLEN-L
SERIES 4000/6000PC boat
trailer plans.
(*) 20' or 24' options provided in plans

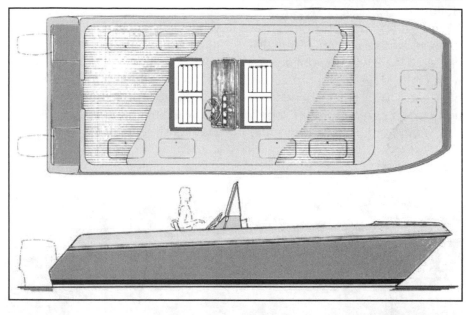

WILDCAT E-X-T CUDDY

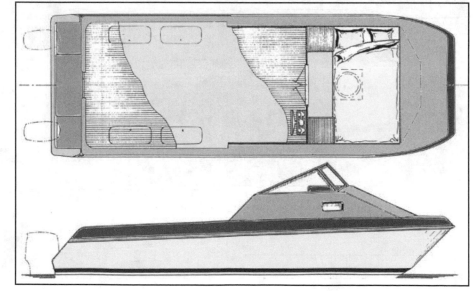

Now the do-it-yourself boatbuilder can save a bundle and still take part in the revival of the proven power catamaran concept. For their size, these boats offer the best combination of a smooth ride in rough seas at high speeds using modest power and minimal fuel.

The advantages of power catamarans result from reduced resistance due to less frontal area of the narrower twin hulls, and a cushion of air compressed within the tunnel that adds to lift for quick acceleration while softening the ride.

In addition, these boats are more inherently stable than monohulls, both at rest and underway. The slender v-bottom hulls minimize pounding. Tracking is straight and true at any speed without roll, yaw,

or lean, even when running before seas or with the wind abeam. Yet turns are tight, secure, and nearly flat even at speed.

Because beam is carried virtually to the bow, the self-bailing cockpit is huge, flat, and uncluttered. A step-over transom gate cut-out leads to a dive-swim step just above water-level. The result is a spacious sportfisher, a super-stable dive platform, or efficient user-friendly workboat.

Hull construction is especially intended for the amateur - either epoxy-glued fiberglass-covered sheet plywood or welded aluminum. Rugged but lightweight bulkhead-type frames feature integral cross beams for strength. FULL SIZE PATTERNS are provided for all hull-forming backbone members and frame contours - no lofting required. Sequential instructions cover all aspects of the design and include hull material listings.

Wildcats Continued...

Build our 22' WILDCAT E-X-T SPORT if an open-cockpit center console appeals to you. Plans include 20' or 24' length options as well. Or if you want the protection of a cabin with sitting headroom that sleeps two on a 4' x 7' berth with space under for a head and cabinets both sides, build our 24' WILDCAT E-X-T CUDDY; it features an express-type windshield control station. Speeds for either with twin outboard motors of listed power will approximate 25 MPH at lower ratings and 50+ MPH at the higher ratings.

AVAILABLE FOR THESE DESIGNS:
- Plans & Patterns
- Bronze Fastening Kit
- Fiberglass Kit
See Price List

BEAR-CAT CUDDY &
BEAR-CAT SPORT

These longer, wider power cats allow greater displacement, tankage, storage, and load-carrying ability than our WILD-CAT design. Besides the extra room, the wider beam only improves upon the superior qualities of power cats, especially stability. Based on v-bottom planing hulls, these boats can also absorb higher horsepower motors. Twin outboards at the higher ratings can provide speed into the 50 MPH range. Even at the minimum power ratings, planing speeds will range in the mid-to-upper 20's depending on all-up weight.

Construction methods in sheet plywood or welded aluminum use amateur-proven techniques similar to our WILDCAT design, but with beefier scantlings in keeping with the boat's greater heft. Full-size patterns are provided for all hull-forming backbone members and frame contours - lofting is not required. Nor are any special or esoteric building techniques. Instructions with hull material listings cover all aspects of the project, and include a fastening schedule with plywood hulls.

BEAR-CAT SPORT features a huge open- cockpit center-console arrangement with raised casting platform at the bow. Plans include length options of 24'6", 25'6", and 27'10".

BEAR-CAT CUDDY features a cabin with walk-around side decks and express-type windshield control station. In the cabin is sitting headroom above the 6'9" x 4' double berth and space for a portable head.

NOTE: When you buy the CUDDY version, you also receive a complete set of the SPORT plans as well.

AVAILABLE FOR THIS DESIGN:
- **Plans & Patterns**
- **Bronze Fastening Kit**
- **Fiberglass Kit**
  See Price List

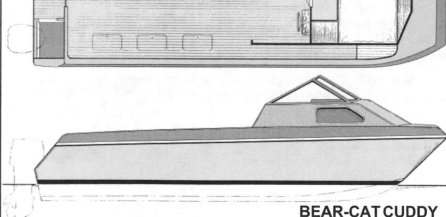

BEAR-CAT SPORT

BEAR-CAT CUDDY

CHARACTERISTICS	Sport	Cuddy
Length overall	25'6"(*)	27'10"
Beam	10'0"	10'0"
Draft	14"	14"
Hull depth max.	5'1"	5'1"
Displacement	6000 lbs.	6700 lbs.
Boat weight ply. approx.	3000 lbs.	3400 lbs.
Boat weight alum. approx.	3200 lbs.	3650 lbs.
Fuel capacity	150 gals.	170 gals.
Cockpit size (nominal)	20' x 9'	16 1/2' x 9'
Cockpit depth	28" - 32"	28" - 32"
Recommended total HP (Twin outboards, 25" shaft required)	150-400	180-450

(*) 24'6" or 27'10" options provided in plans

ROUSTABOUT

A 17' DEEP VEE RUNABOUT

CHARACTERISTICS

Length overall .... 17'-0"
Beam .... 7'-6"
Hull draft .... 11"
Hull depth .... 3'-4"
Hull weight (approx.) .... 700 lbs.
Average passengers 4-6
Cockpit size .... 10'-3"x 6'-6"
Hull type: Full length, high deadrise, deep vee hull developed for sheet plywood planking.
Power: Single or twin outboard motors to 135 HP, or single inboard/outboard drive to 650 lbs. maximum.
Trailer: Designed for use with GLEN-L SERIES 1200/1800 boat trailer plans.

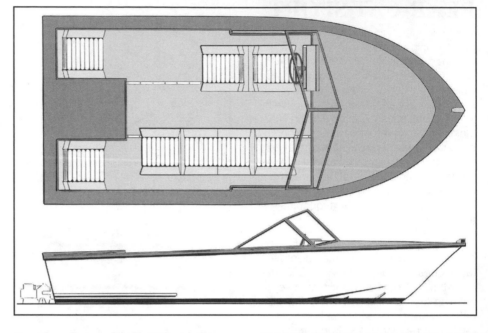

Here's a modern styled runabout capable of fulfilling a variety of your water sport needs in admirable fashion. Whether you want to fish, water ski, or venture offshore, the **ROUSTABOUT** can take it all in stride. This is due to her full length deep vee hull which provides a comfortable ride even in late afternoon chops. With her reverse curve at the chine in the aft sections, she's always stable and dry. For easy handling, we've incorporated a bulbous section into the keel and lift strakes are provided.

There are several power options. Single or twin outboards, or a single inboard coupled to an outdrive unit or vee drive are all detailed in the plans. For versatility, look at those lounge seats! There's two of them that will seat two people each, and they convert to form full length lounges for sun bathing. They can even be used for berths if you want to stay over at your favorite fishing hole. A navy-type folding top can be added for protec-

tion from the elements. With that huge cockpit, there's plenty of room for all the gang and their gear.

COMPLETE PLANS include FULL SIZE PATTERNS for the stem, breasthook, and half-section patterns for each of the frames and transom. Includes instructions, Bill of Materials, and Fastening Schedule.

AVAILABLE FOR THIS DESIGN:
- **Plans & Patterns**
- **Bronze Fastening Kit**
- **Fiberglass Kit**
See Price List

DRAGONFLY A 17' 6" GARVEY FLATS BOAT

CHARACTERISTICS

Length overall .... 17'-6"
Beam .... 7'
Hull depth midship .... 21"
Average passengers 3
Hull weight (approx.) .... 550 lbs.
Displacement ....6" @ 1850 lbs.
Cockpit size .... 42" x 54"
Power: Outboard motors 40-60 HP for normal use: 135 HP maximum.
Hull type: Garvey, developed for sheet plywood planking with flat bottom aft and vee forward.
Can the hull be extended or shortened? No. We also do not recommend increasing the beam.
Trailer: Designed for use with GLEN-L SERIES 1200/1800 boat trailer plans.

COMPLETE PLANS include Instructions, Fastening Schedule, Bill of Materials, Stitch-N-Glue Manual, plywood utilization drawings, full dimensional planking layouts, and PATTERNS for transom, bow, form, deck crown, and knee.

The Dragonfly is a garvey-type hull that is built from plywood by the Stitch and Glue method. A garvey hull with a squared transom bow provides more room than conventional hulls. With the deck recessed slightly below the sheer, a roomy play and work area results. Plenty of walk-around room for fishing, whatever type you're after. Yet when traveling, you sit in a spacious cockpit protected by a windscreen.

The hull is sheet plywood planking in standard 4' x 8' panels fabricated to shape by the simple and practical Stitch and Glue method. The sides and bottom are fully dimensioned and a complex building form is not needed. Lay out the sides and bottom on the plywood, saw to shape, wrap the planking around the single building form, hold the seams together with wire stitches, and follow with fillets (glue) and reinforce with fiberglass laminates. Full-length longitudinal members are added to further stiffen the hull. A proven, easy to build method attested to by the many first time amateurs that have used the procedure.

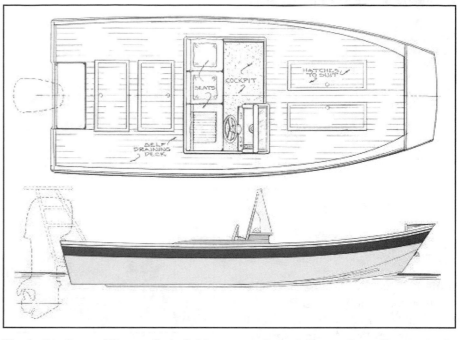

The hull bottom of Dragonfly is flat in the aft section going into a moderate vee forward. This provides maximum buoyancy, and this boat can get to those shallow areas in the backwaters and slither over areas that most vee bottoms can't navigate. These hulls are remarkably stable; no severe rocking from side to side when moving across the boat. Plus, a stable casting platform allows the angler to concentrate on casting rather than on balancing.

AVAILABLE FOR THIS DESIGN:
- **Plans & Patterns**
- **Stitch & Glue Kit**
- **Fiberglass Kit**
- **Stitch & Glue DVD**
See Price List

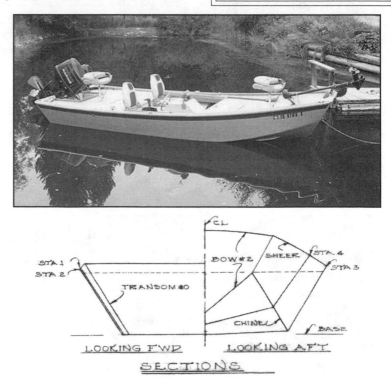

SECTIONS

FLATS FLYER
AN 18-1/2' FLORIDA FLATS BOAT

CHARACTERISTICS

Length overall .... 18'6"(*)
Beam .... 7'6"
Bottom width .... 7'0"
Hull draft .... 6"-7"
Hull depth - fore/aft .... 27"/24"
Cockpit size: 7'3" x 5'2" x 15" deep
Average passengers .... 2 - 3
Hull weight (dry/approx.)800-900 lbs.
Displacement at 7" draft.... 1980 lbs.
Fuel capacity .... 40 gals.
Horsepower range .... 50-175(**)
Trailer: Designed for use with GLEN-L
          SERIES 2500/2800 boat trailer
          plans.
(*) 17'6" & 19'9" hull length options
also in plans
(**) 20" or 25" shaft lengths optional

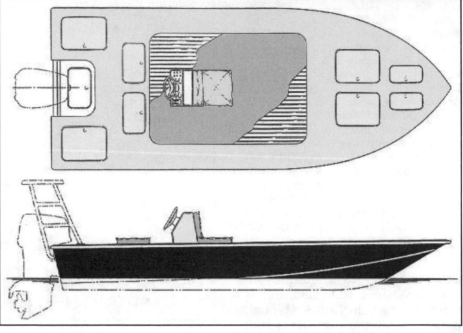

If the high cost of factory-built flats boats is crimping your fishing style, then build our FLATS FLYER. You'll get a flats boat exactly the way you want it at a fraction of the cost and will rival production boats in many ways. For example, FLATS FLYER weighs hundreds of pounds less than typical fiberglass boats. Which means less draft, better access to skinny waters, easier poling, higher speeds with less power, more range, and better economy. While max-rated at 175 HP per the USCG method, most will find lower-rated motors more than ample. For example, a 75 will put you in the 40's, while a 100 HP (plus or minus a bit) can get you into the 50's depending on load.

Regardless of power, FLATS FLYER pops on plane in an instant without noise-inducing lift strakes. The vee-hull features a 25-degree chop-deflecting bow entry decreasing to a 5-degree transom dihedral for superior stability at rest or underway with minimal drag.

Because FLATS FLYER requires less flotation volume than glass boats (wood floats!), you get more volume for compartment capabilities. So there's plenty of space for anchors, batteries, coolers, dry storage, live wells, fish/crustacean wells, tackle, and more. And you can stow several 10' rods below the 14" wide gunnel decks.

Construction is specially intended for FIRST-TIME do-it-yourselfers. The strong, stiff, yet lightweight, sheet plywood hull is built over simple sawn wood frames from FULL SIZE PATTERNS to assure an accurate bottom. This TIME-PROVEN & FATIGUE-RESISTANCE form of construction is QUICK & EASY even if you are working alone.

No special tools or woodworking operations required! Exterior hull surfaces are covered later with epoxy/fiberglass for durability, superior appearance, abrasion resistance, and reduced matinenance.

AVAILABLE FOR THIS DESIGN:
- **Plans & Patterns**
- **Bronze Fastening Kit**
- **Fiberglass Kit**
See Price List

Plans include FULL SIZE PATTERNS for all backbone members such as frames, stem, and transom - NO LOFTING REQUIRED! Plans also include SEQUENTIAL INSTRUCTIONS covering all aspects of the project, PLUS hull material listing and fastening schedule.

PARTY BOAT A 20' OR 22' DECK BOAT

CHARACTERISTICS

Length overall .... 20'-6" or 22'-4"
Beam .... 8'-3"
Hull depth .... 3-8"
Hull weight (approx.) .... 1500 lbs.
Displacement @designed
waterline .... 3100 lbs.
Length, seat bk to seat bk: .... 13'-9"
Cockpit Width, max .... 7'
Passengers 8
Hull type: Vee bottom 15° hard chine hull developed for sheet plywood.
Power: Outboard power: Single 20" Single or twin outboard motors; long or extra-long shaft for single, extra-long for twins. Optional power stern mounted inboard/outboard, v-drive or jet pump optional but not detailed.
Trailer: Designed for use with GLEN-L SERIES 5000/6000 boat trailer plans.

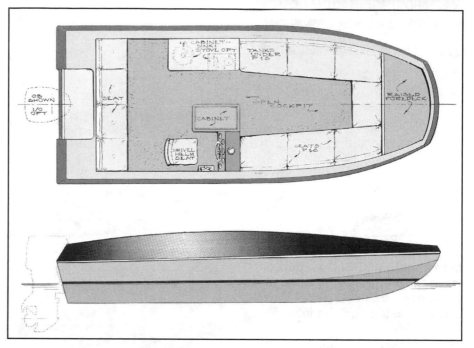

PARTY BOAT, deck boat, fun boat, call it what you will. It's a spacious wide open cockpit sitting atop an efficient hull. Pack it with passengers and take off to a remote area for picnics. Tow water skiers? Right on, and there is plenty of room for kibitsing passengers. Fishing? Sure, add a trolling motor and equip the bow deck with a chair and you're set up for some wicked fly, bass or walleye chasing... and catching.

The interior layout shows cabinetry that can contain sink, stove, and ice box. The layout is versatile; the seats could be converted to berths, and with a canopy you have an overnighter. Or, modify the interior to suit the needs of your family.

The hull has a generous vee with flat area at the chine to cut down the spray on a windy day and stabilize the hull at rest. The full length 15 degree monohedron bottom assures flat running at all speeds and a soft ride when that afternoon chop kicks up. The forward deck area extends beyond the hull underbody to knock down spray and provide a roomy area for fishing or just plain relaxing.

The bottom is 3/4" thick reinforced with bulkhead type frames with vertical longitudinals between. And for ease of construction, the forward portion of the sheer is a patterned sawn harpin to eliminate bending wood around the curvature. This is a tough rugged hull. Power it with a total of 200 shaft horsepower and you'll hit speeds in the 35 mph range, or for economy, 65 HP will get you in the mid 20 mph range.

And the building should be well within the abilities of the average handy person. The complete plans include progressive written instructions, size, type, and number of fasteners to use at each junction is given and complete specifications

for the lumber and plywood. Plus full size patterns with each frame fully detailed simplifies the building even more; no lofting or dimensional layouts are required when you build the PARTY BOAT.

AVAILABLE FOR THIS DESIGN:
- **Plans & Patterns**
- **Bronze Fastening Kit**
- **Fiberglass Kit**
  See Price List

COMPLETE PLANS include FULL SIZE PATTERNS for stem, bulwark frames, transom knee and half-section patterns for the frames, bulkhead, harpin, foredeck and transom. Includes instructions, Bill of Materials and Fastening Schedule.

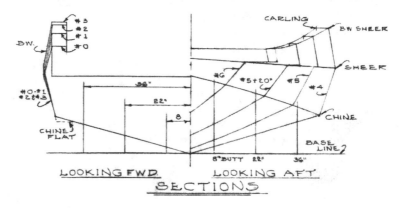

LOOKING FWD   LOOKING AFT

SECTIONS

TINY MIGHT

A 12' MID ENGINE RUNABOUT

BUILD IN PLYWOOD

CHARACTERISTICS

Length overall	12'-0"
Beam	5'-1"
Hull depth	24"
Hull weight (approx.)	250 lbs.
Average passengers	1-2

Hull type: Vee bottom, hard chine hull, developed for sheet plywood planking.

Power: Centrally located inboard motor to 300 lbs.

COMPLETE PLANS include FULL SIZE PATTERNS for stem, breasthook, and half-section patterns for the frames and transom. Includes instructions, Bill of Materials, and Fastening Schedule.

TINY MIGHT may aptly be called a marine "hot rod". Only 12' long, but this little boat packs a lot in a small package. The hull is light and compact for easy trailering and launching, but capable of towing skiers at a good clip. She turns on a dime and gives you change. When on a plane, the water breaks so far to the rear that you have the sensation of being entirely out of the water. Power comes from a compact mid-located engine for optimum performance. You'll think you are handling a classic road racing machine when you sit behind a peppy powerplant in your own **TINY MIGHT**. The aft seating location gives a great sensation of speed, and yet is located at the smoothest riding point in the boat. Plus, there's room for a friend... if he's not too timid.

AVAILABLE FOR THIS DESIGN:
- **Plans & Patterns**
- **Bronze Fastening Kit**
- **Fiberglass Kit**
  See Price List

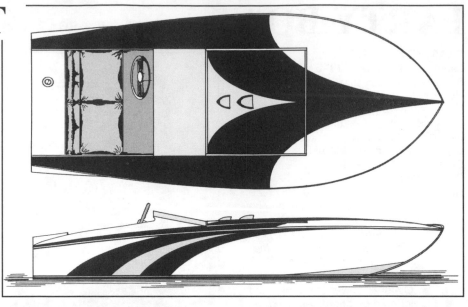

CRACKER BOX A 15' INBOARD SPEEDSTER

BUILD IN PLYWOOD

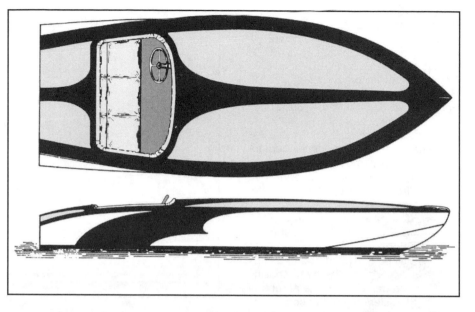

CHARACTERISTICS

Length overall .... 15'-0"
Beam .... 6'-0"
Hull depth .... 28"
Hull weight (approx.) .... 500 lbs.
Average passengers 1-2
Hull type: Vee bottom hard chine hull developed for sheet plywood planking.
Power: Centrally located inboard motor.
Trailer: Designed for use with GLEN-L SERIES 2300/2800 boat trailer plans.

It *looks* like a hot-rod; you can almost imagine a fox tail streaming behind. It's a boat that has a look that will draw spectators wherever she goes. But the **CRACKER BOX** offers more than good looks. It has been used in competition, achieving speeds in excess of 70 mph with a small block Chevy. When you stomp on the accelerator it's easy to imagine you've left the "pack" and are about to take the checkered flag. She can easily handle a skier and is an ideal boat for cruisin' down the main drag.

A mid-mounted inboard engine drives through a reliable and efficient propeller to really dig in and move out. The aft seat location makes the riding easy. The compact **CRACKER BOX** is easy to trailer and handle, too. This proven design can be built even if you're on a budget. You can do your own automotive motor conversion using components available from GLEN-L..

AVAILABLE FOR THIS DESIGN:
- **Plans & Patterns**
- **Bronze Fastening Kit**
- **Fiberglass Kit**
See Price List

COMPLETE PLANS include FULL SIZE PATTERNS for stem, breasthook, and half-section patterns for the frames and transom. Includes instructions, Bill of Materials, and Fastening Schedule.

SKI KING
A 15' INBOARD/DIRECT-DRIVE SKI BOAT

CHARACTERISTICS

Length overall .... 15'-0"
Length waterline .... 13'-9"
Beam .... 6'-0"
Maximum hull depth .... 33"
Depth at the transom .... 21"
Hull weight (approx.).............. 700 lbs.
Forward cockpit size .... 30" x 5'-6"
Aft cockpit size .... 4'-3" x 4'
Average passengers 2-4
Hull type: Vee bottom, developed for sheet plywood planking.
Power: Compact lightweight inboard from 45 hp to 100 hp, center mounted.
Trailer: Designed for use with GLEN-L SERIES 2300/2800 boat trailer plans.
Can the hull be extended or shortened? Yes. Up to 10% by re-spacing the frames from the aft end of the stem to the transom a proportional amount. We do not recommend increasing the beam.
Approx Speeds:
   50hp = 31 mph
   60hp = 33 mph
   75hp = 37 mph
   90hp = 39 mph

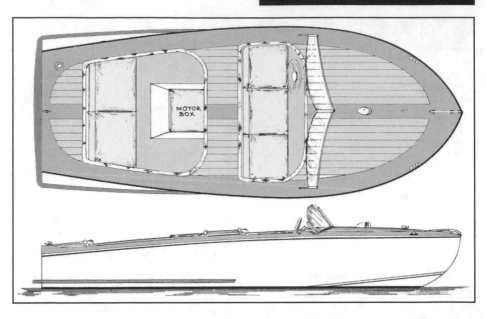

Back by popular demand... because of the interest expressed by web site visitors, we have brought her back.

The following copy appeared in our 1962 catalog:

SKI KING is a flashingly modern, high speed inboard utility for plywood planking. The conendrically developed vee bottom is fast and very stable. Note the adequate beam on this boat. Plenty of room for any type of boating pleasure and ideally suited for towing water skiers. Not a new untested design, but a proven boat in every respect

SKI KING can be powered with motors from 50 hp to 100 hp. The boat photographed clocked 38 mph with 85 hp. Converted automobile motors can be used. The Jeep is ideal and a Ford V8 could be used, however the shaft angle

will be very steep and the space will be cramped. The size of the motor is the important thing and in most motors the 4-cylinder jobs are short and will fit in the space provided.

Glen-L Marine has designed this hull especially for building by the amateur. Construction uses our special lock-in frame method that simplifies and makes this hull almost like a kit to build. All frames, the transom, breasthook, and stem are fully dimensioned, eliminating lofting that so often stops the amateur in his tracks. All frames, stem, motor stringers, motor installation and construction components are shown in detail. Since the original

hull was built by an amateur, we are able to furnish all of the details exactly as the hull was built. The plan set will enable you to build a hull that has more flare, and an appearance better than the average stock runabout of today. In addition she will show her heels to most of them when it comes to speed.

Beauty, speed, and performance are combined with special simplified building instructions and methods for the amateur builder.

This a great boat for those who like to tinker and innovate and would be an eye catcher wherever she went.

Complete Plans with fully dimensioned framework. Instructions include bill of materials and fastening schedule. NOTE: Full Size patterns not available.

AUDEEN
A *CLASSIC* MID ENGINE SKI BOAT

CHARACTERISTICS

Length overall .... 16'-3"
Beam .... 7'-0"
Hull depth .... 37"
Hull weight (approx.)............... 800 lbs.
Average passengers 1-4
Hull type: Vee bottom, hard chine hull, developed for sheet plywood planking.
Power: Centrally located inboard motor.
Trailer: Designed for use with GLEN-L SERIES 2300/2800 boat trailer plans.

COMPLETE PLANS include FULL SIZE PATTERNS for stem, breasthook, transom knee, and half-section patterns for the frames and transom. Includes instructions, Bill of Materials, and Fastening Schedule.

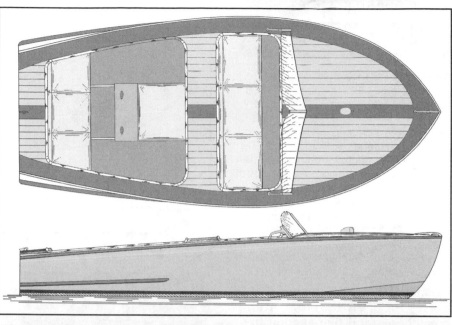

The **AUDEEN** features classic styling and rugged construction. This is a perfect ski and utility boat in one. Constructed from sheet plywood for lightweight and ease of construction, the hull is both dry and quick, and just the right size for easy trailering. The current interest in classic runabouts have led many builders to finish **AUDEEN** with highly varnished mahogany decks and cockpit trim. Her centrally mounted inboard is the type of installation favored by many of the professional skiing teams. Power can be just about any converted lightweight auto engine coupled with a time proven straight shaft set-up. The most common installation being a small block Chevy V-8.

AVAILABLE FOR THIS DESIGN:
- Plans & Patterns
- Bronze Fastening Kit
- Fiberglass Kit
See Price List

HOT ROD

A 17' INBOARD SKI BOAT

BUILD IN PLYWOOD

CHARACTERISTICS

Length overall .... 16'-6"
Beam .... 6'-11"
Hull depth .... 28"
Hull weight (approx.)............... 600 lbs.
Average passengers 2-4
Hull type: Vee bottom hard chine hull de-
veloped for sheet plywood
planking.
Power: Inboard, stern mounted engine
driving through a vee drive, 800
lbs. maximum.
Trailer: Designed for use with GLEN-L
SERIES 2300/2800 boat trailer
plans.

**COMPLETE PLANS include FULL
SIZE PATTERNS for stem,
breasthook, and half-section patterns for the frames and transom.
Includes instructions, Bill of Materials, and Fastening Schedule.**

The **HOT ROD** is a tough boat intended
for speed. It has been used in competition and scored a string of successes.
Because of its rugged construction, the
HOT ROD always comes back for more.
She is an excellent ski boat as well. Pack
a big engine (under 1000 lbs.) and connect to a reliable v-drive system, and the
prop will really dig in and move out. While
not designed for rough waters, your **HOT
ROD** is still a safe boat when handled
within the limits of its design.

Glen-L has engineered this hull for amateur construction. With the FULL SIZE
PATTERNS there is no reason to put off
building your own classic drag boat.

AVAILABLE FOR THIS DESIGN:
- **Plans & Patterns**
- **Bronze Fastening Kit**
- **Fiberglass Kit**
See Price List

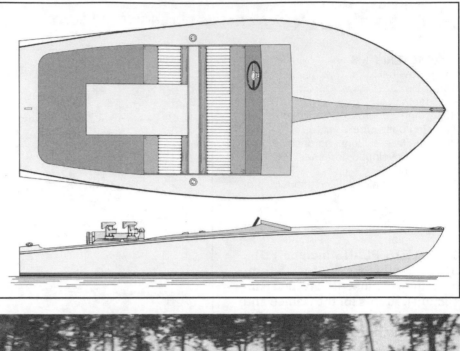

160

MIST MISS

A *CLASSIC* INBOARD RUNABOUT

BUILD IN PLYWOOD

CHARACTERISTICS

Length overall .... 18'-2"
Beam .... 7'-1"
Hull depth .... 3'-2"
Hull weight (approx.).............. 850 lbs.
Average passengers 4-6
Hull type: Vee bottom hard chine hull developed for sheet plywood planking.
Power: Centrally located inboard motor.
Trailer: Designed for use with GLEN-L SERIES 2300/2800 boat trailer plans.

COMPLETE PLANS include FULL SIZE PATTERNS for stem, breasthook, and half-section patterns for the frames and transom. Includes instructions, Bill of Materials, and Fastening Schedule.

The **MIST MISS** is a husky, practical inboard utility runabout with traditional styling reminiscent of classics of the past. Sit in her comfortable cockpit, protected by a fixed windshield. When you push the starter button and ease away from the dock, you will be the envy of all. Pull back on the throttle and give her the gun, she instantly responds; up on a plane and away, with the pilings flying by like a picket fence. The generous vee cushions the ride and the generous flare flattens the spray, making for a dry, safe boat.

MIST MISS can be powered with just about any converted automotive engine, coupled to a marine transmission and straight shaft. Since the motor is directly over the center of bouyancy, changes in the weight of the motor do not affect the trim.

AVAILABLE FOR THIS DESIGN:
- **Study Plans**
- **Plans & Patterns**
- **Bronze Fastening Kit**
- **Fiberglass Kit**
See Price List

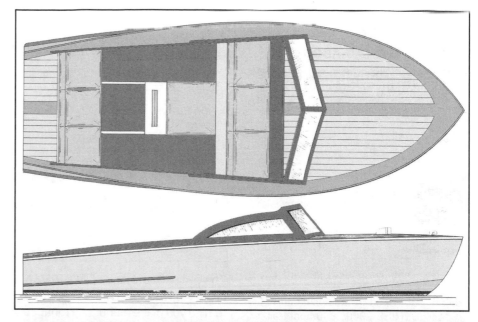

BONANZA

A 17' INBOARD RUNABOUT

BUILD IN PLYWOOD

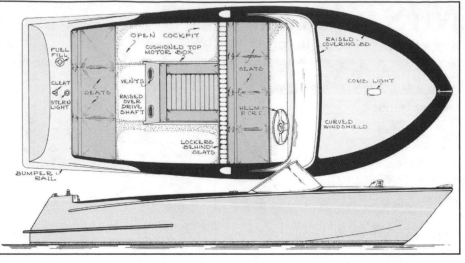

CHARACTERISTICS

Length overall .... 17'-0"
Beam .... 6'-11"
Hull depth .... 35"
Hull weight (approx.).............. 850 lbs.
Average passengers 4-6
Hull type: Double curvature bottom with hard chine for double diagonal plywood planking. Sides developed for sheet plywood planking.
Power: Centrally located inboard motor to 900 lbs.
Trailer: Designed for use with GLEN-L SERIES 2300/2800 boat trailer plans.

COMPLETE PLANS include FULL SIZE PATTERNS for stem, breasthook, chine blocking, and half-section patterns for the frames and transom. Includes instructions, Bill of Materials, and Fastening Schedule.

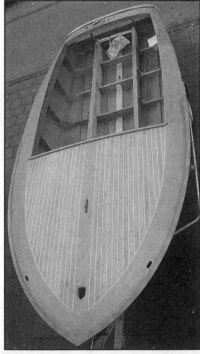

The distinctive styling of **BONANZA's** clipper bow and raked transom may remind you of the mahogany runabouts of the 50's. But she's more than a pretty face. The hull design incorporates the easy riding bulbous forefoot and reverse wave-dampening curve along the chine that we use on many of our large, high speed cruising yachts. Her shapely bottom is formed using double diagonal plywood in which two layers of 1/4" plywood are applied in strips. Sides are applied in sheets of 1/4" plywood.

The motor is mounted in the center; the type of installation preferred by professional skiers. The reliable straight shaft inboard can be any automotive conversion, with great performance possible using a readily available small block Chevy.

For those who want something more *conventional*, the plans detail a straight transom. But who wants to be conventional. Add a mahogany deck and plush seating and start cruising your local aquatic boulevard. The un-conventional **BONANZA** will stand out from the crowd. She's a classic dreamboat that you can have for a non-classic price. Start building now and be ready for next season.

THUNDERBOLT
A 17' INBOARD SKI BOAT

CHARACTERISTICS

Length overall .... 17'-3"
Beam .... 6'-11"
Hull depth .... 25"
Hull weight (approx.).............. 650 lbs.
Average passengers 2-4
Hull type: Vee bottom with flaring sides that act as anti-trip chines. Developed for sheet plywood planking.
Power: Inboard, stern mounted engine driving through a v-drive.
Trailer: Designed for use with Glen-L Series 2300/2800 boat trailer plans.

COMPLETE PLANS include FULL SIZE PATTERNS for stem, breasthook, and half-section patterns for the frames and transom. Includes instructions, Bill of Materials, and Fastening Schedule.

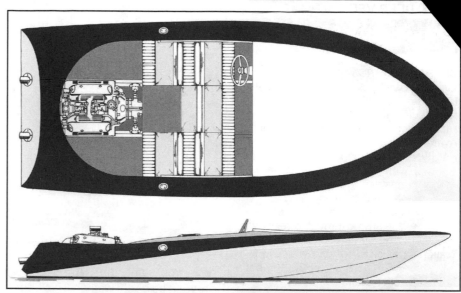

The **THUNDERBOLT** is a boat designed for one thing, speed. Two brothers on the Australian racing circuit held three gold cups with their **THUNDERBOLT**, equipped with a big block Chevy. You can use her for dragging, ski towing, or just plain old getting out and going fast.

The appearance of the **THUNDERBOLT** is impressive. The plans show a unique slanted transom as standard, with details for an optional vertical transom if preferred. All of the details are provided for the building with step-by-step photos of the actual construction of the prototype. The motor is mounted at the stern of the boat and connected to a v-drive to maintain the proper hull balance. The motor in this type of boat is usually left exposed and a good amount of chrome plate and paint used to enhance its appearance.

AVAILABLE FOR THESE DESIGNS:
- **Plans & Patterns**
- **Bronze Fastening Kit**
- **Fiberglass Kit**

See Price List

DESPERADO
AN 18' OR 19' PERFORMANCE INBOARD OR OUTBOARD SKIBOAT

CHARACTERISTICS

Length overall .... 18'0" or 19'0"
Beam .... 7'10"
Depth (max.) .... 2'6"
Weight (approx.) .... 800 lbs.
Power (outboard max.) ..... 190/205 HP
Trailer: Designed for use with Glen-L Series 2300/2800 boat trailer plans.

This stylish high-performance ski runabout has enough depth for peace of mind along with the comfort of a beamy deep-v hull that - unlike most ski boats - actually rides well. The vee at the bow is a wave-splitting 24°, blending in to 15° at the transom. Integral lift strakes make for a quick hole shot, while knocking down spray and adding control in the process. You can power with a single I/O, or one or two outboards.

There's plenty of seating and space in the cockpit. The arrangement shown is only a suggestion - you can vary it to suit your needs. For strength and durability, construction is over five sawn frames reinforced by stringers that stay in the boat as part of the simple building jig. Yet assembly is easy, quick, lightweight, low cost, and suitable even for first-timers. Sheet plywood planking totals 1/2" on the bottom and 3/8" in the sides. Fiber-

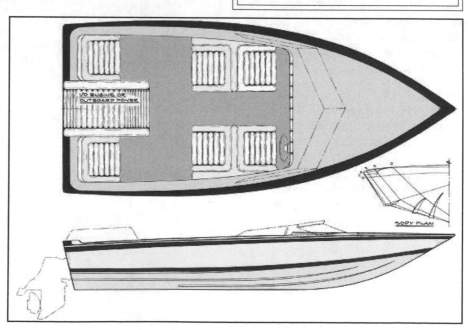

glass sheathing is used on the exterior for low maintenance, added durability, and a quality appearance.

Plans include instructions, material listing, fastening schedule, and FULL SIZE PATTERNS.

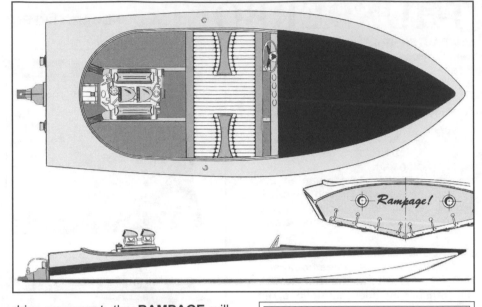

...CTERISTICS

Length overall	18'-0"
Beam	7'-1"
Hull depth	23"
Hull weight (approx.)	750 lbs.
Average passengers	2-4

Hull type: A 12° deep deadrise bottom with lift strakes and flaring topsides. Developed for sheet plywood planking.

Power: Inboard, stern mounted engine driving through a vee drive or jet pump.

Trailer: Designed for use with GLEN-L SERIES 2300/2800 boat trailer plans.

COMPLETE PLANS include FULL SIZE PATTERNS for stem, breasthook, and half-section patterns for the frames and transom. Includes instructions, Bill of Materials, and Fastening Schedule.

This low profile inboard features a full 12° vee bottom that flattens out bumps in the water like a steam roller over hot asphalt! The lift strakes on the bottom of the **RAMPAGE** are just like the ones proven on the hot competition ocean racing boats which make all the headlines. They give you a flat, dry ride with easy steering, besides letting you get out of the hole like buckshot out of the barrel.

Designed specifically for use with jet pump units, the **RAMPAGE** makes an ideal ski boat for the whole family. Unlike most flat bottom ski boats, you can stay out when a little breeze kicks up, because this beauty can take it in stride. The sides feature a broad flare which is carried all the way aft for good turning ability and safety. Plus, there's plenty of beam which means more room inside than similar sized boats.

The radiused cockpit makes an ideal showcase for your motor; the plans include options for a straight cockpit if you desire. For those who want a vee drive, full details for the installation of this unit are provided on the plans and in the instructions. Whichever type of

drive you want, the **RAMPAGE** will prove to be a real winner. This boat is ruggedly built, but not hard to build. As with our other boats in this category, the motor stringers are used as the building form which makes setting-up easy and accurate.

TORNADO

AN 18' INBOARD SKI BOAT

BUILD IN PLYWOOD

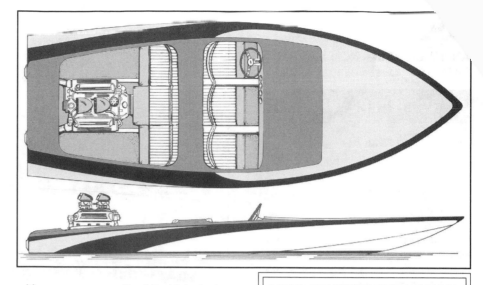

CHARACTERISTICS

Length overall .... 18'-6"
Beam .... 7'-0"
Hull depth .... 20"
Hull weight (approx.).............. 725 lbs.
Average passengers 1-4
Hull type: Vee bottom with flaring sides that act as anti-trip chines. Developed for sheet plywood planking.
Power: Inboard, stern mounted engine to 800 lbs. driving through a vee drive.
Trailer: Designed for use with GLEN-L SERIES 2300/2800 boat trailer plans.

COMPLETE PLANS include FULL SIZE PATTERNS for stem, breasthook, and half-section patterns for the frames and transom. Includes instructions, Bill of Materials, and Fastening Schedule.

The **TORNADO** is for the person with a yen to show his transom to the rest of the crowd. Put your super hot power plant or even a healthy stocker in the **TORNADO** and you have the perfect mating for the man who likes speed over the water.

The sleekness of the **TORNADO** is obvious in the lines. A low profile with a healthy beam and adequate length to provide stability at the higher speeds. The sides carry a generous flare back to the transom for safety on turns. Near the transom, however, the sides of the boat virtually disappear as the deck and sides form a smooth curving tumblehome to the crown of the deck. The low cowl with the "buckets" for the driver and passengers further carry through the clean lines. The motor, the pride of the fast boat enthusiast, is exposed and best equipped with chromed and polished appendages.

The engine in the **TORNADO** must be stern mounted and is usually connected to a vee drive that overdrives the propeller. She is ruggedly constructed but relatively simple to build. The construction is carried through

with our proven method that interlocks the motor stringers with the frames. In this type of construction, the motor stringers *are* the building form.

AVAILABLE FOR THIS DESIGN:
- **Plans & Patterns**
- **Bronze Fastening Kit**
- **Fiberglass Kit**
See Price List

BASS

NATION BASS &

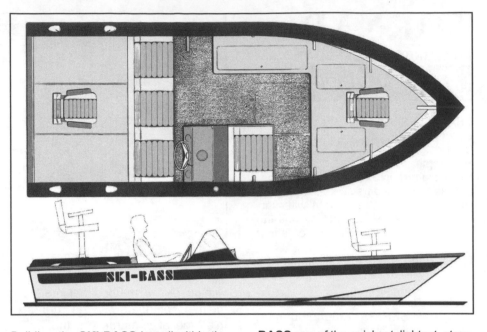

CHARACTERISTICS

Length overall .... 18'-0"
Beam .... 7'-4"
Hull draft .... 10"
Hull depth .... 34"
Hull weight (approx.)............... 800 lbs.
Average passengers 1-4
Cockpit size .... 12'-10"x 6'-2"
Hull type: Full length, deep vee hull developed for sheet plywood planking.
Power: Single long shaft outboard motor to 175 HP, or single inboard engine driving through an outdrive or jet not to exceed 750 lbs. Trim tabs recommended for high speed use.
Trailer: Designed for use with GLEN-L SERIES 2300/2800 boat trailer plans.

COMPLETE PLANS includes FULL SIZE PATTERNS for the stem, breasthook, and half-section patterns for each of the frames and transom. Includes instructions, Bill of Materials, and Fastening Schedule.

The evolution of the American bass boat is carried one giant step forward with our **SKI BASS** design. Here is a boat that doubles as a bass boat and a ski boat, all in one! The hull features a full length modified gull wing vee bottom for exceptional speed and ride, even in rough water conditions. A bulbous keel section splits choppy waters, while a reverse curvature at the chine gives the stability that fishermen require. Lift strakes on the bottom deflect spray and lift the hull onto a plane quickly, with minimal power.

You can power your **SKI BASS** with a single outboard or inboard engine using either an outdrive or jet drive to suit your special conditions. There is plenty of speed potential with any drive option, and with 25 gallons of fuel, you will be able to run for long periods before refuelling. Special features include fore and aft casting decks, seating for four, a large control console for locating electronic aids, and built-in wells for storage of rods, fish, bait, ice, and other gear. Because you build the boat yourself, you can fit out and customize your **SKI BASS** to suit your own special needs, for a real one-of-a-kind fishin' machine.

Building the **SKI BASS** is well within the skills of the average amateur. Our PLANS, with FULL SIZE PATTERNS, simplify the work and keep costs to a minimum. Strong, lightweight plywood hull construction coupled with a fiberglass cloth covering will make your **SKI**

BASS one of the quickest, lightest, strongest, and easiest to maintain bassboats available at any price. With all of its virtues as a bass boat, it's hard to believe the **SKI BASS** is one of the best waterski hulls around. Your friends, family, and bystanders will be amazed that you built this versatile dual-use boat.

AVAILABLE FOR THIS DESIGN:
- **Plans & Patterns**
- **Bronze Fastening Kit**
- **Fiberglass Kit**
See Price List

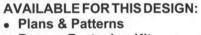

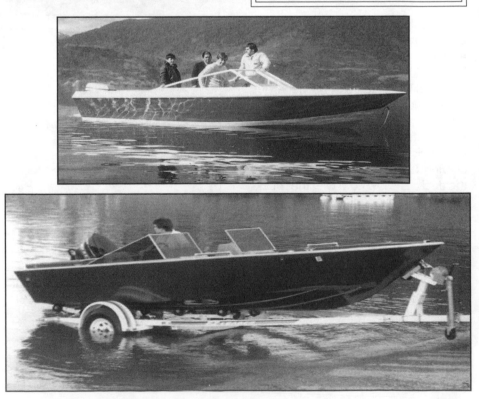

GENTRY

A 17' GENTLEMAN'S RUNABOUT

BUILD IN COLD-MOLDED WOOD

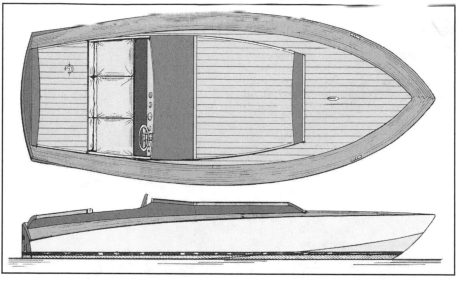

CHARACTERISTICS

Length overall .... 17'-4"
Beam .... 7'-2"
Hull depth midship .... 26"
Depth under hatch .... 35"
Hull weight (approximate) ...... 900 lbs.
Cockpit size .... 31" x 60"
Passengers .... 2 or 3

Hull Type: Cold-molded plywood with longitudinal veneers. Convex vee bottom with concavity along the chine and generous flaring sides forward blending into a barrel back styled transom tumble home aft.

Power: Centrally located inboard inline marine or auto conversion to about 5.6 liters or 350 cu. in.

Can the hull be extended or shortened? Yes. Up to 10% by re-spacing the frames from the aft end of the stem to the transom a proportional amount. We do not recommend increasing the beam.

Trailer: For use with GLEN-L SERIES 2300/2800 trailer plans.

COMPLETE PLANS and FULL SIZE PATTERNS include plans on all details of the construction, plus sequential Instructions, Bill of Materials, and Fastening Schedule. Full patterns are given for the deck beam arc, stem and breasthook with half section templates for each of the frames and transom showing both inner and outer contours and detailed joining members.

The GENTRY is a modern day adaptation of these classic boats. The mahogany hull and general appearance emulates its predecessors. A gleaming mahogany deck with outer finishing board, made from laminations of solid wood, attracts attention at the dock and underway. However, there are subtle changes made to improve the structure. The epoxy cold-molded hull is stronger and more durable than those of yesteryear. The old batten seam planking leaked like a sieve, that is, until the planking swelled, and even then a dry bilge was rare. Thus the boats were not practical to trailer as for the first day after launching, pumping was required to keep them afloat. GENTRY uses modern planking methods that eliminate this problem. The cold-molded hull planking uses laminates of diagonal plywood or solid wood veneers, covered with mahogany veneers all bonded with epoxy. This method eliminates the leaking problem and makes a superior hull.

We've also tweaked the hull design to suit modern conditions of use and lighter, more powerful, motors. The forward entry features a convex area along the keel, flattening out to a reverse curve at the chine; thus providing a softer, drier ride. The forefoot has been lifted to prevent the bow from hooking when crossing a wake or wavelet obliquely; a common tendency of the older boats at the top end of their speed range. In short, it may look like the old gentleman's runabout, but it's much more.

The construction method starts by mounting the frames on longitudinals that are used as motor stringers. The plans even detail the simple stand or building form that holds these stringers in place; complete with a bill of materials for the form.

The diagonal planking is relatively easy to apply, although more time consuming than sheet plywood. But the sexy, curving hull shape makes it worth the trouble. The outer mahogany planking along with the finishing board around the deck perimeter is also more time consuming than using sheet material, but is well within the range of the typical builder. Check the price of one of these boats, ready-made in one of the upscale boating magazines. They will usually be custom built if even available. After you recover from the sticker shock, realize that with time and effort, this beautiful mahogany craft can be built at a fraction of the retail price. Look at the photos and comments on the web site about the other mahogany runabouts. Now imagine yourself being surrounded by an admiring crowd listening to how you built it yourself.

AVAILABLE FOR THIS DESIGN:
- **Plans & Patterns**
- **Bronze Fastening Kit**
- **Fiberglass Kit**

See Price List

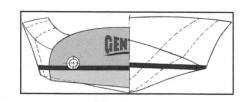

BISCAYNE 18 & 22

The BISCAYNE 18 & 22 classic mahogany runabout designs capture the look and feel of production runabouts built in the several years either side of 1940, and incorporate similar hull shapes accordingly. That means reverse-curved flaring topsides at the bow blending gracefully aft to a generous tumblehome at the transom. Such attractive contours are impossible to build using sheet plywood alone, yet easily reproduced using our carefully detailed building methods.

Also, notice the gentle reversed sheer profile lines of these designs. They incorporate enough "heft" within the specially-designed structure so you can create that soft "rolled edge" gunnel. That's a prime feature giving these boats the elegance missing in more "ordinary" runabouts of similar size. Couple this with the authentic "plumb" stem and careful cockpit/deck detailing and you have a boat with true classic authenticity.

But beyond the authentic styling of our Biscayne 18 & 22 is both a superior boat and one that will cost a fraction of a new replica or restored original. It's all due to our modern wood-epoxy "cold-molded" planking method that prevents leaking joints and flexing hulls that can detract from performance and longevity. If boats of the past had had such technology, they would have been built this way.

Using double diagonal ply/veneer planking, there are no rabbets to cut, no steam bending, no caulked seams, and no lofting. Bottom thickness totals 1/2" (four layers) with 3/8" topsides (three layers with the final appearance layer applied lengthwise). Planking is reinforced inside by a series of longitudinal stiffeners wrapped around a series of husky sawn wood frames and other backbone members. The result? A stiff, strong, durable yet lightweight hull that's free from rot and easy to maintain.

Power comes from a direct drive motor located amidships. We prefer a contemporary power plant over traditional motors that are sometimes still available because they are lighter in weight, more compact, more reliable, and offer higher output for their size. Usually gasoline motors are used, but diesel is an option as long as weight won't exceed that of the largest gasoline type.

However, we advise against overpowering these boats; practical speeds should be limited to the 30's and 40's. And if using longer in-line motors, and/or those that may be on the heavy side, we would recommend considering building the longer option hull included with both designs. This is done by respacing frames proportionately so appearance features are retained. Shortening these boats, however, is not recommended.

Plans with instructions aimed at the amateur craftsman include all the details along with

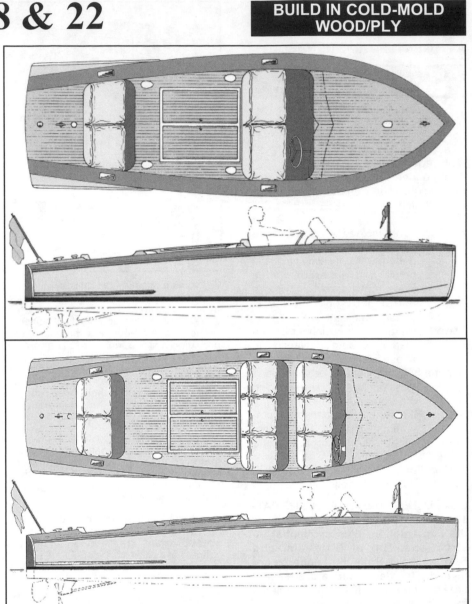

material listing and fastening schedule. Also provided are FULL SIZE PATTERNS for the sawn frame and backbone members so lofting is not required.

CHARACTERISTICS	Biscayne 18	Biscayne 22
Length overall	18'2"	21'10"
Length option	19'1"	22'11"
Beam	6'1"	6'8"
Draft w/prop	19"	21"
Freeboard fwd	2'2"	2'5"
Freeboard aft	1'4"	1'6"
Passengers	4	8
Motor type	4; V6	V6; V8
Motor cu in	120-200	220-330
Fuel capacity	25 gals.	40 gals.
Hull wt approx.	850 lbs.	1000 lbs.
Cockpit size - L x W - Forward	3'0"x4'8"	2'6" x 5'5"
Cockpit size - L x W - Aft	2'3"x3'11"	2'5" x 4'3"
Cockpit size - L x W - Mid	-	2'5" x 5'6"

Trailer: Designed for use with GLEN-L SERIES 2900/3800 trailer plans.

AVAILABLE FOR THESE DESIGNS:
- **Plans & Patterns**
- **Bronze Fastening Kit**
- **Fiberglass Kit**
See Price List

MONACO

19' CLASSIC INBOARD MAHOGANY RUNABOUT

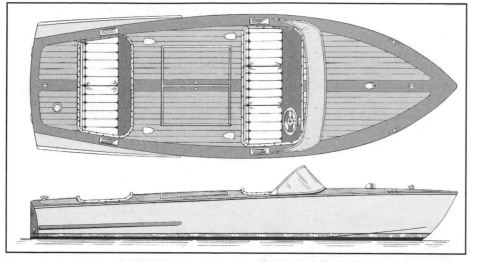

CHARACTERISTICS

Length overall	19'-4"
Beam	6'-7"
Hull depth midship	33"
Hull depth aft	27"
Hull weight (approximate)	950 lbs
Cockpit size:	
Forward	31"x62"
Aft	31"x48"
Passengers	5

Hull Type: Cold-molded veneers and plywood. Convex vee bottom with flaring sides and generous transom tumblehome.

Power: Centrally located inboard marine engine or automotive conversion, 250-350 cu. in.

Trailer: Designed for use with GLEN-L SERIES 2300/2800 trailer plans.

AVAILABLE FOR THIS DESIGN:
- **Study Plans**
- **Plans & Patterns**
- **Utility Supplement**
- **Bronze Fastening Kit**

See Price List

There is something about a classic mahogany runabout that attracts attention and admiration. The flaring concave sides flowing into a reverse barrel tumblehome at the transom, combined with the gleaming mahogany finish, accentuate the sleek flowing lines and conjure up the feeling of what *real* boating is supposed to be.

The **MONACO** is a modern version of these classic runabouts. Epoxy adhesives, encapsulation and advanced construction techniques have brought building one of these classics within the capabilities of most amateur builders. The hulls are built by cold-molding methods, plywood and thin veneers (or solid veneers) laminated over closely spaced framing members; a proven structurally sound concept that eliminates most of the maintenance and problems associated with yesteryear's methods.

The plans specify the underwater hardware required such as strut, rudder, shaft log, etc. All of these fittings, custom designed for inboard runabouts, are available directly from GLEN-L; searching for the proper hard to find fittings is not required.

Building is simplified by the use of longitudinal motor stringers that lock into each frame, a method pioneered by GLEN-L that assures accurate duplication of the hull lines. The complete PLANS provide drawings on all phases of the construction with numerous enlarged details, sections, Fastening Schedule, Bill of Materials, and step by step Instructions. FULL SIZE PATTERNS give templates for structural members and eliminate lofting or the use of complex dimensional layouts.

COMPLETE PLANS include FULL SIZE PATTERNS on all details of the construction, plus instructions, Bill of Materials, and Fastening Schedules. Full patterns are given for the stem, breasthook with half section templates for each of the frames and transom.

Optional Utility Version:

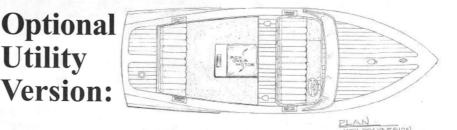

Now you can build the MONACO as an open utility to provide a large aft cockpit area. This provides more usable space for skiing, fishing or just moving around. Yet, the classic runabout styling is retained so you have the best of both worlds; appearance and more room. The aft cockpit is approximately 6' x 5'.

The plans for the two cockpit version of the MONACO have been revised by an Addendum sheet to illustrate the changes that are required to build the utility version of the MONACO. Alteration to the written instructions and Bill of Materials are also included. Order the Utility version in addition to the Plans & Patterns.

BARRELBACK 19

A 19' or 20' *CLASSIC* DOUBLE COCKPIT INBOARD BARRELBACK RUNABOUT

CHARACTERISTICS

Length overall	19'1"
Length option	20'1"
Beam	6'1"
Draft w/prop	17"
Freeboard fwd	2'3"
Freeboard aft	1'6"
Passengers	6
Motor type	4; V6, V8(*)
Motor cu in	150-290
Fuel capacity	30 gals.
Hull wgt approx.	875 lbs.
Cockpit size - L x W - Forward	2'9"x5'2"
Cockpit size - L x W - Aft	2'5"x5'2"
Trailer:	Designed for use with GLEN-L SERIES 2900/3800 trailer plans.

(*) 20'-1" length recommended if using V8. 265 cu. in. max for 19'-1" length.

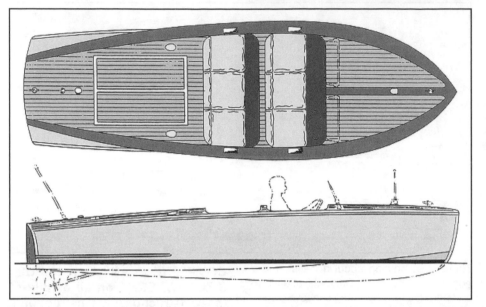

Nothing causes aficionados of classic mahogany runabouts to salivate more than the sight of the famous barrel-stern examples built by Chris Craft long ago. For those unfamiliar with the type, the stern is a semi-circular or elliptical like half a barrel, with a lovely seamless blending of the tumble-home topsides into the deck, side to side.

Of all the half-dozen or so sizes built by Chris Craft, the 19' Custom Runabout model produced between 1939 and 1942 seems to generate the most interest today. Yet with purportedly less than 400 ever produced, any remaining boats given care and restoration trade hands for big bucks, if at all.

But now you can build your own near-replica with our carefully-detailed Barrelback 19 design for a fraction of the cost and actually end up with a better boat. Beyond its authentic styling is a modern wood-epoxy hull that's honestly easier to build. Unlike old boats that suffer from leaking seams and flexing hulls, ours come out stiff, tight, and strong, yet lightweight.

Our system of double diagonal ply/veneer planking requires no rabbets to cut, no steam bending, no caulked seams, and no lofting, yet looks like the genuine article and is much easier to maintain.

Engine recommendations listed apply to the 19' option. But if you want to use a small block V-8 up to 290 cubic inches, we recommend building the boat at the 20' option included in the plans.

Plans with instructions aimed at the amateur craftsman include all the details along with material listing and fastening schedule. Also provided are FULL SIZE PATTERNS for the sawn frame and backbone members so lofting is not required.

AVAILABLE FOR THIS DESIGN:
- Study Plans
- Plans & Patterns
- Bronze Fastening Kit
- Fiberglass Kit

See Price List

KEY LARGO 19
A 19' or 20' *CLASSIC* DOUBLE COCKPIT INBOARD BARRELBACK RUNABOUT

CHARACTERISTICS

Length overall .... 19'1"
Length option .... 20'1"
Beam .... 6' 1"
Draft with prop .... 17"
Freeboard forward .... 2' 3"
Freeboard aft.............................. 1' 6"
Passengers 5
Hull weight (approx) .... 875 lbs.
Motor type .... 4; V6; V8 (*)
Motor (cu. in.)...................... 150-290
Fuel capacity .... 30 gals.
Cockpit size - L x W............ 10'6" x 5'2"
Hull wgt approx. .... 875 lbs.
Cockpit size - L x W - Forward 2'9"x5'2"
Cockpit size - L x W - Aft .... 2'5"x5'2"
Trailer: Designed for use with GLEN-L
            SERIES 2900/3800 trailer plans.
(*) 20'1" length recommended if using

Based on our proven Barrelback 19 hull, Key Largo features the added versatility of a big open cockpit forming what is better known as a "sport-utility" type runabout. Many prefer such an arrangement especially where watersports or fishing may be desired activities.

Additional benefits include easier motor access, room for everyone to move about, and space to carry skis, fishing gear, and such. Otherwise, construction methods and features are the same as our Barrelback 19, including that gorgeous barrelback stern and our proven "cold molded" wood/ply/veneer hull construction method well suited to the average do-it-yourself builder.

The results are a tight, stiff, strong, lightweight hull free of leaking seams and flexing joints. In other words, a boat both easier to build and superior to those of the past, all at a fraction of the cost of production replicas or restored originals. As we often say, had such technology been available in the past, this is the way boats would have been built then.

Plans with instructions aimed at the amateur craftsman include all the details, along with material listing and fastening schedule. Also provided are FULL SIZE PATTERNS for the sawn frame and backbone members so lofting is not required.

CUDDY SPORT
A 24' WALKAROUND DECK CUDDY CABIN SPORTFISHER

CHARACTERISTICS

Length overall (standard) .... 24'1"
Length waterline .... 20'8"
Beam .... 8'6"
Draft (hull) .... 14-1/2"
Hull depth (max) .... 4'7"
Displacement .... 4300 lbs.
Hull weight (approx.)............. 1300 lbs.
Fuel capacity .... 105 gals.
Headroom (cabin) .... 4'10"
Sleeping capacity 2

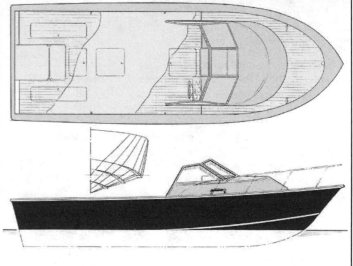

Here's a no-nonsense boat for anglers who want lots of room and total access around the boat, along with some overnight accommodations. An enclosed cabin includes a full-size v-berth with space for a head below. Yet there's a full-access recessed deck around the cabin outside. A windshield with side wings protects the helm from wind and spray, and the self-bailing aft cockpit is nearly 14' long.

A variable-angle deep-v hull smooths out the rough stuff with a 40+° v-entry leading aft to a stable 18-1/2° transom vee. Wide chine flats and two lift strakes per side keep her pointed ahead while assuring optimum performance. You can use I/O units to 1300 lbs., or single or twin outboards (25" shaft lengths for singles; 20" or 25" for twins). Other power systems (v-drives, jets, bracket-mounted outboards, etc.) may be suitable with minor modifications. Ample fuel capacity is available in any case.

Plywood hulls use 1/2" total bottom thickness and 3/8" on the sides. Aluminum hulls feature 3/16" bottoms and 1/8" sides. Plans include FULL SIZE PATTERNS for frame member contours, and include instructions, material listings, and fastening schedule (wood hulls).

AVAILABLE FOR THIS DESIGN:
- **Plans & Patterns**
- **Bronze Fastening Kit**
- **Fiberglass Kit**

TAHOE 19 & 23
19' TO 24' CLASSIC DOUBLE & TRIPLE COCKPIT INBOARD RUNABOUTS

Looking for a classic mahogany runabout in a more modern theme typical of runabouts built in the period from the mid 1950's through the early 1960's? Then look no further than our Tahoe 19 & 23 designs. They exude luxury and elegance together with authentic styling cues and hull forms similar to those from the leading domestic and European builders of the time.

Note their lean lines and trim profiles with generous "rolled funnel" deck edges, coupled to near-rakish elements such as forward-inclined transoms and forward-raked double curvature "clipper" bow profiles. These hull shapes also have even greater bow flare and sophisticated bottom shapes compared to boats of earlier decades, which result in the ability to accommodate larger motors and higher speeds.

Such hulls can't be planked with full sheets of plywood as such, and would be ugly if that were possible. While perhaps more complex as a result, their beauty is easy to reproduce using our modern wood-epoxy "cold molded" planking methods. The result is a hull free of leaking joints and flex that can detract from performance and longevity. In other words, a superior boat, but still at a fraction of the cost of a new production replica or restored original, assuming you could even find one.

With our "cold molded" epoxy/ply/veneer planking method, there are no rabbets to cut, no steam bending, no caulked seams, and no lofting. Bottom thickness totals 1/2" (four layers) with 3/8" topsides (three layers with the final appearance layer applied lengthwise). Planking is reinforced inside by a series of longitudinal stiffeners wrapped around husky sawn wood frames and related backbone members. The completed hull is stiff, strong, and durable yet lightweight, free from rot and easy to maintain.

These boats use a single direct-drive inboard motor located amidships. While gasoline power is typically used, diesel is an option as long as weight won't exceed that of the largest gasoline type.

However, we advise against overpowering these boats; speeds over 50 MPH should not be attempted at least without some trials and a backlog of experience with the boat first. If using longer "in-line"

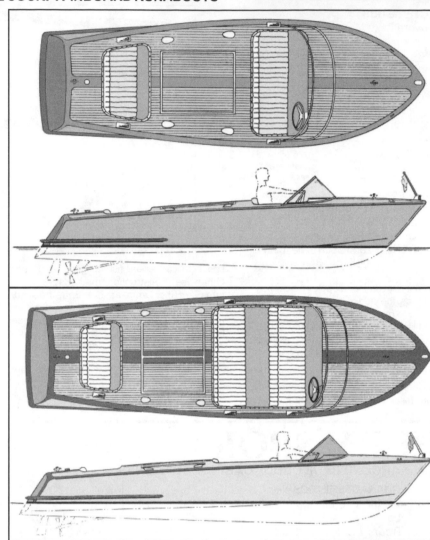

CHARACTERISTICS	Tahoe 19	Tahoe 23
Length overall	19'2"	22'9"
Length option	20'5"	24'0"
Beam	6'2"	6'9"
Draft w/prop	21"	22"
Freeboard fwd	2'2"	2'4"
Freeboard aft	1'4"	1'5"
Passengers	5	8
Motor type	V6; V8	V8
Motor cu in	260-330	300-360
Fuel capacity	30 gals.	40 gals.
Hull wgt approx.	850 lbs.	1000 lbs.
Cockpit size - L x W - FWD	2'9"x5'3"	6'1" x 5'8"
Cockpit size - L x W - Aft	2'4"x3'10"	2'4" x 3'11"
Trailer: For use with GLEN-L series 2900/3800 trailer plans.		

motors, and/or those that may be on the heavy side, we would recommend considering building the longer option hull included with both designs. Such a change is done by respacing frames proportionately so appearance features are retained. Shortening these boats, however, is not recommended.

Plans with instructions especially intended for the do-it-yourself craftsman include all the details along with material listing AND fastening schedule. Also provided are FULL SIZE PATTERNS for the sawn frame and backbone members so lofting is not required.

RIVIERA

20' CLASSIC INBOARD MAHOGANY RUNABOUT

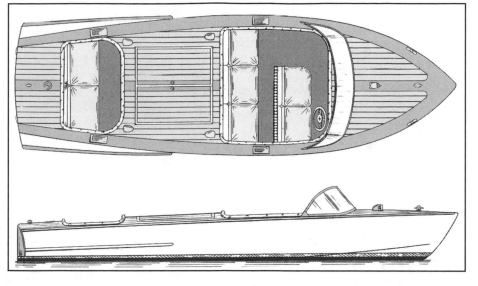

CHARACTERISTICS .... RIVIERA
Length overall .... 20'-3"
Beam .... 6'-7"
Hull depth midship .... 33"
Hull depth aft .... 27"
Hull weight (approximate) .... 1100 lbs.
Cockpit size:
    Forward .... 60"x 60"
    Aft .... 31"x 48"
Passengers 7
Hull Type: Cold-molded veneers and plywood. Convex vee bottom with flaring sides and generous transom tumblehome.
Power: Centrally located inboard marine engine or automotive conversion, 250-350 cu. in.
Trailer: For use with GLEN-L SERIES 2300/2800 trailer plans.

COMPLETE PLANS include FULL SIZE PATTERNS and all details of the construction, plus instructions, Bill of Materials, and Fastening Schedules. Full patterns are given for the stem, breasthook with half section templates for each of the frames and transom.

The RIVIERA is a larger version of our Monaco offering additional seating in the forward cockpit. This classically styled hull, frequently called a "gentleman's runabout", has the same mystique about it that makes the originals sought out by collectors, but at an affordable price.

This is a boat that allows the craftsman to shine. Many builders have gone to great lengths to give their boat the "look"; installing antique hardware and putting in extra time on finishes and other details. The results have drawn stares at boat shows from owners of antique boats and other lovers of traditional wooden boats.

The RIVIERA offers the best of traditional design but using lower maintenance contemporary construction techniques. The hull is built by cold-molding methods, plywood and thin veneers (or solid veneers) laminated over closely spaced framing members; a proven structurally sound concept that eliminates most of the maintenance associated with the methods used in the originals.

The plans specify the underwater hardware required such as strut, rudder, shaft log, etc. All of these fittings, custom designed for inboard runabouts, are available directly from Glen-L; searching for the proper hard to find fittings is not required.

Building is simplified by the use of longitudinal motor stringers that lock into each frame, a method pioneered by GLEN-L that assures accurate duplication of the hull lines. The complete Plans provide drawings on all phases of the construction with numerous enlarged details, sections, Fastening Schedule, Bill of Materials, and step by step Instructions. Full Size Patterns give templates for structural members and eliminate lofting or the use of complex dimensional layouts.

AVAILABLE FOR THIS DESIGN:
- **Study Plans**
- **Plans & Patterns**
- **Bronze Fastening Kit**
See Price List

BELLE ISLE 23

A 23' OR 22' CLASSIC TRIPLE COCKPIT INBOARD BARRELBACK RUNABOUT

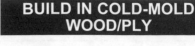

CHARACTERISTICS

Length overall .... 23'
Length option .... 22'
Beam .... 6' 8"
Draft with prop .... 21"
Freeboard forward .... 2' 5"
Freeboard aft .... 1' 6"
Passengers 8
Hull weight (approx) .... 1100 lbs.
Motor type V6; V8
Motor (cu. in.)..................... 220-360(**)
Fuel capacity .... 45 gals.
Cockpit size - L x W - Forward 2'6"x5'8"
Cockpit size - L x W - Mid ..... 2-5" x 5'8"
Cockpit size - L x W - Aft .... 2'5"x4'5"
Trailer: . For use with GLEN-L SERIES 2900/3800 trailer plans.
(**) 330 cu. in max for 22' length

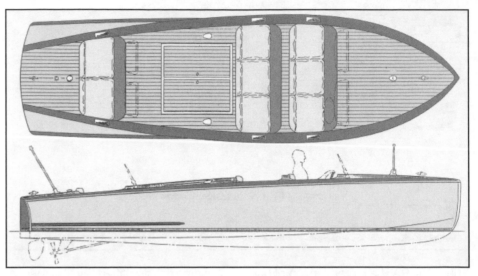

Belle Isle... our largest authentic barrelback design... uses the same type of amateur-proven construction as all our other classic mahogany runabouts and can be built in two different lengths. Husky full-length motor stringers and 1/2" bottom combine to allow for ample powering and load carrying ability.

For those unfamiliar with the type, the barrelback stern is a semi-oval or elliptical shape, like half a barrel, with a lovely seamless blending of the tumblehome topsides into the deck, side-to-side.

You can build your own Belle Isle for a fraction of the cost of restoring some questionable original or buying a new production replica, all while ending up with a better built boat. No rabbets, steam bending or lofting is required.

Beyond its authentic styling is a modern wood/epoxy hull that's actually well within the abilities of the first-time do-it-yourselfer. We say it will be a better boat because, when compared to boats of the past built with traditional planking methods, our boats are free of leaks, rot, high maintenance, flexing hulls, and other

problems resulting from such outdated planking methods. Our methods result in leak-free hulls that are stiff, strong, lightweight, durable, and easy to take care of without need for any caulking.

Power comes from a direct drive motor located amidships. Usually gasoline motors are used, but diesel is an option as long as weight won't exceed that of the largest gasoline type. However, we advise against overpowering the boat; practical speeds should be limited to the 30's and 40's.

Plans with instructions aimed at the amateur craftsman include all the details along with material listing, fastening schedule. Also provided are FULL SIZE PATTERNS for the sawn frame and backbone members, so lofting is not required.

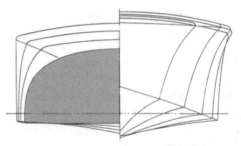

MONTE CARLO

A 24' 6" CLASSIC MAHOGANY RUNABOUT

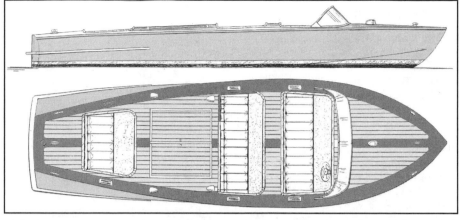

CHARACTERISTICS

Length overall	24'-6"
Beam	7'-6"
Hull depth midship	36"
Hull depth aft	27"
Hull weight (approx.):	1400 lbs.
Fwd cockpit	36" x 5'-10"
Center cockpit	36" x 5'-8"
Aft cockpit	36" x 40"
Opt. combined ctr/fwd cockp .	4'-9"x81"
Passengers	8

Hull Type: Cold-molded veneers and plywood. Convex vee bottom with flaring sides and a "barrel-back" transom tumblehome.

Power: Centrally located inboard marine engine or automotive conversion, 300-450 cu. in.

Can the hull be extended or shortened? Yes. Up to 10% by re-spacing the frames from the aft end of the stem to the transom a proportional amount. We do not recommend increasing the beam.

Trailer: For use with Glen-L Series 5000/6000 trailer plans.

COMPLETE PLANS plus FULL SIZE PATTERNS include all details of the construction, plus sequential instructions, Bill of Materials and Fastening Schedule. Full patterns are given for the deck beam arc, stem and breasthook with half section templates for each of the frames and transom showing both inner and outer contours and detailed joining members.

Sleek and long, a classic barrelback inboard 24' 6" runabout; that's the MONTE CARLO. As seen from the stern, the sides flow into the deck in a seamless circular arc resembling a half barrel. A styling typical of the finer Chris Craft of yesteryear and, when finished in gleaming mahogany, craft of this type were the choice of the affluent and the envy of others. Now you can build one of these craft by incorporating modern construction methods and have an improved hull for better performance.

Although shown as two cockpits forward and one aft, the design is such that the forward cockpits can be combined to form an 81" long single cockpit for lounge or other optional seating. Because the original craft of this type were planked and modern epoxy adhesives unknown, they leaked and had to remain in the water or the seams would open up. Our updated building method uses cold molded plywood/ veneers applied in laminations, completely glued and encapsulated with epoxy. The hull is virtually monocoque and thus, very strong and leak proof. Best of all, the building method is not difficult and eliminates the typical tedious cutting of rabbets and seam caulking that wouldn't stay put. Yet the final appearance is equal or better than the forerunners.

The construction is simplified by the use of full size patterns, detailed plans, instructions, bill of materials and fastening schedule. The frame patterns are not just the exterior contour of the frames furnished by most. Our patterns show inner and outer frame contours and the sizes and type of corner gussets and other reinforcing members shown in place. No need to loft or look on the plans for necessary dimensions, it's all drawn out on the patterns. Each frame is mounted on longitudinal motor stringer beams keyed to form the contour of the boat; a method pioneered during our many runabout construction projects over the years and emulated by many.

The propulsion is an in-line inboard marine motor or conversion, minimal of about 4.8 liters or 300 cu.in. and about 7.4 liters or 450 cu. in. displacement maximum. Powering for speeds much beyond 50 MPH is not recommended. The plans specify the underwater hardware required such as strut, rudder, shaft log, etc. All of these fittings, custom designed for inboard runabouts, are available directly from GLEN-L; searching for the proper hard-to-find fittings is not required.

> ### AVAILABLE FOR THIS DESIGN:
> - **Plans & Patterns**
> - **Bronze Fastening Kit**
> - **Fiberglass Kit**
> **See Price List**

MISS CHRIS
A 28' or 26' CLASSIC TRIPLE COCKPIT INBOARD RUNABOUT

Characteristics

Length overall	28'0"
Length option (*)	26'3"
Beam	7'0"
Draft w/prop	2'3"
Freeboard fwd	2'10"
Freeboard aft	1'9"
Passengers	8
Motor type	V8
Motor cu in	325-460
Fuel capacity	50 gals.
Hull wgt approx.	1000 lbs.
Cockpit size - L x W - Forward	6'6" x 5'6"
Cockpit size - L x W - Aft	2'6" x 4'0"
Cockpit size - L x W - Mid	2'5" x 5'6"
Trailer:	Designed for use with GLEN-L SERIES 5000/6000 boat trailer plans.

(*) Length option is done by respacing frames proportionately. These procedures are covered in the instructions, and the option comes automatically with the plans - no need to specify on your order.

You and your thrilled passengers will be hard pressed to tell the difference in our long and shapely Miss Chris design from the famous grand triple cockpit classics of the early 1930's. And while we've replicated the "look and feel" of these renowned craft, ours is a superior boat because it incorporates our stiff, strong and tight "cold molded" wood/epoxy construction methods.

Better yet, we've simplified the procedures so that any caring do-it-yourself woodworker can tackle the project without need for special skills or unique tools. Likewise, no difficult operations, such as steam bending, cutting rabbets, caulking seams, or lofting hull lines, are required.

Double diagonal planking using a combination of 1/8" wood veneers and plywood totals 5/8" thick on the bottom and 1/2" on the sides. Both are applied over closely-spaced longitudinal battens bent around the boat's frames and backbone members. On the sides, the final planking layer is applied in lengthwise strips emulating the look of genuine planking, but without the maintenance and structural weaknesses inherent with such obsolete past methods.

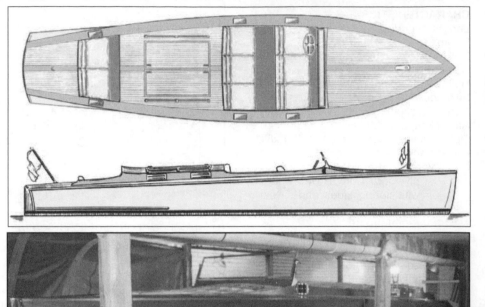

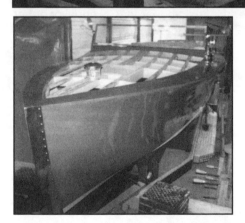

Husky motor stringers double as jig members to key in the frames for accuracy, and run nearly the length of the boat for strength. Speeds in the 40's are possible with the larger displacement automotive-type motor located amidships in the traditional in-line set-up.

Plans come with instructions, material listing, fastening schedule, and resource list, as well as FULL SIZE PATTERNS for frame, transom, and stem contours.

AVAILABLE FOR THIS DESIGN:
- **Plans & Patterns**
- **Bronze Fastening Kit**
- **Fiberglass Kit**

See Price List

RENEGADE
A 20' DEEP VEE SKI BOAT

BUILD IN PLYWOOD

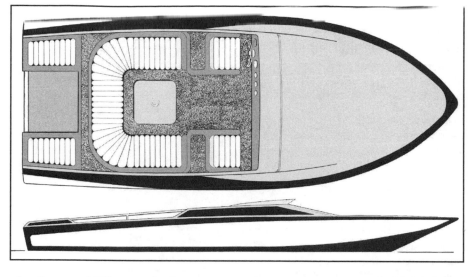

CHARACTERISTICS
Length overall .... 20'-8"
Beam .... 7'-11"
Hull depth .... 31"
Height overall .... 3'-4"
Hull weight (approx.)............... 1000 lbs.
Cockpit size .... 6'-6"x 9'-4"
Average passengers 2-4
Hull type: Full length deep vee with 12° deadrise bottom and flaring sides. Developed for sheet plywood planking.
Power: Outboard power: Single 20" or 25" long shaft motor to 220 HP. Twins may be used as long as the total weight does not exceed 500 lbs. Inboard power: Single stern mounted engine driving through a vee drive, jet pump, or outdrive, 1000 lbs. maximum combined weight.
Trailer: Designed for use with GLEN-L SERIES 2300/2800 boat trailer plans.

COMPLETE PLANS include FULL SIZE PATTERNS for stem, breasthook, transom knee, and half-section patterns for the frames and transom. Includes instructions, Bill of Materials, and Fastening Schedule.

A luxurious runabout... a mini daycruiser... a high-performance ski boat... call it what you will, because the **RENEGADE** is all these things wrapped up in a long, lean, rakish package of dynamite that will turn heads wherever you go. We specifically designed this boat for the big, powerful outboard motors available, *but* the **RENEGADE** can also be fitted out as an inboard equally well. In fact, you can couple a stern-mounted inboard to any of the popular drive methods whether it be a jet pump, vee drive, or an I/O unit. How's that for versatility! The plans and instructions cover all these possible variations.

The hull design of the **RENEGADE** is a full length deep vee type specifically modified to provide an ideal compromise for a smooth, comfortable ride,

plus the capabilities required to tow a gang of water skiers without bogging down. Longitudinal lift strakes assure quick acceleration out of the "hole" with a minimum of fuss and spray. Even with a load of passengers aboard in that big, luxurious cockpit, you'll still be amazed by the performance of your **RENEGADE**. The super strong, but lightweight, plywood construction means higher speeds with less power and greater economy, plus it makes the building of the boat well within the abilities of the average amateur.

So be the envy of your friends. Build your own **RENEGADE** using our comprehensive plans and full size patterns. Our sequential instructions allow you to build a boat that can equal *or* exceed the quality of similar stock boats, *and* you'll save a bundle in the process.

AVAILABLE FOR THIS DESIGN:
- **Plans & Patterns**
- **Bronze Fastening Kit**
- **Fiberglass Kit**
See Price List

KINGPIN

A 21' DEEP VEE SKI CRUISER

BUILD IN PLYWOOD

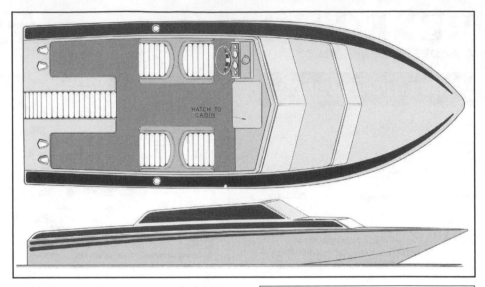

CHARACTERISTICS

Length overall .... 21'-0"
Beam .... 7'-11"
Hull depth .... 31"
Height overall .... 4'-0"
Interior headroom (max.) .... 3'-6"
Hull weight (approx.)............. 1200 lbs.
Average passengers 4
Sleeping capacity 2
Cockpit size .... 6'-6"x 9'-0"
Fuel capacity .... 50 gals.
Hull type: Full length deep vee with 12°
       deadrise bottom and flaring
       topsides. Developed for sheet
       plywood planking.
Power: Inboard, stern mounted engine
       driving through a vee drive, jet
       pump, or outdrive unit.
Trailer: Designed for use with GLEN-L
       SERIES 2900/3800 boat trailer
       plans.

COMPLETE PLANS include FULL SIZE PATTERNS for stem, breasthook, and half-section patterns for the frames and transom. Includes instructions, Bill of Materials, and Fastening Schedule.

The **KINGPIN** is the latest in high performance ski boats. There's plenty of fuel in this beauty, enough in most cases to run all day. When the sun sets, just pick out a secluded cove and bunk down in the cabin. There's room for two or three adults in a full length vee berth. The next day you can rise early and hit the ski trail again.

The **KINGPIN** will really let you stretch your skiing time. The full length deep vee hull smoothes out rough water so you can ignore those short snappy wind blown chops; and crossing wakes will no longer be the bone jarring experience it once was. Those lift strakes on the bottom make for dry riding, good steering, and quick acceleration to lift a gang of skiers up quickly and smartly.

You can power your **KINGPIN** with just about any marine or auto conversion engine. This job is meant to take power. You can use either a jet pump,

v-drive with conventional propeller, or an outdrive unit to get the power to the water. The motor can be covered with the stylish motor compartment detailed on the plans, or leave it exposed if you're the chrome-polished motor type.

AVAILABLE FOR THIS DESIGN:
- **Plans & Patterns**
- **Bronze Fastening Kit**
- **Fiberglass Kit**
See Price List

BOLERO

A 24' DEEP VEE RUNABOUT

BUILD IN PLYWOOD

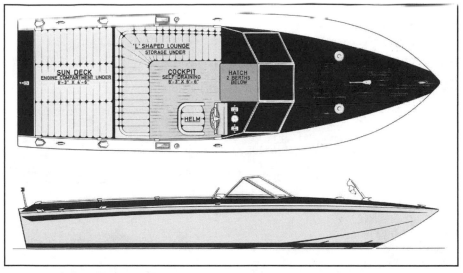

CHARACTERISTICS

Length overall .... 24'-5"
Beam .... 7'-11"
Draft .... 14"
Displacement .... 3989 lbs.
Hull weight (approx.)............. 1500 lbs.
Freeboard forward .... 2'-2"
Freeboard aft .... 2'-0"
Hull depth .... 4'-2"
Average passengers 4
Sleeping capacity 2
Cockpit size .... 6'-3"x 6'-6"
Fuel capacity .... 90 gals. standard
.... 120 gals. optional
Hull type: Full length deep vee with lift strakes and 20° deadrise bottom. Developed for sheet plywood planking on the sides and double plywood planking on the bottom.
Power: Inboard, stern mounted engine driving through a vee drive or outdrive unit. While most engines will drive direct, reduction gears may be required on some. Combined weight of engine and transmission equipment should be as follows:
I/O units should be at least 600 lbs., but not more than 1200 lbs. Vee drive units should be at least 800 lbs., but not more than 1600 lbs.
Jet drives may be used with minor modifications.
Trailer: Designed for use with GLEN-L SERIES 5000/6000 boat trailer plans.

COMPLETE PLANS include FULL SIZE PATTERNS for stem, breasthook, and half-section patterns for the frames and transom. Includes instructions, Bill of Materials, and Fastening Schedule.

There's no doubt about it. The big luxury runabouts are the smash hits at the nation's boat shows. There's no doubt about the price of these high performance jobs either. The factory built ones are a rich man's toy. But now GLEN-L brings this high performance luxury runabout within the reach of the masses of amateur builders.

The **BOLERO** is a thoroughbred in all respects. She features a full length deep vee hull with a 20° deadrise. The critically placed lift strakes deflect spray, provide quick planing, and aid directional stability. Lightweight strong double diagonally planked plywood on the bottom permits a bulbous keel section for a soft entry, and a reverse curve at the chine for a dry ride. The reversed sheer line permits unobstructed vision across the bow of the boat at any speed. Plush comfort and fun begins on the sun deck which is roomy enough for two adults. Forward of this is a self-draining cockpit complete with L-shaped lounge seat and a business-like control station in keeping with the high performance concept. If you decide to spend the night,

there's a two-berth cabin below the foredeck. Below the sun deck, at the heart of this beauty is the powerplant. There's plenty of room down there for single or twin engines either gasoline or diesel powered.

AVAILABLE FOR THIS DESIGN:
- **Plans & Patterns**
- **Bronze Fastening Kit**
- **Fiberglass Kit**

See Price List

SIROCCO

A 20' DEEP VEE SPORT CRAFT

BUILD IN PLYWOOD

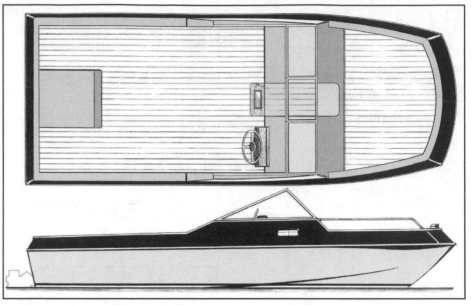

CHARACTERISTICS

Length overall	20'-0"
Length waterline	17'-3"
Beam	7'-10"
Draft	11"
Hull depth	4'-0"
Displacement	2540 lbs.
Hull weight (approx.)	1200 lbs.
Freeboard forward	2'-7"
Freeboard aft	2'-3"
Height overall	5'-4"
Fuel capacity	40 gals.
Aft cockpit size (approx.)	10'-6"x 6'-9"
Aft cockpit depth	24" to 35"
Fwd cockpit size (approx.)	4'-3"x 6'-6"
Forward cockpit depth	8"
Sleeping capacity	2

Hull type: Full length deep vee, developed for sheet plywood planking.

Power: Single or twin outboard motors or single I/O. Minimum recommended HP: 50. Maximum total engine weight: 700 lbs.

Trailer: Designed for use with GLEN-L SERIES 2900/3800 boat trailer plans.

COMPLETE PLANS include FULL SIZE PATTERNS for stem, breasthook, and half-section patterns for the frames and transom. Includes instructions, Bill of Materials, and Fastening Schedule.

The **SIROCCO** features a full length, moderate deep vee hull ideal for fishing, skiing, and diving. The boat really shines as a fishing boat. Huge fore and aft cockpit areas connect with a passageway through the windshield. The foredeck extends beyond the sheer to provide a large casting platform or for installing a pedestal chair. The forward cockpit can be eliminated (as shown on this page) for a more sporty look. The **SIROCCO** has enough power capability to get to that faraway fishing spot before the sun comes up or to effortlessly get a skier up.

If you want to spend the night on the water so that you can be on the spot for the best evening and early morning fishing, there is a cuddy cabin under the foredeck and the console that sleeps two.

The **SIROCCO** is a dry running boat that is light in weight for economical powering and maximum performance. Power with either inboard stern drive or outboard engines (100 SHP will yield approximately 30 mph). Features like a self-draining cockpit and plenty of hull depth allow this boat to take rough weather in stride.

AVAILABLE FOR THIS DESIGN:
- **Plans & Patterns**
- **Bronze Fastening Kit**
- **Fiberglass Kit**

See Price List

BANDIDO

a 30' inboard deep vee runabout

CHARACTERISTICS

Length overall .... 30'-2"
Length waterline .... 24'-8"
Beam .... 8'-0"
Hull draft .... 15 1/2"
Displacement @ DWL .... 5350 lbs.
Hull weight (approx.) fbgls 1900-3200 lbs.
Hull weight (approx.) wood .. 2700 lbs.
Hull depth .... 5'-0"
Freeboard forward .... 3'-3"
Freeboard aft................................ 2'-10"
Height overall (to top of windshield) 6'-5"
Cabin headroom.......................... 4'-4"
Cockpit size .... 8'-0" x 6'-6"
Sun deck size .... 6'-0" x 6'-6"
Fuel capacity (varies with power system)Fiberglass versions: 155 to 220 gals.
Wood version: 140 to 220
Average passengers 2-5
Sleeping accommodations 2-3
Hull type: Full length deep vee with 22° min. deadrise with radiused keel section and double curvature, flaring topsides.

Power: Single or twin inboard gasoline or diesel engines using I/O units, surface propeller drives, or v-drives. Jet drives optional but not detailed. Outboard motors optional and detailed.

Can the hull be extended or shortened? Yes. Up to 10% by re-spacing the frames from the aft end of the stem to the transom a proportional amount. We do not recommend increasing the beam.

BANDIDO is a luxury offshore performance boat offering high-tech performance and construction methods to match the exotic production boats, at a fraction of the cost. You can build yours in Wood or Fiberglass with a wide array of powering options. The trailerable hull, capable of 50+ knot speeds in offshore conditions, features a 22° minimum deep vee with radiused keel section and lift strakes.

Your BANDIDO can be set up with single or twin inboards (either diesel or gasoline), driving through I/O units, vee-drives, surface propeller drives, or with jets with minor modifications (although not specifically detailed). Or use twin outboards if you like (a single outboard engine is also possible within certain limitations as explained in the plans.) The choice is yours, and a large fuel capacity means long range even with larger motors.

Because of the high performance po-

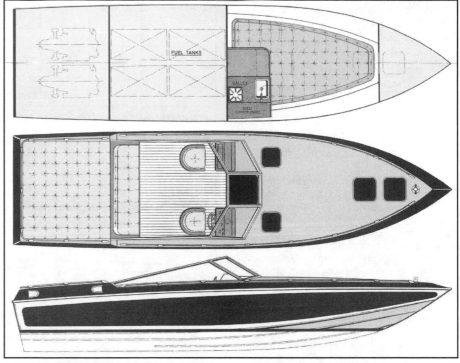

tential of the BANDIDO, construction is aimed at the conscientious builder willing to follow instructions and use the best materials. With the Wood Version, we specify cold-molded wood veneers or plywood strips laid up in multiple layers diagonally applied, all bonded together preferably with an epoxy bonding and encapsulating system. A layer of fiberglass on the exterior is used for abrasion resistance and added durability. A carefully designed structural "grid" framing system emphasizing longitudinal stringer webs makes a strong, yet lightweight hull.

With the Fiberglass Version, several materials and "one-off" methods are detailed, depending on the builder's budget, abilities, and desires. The fiberglass planking option is probably easiest and cheapest of the fiberglass methods for the novice, but not the lightest in weight. The sandwich core option, using a core material of PVC foam or end-grain balsa, is perhaps a bit more costly, but somewhat lighter in weight. Both systems result in strong boats well within the average amateur's abilities.

The High-Tech version is for the builder who wants the ultimate in light weight and performance potential. The fiberglass hull consists of a sandwich core using rigid PVC foam or end-grain balsa. The super-thin high strength skins are made from aerospace-type S-Glass uni-directional and triaxial fiberglass reinforcements. The high-tech version can be built using conventional "one-off" methods, or for the more ad-

venturous type, vacuum bag methods suitable for many amateurs more fully explained in our text, FIBERGLASS BOATBUILDING FOR AMATEURS. This system can result in a structure that weighs less than 2000 lbs! Procedures used to build the high-tech version are not any more difficult than the other methods, however, they do require care and attention to detail.

Regardless of the construction method, all BANDIDO's feature a plush cabin with galley provisions and a head, a spacious and safe cockpit, and a roomy sun deck lounge. All plans include Full Size Patterns and comprehensive instructions to simplify construction. So why wait? Fulfill that dream now and save thousands.

AVAILABLE FOR THIS DESIGN:
- **Study Plans**
- **Plans & Patterns**
- **Bronze Fastening Kit**
- **Fiberglass Kit**
See Price List

CRUISE MISSILE

A 32' HIGH-SPEED TRAILERABLE WEEKEND EXPRESS CRUISER WITH TUNNEL SLOT HULL

CHARACTERISTICS

Length overall .... 32'0"
Beam .... 8' 6"
Draft .... 1' 3"
Headroom .... 4'6"
Displacement .... 5360 lbs.
Sleeping capacity 4
Fuel capacity .... 180 gals.
Trailer: Designed for use with GLEN-L SERIES 7000/10,00 boat trailer plans.

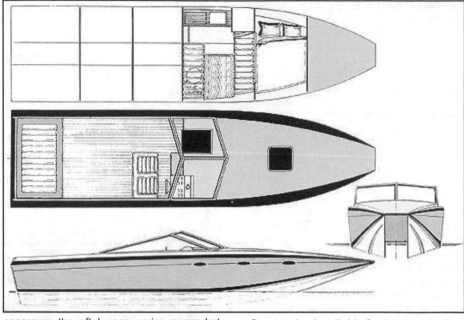

Incorporating our proven tunnel slot concept, this exciting design is a more compact and trailerable rendition of our successful SLOT MACHINE. Construction materials and methods are virtually identical, as are general performance and handling qualities. Power options include twin outboards, I/O's, or surface piercing drives. Speeds in the range of 50-60 MPH require approximately 350 to 450 HP total.

While performance is impressive, this boat is suited to practical uses. Accommodations equal or exceed those found on similar type monohulls, including a forward double berth, and a galley. There is sitting headroom above the berth and seat tops. Cockpit space is also generous; the aft lounge varies somewhat when transom-mounted outboards are used. However, if desired, the cabin could be omitted and the area opened up into a gigantic cockpit.

Construction is suitable for the conscientious do-it-yourself builder. Complete plans include FULL SIZE PATTERNS, laminate schedule, hull material estimates, all working drawings, and details for all powering options.

SLOT MACHINE

A 46' HIGH-SPEED LUXURY EXPRESS CRUISER WITH TUNNEL-SLOT HULL

Characteristics
Length overall .... 45' 11"
Beam .... 12' 6"
Draft .... 2' 0"
Headroom .... 6'3"-6'6"
Displacement .... 14,200 lbs.
Sleeping capacity 4
Fuel capacity .... 330 gals.
Water capacity .... 60 gals.

Sea trials on this stylish vessel exceeded all our performance expectations and validated our tunnel slot concept. Originally a custom design, plans are now available at a fraction of the original design fee. And while the first was custom built, this is not a project beyond the abilities of a qualified do-it-yourselfer.

Construction uses the latest in modern composite technology - vinylester resins, nonwoven unidirectional reinforcements, vacuum bagged PVC or balsa coring, and carbon fiber reinforcements at critical areas.

With laminates laid up over a simple male mold, the resulting structure is amazingly strong and stiff, yet super lightweight. There is absolutely no wood or plywood used anywhere in the completed vessel; even non-structural interior members are foam-cored sandwich for the ultimate in light weight.

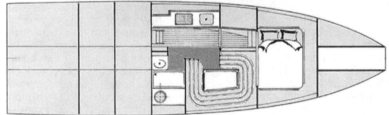

Power is by twin stern-mounted motors using either surface-piercing drives or I/O units. Horsepower in the range of 900-1100 gives speeds in the 50-60 MPH range depending on load, and with a generous fuel capacity to insure ample range.

Instead of being an out-and-out race boat, Slot Machine is intended for practical watersport uses. Accommodations are spacious and the cockpit is huge, with a convenient swim step and room to carry a large inflatable dinghy. The cabin includes a queen-size bed and huge dinette that seats six, plus a complete galley and enclosed head with shower, all with full standing headroom.

NOTE: COMPLETE PLANS include hull lines, offsets (corrected so you can lay out members directly without complete lofting), laminate schedule, all working drawings and required details. Full-size patterns are NOT available. REVIEW PLANS are also available; these include all the above except for hull lines, offsets, and laminate schedule. The price of REVIEW PLANS can later be applied to the purchase of COMPLETE PLANS (required to build the boat) if you decide to build. Our typical STUDY PLAN PAK is NOT available otherwise.

VEE GULL
A 20' DEEP VEE SPORT CRAFT

BUILD IN PLYWOOD

CHARACTERISTICS

Length overall	20'-2"
Length waterline	17'-4"
Beam	8'-0"
Draft	13"
Hull depth	3'-9"
Displacement	3075 lbs.
Hull weight (approx.)	1350 lbs.
Freeboard forward	2'-11"
Freeboard aft	2'-4"
Height overall	5'-7"
Headroom	4'-4"
Fuel capacity	40 gals.
Cockpit size	7' x 10'
Sleeping capacity	2

Hull type: Full length deep vee with 16° min. deadrise and lift strakes. Hard chine, developed for sheet plywood planking.

Power: Single or twin outboard motors or single inboard stern mounted motor, connected to an outdrive or vee drive. Maximum total engine weight: 800 lbs.

Trailer: Designed for use with GLEN-L SERIES 2900/3800 boat trailer plans.

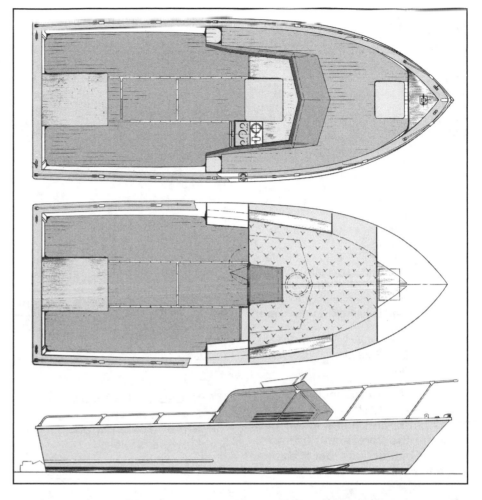

COMPLETE PLANS include FULL SIZE PATTERNS for stem, sheer harpin, and half-section patterns for the frame/bulkheads and transom. Includes instructions, Bill of Materials, and Fastening Schedule.

A complete walk-around deck... a 7' x 10' aft cockpit... sleeping accommodations for two... a trailerable boat... these are but a few of the unique features of the **VEE GULL**. All of these features are on a deep vee hull that is both fast and able, for a unique soft riding boat.

The cabin on the **VEE GULL** has adequate accommodations for two with space for a water closet under the berths. The forward chain locker is entirely separate from the cabin but readily accessible from the forward deck area.

The **VEE GULL** can be powered with single or twin long shaft outboard motors, or a stern mounted inboard motor connected to an outdrive or vee drive assembly. Details on either type of mounting is covered in the plans.

The construction is unique; the bulkhead frames are mounted on a sawn sheer member or harpin. This latter member eliminates any bending of the sheer and provides a positive accurate building method. The drawings carry the builder through all construction from building form to the cabin.

AVAILABLE FOR THIS DESIGN:
- Plans & Patterns
- Bronze Fastening Kit
- Fiberglass Kit
See Price List

KINGFISHER

AN 18' CENTER CONSOLE SPORTFISHER

CHARACTERISTICS

Length overall .... 18'-0"
Beam .... 7'-6"
Hull depth .... 3'-3"
Draft .... 10"
Hull weight (approx.) .... 800 lbs.
Cockpit size (approx.) .... 14'-8"x 6'-5"
Sleeping capacity 2
Fuel capacity .... 40 gals. max.
Average passengers 2-4
Hull type: Full length 18° deep vee with lift strakes, reverse curve at chine, and radiused keel section; developed for sheet plywood planking.
Power: Single or twin outboard motors to 175 HP, or single I/O, 750 lbs. max. Power trim and/or trim tabs recommended for high speed use and/or larger power plants.
Trailer: Designed for use with GLEN-L SERIES 2900/3800 boat trailer plans.

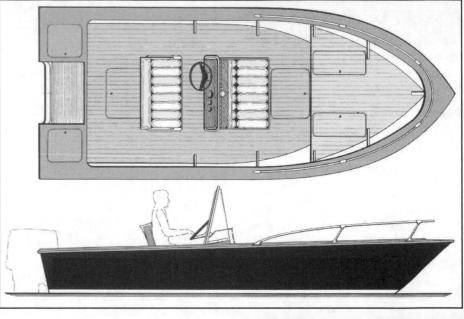

COMPLETE PLANS include FULL SIZE PATTERNS for stem, breasthook, and half-section patterns for the frames and transom. Includes instructions, Bill of Materials, and Fastening Schedule.

AVAILABLE FOR THIS DESIGN:
- **Plans & Patterns**
- **Bronze Fastening Kit**
- **Fiberglass Kit**
See Price List

Why pay the high prices asked for production center console sportfishers when you can build your own? Our **KINGFISHER** design lets you do it at a fraction of the cost. Our instructions with material listing and fastening schedule help you achieve professional results you'll be proud of.

The **KINGFISHER** is virtually all cockpit with plenty of nooks and crannies for stowing gear, food, drink, ice, bait, and the catch. There's a raised casting deck forward and a helmsman's seat with a pivoting backrest for use as a dual fighting chair. It's the perfect boat for all sorts of fresh and salt water angling as well as diving or water skiing activities.

The **KINGFISHER** features a full length 18° deep vee hull with lift strakes for quick planing with minimum power. The hull incorporates a radiused keel section for a smooth ride, and a reverse curve at the chine to knock down spray and improve stability at rest. Power choices include single or twin outboards, or single I/O units (stern drive inboards).

SCRAMBLER

A 15' OUTBOARD WHITEWATER SLED BOAT

CHARACTERISTICS

Length overall .... 15'6"(*)
Beam .... 6'8"
Bottom width .... 5'0"
Hull depth aft .... 2'1"
Hull weight (approx.).............. 550 lbs.
Power (outboard HP)........... 35 to 100
Trailer: . Designed for use with GLEN-L SERIES 1200/1800 boat trailer plans.
(*) 14'6" to 16'6" optional

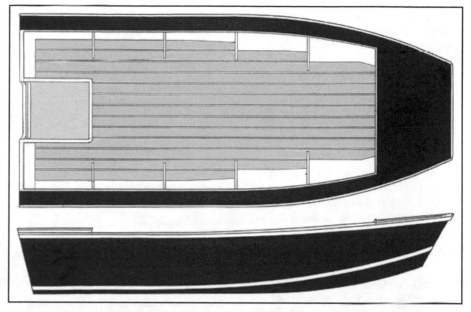

This compact whitewater sled offers quick and nimble maneuvering in tight quarters on fast-moving streams and rivers, or use on other waters just like any boat. Its smaller size makes it easy to trail, easy to build, and easy on the wallet. Yet it's strong and rugged whether built in sheet plywood or welded aluminum. Both versions feature five husky frames. Bottoms are 1/2" total with 3/8" sides on plywood hulls. Aluminum hulls use 3/16" bottom and 1/8" sides - heavier scantlings than most boats this size and in keeping with the tough intended usage. Power comes from a 20" or 25" shaft length outboard fitted with jet pump for whitewater use, or standard propeller otherwise. A slight "vee" in the bottom aft keeps the pump primed and assures responsive steering. The vee increases forward, much more so than other boats this size. Combined with an upswept pram bow and flaring topsides, the ride is surprisingly smooth and dry. An integral splash well keeps out any backwash while adding extra transom stiffness.

A spacious open cockpit with minimal foredeck lets you add a control console, seating, and amenities to suit your needs. And it's easy to vary boat length a foot or so either way.

FULL SIZE PATTERNS for frame and transom contours, together with instructions and material listings especially for do-it-yourselfers makes building quick and easy. Plywood plans show joining methods making it easy to use 8' panels throughout

AVAILABLE FOR THIS DESIGN:
- Plans & Patterns
- Bronze Fastening Kit
- Fiberglass Kit
See Price List

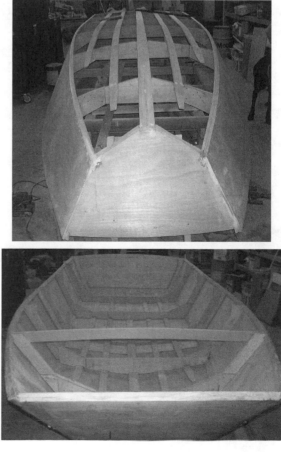

ROGUE RUNNER
A 17' INBOARD OR OUTBOARD WHITEWATER SLED BOAT

CHARACTERISTICS

Length overall (standard) .... 17'6"(*)
Beam .... 7'0"
Bottom width .... 5'0"
Hull depth (aft) .... 2'3"
Hull weight (approx.)............... 700 lbs
Power (outboard HP) .... 40 to 125
Trailer: . Designed for use with GLEN-L SERIES 1200/1800 boat trailer plans.
(*) 16' to 20' optional

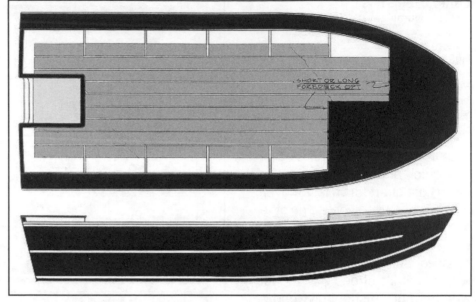

You can readily navigate wide, fast-moving, rock-strewn rivers in this whitewater sled. An upswept pram bow with some "vee" in the bottom, flaring topsides, and flat run aft assure rapid, safe motivation, even in the shallows. Power comes from an outboard retro-fitted with a jet pump lower unit (20" or 25" shaft length), or an inboard with jet drive. If you like, you can also use propeller-drive in outboard or I/O's where water depths permit - all these options are detailed and/or covered. Plywood construction is simple, inexpensive, and robust, but not over-weight. Bottom is 1/2" with 3/8" sides, with heavier options possible to a point. The backbone includes six sawn wood frames crossed by inner longitudinals--a husky internal structure to which you can mount seats, consoles, motors, etc. Outer hull surfaces get sheathed with fiberglass and epoxy for durability, easy maintenance, and top appearance.

Aluminum hulls use a similar all-aluminum framing configuration with 3/16" bottom and 1/8" side plating - all materials are standard types and shapes requiring no special fabrication techniques.

Whichever material is used, plans include FULL SIZE PATTERNS for the backbone member contours so no lofting or layouts are required. Hulls are built over a simple jig, and include easy methods for varying boat length by respacing frames or duplicating frames aft. The huge open interior allows builders to outfit the boat to suit their needs. You can build the foredeck in either a short or long option.

AVAILABLE FOR THIS DESIGN:
- **Plans & Patterns**
- **Bronze Fastening Kit**
- **Fiberglass Kit**
See Price List

SLITHER
A 17' OR 18' WHITEWATER SLED BOAT

CHARACTERISTICS

Length overall .... 17' or 18'
Beam .... 7'0"
Bottom width .... 5'6"
Hull depth (fore/aft) .... 35"/30"
Cockpit depth aft .... 24"
Hull weight (approx.).............. 700 lbs.
Fuel capacity .... 30 gals.
Power (outboard HP)........... 50 to 165
Trailer: . Designed for use with GLEN-L SERIES 2300/2800 boat trailer plans.

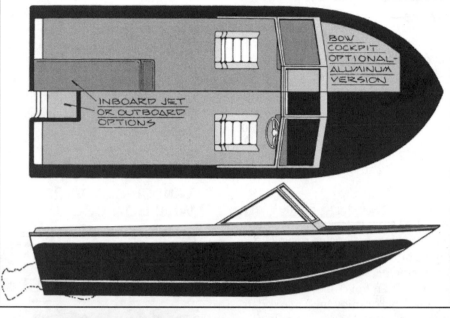

BOW COCKPIT OPTIONAL-ALUMINUM VERSION

INBOARD JET OR OUTBOARD OPTIONS

For whitewater river running, not much matches our SLITHER and SNAKE SHOOTER VEE sleds. Each design includes two V-bottom options. For ultimate shallow water use, build the 6° transom vee (12° bow entry). For deeper rivers or more open waters such as lakes, bays, sounds, or other choppy waters, build the 12° transom vee (20° bow entry). In all cases you get a beamy hull deep enough for safety, with generous full-length flare for dry running.

With SNAKE SHOOTER VEE you can also build an open-cockpit CENTER CONSOLE VERSION or pass-thru WINDSHIELD VERSION with forward cockpit. With SLITHER you can build with standard covered foredeck or with BOW COCKPIT and pass-thru on the Aluminum Version. Power options with both designs detail single 20" or 25" shaft length outboard (jet pump retrofit or prop optional), or stern-mounted inboard with jet or I/O. Weight limits are 1000 lbs. for jet inboards and 900 lbs. for I/O's in the case of SNAKE SHOOTER VEE, and 750 lbs. for jets and 675 lbs. for I/O's in the case of SLITHER.

All plans include FULL SIZE PATTERNS for frame member outer contours; NO LOFTING REQUIRED! Instructions especially for amateurs include material listings. Plans also include easy methods for altering boat length. You can build SLITHER at either 17' or 18' long, and SNAKE SHOOTER VEE between 17-1/2' and nearly 23'.

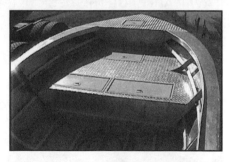

Separate plans are available for sheet plywood or welded aluminum construction for both designs. Plywood hulls total 1/2" bottoms and 3/8" sides over a rugged framework, with fiberglass coverings on the outside. Aluminum hulls have 3/16" bottoms and 1/8" sides over transverse frames reinforced by standard extrusion longitudinals.

Construction is simple yet rugged in either material. Sides and bottom are fully developable for easy application (continued on next page)

SNAKE SHOOTER

A 20' WHITEWATER SLED BOAT

CHARACTERISTICS

Length overall		20'1"(*)
Beam 7'0"		8'0"
Bottom width 5'6"		6'0"
Hull depth (fore/aft)		39"/34"
Cockpit depth aft		26"
Hull weight (approx.)		1050 lbs.
Fuel capacity		40 gals.
Power (outboard HP)		75 to 230

Trailer: . Designed for use with GLEN-L SERIES 2300/2800 boat trailer plans.
(*) 17'6" to 22'10" optional

(continued from Slither)
without special forming. Frames, transom, and stem (all taken from pattern contours), are set upside down over a simple but rigid form. Hull-strengthening longitudinals are then wrapped around. Then hull sheets are leaned against this framework, marked to shape, cut, and fastened or welded in place - it's quick and easy even for first-timers. Yet results can equal or exceed those found on costly production boats.

So whether you want to fish, run rapids, or tow skiers, SNAKE SHOOTER VEE and SLITHER can do it all.

AVAILABLE FOR THIS DESIGN:
- **Plans & Patterns**
- **Bronze Fastening Kit**
- **Fiberglass Kit**
See Price List

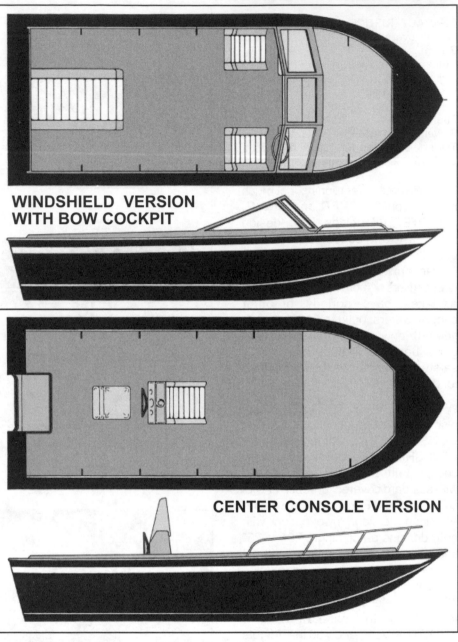

**WINDSHIELD VERSION
WITH BOW COCKPIT**

CENTER CONSOLE VERSION

RIVER RAT

A 20' MODIFIED SLED, RIVER RUNNER

RIVER RAT is a jet sled with an advanced underbody for improved performance and handling. The built-in chine flats or rails deflect the spray which makes for a dry boat regardless of the water condition.

The hull can be built in durable fiberglass covered sheet plywood or welded aluminum. Separate plans detail building with aluminum or wood. This design can also be lengthened or shortened about 10% with minor changes, as detailed in the plans and instructions.

The **RIVER RAT** is powered using the popular water jet pump coupled to an inboard motor, or a conventional or jet outboard. An optional variation on the aluminum plans detail a "shoe" or "ski" flat area along the keel for a jet pump installation. Details are also provided for a stern mounted inboard coupled to an outdrive.

The **RIVER RAT** can be built as an open hull with center console to provide a huge open cockpit, or an optional version utilizes a slightly longer deck with a windshield and provisions for a folding "navy" top. Both versions are detailed in the plans.

The large scale plans are very complete, providing many enlarged sections and details along with precise information on the simple building form. The complete plan and pattern package comes with full size patterns for framing members; no lofting or dimensional layouts are required. Everything needed to make building your own **RIVER RAT** easy and quick is included.

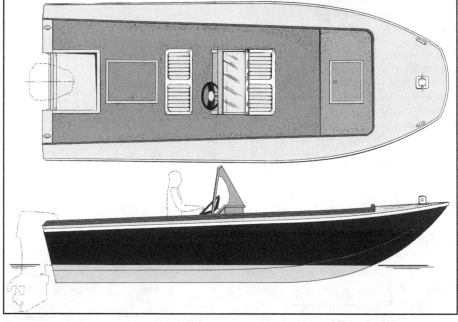

CHARACTERISTICS

Length overall	20'-2"
Beam	8'-0"
Hull Draft	11"
Hull Weight - Approx	1100 lbs.
Displacement	3040 lbs.
Freeboard Forward	3'-0"
Freeboard Aft	2'-0"
Hull Depth, Amidship	3'-3"
Cockpit Size (approx)	6' x 13'-6"
Average passengers	2-4

Hull type: Modified sled/garvey with 12° deadrise. Developed for sheet plywood or aluminum with built-in chine flat spray rail.

Power: Single or twin outboard motors or inboard stern mounted engine coupled to an outdrive or water jet pump. Vee drive optional but not detailed.

Trailer: Designed for use with GLEN-L SERIES 2900/3800 boat trailer plans.

PLYWOOD VERSION
COMPLETE PLANS include **FULL SIZE PATTERNS** for stem, knee, sawn chine, and half section patterns of each frame, transom and bow piece plus detailed instructions, Bill of Materials, Fastening Schedule, and Build it Yourself the GLEN-L Way pictorial.

ALUMINUM VERSION
COMPLETE PLANS for welded sheet aluminum construction include **FULL SIZE PATTERNS** for the stem, and half section patterns for the bow piece, transom, and frames, with instructions, material listing and **ALUMINUM BOATBUILDING GUIDE.**

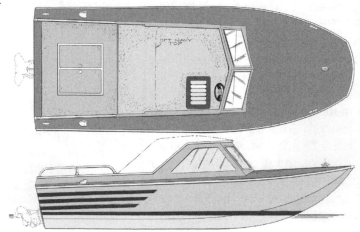

AVAILABLE FOR THIS DESIGN:
- Plans & Patterns
- Bronze Fastening Kit
- Fiberglass Kit
- See Price List

CANYON CRUISER
A 21' WHITEWATER JET SLED CRUISER

CHARACTERISTICS

Length overall (standard) .... 21'3"(*)
Beam .... 8'0"
Bottom width .... 6'0"
Hull depth (fore/aft) .... 42"/37"
Cockpit depth aft .... 26"
Hull weight (approx.).............. 1400 lbs.
Cabin headroom........................ 6'-6'2"
Fuel capacity .... 80 gals.
Power: ....Inboard jets to 1100 lbs.
.... I/O's to 1000 lbs.
Trailer: Designed for use with GLEN-L
           SERIES 2300/2800 boat trailer
           plans.
(*) 20'3" to 21'11" optional

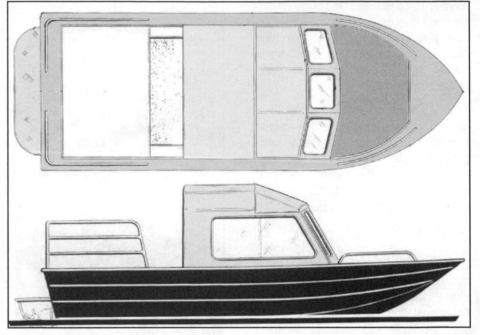

Blistering sunshine or torrential downpours won't keep you from running your favorite whitewater rivers aboard our CANYON CRUISER. A hardtop cuddy cabin with full standing headroom protects you from the elements, but includes a removable soft-top sunroof that's great for standing at the helm when extra visibility and ventilation are required. And it makes passing through to the forward cockpit a breeze.

An inboard motor driving through a jet pump or I/O is located below the raised aft deck, making the perfect fishing perch, and with ready access to the transom swim step aft. Plus there's plenty of fuel to get you where you want to go and back.

While ideal for the big fast-moving rivers out west, CANYON CRUISER is also suited to other waters that can kick up a fuss, whether on oceans or lakes. Depending on your needs, plans include two V-bottom options. For ultimate speeds or where draft is a concern in shallower waters, pick the 6° transom vee (12° bow entry). For more open waters or bigger rivers we recommend our 12° transom vee (20° bow entry). Both options are a part of the plans. In either case, the beamy

hull has generous depth for safety and dry running. And options on the plans make it easy to vary boat length within the limits noted.

Plans are available for either sheet plywood or welded aluminum construction. Plywood hulls total 1/2" bottom and 3/8" sides over a husky framing with fiberglass

sheathing on the outside. Aluminum hulls have 3/16" bottoms and 1/8" sides over transverse frames reinforced by standard extrusion longitudinals. Either hull includes plenty of rub rails for protection against bumps and scrapes.

With available FULL SIZE PATTERNS for frame member outer contours, NO LOFTING or redrawing hull lines is required. Instructions with material listing assure professional results even if you've never built a boat before.

AVAILABLE FOR THIS DESIGN:
- Study Plans
- Plans & Patterns
- Bronze Fastening Kit
- Fiberglass Kit
See Price List

JET SETTER

A 20' INBOARD OR OUTBOARD WHITEWATER SLED WITH PRAM BOW

BUILD IN PLYWOOD or ALUMINUM

CHARACTERISTICS
Length overall .... 20'3"(*)
Beam .... 7'11"
Bottom width .... 6'0"
Hull depth (min.) .... 31" or 33"
Cockpit depth aft .... 24"
Hull weight (approx.).............. 950 lbs.
Fuel capacity .... 36 gals.
Power (outboard HP) .... 75 to 230
Trailer: Designed for use with GLEN-L SERIES 2300/2800 boat trailer plans.
(*) 17'7" to 22'11" optional

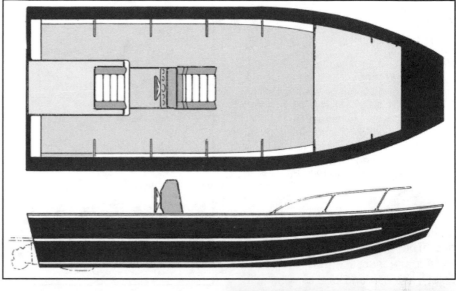

Equally at home in whitewater rivers, fishing on lakes and bays, or towing skiers, our JET SETTER whitewater sled plans come in either a "Windshield Version" with hinged center section, bow cockpit, or raised casting deck; or as a "Center Console" with raised casting deck forward. Power can be a 20" or 25" shaft outboard (jet pump or prop type), or inboard with I/O to 900 lbs., or jet to 1000 lbs. In any case, the v-bottom hull with three rub rails per side can handle turbulent waters while fending off rocks and hazards with aplomb.

AVAILABLE FOR THIS DESIGN:
- **Plans & Patterns**
- **Bronze Fastening Kit**
- **Fiberglass Kit**
See Price List

Ply hulls use 1/2" bottom and 3/8" sides over husky sawn frames. Aluminum hulls use welded 3/16" bottom and sides backed by standard shape longitudinals and transverse frames. Plans show easy ways for varying boat length. FULL SIZE PATTERNS are provided for hull framing members. Instructions especially for do-it-yourself builders include material lists so construction is fast and easy even for first-timers.

WEE HUNK

A 16' FLAT BOTTOM PACIFIC DORY

CHARACTERISTICS

Length overall .... 16'-0"
Beam .... 6'-7"
Hull depth midship .... 24"
Bottom width .... 4'-7"
Hull weight (approximate) ...... 380 lbs.
Average passengers .... 2 - 4
Hull Type: Flat bottom power dory developed for Stitch-N-Glue sheet plywood construction.
Power: Intended for outboard motors, short or long shaft to 40 HP.
Trailer: Designed for use with GLEN-L SERIES 1200/1800 boat trailer plans.

WEE HUNK is a simple, sturdy boat, patterned after the popular Pacific dories. The upswept bow with flaring topsides assures stability, speed, safety, dryness, and load carrying ability. The hull will support a gross weight of about 1450 lbs. with only 6" draft!

The Stitch-N-Glue construction method furnishes full size patterns for virtually *every* part in the boat, *including* planking. No lofting or dimensional layouts are required; just duplicate the patterns to the plywood and you're on your way. The **WEE HUNK** uses standard 4' x 8' plywood panels throughout, 3/8" on the side and 1/2" minimum for the bottom planking. Planking parts are assembled flat on the ground and bent around a single form to shape the boat. No complex building forms or jigs are required to build the **WEE HUNK**. With the simplified Stitch-N-Glue method, frames, internal backing member requiring bending and fairing, and most fasteners are eliminated. The composite construction utilizes plywood stitched together at seams and bonded with an adhesive fillet reinforced both inside and out, with laminates of fiberglass. A proven, simple, very strong, building method that

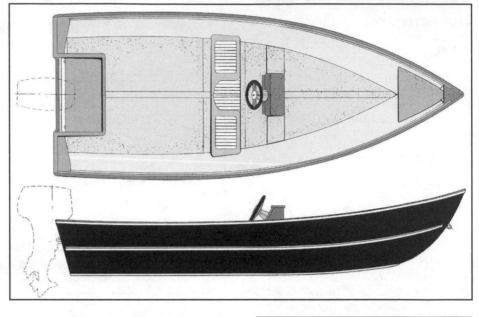

makes boatbuilding practical for almost everyone.

A console steering helm with bench seat is detailed in the plans, but the wide open hull, unimpaired by structural members, allows custom modifications to suit the builder's needs. Side, aft, or center seating, extra storage compartments, or raised forward sole are all simple modifications the builder can make.

COMPLETE PLANS include FULL SIZE PATTERNS for side and bottom planking, butt blocks, breasthook, knee, motorwell sides, corner knee, bow seat, bulkhead, form, and transom *plus* **full material list, plywood layouts, instructions, and Stitch-N-Glue Manual.**

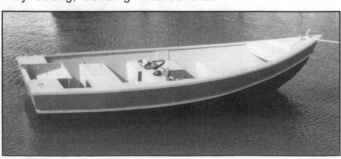

LITTLE HUNK
AN 18' FLAT BOTTOM PACIFIC DORY

CHARACTERISTICS

Length overall (inboard well) .... 18'-3"
Length overall (other options) ... 17'-6"
Beam .... 7'-6"
Hull depth forward .... 3'-11"
Hull depth aft .... 2'-6"
Bottom width .... 4'-6"
Hull weight (approximate) ..... 700 lbs.
Minimum recommended HP .... 25 HP
Maximum engine/drive weight 500 lbs.
GLEN-L Trailer Plans Series 1200/1800
Hull type: Flat bottom dory-type hull aft. Developed for sheet plywood planking with outer rub strakes.
Power: Single well-mounted outboard standard. Transom mounted single outboard. Short shaft motors not recommended. Inboard driving through outdrive or jet pump optional.

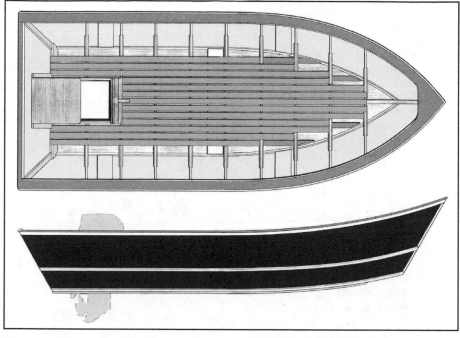

The LITTLE HUNK can be launched directly into the surf by virtue of its raised bow and broad flaring topsides. Like our other power dories and dories in general, LITTLE HUNK has tremendous load carrying ability while the flat bottom assures a stable boat when loaded. The wide open hull allows unrestricted movement and is readily adapted to a variety of uses. Cabins and center consoles, fish holds, bait tanks, or other accessories can easily be added.

The shallow draft and stable flat bottom makes an ideal dive or fishing boat that can get into places that deep vees and other hulls cannot. The well-mounted outboard makes beach launching and retrieving easy and safe, while keeping the motor entirely within the boat when "kicked up". The well-mounted outboard also allows for working nets, setting lobster pots, or handling fish without worrying about tangling the lines around a transom mounted outboard. For those with other applications, the plans detail an optional transom-mounted outboard as well as stern-mounted inboard engines driving through an outdrive or jet pump.

The hull drives easily with minimum power and maximum economy.

The simple hull shape makes building easier and quicker than other designs in this size range. Virtually all bevels can be pre-cut so that little fairing is required. The contours of the frames are straight and planking is simple sheet plywood. No steam bending or lofting is required and material waste is minimal. The LITTLE HUNK can be increased or decreased in length by up to 3' by simply adding or deleting one or two of the duplicate aft frames.

The plans include instructions, material listings, and fastening schedule, as well as Full Size Patterns, which make LITTLE HUNK, as well as the larger Hunky Dory or Big Hunk, well suited to the first-time builder. These are tough, durable boats well within the budget and ability of just about any fisherman.

AVAILABLE FOR THIS DESIGN:
- **Plans & Patterns**
- **Dory Cabin Plans**
- **Bronze Fastening Kit**
- **Fiberglass Kit**

See Price List

HUNKY DORY

A 22' FLAT BOTTOM PACIFIC DORY

CHARACTERISTICS

Length overall (inboard well) . 22'-10"
Length overall (other options) ...22'-0"
Beam ....8'-0"
Hull depth forward ....4'-2"
Hull depth aft ....2'-8"
Bottom width ....5'-0"
Hull weight (approximate) ...1000 lbs.
Minimum recommended HP ....30 HP
Maximum engine/drive weight700 lbs.
GLEN-L Trailer Plans Series 2900/3800
Hull type:Flat bottom dory-type hull aft. Developed for sheet plywood planking with outer rub strakes, or welded aluminum construction.
Power: Single well-mounted outboard standard. Single or twin transom mounted outboard. Short shaft motors not recommended. Inboard driving through outdrive or jet pump optional.

The HUNKY DORY is a type of powered fishing dory that evolved on the Pacific coast where boats of this type are commonly used for pleasure and commercial fishing. This trailerable craft is quickly and easily launched directly into the surf due to its abruptly raised bow and broad flaring topsides. The dory hull has tremendous load carrying ability while the flat bottom assures a stable boat when loaded. The wide open hull allows unrestricted movement for easy gear handling and versatility. The boat can be outfitted with control console, seating, fish holds, bait tanks, or any manner necessary to suit the special requirements of the owner. There are several Dory Cabin Plans available from Glen-L that can be adapted to the HUNKY DORY.

While this may seem to be a specialized craft, the virtues can readily be appreciated where shallow draft operation is necessary, ease of beaching required, or where rapid river running is a prerequisite. The well-mounted outboard makes beach launching and retrieving easy and safe, and does not interfere with fishing gear as the motor

can "kick-up" entirely within the boat. However, options are shown on the plans for transom-mounted outboards as well as stern-mounted inboard engines driving through an outdrive or jet pump. In any case, the hull drives easily with minimum power and maximum economy.

The HUNKY DORY is also quick, easy, and inexpensive to build. Virtually all bevels can be pre-cut so that little fairing is required. The hull uses 12 straight contoured frames, and 12 sheets of standard 4' x 8' plywood. No steam bending or lofting is required and material waste is minimal. The 1/2" plywood bottom has inner and outer bottom strakes for stiffness and protection, while the 3/8" plywood sides feature husky rub rails at critical points. The craft can be increased or decreased in length by up to 3' by

simply adding or deleting one or two of the duplicate aft frames or by re-spacing them a proportional amount. The HUNKY DORY is also available for aluminum construction.

The instructions cover all phases of contruction including material listings, fastening schedule, and full size patterns for all frame members. She is truly a tough, durable boat well within the budget and abilities of just about any fisherman. See Little Hunk and Big Hunk for larger and smaller versions of the HUNKY DORY.

CHUNKY DORY

A 23' MODIFIED PACIFIC CITY-TYPE POWER DORY

CHARACTERISTICS

Length overall (standard) .... 23'0" (*)
Beam .... 8'6"
Bottom width .... 5'6"
Depth aft .... 2'8"
Hull weight (approx.)... 1200/1500 lbs.
Power (minimum) .... 40 HP
Trailer: Designed for use with GLEN-L SERIES 2900/3800 boat trailer plans.
(*) 20'4" & 25'8" optional

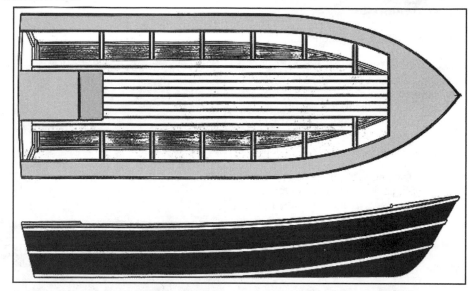

Here's a versatile, roomy, simple, and able craft. Plans include two bottom options: A smoother riding v-entry version much improved over other Pacific dory types, or the simpler all-flat bottom option. Plans also let you build in any of three lengths: 20'4", 23'0" (standard), or 25'8". A deep cockpit and wide bottom assure safety and stability. Three power options include I/O, transom-mounted outboards (single or twin), or single well-mounted outboard. Planing occurs with about 40 HP, and bigger engines up to 1000 lbs. total are okay.

Construction is rugged but simple and inexpensive. Plans are available in either sheet plywood or welded aluminum. Plywood hulls have 1/2" standard or 3/4" optional thickness bottoms over 2" sawn wood frames. Aluminum hulls use 3/16" on the bottom and 1/8" sides.

Outfit the huge interior as you wish - center console, cuddy cabin, trunk cabin, foredeck , etc. Or just leave it wide open.

All plans include FULL SIZE PATTERNS, instructions, material list, and fastening schedule on wood version.

AVAILABLE FOR THIS DESIGN:
- Plans & Patterns
- Dory Cabin Plans
- Bronze Fastening Kit
- Fiberglass Kit
See Price List

BIG HUNK
A 26' FLAT BOTTOM PACIFIC DORY

CHARACTERISTICS

Length overall (inboard well) .... 26'-7"
Length overall (other options) ... 25'-8"
Beam .... 9'-8"
Hull depth forward .... 5'-2"
Hull depth aft .... 3'-3"
Bottom width .... 6'-0"
Hull weight (approximate) ... 1800 lbs.
Minimum recommended HP .... 50 HP
Maximum engine/drive weight 1000 lbs.
Hull type: Flat bottom dory-type hull aft. Developed for sheet plywood planking with outer rub strakes
Power: Single well-mounted outboard standard. Single or twin transom mounted outboard. Short shaft motors not recommended. Inboard driving through outdrive or jet pump optional.

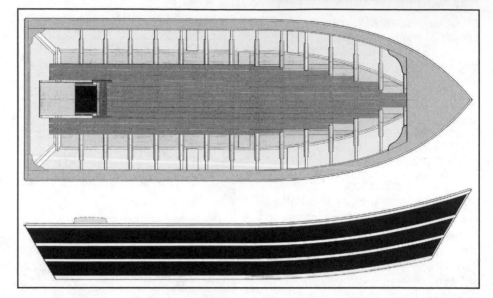

The BIG HUNK is the largest of our Pacific dories. With a 9'-8" beam it is not trailerable. This is a serious work boat. In the harbor, at sea, or on lakes and rivers, the BIG HUNK provides a stable platform for all sorts of commercial activities. This is an ideal boat for many fishing activities, shrimping in Louisiana, diving off the coast of southern California or Florida, or hauling in the salmon from the Pacific northwest to Alaska. The stability of the hull is most noticeable when the boat is being worked hard with a lot of activity. The dory hull has tremendous load carrying ability. The wide open hull allows unrestricted movement for easy gear handling and versatility. There are several Dory Cabin Plans available from Glen-L that can be adapted to the BIG HUNK to keep out the rain and weather or to provide a place for the crew to lay down or relax at the end of a long day.

The characteristics that make this a good commercial boat also make it ideal for the sportsman in any application where shallow draft operation is necessary, or the ability to be easily beached. The well-mounted outboard makes beach launching and retrieving easy and safe, and does not interfere with fishing gear as the motor can "kick-up" entirely within the boat. However, options are shown on the plans for transom-mounted outboards as well as stern-mounted inboard engines driving through an outdrive or jet pump. In any case, the hull drives easily with minimum power and maximum economy.

Like our other Pacific dories, BIG HUNK is quick, easy, and inexpensive to build. Virtually all bevels can be pre-cut so that little fairing is required. No steam bending or lofting is required and material waste is minimal. The 3/4" plywood bottom has inner and outer bottom strakes for stiffness and protection, while the 1/2" plywood sides feature husky rub rails at critical points. The craft can be increased or decreased in length by up to 3' by simply adding or deleting one or two of the duplicate aft frames or by re-spacing them a proportional amount.

The instructions cover all phases of contruction including material listings, fastening schedule, and full size patterns for all frame members. She is truly a tough, durable boat well within the budget and abilities of just about any fisherman. See Little Hunk and Hunky Dory smaller versions of the BIG HUNK.

AVAILABLE FOR THIS DESIGN:
- **Plans & Patterns**
- **Dory Cabin Plans**
- **Bronze Fastening Kit**
- **Fiberglass Kit**
See Price List

V-DORY
A 22' DORY WITH A VEE BOTTOM FORWARD

CHARACTERISTICS

Length overall (inboard well) ... 22'-10"
Length overall (other options) .... 22'-0"
Beam .... 8'-5"
Hull depth forward .... 4'-2"
Hull depth aft .... 2'-8"
Bottom width .... 5'-8"
Hull weight (approximate) .... 1100 lbs.
Displacement @7" draft .... 3250 lbs.
Min. recommended horsepower30 HP
Power: Single well-mounted outboard standard. Optional and detailed transom mounted outboard, outdrive (I/O), jet drive, or in-line inboard.
Hull type: Flat bottom dory-type hull aft flowing into a vee bottom forward. Developed for sheet plywood planking with outer rub strakes.
Trailer: Designed for use with GLEN-L SERIES 2900/3800 boat trailer plans.

COMPLETE PLANS include FULL SIZE PATTERNS for the stem, breasthook, transom for inboard and outboard versions, motorwell sides, knees, all frames plus detailed plansheets, Instructions, Bill of Materials, & Fastening Schedule.

The flat bottom Pacific Coast dories are renowned for their ability to navigate shoal water, carry a load, and building simplicity. The **V-DORY** is an evolutionary step forward in our line of craft of this type.

The flat bottom aft has remained unchanged, as has the distinctive upsweep at the bow. *But*, a vee has been incorporated in the forward bottom sections for a smoother ride in a choppy sea. The raised forefoot was retained to eliminate hooking or tracking when quartering a sea or wake. The beam was increased, adding more room and greater load carrying ability. At a mere 7" of draft, the hull will support a total weight of 3250 lbs.

The forward vee bottom plywood is fully developed to bend simply in place *and* two layers are used to make forming even easier. All materials are readily available, using standard 4' x 8' plywood panels.

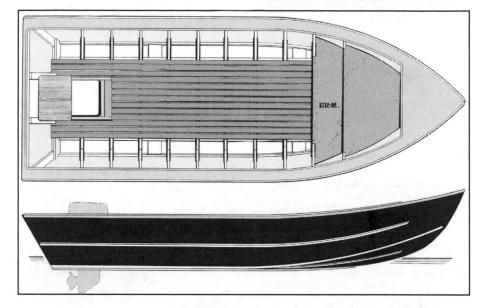

There are various power options; the standard version uses an outboard motor mounted in a well, however, complete details are provided for transom mounted outboard(s). A stern mounted motor can be used with either an I/O or outdrive, or if running in shallow water is required, a jet drive installation is also detailed. For the conventional in-line inboard power enthusiast, a centrally located conversion, or marine engine is depicted.

The hull is left wide open so you can easily make custom modifications or add a cabin from the GLEN-L DORY CABIN PLANS group. To balance out such modifications, a method of keeping the boat in equilibrium over the center of buoyancy is given. The hull can be lengthened or shortened a couple of feet by adding or subtracting frames in the aft section of the boat. Of course, the plans include Bill of Materials and Fastening Schedule along with progressive instructions, plus full size or half section patterns for essential parts.

AVAILABLE FOR THIS DESIGN:
- Plans & Patterns
- Dory Cabin Plans
- Bronze Fastening Kit
- Fiberglass Kit
See Price List

DORY CABIN PLANS

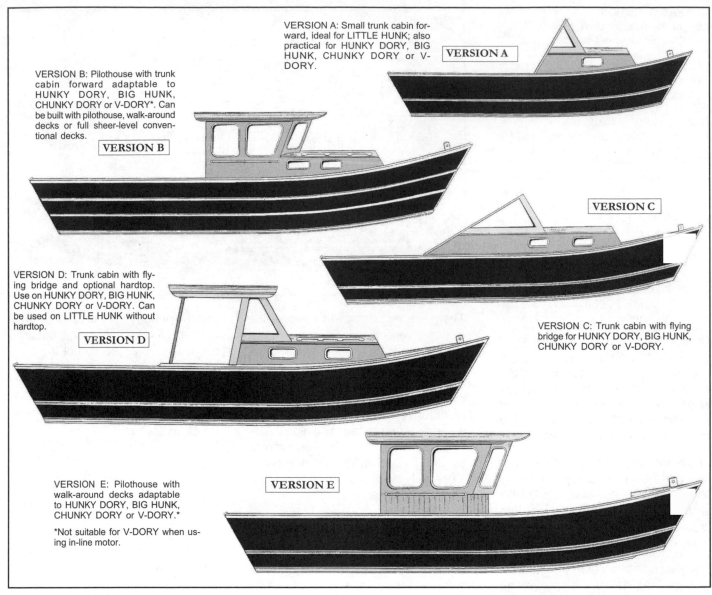

VERSION A: Small trunk cabin forward, ideal for LITTLE HUNK; also practical for HUNKY DORY, BIG HUNK, CHUNKY DORY or V-DORY.

VERSION A

VERSION B: Pilothouse with trunk cabin forward adaptable to HUNKY DORY, BIG HUNK, CHUNKY DORY or V-DORY*. Can be built with pilothouse, walk-around decks or full sheer-level conventional decks.

VERSION B

VERSION C

VERSION D: Trunk cabin with flying bridge and optional hardtop. Use on HUNKY DORY, BIG HUNK, CHUNKY DORY or V-DORY. Can be used on LITTLE HUNK without hardtop.

VERSION D

VERSION C: Trunk cabin with flying bridge for HUNKY DORY, BIG HUNK, CHUNKY DORY or V-DORY.

VERSION E: Pilothouse with walk-around decks adaptable to HUNKY DORY, BIG HUNK, CHUNKY DORY or V-DORY.*

*Not suitable for V-DORY when using in-line motor.

VERSION E

Put a cabin on your GLEN-L dory. Convert HUNKY DORY, LITTLE HUNK, BIG HUNK CHUNKY DORY or V-DORY to a deluxe cruiser with a choice of five different cabin styles. *Details on all versions are furnished* in **DORY CABIN PLANS**; with dimensional layouts for cabin exterior, interior joinery, control console, plus structural details, lumber sizes, fastening schedule, and instructions. Only minor modifications are required, so add a cabin while building, *or* retrofit one after hull completion.

A floor plan is given in the **DORY CABIN PLANS** along with suggested cabinetry. All trunk versions feature large vee berths forward with sitting headroom. Versions B, C, and E have space for port and starboard cabinets or head and cabinet. Pilothouse versions have 6' plus headroom, helm station, cabinets and space for stove and sink.

Although specifically for GLEN-L dories, it is probable, with minor variations, that these CABIN PLANS could be used to build a cabin on similar craft.

Version "D" on Hunky Dory

SWEET CAROLINE

A 20' TRADITIONAL DORY/SKIFF

BUILD IN PLYWOOD

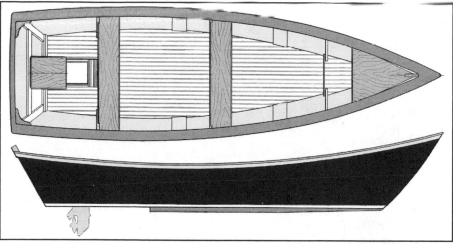

CHARACTERISTICS

Length overall .... 20'-1"
Bottom length .... 16'-0"
Beam overall .... 6'-0"
Bottom width (max.) .... 4'-0"
Transom width .... 5'-4"
Hull depth forward .... 3'-4"
Hull depth aft .... 2'-4"
Hull depth amidships (min.) ...... 1'-10"
Displacment (at 6" draft) ...... 1600 lbs.
Hull weight (approx.) .... 640 lbs.
Average passengers 4-6
Hull type: Flat bottom dory-type, developed for sheet plywood planking.
Power: Single shortshaft (15" nominal) outboard motor from 10 to 40 HP, mounted in a motor-well. Longshaft motor optional with minor modifications.
Trailer: Designed for use with GLEN-L SERIES 2300/2800 boat trailer plans.

COMPLETE PLANS include FULL SIZE PATTERNS for stem, breasthook, motorwell sides, and half-section patterns for the frames and transom. Includes instructions, Bill of Materials, and Fastening Schedule.

Our **SWEET CAROLINE** is an improved version of the traditional dory/skiff commonly found along the coast of the Southeastern Atlantic seaboard. We've refined the design to be even simpler and less expensive to build, and have enhanced the qualities that have made this type of craft so popular.

For example, we've simplified the construction to the point where even the beginner should have no difficulty. The FULL SIZE PATTERNS eliminate the need for lofting and layouts. The plans are supplemented with sequential instructions, a material listing and utilization layouts, plus fastening schedule so nothing is left to chance. With our stress-skin plywood planking, there are only three frames required, and these have been carefully located so that they don't trip up any passengers. Careful design using pre-beveling wherever possible keeps fairing to an absolute minimum. The result is a strong boat that is amazingly light in weight for its size. It only takes eight standard 4' x 8' sheets of 1/2" plywood to build the boat, plus a few lengths of lumber for the

longitudinals and framing.

The flat, straight bottom on the **SWEET CAROLINE** accounts for the low power requirements of this craft. For example, speeds approaching the 30 MPH bracket are possible with a 40 HP outboard. In fact, this boat makes a good rowboat, with either a single or double bank of oars. The hull is amazingly stable and seaworthy, making this an ideal boat for fishermen. The motor is located in a well that allows the shortshaft motor to kick up entirely within the boat to prevent snagging lines and nets.

We doubt you'll find an easier boat to build in the 20' range, or one that is more ecomonical to build, own or operate.

AVAILABLE FOR THIS DESIGN:
- **Plans & Patterns**
- **Bronze Fastening Kit**
- **Fiberglass Kit**
See Price List

PLAY 'N JANE

A 22' TRAILERABLE UTILITY CRAFT

CHARACTERISTICS

Length overall	21'-9"
Length waterline	19'-8"
Beam	7'-11 1/2"
Draft	24"
Hull Weight (approx.)	1500 lbs.
Displacement	4868 lbs.
Freeboard forward	5'-0"
Freeboard Aft	3'-2"
Hull depth	6'-9"
Height overall	9'-5"
Hold volume	28 cu. ft.
Fuel capacity	70 gals.
Cockpit size	6'x 13'-3"
Cockpit depth (min.)	32"
Sleeping capacity	2

Hull type: Semi-displacement, hard chine hull with practical cruising speed of 6 1/2 knots, and a maximum hull speed of approx. 9 knots. Bottom design features bulbous forefoot with a reverse curve at the chine, double diagonally planked to a total thickness of 1/2". Topsides planked with sheet plywood to a total thickness of 3/8". Carvel planking or other conventional types are optional but not detailed in the plans.

Power: Single centrally mounted diesel or gasoline inboard; 10 SHP for 6 1/2 knot cruising speed, 25 SHP for maximum 9 knots intermittently. Reduction gear may be required. Engines rated over 35 SHP not recommended. Total engine and gear max. 600 lbs.

Trailer: Designed for use with GLEN-L SERIES 5000/6000 boat trailer plans.

COMPLETE PLANS include FULL SIZE PATTERNS for stem, breasthook, and half-section patterns for the frames and transom. Includes instructions, Bill of Materials, and Fastening Schedule.

PLAY 'N JANE might look plain, but she's no ordinary boat. She's versatile and economical to boot! Whether for business or pleasure, she'll take either in stride. Use her for a club launch, buoy tender, patrol craft, yard tug, fishing boat, or just about any other task you can dream up. The true beauty of this no-nonsense craft will soon become apparent once you put her to work.

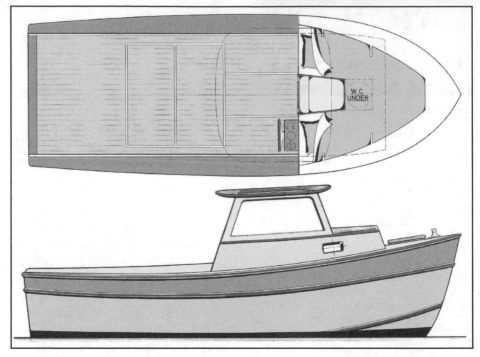

Consider these features: Your **PLAY 'N JANE** can be trailered anywhere because she's trim in the beam (under 8'!). The double sheer rails handle bumps and scrapes, and a husky deadwood protects her underwater gear. The cockpit is huge and the sole completely flush. The plans include provisions for a hold suitable for carrying about 3/4 ton of fish or anything else you would like to stow. If you want to lay over, the cabin features full standing headroom, two full size berths, and a head!

Best of all, your **PLAY 'N JANE** doesn't have an expensive appetite like her fancy frilled relatives. All you need is minimal power to reach cruising speed range, and you'll take her 500 miles on one filling of diesel fuel. She won't make it in fast company, but her sea-worthy hull with high freeboard and deep forefoot makes her comfortable and safe in any sea a boat this size should be out in. All the methods and materials used in her construction are basic, for low costs. The plywood planking over sturdy sawn frames are the perfect materials for the amateur builder or small custom yard. The plans for the **PLAY 'N JANE** come complete with full size patterns so no lofting is required.

AVAILABLE FOR THIS DESIGN:
- **Plans & Patterns**
- **Bronze Fastening Kit**
- **Fiberglass Kit**

See Price List

NOYO TRAWLER

A 24' TRAILERABLE WORKBOAT

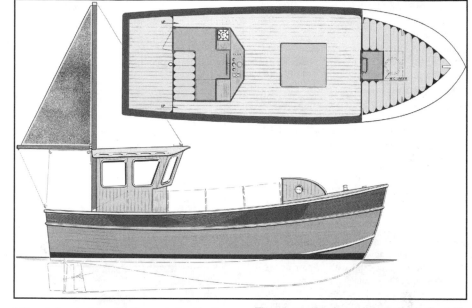

CHARACTERISTICS

Length overall	24'-1"
Length waterline	22'-0"
Beam	7'-11 1/2"
Draft	27"
Hull Weight (approx.)	1600 lbs.
Displacement	5532 lbs.
Freeboard forward	5'-0"
Freeboard Aft	3'-2"
Hull depth	6'-9"
Height overall	9'-9"
Hold volume	140 cu. ft.
Fuel capacity	80 gals.
Headroom (min.)	6'-1"
Sail area	24 sq. ft.
Sleeping capacity	2

Hull type: Semi-displacement, hard chine hull with practical cruising speed of 7 to 8 knots, and a maximum hull speed of approx. 9 knots. Bottom design features bulbous forefoot with a reverse curve at the chine. Double diagonally planked to total thickness of 1/2" (3/4" optional). Topsides planked with sheet plywood to a total thickness of 3/8" (1/2" optional). Carvel planking or other conventional types are optional but not detailed in the plans.

Power: Single centrally mounted diesel or gasoline inboard; 10 SHP for 7 knot cruising speed, however, 20 -25 SHP advised where wind and sea conditions are against the vessel. Engines rated over 35 SHP not recommended. Total engine and gear should be 600 lbs. plus or minus 10%.

Trailer: Designed for use with GLEN-L SERIES 7000/10000 boat trailer plans.

COMPLETE PLANS include FULL SIZE PATTERNS for stem, breasthook, and half-section patterns for the frames and transom. Includes instructions, Bill of Materials, and Fastening Schedule.

Our **NOYO TRAWLER** is a sensible and appealing craft, especially for those who might be interested in turning hobby fishing into a profit making activity, at least part of the time. While compact in size and trailerable, the hold has a surprising 140 cubic feet of volume that will take on a couple of tons of fish or other cargo with ease. Just think! you can trailer your own **NOYO TRAWLER** anywhere, following the fishing grounds as they change and eliminating the cost of a full-time slip. You can operate on a shoestring since this economical vessel requires only nominal power using just a little more than one gallon of diesel fuel per hour for a range of about 500 miles!

Our naval architects incorporated a hard-chine semi-displacement hull in the **NOYO TRAWLER** design for easy construction and superb sta-

bility. A long, deep keel coupled with the steadying sail provides sure-footed handling underway or at rest while fishing. The deep forefoot and double curvature bottom combined with high freeboard, protective bulwarks, and watertight decks, instills peace-of-mind normally associated only with much larger boats. Husky sawn frame construction with double diagonally planked plywood bottom and sheet plywood sides assures a strong craft capable of taking rough weather conditions that would send less able boats back to the protection of their harbors.

The cuddy cabin forward sleeps two and has full headroom plus a head. The anchor rode stows below the berths and passes up through a pipe to the foredeck. The pilothouse provides shelter and sitting space, plus a small galley worked in along with the control console, hinged table, and storage spaces.

The tabernacle-stepped mast pivots aft quickly and easily to clear low bridges, and full length double rub rails take the brunt of bumps and scrapes so common to workboat conditions. Construction materials and methods are well within the realm of the average amateur. There is no steam bending required and materials are standard sizes and types. Plans come with Table of Offsets for those who desire to loft the lines to full size, or FULL SIZE PATTERNS are available with the plans to eliminate this process.

AVAILABLE FOR THIS DESIGN:
- **Study Plans**
- **Plans & Patterns**
- **Bronze Fastening Kit**
- **Fiberglass Kit**
- **See Price List**

KOKANEE

A 20' CENTER CONSOLE SPORTFISHER

CHARACTERISTICS

Length overall .... 20'6"(*)
Beam .... 8'2"
Draft (hull) .... 13"
Hull depth (max) .... 4'7"
Displacement .... 3500 lbs.
Hull weight (approx) .... 1400 lbs.
Fuel capacity .... 70 gals.
Horsepower (max) 200
Cockpit size (nom) .... 17'4" x 7'
Trailer: . Designed for use with GLEN-L SERIES 2900/3800 boat trailer plans.
(*) 19'0" Optional

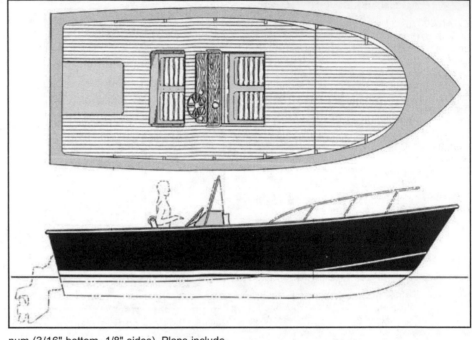

Our KOKANEE is based on a beamy, fast "WIDE-TRACK" hull design that's plenty stable for sportfishing, yet easy riding. A deep-v (45° bow deadrise) forefoot blends into a semi-v (13° transom deadrise) aft for stability and economy. Flaring topsides with integral chine flats knock down spray for a dry ride. A huge self-bailing cockpit with center console and raised casting deck forward can hold a gang of anglers and their gear. Fuel capacity is generous for long range. Power can be single outboard or I/O's to 900 lbs. (700 lbs. with 19' length).

Construction is especially aimed at the do-it-yourself builder, even first-timers. Hull options include sheet plywood (1/2" bottom, 3/8" sides) over sawn frames, or welded aluminum (3/16" bottom, 1/8" sides). Plans include FULL SIZE PATTERNS for frame members, instructions especially for do-it-yourselfers, material listings, plus a fastening schedule on the wood version.

BARRACUDA

A 23' TRAILERABLE PILOTHOUSE SPORTFISHER

CHARACTERISTICS

Length overall .... 23'1" (*)
Length waterline .... 19'8"
Beam .... 8'6"
Draft (hull) .... 14-1/2"
Hull depth (max.) .... 4'7"
Displacement .... 4100 lbs.
Hull weight (approx.) .... 1250 lbs.
Fuel capacity .... 100 gals.
(*) Optional 22' or 24'

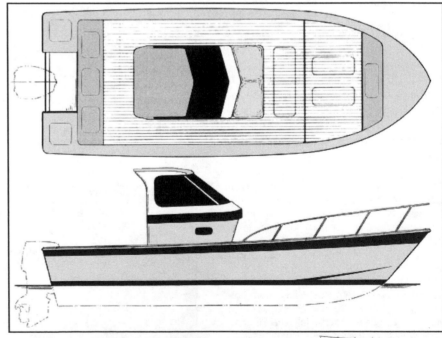

With a semi-enclosed pilothouse, there's no need to cut your day short on the water due to blistering sun, unrelenting rain, or freezing wind. Two adults can escape these elements in full standing headroom. And equally important, there is an enclosed head forward and below the offset control station with generous headroom above the "throne". Other features include self-bailing cockpit, full walk-around access, forward casting deck, and lots of space for built-in wells, fish boxes, and integral seating areas.

The easy riding hull features a 40° bow entry and 18-1/2° transom vee. Integral chine flats and double lift strakes each side of the centerline on the bottom pop the hull onto plane with little fuss. Plans detail single or twin outboards, or I/O units up to 1250 lbs., all with plenty of fuel available. Plywood sheet planking is easy to build and features double 1/4" bottom and 3/8" sides. Aluminum hulls are 3/16" on bottom and 1/8" sides. All plans includes FULL SIZE PATTERNS for framing backbone members, plus instructions, material list, and fastening schedule (wood hulls).

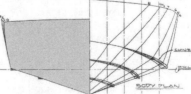

LA PAZ 22 — A 22' TRAILERABLE CENTER CONSOLE SPORTFISHER

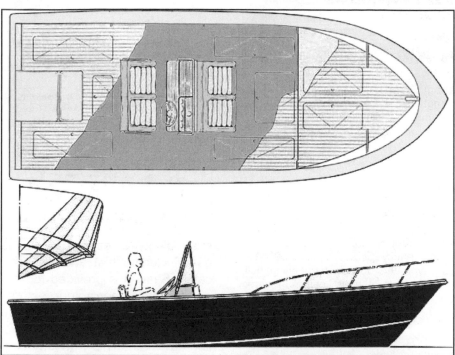

CHARACTERISTICS

Length overall	22'1" (*)
Length waterline	18'8"
Beam	8'6"
Draft (hull)	14½"
Hull depth (max.)	4'7"
Displacement	3800 lbs.
Hull weight (approx.)	1200 lbs.
Fuel capacity	100 gals.

Trailer: . Designed for use with GLEN-L SERIES 7000/10000 boat trailer plans.
(*) 20' to 24' Optional

This fisherman's delight has an agile, superb-riding variable-angle deep-v hull with a 40+° forefoot angle and 18-1/2° transom angle. Wide chine flats and two lift strakes per side assure directional control, quick and economical performance, and the rock-solid stability that fishermen demand.

A huge self-bailing cockpit includes raised casting platform forward, space for a portable head, plenty of storage, and seating for four including fore-or-aft facing helm seat. Power is by I/O units to 1200 lbs., or single or twin outboards (25" shaft length singles; 20" or 25" twins). Other power systems (v-drive, jets, bracket-mounted outboard, etc.) may be suitable with minor modifications. Fuel capacity is generous regardless.

Plywood planking is double 1/4" bottom, 3/8" sides, all sheathed with fiberglass. Aluminum hulls use 3/16" bottom and 1/8" sides. Plans with instructions show how to vary length 2' shorter or longer, and include FULL SIZE PATTERNS, instructions, material listings, and fastening schedule (wood plan). A carefully planned structure emphasizing longitudinal stiffeners minimizes the need for side frames encroaching upon cockpit space.

AVAILABLE FOR THIS DESIGN:
- Study Plans
- Plans & Patterns
- Bronze Fastening Kit
- Fiberglass Kit

See Price List

KEY WEST

A 23' CENTER CONSOLE SPORTFISHER

BUILD IN PLYWOOD

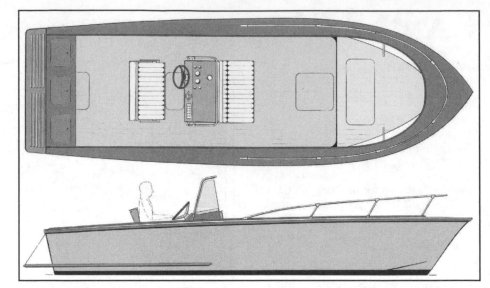

CHARACTERISTICS

Length overall	22'-9"
Length waterline	19'-10"
Beam	7'-11"
Draft	15"
Hull depth	4'-1"
Displacement	4000 lbs.
Hull weight (approx.)	1300 lbs.
Freeboard forward	2'-11"
Freeboard aft	2'-3"
Height overall	6'-5"
Cockpit size	20'x 6'
Cockpit depth	24" to 30"
Fuel capacity	60 gals.

Hull type: Vee bottom, hard chine hull, with bulbous keel and reverse curve at chine. Bottom designed for double diagonal planking, sides developed for sheet plywood planking.

Power: Single centrally mounted inboard engine to 1200 lbs., single or twin outboards to 400 lbs., or stern mounted inboard driving through an outdrive, jetdrive, or v-drive, not exceeding 700 lbs. Reduction gear may be required for inboard engines.

Trailer: Designed for use with GLEN-L SERIES 5000/6000 boat trailer plans.

COMPLETE PLANS include FULL SIZE PATTERNS for stem, breasthook, harpin, and half-section patterns for the frames and transom. Includes instructions, Bill of Materials, and Fastening Schedule.

The **KEY WEST** is a sportfisherman's dream come true! This boat is *all* cockpit! And that means plenty of room for a gang of anglers without tripping over each other. There's even plenty of space for all the gear including bait and the prize catch. Seating is provided for four and the helmsman's seat features a pivoting backrest so it can be used in equal comfort as a dual fishing chair. The transom step hinges up and out of the way when necessary and there is a compartment for carrying a portable head.

The **KEY WEST** can be powered in a variety of ways. Standard power is by a centrally located inboard under the removable control console. An optional deep skeg can be used for protection of underwater gear and for excellent directional stability at slow trolling speeds. Optional power can be provided by single or twin outboard motors, or even stern mounted inboards driving through an outdrive, jet-drive, or v-drive.

The **KEY WEST** is a rugged and seaworthy craft with a good turn of speed. The vee bottom hull features a bulbous entry for soft riding while the chine has a reverse curvature to deflect spray for a dry ride. The hull aft is modified to provide a stable fishing platform unlike the many tippy extreme vee hull types. Hull construction features strong but simple double diagonal plywood bottom planking with convenient sheet plywood used on the sides for economical construction. Not only will the **KEY WEST** cost far less than a comparable stock boat, but by building your own, you can get a boat just the way *you* want it that's truly custom built! And you can have the pride of stating, "I built it myself".

AVAILABLE FOR THIS DESIGN:
- **Plans & Patterns**
- **Bronze Fastening Kit**
- **Fiberglass Kit**
See Price List

EAGLE
A 22' TRAILERABLE LOBSTER BOAT

STRIP PLANKED, COLD-MOLDED, OR FIBERGLASS

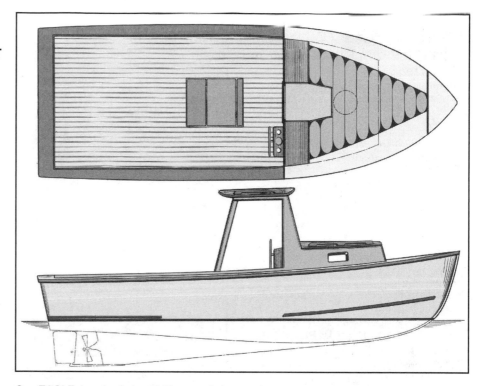

CHARACTERISTICS

Length overall	22'-0"
Length waterline	20'-0"
Beam	7'-11"
Draft (inboard version)	2'-2"
Draft (outboard and I/O version)	1'-3"
Hull depth	4'-7"
Displacment	3600 lbs.
Hull weight (approx.)	1000 lbs.
Headroom (cabin)	4'-4"
Freeboard forward	3'-6"
Freeboard aft	2'-1"
Height overall (max.)	8'-11"
Cockpit size	6'-8"x 12'-6"
Cockpit depth	2'-0" to 2'-4"
Sleeping capacity	2
Fuel capacity	80 gals.

Hull type: Round bilge hull with flat run aft, skeg, and flaring topsides characteristic of New England lobster boats. Hull can be built in wood using conventional strip planking or cold-molded epoxy strip planked with double laminated wood outer veneer. Alternately, hull may be built in "one-off" fiberglass planking or PVC foam or Balsa-core sandwich construction.

Power: Single diesel or gasoline inboard motor, centrally located up to 875 lbs., driving through a straight shaft; or stern mounted motor driving through an outdrive between 400 and 600 lbs. total; or outboard (single or twin) to 450 lbs.

Trailer: Designed for use with GLEN-L SERIES 5000/6000 boat trailer plans.

PLANS & PATTERNS - WOOD AND FIBERGLASS VERSIONS INCLUDE: COMPLETE PLANS plus FULL SIZE PATTERNS for stem, breasthook, and half-section patterns for the station forms and transom. Includes instructions, Bill of Materials, and Table of Offsets. *Fiberglass version includes Fiberglass Manual.*

Our **EAGLE** has landed and it's a scaled-down trailerable replica of those quick, nimble, easy riding, and seaworthy round bilge boats from New England better known as lobster boats. Modern materials and specially adapted construction methods make this boat ideal for the home builder who may have been put off by the idea of building such a boat using the more difficult and expensive traditional methods. The hull can be built in wood or fiberglass, with plans separately available for each. In wood, the plans for **EAGLE** show the hull built over temporary forms. Planking is the conventional strip type noted in popular boatbuilding texts, or a strip planked inner core with solid wood veneers applied in double layers on the outside, bonded with epoxy and sheathed with fiberglass. Either method results in a light, strong, cold-molded hull having a total thickness of 3/4" minimum.

With fiberglass, **EAGLE** can be built using the "one-off" male mold materials like fiberglass planking (C-FLEX), PVC foam core or Balsa core, with fiberglass laminates. In both the wood and fiberglass options, deck and cabin structures are simple, low-cost lumber and plywood, with exterior surfaces covered by fiberglass. Whether you choose wood or fiberglass, you can power **EAGLE** with the proven reliable inboard centrally located and driving through a straight shaft with the un-derwater gear all protected by a long, deep skeg. Or you can choose a stern mounted inboard engine driving through a stern drive (I/O unit), or even single or twin outboards hung on the transom, with either option using a skeg of less depth for propeller efficiency. No matter how you power, this boat takes little effort to drive so that economy will be a pleasant surprise. And when coupled with huge tank capacities, the range of your **EAGLE** will let you go where you want, when you want.

While **EAGLE** is easily trailered, there's plenty of room to make this a serviceable boat. The cockpit lends itself to all sorts of commercial and pleasure fishing operations, and is a good load carrier. The canopy offers a bit of weather protection, but can be easily deleted for fairer climates. If you want to lay over, the compact cabin offers two berths, a space for a head, and a couple of hanging lockers with tops that could provide a minimal galley. The plans include a simple method for varying the length plus or minus 10%. A Table of Offsets is provided for those who wish to loft the lines to full size, however, the full size patterns included make this job unnecessary. Instructions include hull material listings to make building your own **EAGLE** a rewarding and enjoyable experience, resulting in a boat for much less than one you would buy.

DOUBLE EAGLE

A 23' TRAILERABLE LOBSTER BOAT

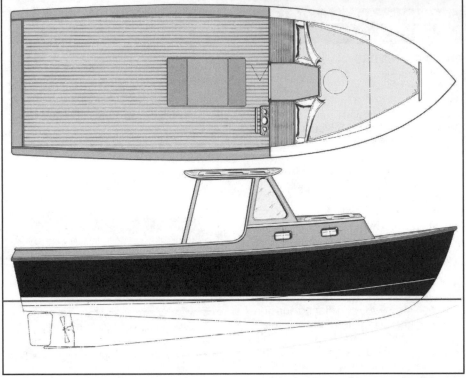

CHARACTERISTICS

Length overall .... 23'-0"
Length waterline .... 20'-8"
Beam .... 7'-11"
Draft (inboard version) .... 2'-5"
Draft (outboard and I/O version) .. 1'-6"
Hull depth .... 4'-11"
Displacment .... 4200 lbs.
Hull weight (approx.) .... 1200 lbs.
Height overall .... 9'-2"
Headroom (cabin, approx.) .... 4'-9"
Headroom (shelter top, approx.) . 6'-3"
Freeboard forward .... 3'-8"
Freeboard aft .... 2'-3"
Height overall (max.) .... 9'-2"
Cockpit size .... 7'x 13'
Cockpit depth .... 2'-5" to 2'-9"
Sleeping capacity 2
Fuel capacity (approx.):

	ALUMINUM VERSION	PLYWOOD VERSION
Inboard option	76 gals.	64 gals.
I/O option	82 gals.	68 gals.
Outboard option	88 gals.	66 gals.

Hull type:Hard chine, vee bottom with skeg, developed for sheet plywood or aluminum.

Power: Single inboard engine to 875 lbs., or single I/O engine from 400 to 600 lbs., or outboard (single or twin) from 200 to 325 lbs.

Trailer: Designed for use with GLEN-L SERIES 5000/6000 boat trailer plans.

COMPLETE PLANS include FULL SIZE PATTERNS for stem, and half-section patterns for the station forms and transom. Includes instructions, Bill of Materials, and all powering options. *Aluminum version includes "Aluminum Boatbuilding Guide".*

Don't be fooled by the traditional, well balanced lines of our **DOUBLE EAGLE** design. Underneath her timeless appearance lies a modern power-efficient hull that can be built in either sheet plywood or sheet aluminum, two of the lightest and strongest boatbuilding materials.

How is our **DOUBLE EAGLE** different from the traditional down east lobster boat? Primarily because of a hard-chine vee bottom hull that has a higher performance potential than the typical round bilge type. This feature also deflects spray at speed more efficiently, and the flatter bottom aft gives greater stability at rest. Yet the classic easy ride and positive handling characteristics are all retained.

You can power your **DOUBLE EAGLE** with a reliable centrally located inboard which has the underwater gear protected by a long, deep skeg. Or, details are included for a stern mounted inboard driving through a stern drive. Or, you can use single or twin outboards. In the latter two cases, the skeg is of less depth for propeller efficiency. Regardless of your power choice, you'll be amazed by her performance and sea kindliness.

You can select PLYWOOD or ALUMINUM construction. With PLYWOOD PLANS, the hull is built over sturdy sawn wood frames reinforced with longitudinal members and planked with sheet plywood. Decks and superstructure are also plywood, reinforced with solid wood members, and all exterior surfaces sheathed with fiberglass. No difficult woodworking methods are required. With ALUMINUM PLANS, the hull is all-welded 100% aluminum, including the superstructure. The hull consists of marine alloy plating, reinforced by a sturdy system of athwartship frames and longitudinal stiffeners.

The spacious single-level cockpit on the **DOUBLE EAGLE** is near the water, yet self-draining and deep for safety. Two people can sleep in the cabin and there are two hanging lockers (a small galley could be worked in if desired), plus space for a head. The helm area is well protected from the elements and fuel capacity is generous. Length of the boat can be increased or decreased by about 10% simply by respacing the frames a proportional amount if desired. Best of all, the **DOUBLE EAGLE** is legally trailerable.

EUREKA

A 26' FIBERGLASS WORKBOAT

BUILD IN FIBERGLASS

CHARACTERISTICS

Length overall .... 26'-0"
Length waterline .... 23'-4"
Beam .... 9'-10"
Draft .... 3'-6"
Displacement .... 10,200 lbs.
Freeboard forward .... 4'-9"
Freeboard Aft............................ 2'-11"
Height overall (approx. no mast) 11'-0"
Hold volume .... 180 cu. ft.
Fuel capacity .... 150 gals.
Fresh water capacity .... 20 gals.
Cruising range (approx.) 1000+ miles
Headroom (nominal) .... 6'-3"
Sail area .... 33 sq. ft.
Sleeping capacity 2
Hull type: Full displacement round bilge hull form with maximum hull speed of approx. 6 1/2 knots. Designed for "one-off" fiberglass construction using fiberglass planking or PVC foam sandwich core with fiberglass laminate.

Power: Single diesel or gasoline inboard of approx. 15 continuous SHP (20 to 30 brake HP) not exceeding 600 lbs. Reduction gear may be required, driving through straight shaft to 24" max. diameter propeller.

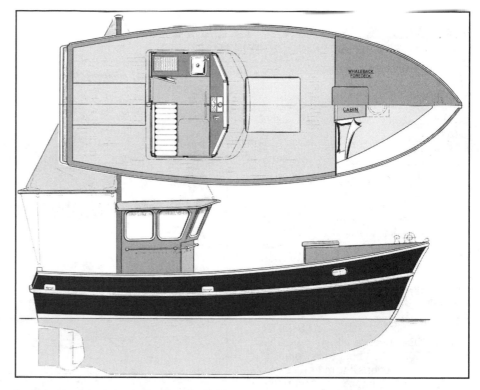

Inspired by traditional motor fishing vessels of North Sea fame, the **EUREKA** is a contemporary answer to the need for a sturdy, compact, and economical vessel suitable for commercial and pleasure use. While maintaining the character of these proven vessels, our designers have included features and modifications that experienced skippers will quickly appreciate. For example, a transom stern with reverse curved running lines aft increases deck space, minimizes pitching, adds reserve buoyancy under loading, and reduces squatting, thereby lowering power requirements for better economy as opposed to traditional canoe stern types. Unlike the chubby hulls of yesteryear, the **EUREKA** is trim where it should be, up forward for a smooth ride, yet with a deep forefoot and long keel for directional stability, and with plenty of flare

to reduce plunging, deflect spray, and improve the appearance.

But, the time-tested features of safety and reliability have not been sacrificed. These include a strong whaleback foredeck, reverse raked windshield, steadying sail, husky rub rails, watertight decks with protective bulwarks, raised rudder heel with straight keel shoe for grounding protection, emergency tiller, and tabernacle-stepped mast. Best of all, the hull can be divided into three watertight compartments. The pilothouse has amenities for two crew members, plus a double cabin with head forward, both with full standing headroom. Usable hold volume is about 180 cubic feet, capable of carrying 3 tons of cargo. Coupled with a 1000+ mile range and modest power needs, the **EUREKA** makes sense in these days of high fuel and equipment costs.

The extra heavy fiberglass hull construction uses proven "one-off" materials and methods, and features an inner gridwork reinforcement system. The balance of the structure uses a composite of standard materials with fiberglass well suited to the abilities of the experienced amateur or small custom yard. The plans cover all aspects of

the construction, and include complete instructions plus the illustrated manual, "Fiberglass Boatbuilding the GLEN-L Way". No lofting of the hull lines is required since full size patterns are provided for all the members used for the hull configuration.

COMPLETE PLANS include FULL SIZE PATTERNS for stem contour and half-section patterns for the station sections, bulkheads (form contours), whaleback forms, and deck camber pattern. Includes instructions, Hull Materials Listing, and GLEN-L Fiberglass Manual.
STUDY PLANS AVAILABLE

ATLANTIC SKIFF

A 24' TRAILERABLE OPEN-COCKPIT INBOARD SPORTFISHER

CHARACTERISTICS

Length overall .. 24' 6" (25' 3" optional)
Length waterline .... 22' 0"
Beam .... 8' 6"
Draft .... 1' 7" (Standard skeg)
.... 2' 7" (Deep skeg)
Freeboard forward .... 3' 7"
Freeboard aft................................ 2' 1"
Hull depth (w/out skeg) .... 3' 6"
Displacement .... 5100 lbs.
Hull weight (approx) .... 2500 lbs. (*)
Fuel capacity .... 80 or 100 gals.
Motor weight max. .... 1300 lbs.
Cockpit size .... 17-1/2' x 7'
Speed/power recommendations:
Minimum (20 knots) .... 130 SHP (**)
30 Knots .... 225 SHP (**)
40 Knots .... 300 SHP (**)
Trailer: . Designed for use with GLEN-L SERIES 5000/6000 boat trailer plans.(*) May vary with options and materials used (**) Estimation is based on shaft horsepower

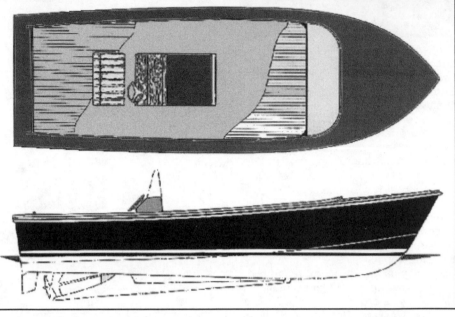

Seaworthiness and traditional good looks separate this design from others her size. Just like the traditional sportfishing boats often seen along the Eastern Atlantic seaboard states, our ATLANTIC SKIFF features a prominent reverse-curved bow flare along with a sharply "vee'd" hull entry for a smooth, dry ride and attractive appearance that can't be duplicated in hulls built from ordinary sheet plywood. Bottom lines flatten out to a moderate transom vee for the stability fisherman appreciate while also reducing fuel consumption and power needs in the process. Hull options include a shallower "standard" skeg for use when speed and minimal draft are paramount, or a longer deep skeg option that offers optimum maneuverability and protection for underwater hardware in the event of debris or grounding.

Power comes from a centrally-located "direct drive" inboard (gas or diesel) housed within the center console. This is a proven, reliable set-up that's easy to maintain and doesn't get in the way when working or landing the catch. And there is plenty of fuel possible for extended range. The spacious self-bailing cockpit is close to the water, but with adequate depth (24"-27") for security.

Construction is well-suited to the do-it-yourself woodworker, even for those who have not built a boat. No special materials or methods (such as steam bending) are required. Hull planking is "cold molded" double diagonal type using either solid wood veneers or plywood cut into strips.

Frames are sawn to shape from ordinary lumber and plywood. Optionally, topsides can be strip planked from solid wood. Husky motor stringers run almost the entire length of the hull. Building the hull is done upside down over a building form of ordinary lumber fully detailed in the plans. Epoxy resins and adhesives are highly advised throughout the construction, using encapsulation techinques for added longevity, durability, and reduced maintenance. Fiberglass cloth/epoxy hull sheathing is recommended on the final hull exterior to enhance such qualities while adding to appearance.

Plans cover all options, including length options, and sequential instruction manual with fastening schedule and materiial list. Also included are FULL SIZE PATTERNS for all the "backbone" members such as frames, stem, and transom; NO LOFTING IS REQUIRED. STUDY PLANS show more details of the construction, features, and building methods used.

AVAILABLE FOR THIS DESIGN:
- **Study Plans**
- **Plans & Patterns**
- **Fiberglass Kit**
See Price List

A-LURE

A 25' X 8 1/2' WALKAROUND SPORTFISHER

BUILD IN PLYWOOD OR ALUMINUM

CHARACTERISTICS

Length overall .... 25'-2"
Length waterline .... 20'-8"
Beam .... 8'-6"
Draft.. 15"
Hull depth .... 4'-10"
Displacement .... 6450 lbs.
Hull weight (approx.) .... 1500 lbs.
Headroom (approx.) .... 6'-0"
Freeboard forward .... 3'-7"
Freeboard aft .... 2'-7"
Height overall .... 8'-1"
Cockpit size (approx.) .... 12'-6"x 7'-6"
Sleeping capacity 2
Fuel capacity .... 200 gals.
Fresh water capacity .... 20 gals.
Hull type:Hard chine full length deep vee
        with 18° min. deadrise, bulbous
        keel section, and lift strakes. De-
        veloped for sheet plywood
        planking (1/2" bottom, 3/8" sides),
        or welded aluminum plating (3/
        16" bottom, 1/8" sides).
Power: Stern mounted diesel or gasoline
        inboard motor connected to an
        outdrive or vee drive. Motor weight
        with outdrive: 600-1200 lbs; with
        vee drive: 800-1400 lbs. Other
        transom or bracket-mounted drive
        systems may be used, but are not
        detailed. Twin motors also optional
        within weight ranges stated, but
        not detailed, and motor boxes may
        be required in cockpit.
Trailer: Designed for use with GLEN-L
        SERIES 7000/10000 boat trailer
        plans.

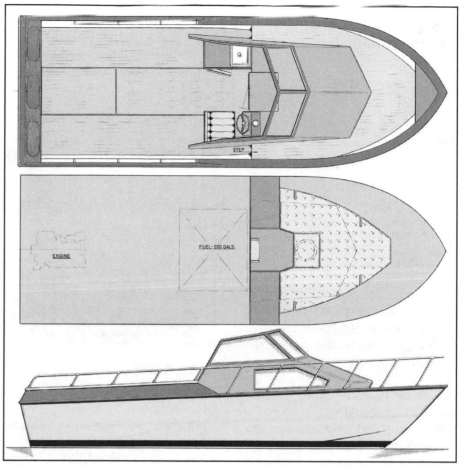

PLYWOOD VERSION
COMPLETE PLANS include FULL SIZE PATTERNS for stem and half-section patterns for the frames, sheer harpin, and transom. Includes instructions, Bill of Materials, and Fastening Schedule.

ALUMINUM VERSION
COMPLETE PLANS for welded aluminum construction include **FULL SIZE PATTERNS** for the stem and harpin contours, and half sections for the frames and transom. Includes Material Listing and "Aluminum Boatbuilding Guide".

A-LURE was designed to catch fish. She's a no nonsense, no frills sportfisher that makes no compromises to its purpose. A huge single level self-draining flush cockpit adjoins port and starboard by a step up to a full walkaround deck so a gang of anglers need not tangle or bump elbows.

What's more, our **A-LURE** has the capabilities you need to get to your favorite fishing grounds even if they're far offshore; a tremendous fuel capacity sees to that. If the going gets tough, this tough boat keeps going; a wide 8 1/2' deep vee hull assures that. Equipped with lift strakes and wide chine flats, you get a combination of rock solid stability, quick acceleration, and dryness that's remarkable.

Yet our **A-LURE** doesn't forsake amenities. If you want to lay over, the accommodations offer comfort and spaciousness equal to that of many cruisers this size. Berthing is on a 6 1/2' double in a cabin with full-standing headroom. Space for a head is available, there are twin hanging lockers, and the galley is conveniently located in the cockpit.

Unlike heavier, less economical production boats, **A-LURE** can achieve high speeds with lower power requirements because of technologically advanced construction in either plywood or aluminum, two of the lightest and strongest of boatbuilding materials. With either material, a wide variety of powering options and speeds are possible.

Building your own **A-LURE** is easier than you think. FULL SIZE PATTERNS mean no lofting is required. Comprehensive instruction manuals are especially intended for amateurs. For those with nominal woodworking skills, the PLYWOOD VERSION is built over sawn frames crossed by simple longitudinal battens and extra long motor stringers. Decks and cabin are also plywood, with all exposed plywood surfaces best covered with a sheathing of fiberglass cloth and resin for easy maintenance and abrasion resistance.

If you have welding skills, the ALUMINUM VERSION features an all-welded hull, deck, and superstructure, except for the cockpit sole which is fiberglass covered plywood for economy, simplicity, and non-skid qualities. Lengthening or shortening the boat in either version by up to 10% is easily accomplished by respacing each of the frames a proportional amount. If you want to trailer your A-LURE, we have the plans to build a suitable trailer.

```
AVAILABLE FOR THIS DESIGN:
• Study Plans
• Plans & Patterns
• Bronze Fastening Kit
• Fiberglass Kit
See Price List
```

NOR'WESTER
A 26' TRAILERABLE SPORTFISH CRUISER

CHARACTERISTICS

Length overall .... 25'8" (*)
Length waterline .... 21'3"
Beam .... 8'6"
Draft (hull) .... 15-1/2"
Hull depth (max.)........................... 5'1"
Displacement .... 5900 lbs.
Hull weight (approx.)............. 1500 lbs.
Fuel capacity .... 120 gals.
Headroom .... 6'5"
Sleeping capacity 2
Cockpit size .... 11' x 7'
Trailer: . Designed for use with GLEN-L SERIES 5000/6000 boat trailer plans.
(*) 23' 1" to 28' 3" optional

Based on our popular CORONADO deep-vee hull design, NOR'WESTER is a practical trailerable boat configured for foul weather and rough seas. With an emphasis on practicality, the cabin has full headroom and an inside helm to assure a roomy, warm, dry, and protected environment for passengers and skipper. The forward-raked windshield commonly associated with commercial boats improves visibility while minimizing glare and heat radiation.

Two or three can sleep on the v-berth forward, and there's an enclosed head plus space for a galley or hanging locker. Or you can rearrange the interior to suit your needs. A gang of anglers will find plenty of room in the 11' long self-draining cockpit. Power can be single or twin outboards (25" long shaft for singles; 20" or 25" for twins), or I/O units to 1300 lbs.

Construction is easy with our FULL SIZE PATTERNS for the seven frames. These are combined with longitudinal stringers to further reinforce the rugged 1/2" bottom and 3/8" sides. Or build in welded aluminum using 3/16" bottom and 1/8" sides. Methods are given for varying boat length from about 23' to 28'. Plans include instructions, material list, and fastening schedule (wood plans).

NOTE: When purchasing plans for

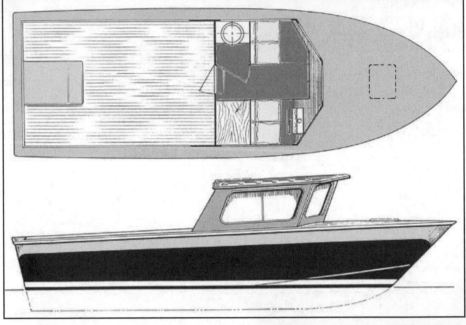

this design, you receive a complete set of plans and patterns for the CORONADO design as well as supplemental plans and instructions for the NOR'WESTER. Plans cover all length options; no need to specify.

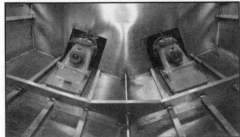

AVAILABLE FOR THIS DESIGN:
- **Study Plans**
- **Plans & Patterns**
- **Bronze Fastening Kit**
- **Fiberglass Kit**
See Price List

CAROLINA ANGLER

A 31' OPEN-COCKPIT INBOARD SPORTFISHER

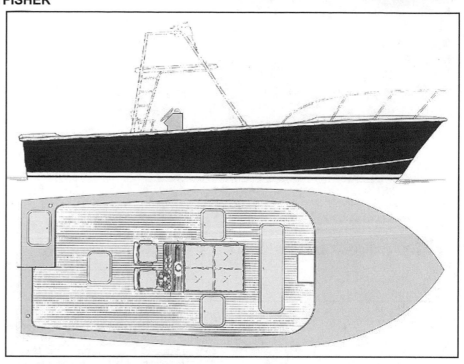

CHARACTERISTICS

Length overall (standard)	30'8"(*)
Length waterline	27'1"
Beam	11'0"
Draft (hull with skeg)	2'8"
Freeboard forward	4'2"
Freeboard aft	2'7"
Cockpit depth fwd/aft	36"/27"
Cockpit size (max)	20'6" x 9'6"

Displacement:
W/Min eng wt . 7960 lbs. (@ D.W.L.-1")
W/Max engine wt 8900 lbs. (@ D.W.L.)
Fuel capacity .... 230 gals.
(*) 29'10" or 31'6" options with plans

Enamored by those flashy sportfishing machines common to ports-of-call along the Southeastern U.S. seaboard, but not their cost? Then CAROLINA ANGLER is the boat for you. With a graceful "S"-curved sheerline, flaring bow topsides, and wave-flattening deep-v forefoot entry, this is one seaworthy hull equal to anything you could buy. Variable v-bottom lines flatten aft for reduced drag, maximum economy, higher speed potential, and the rock-solid stability fishermen want at-rest and underway. A long skeg assures directional control. Power is transmitted through a time-proven reliable single centrally-mounted inboard engine located below the center console motor box. Operating speeds from just over 20 knots up to 36 knots are possible with either gasoline or diesel motors between 1000 and 2200 lbs. These are supported on nearly full-length motor stringers. Power varies with displacement and ultimate boat weight: Lightest engines range from 135 to 350 SHP; Max engines between 150 and 470 SHP.

Features include a spacious self-bailing cockpit close to the water, but plenty deep for security. Cockpit length can be varied to suit your type of fishing layout. In either case, there is plenty of room for bait wells, fish boxes, and a gang of anglers.

Overnight accommodations for two are available under the foredeck along with space for a head; there is sitting headroom above the berth tops. A tower is optional.

Construction is well-suited to the do-it-yourself builder, yet is strong and rugged. FULL SIZE PATTERNS are provided for all the frame contour and other hull-forming members so no lofting is required. The hull is built upside down over a simple jig detailed on the plans. Epoxy resins and adhesives are used throughout the construction, with fiberglass/epoxy sheathing over the hull exterior for added durability, integrity, and appearance.

No special materials, skills, or building methods (such as steam bending) are required. Hull planking is "cold molded" using either plywood cut into strips or solid wood veneers laid in double diagonal format; 3/4" total on the topsides and 1" on the bottom. Ordinary sheet plywood planking isn't appropriate for such a design since it can't conform to the attractive reverse curved hull lines that make this boat what it is.

Plans cover all aspects of the design including hull length options, sequential instruction manual, fastening schedule, and hull material listing. STUDY PLANS are available if you need more information and details prior to purchasing plans; these come with a hull material list for cost estimating purposes.

AVAILABLE FOR THIS DESIGN:
- **Study Plans**
- **Plans & Patterns**
- **Fiberglass Kit**

See Price List

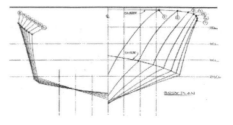

POT LUCK

A 33' LOBSTER-TYPE BOAT

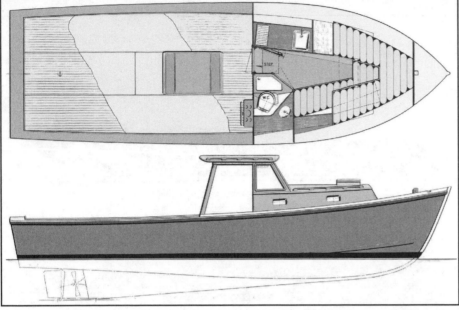

CHARACTERISTICS

Length overall	33'-3"
Length waterline	30'-0"
Beam	10'-7"
Draft	2'-11"
Displacement	9250 lbs.
Freeboard forward	5'-0"
Freeboard aft	2'-11"
Height overall	10'-9"
Headroom (min. at centerline)	6'-2"
Cockpit size (nominal)	9'x 18'
Fuel capacity	200 gals.
Water capacity	100 gals.
Sleeping accommodations	3

Hull type: Round bilge hull form with a flat run aft, long deep skeg, and flaring topsides forward, characteristic of New England lobster boats. Build in wood or one-off fiberglass. The wood version is built using conventional strip planking or cold-molded epoxy strip planked with triple laminated wood outer veneer. Fiberglass version: plans detail fiberglass planking and sandwich core construction.

Power: Single engine, either gasoline or diesel powered, located amidship using conventional straight shaft with reduction gear to suit. Maximum practical speed of 16 to 18 knots using 100 to 120 SHP. Slower speeds with lower horsepower engines are equally suited.

COMPLETE PLANS include FULL SIZE PATTERNS for the stem, breasthook, and transom and station (frame) contours. Includes instructions, Bill of Materials, and Table of offsets. *FIBERGLASS version includes FIBERGLASS MANUAL. STUDY PLANS AVAILABLE*

The **POT LUCK** design brings the renown New England lobster boat within the capabilities of the competent amateur builder. Our modern building methods, coupled with proven materials, make building the characteristic round bottomed hull form much easier than traditional methods more suited to professionals. These easily driven, smooth riding hulls with fine entries and long, flat running lines aft, make money saving sense in these days of increasing fuel costs. That's why our designers included generous sized tanks for plenty of range. For reliability, there's a long, deep skeg to protect the rudder, shaft, and propeller, while at the same time assuring good directional control.

Everyone knows of the traditional beauty of these hulls, and our **POT LUCK** is no exception. Flaring topsides forward are not only attractive, but when coupled with spray rails, these hulls stay dry and have an easy motion when the going gets tough. Use her for a yacht, sport boat, or even commercially. That huge cockpit adapts to a wide variety of uses including sportfishing, diving, various types of specialty fishing (such as lobstering, crabbing, oystering or scalloping), or anywhere you might need a quick, nimble, seaworthy, and economical craft. The cockpit is self-draining and watertight, with a sub-surface drain system for hosing down, and you won't need to worry about covering it if you don't want to.

Unlike some stripped-out utility boats, we made the cabin area yacht-like for comfort. Berths are provided for three, and there's plenty of seating area. The cabin features full headroom with plenty of lockers, drawers, and a hanging locker. The galley is complete and the toilet room features a shower and lavy. The control station is covered and protected, with engine and bilge access readily at hand through centerline hatches.

Hull construction is either by wood or fiberglass, with separate plans available for either material. For WOOD construction, the plans show a hull built over temporary forms which do not remain in the hull. However, a series of full and partial bulkheads, floor timbers, and motor stringers later installed reinforce what amounts to a virtually frameless "monocoque" hull that is strong, but light in weight. Planking is by the conventional strip plank method (seen in numerous boatbuilding books and used for generations), or cold-molded using a combination strip planked inner core with solid wood veneers applied triple diagonally on the outside, all epoxy glued with fiberglass sheathing over. Hull thickness either way is a minimum of 1-1/8".

The FIBERGLASS version details "one-off" methods, either with the fiberglass planking method (C-FLEX), PVC foam core, or Balsa core in conjunction with fiberglass laminates. Regardless of the method used to build the hull, the cabin, cockpit, and deck are made from wood and plywood in the conventional method, sheathed on the outside with fiberglass for low cost, simplicity, and durability.

For those who may want to change the length of the boat, a simple method is given in the instructions to vary the length plus or minus 10%. While a Table of Offsets is provided with the plans for those who may want to loft the lines, the full size patterns provided make this tedious job unnecessary. Voluminous instructions plus hull material listings included with the plans greatly simplify the building of your own **POT LUCK**, giving you a custom boat at a cost far less than a comparable stock boat of this type, if there even is such a thing!

DAUNTLESS

A 36' SEMI-DISPLACEMENT WORKBOAT

BUILD IN PLYWOOD OR FIBERGLASS

CHARACTERISTICS

Length overall	35'-8"
Length waterline	31'-3"
Beam	13'-9"
Draft	3'-6"
Displacement	17,400 lbs.
Freeboard forward	6'-6"
Freeboard aft	3'-3"
Height overall	15'-10"
Fuel capacity	250-375 gals.
Fresh water capacity	20 gals.
Cruising range (approx.)	875 miles
Hold volume (approx.)	200 cu.ft.
Cockpit size	4'x 11'
Headroom (min.)	6'-5"
Sleeping accommodations	2

Hull type: Semi-displacement, hard chine hull with efficient speed range to 10 knots. Construction can be double diagonal cold-molded plywood or solid wood on bottom, and double diagonal plywood or wood on sides. Fiberglass hull construction optional, using either fiberglass planking or PVC foam sandwich construction. Balsa core construction can be used but not detailed.

Power: Single gasoline or diesel motor of approximately 100 continuous shaft horsepower with suitable reduction gear. Twin motors may be used, but are not as practical or economical, and hence not recommended.

Our **DAUNTLESS** design is specifically intended to fill a variety of workboat uses, including various types of commercial fishing, cargo handling, and related activities. Her modest size and power requirements assure profitable operation for the owner-operator who is willing to build his own craft. Here's a proven semi-displacement hull that will give speeds to 10 knots with very modest power requirements adding up to exceptional range and economy. Hold capacity is quite commodious, with over 200 cubic feet of volume.

The **DAUNTLESS** is a flexible design, allowing outfitting and equipment to be installed to suit the owner's requirements. There's plenty of open deck space and a recessed aft cockpit adaptable to many uses. Net reels, masts and booms, out-riggers, and other deck gear can be added just to suit, making for a true custom workboat. High freeboard and protective bulwarks make for a safe, dry running vessel. A long, deep skeg protects the single 28" maximum diameter propeller and assures good directional stability. The deep bulbous forefoot minimizes plunging in a head sea and provides an easy ride.

Accommodations are available for two crew members, including a head, galley space, a hinged table, and settee. Dual control stations and a flying bridge assure safety and comfort in any weather conditions. Plans are available for either plywood and lumber, or "one-off" fiberglass materials for use in building the hull. Either method is well within the abilities of most experienced amateurs, or construction can be done by the small professional yard if desired. Either way,

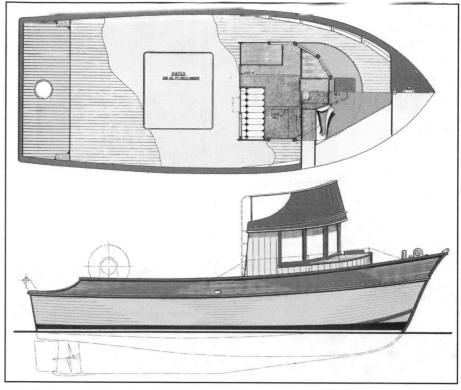

you'll have a genuine custom workboat at a fraction of the cost of expensive production boats.

AVAILABLE FOR THIS DESIGN:
- **Study Plans**
- **Plans & Patterns**
- **Fiberglass Kit**

See Price List

COMPLETE PLANS include FULL SIZE PATTERNS for frames (station contours), stem, transom, and transom knee. Includes builder's specifications, Table of Offsets, and Bill of Materials. *FIBERGLASS version includes FIBERGLASS MANUAL.*

VIGILANT

A 42' SEMI-DISPLACEMENT WORKBOAT

BUILD IN PLYWOOD OR FIBERGLASS

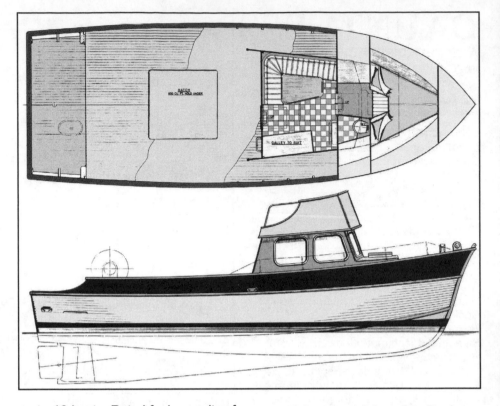

CHARACTERISTICS

Length overall	42'-0"
Length waterline	38'-4"
Beam	15'-3"
Draft	4'-6"
Displacement (at DWL)	25,600 lbs.
Displacement (at LWL)	38,200 lbs.
Freeboard forward (at DWL)	7'-6"
Freeboard aft (at DWL)	3'-10"
Height overall	17'-9"
Fuel capacity	700-1000 gals.
Fresh water capacity	120 gals.
Cockpit size	5'x 13'
Headroom	6'-3" - 6'-7"
Hold capacity (approx.)	850 cu.ft.
Sleeping accommodations	2-3

Hull type: Semi-displacement, hard chine hull with bulbous bow and reverse curve at chine forward. Efficient speed range to 10 knots. Triple diagonal cold-molded plywood or solid wood on bottom to 1 1/8" thick, and double diagonal plywood or wood on sides to 3/4" thick, fiberglass or comparably sheathed. "One-off" fiberglass hull construction optional.

Power: Single diesel motor of approximately 145 continuous shaft horsepower with suitable reduction gear. Twin motors may be used, but are not as practical or economical, and hence not recommended.

COMPLETE PLANS include FULL SIZE PATTERNS for frames (station contours), stem, transom, and transom knee. Includes builder's specifications, Table of Offsets, and Bill of Materials. *FIBERGLASS version includes FIBERGLASS MANUAL.*

The **VIGILANT** makes an ideal workboat that the owner can outfit to exactly suit his needs. This multi-purpose vessel can be used for both commercial and sport fishing, cargo carrying, general yard work, salvage operations, or other similar duties. Hold capacity is a substantial 850 cubic feet for an 8 to 10 ton working load under normal conditions. A single diesel of about 145 SHP driving a 34" maximum wheel will permit speeds up to 10 knots. Rated fuel capacity of 700 gallons allows plenty of range, even though extra capacity up to 1,000 gallons is available at the discretion of the skipper with regard to loading balance and stability.

Construction of the **VIGILANT** is specifically aimed at the amateur or small custom yard. Hull construction is either wood or fiberglass. WOOD methods feature strong and lightweight multi-diagonal plywood or solid wood over substantial wood frames and longitudinals, with exterior surfaces fiberglass sheathed. FIBERGLASS hull construction methods include the "one-off" materials, either the fiberglass planking technique or foam sandwich core with balsa core optional. With wood or fiberglass hulls, decks and superstructure are basic wood and plywood construction with exteriors sheathed with fiberglass for low cost and simplicity.

Features of the **VIGILANT** include a beamy hull, noticeable flare forward, a bulbous forefoot, and protective bulwarks for stay-at-sea ability. Accommodations include berths for 2 (3 in a pinch by using the settee), enclosed head with optional shower, hanging locker, roomy settee with table, and space for a complete galley. Dual controls with flying bridge allow continuous operation in fair weather or foul, and a recessed aft cockpit lends itself to many uses. Although a Table of Offsets is provided, lofting the lines of the **VIGILANT** is not necessary if using our available FULL SIZE PATTERNS. In addition, instructions, complete with hull material listings, are a part of all plan options.

> **AVAILABLE FOR THIS DESIGN:**
> - **Study Plans**
> - **Plans & Patterns**
> - **Fiberglass Kit**
>
> **See Price List**

GYPSY
A 20' TRAILERABLE HOUSEBOAT

BUILD IN PLYWOOD

CHARACTERISTICS

Length overall	20'-1"
Length waterline	17'-0"
Beam	7'-11"
Hull draft	9"
Freeboard forward	2'-10"
Freeboard aft	2'-7"
Hull depth	3'-5"
Height overall	7'-5"
Displacement	3250 lbs.
Hull weight (approx.)	1700 lbs.
Fuel capacity	70 gals. max.
Fresh water capacity	34 gals. max.
Headroom minimum	6'-4"
Sleeping capacity	4
Cockpit size	7' x 7'

Hull type: Full length, high deadrise, deep vee hull developed for sheet plywood planking.

Power: Single or twin outboard motors to 135 HP, or single inboard/outboard drive to 600 lbs. maximum.

Trailer: Designed for use with GLEN-L SERIES 2900/3800 boat trailer plans.

COMPLETE PLANS include FULL SIZE PATTERNS for the stem, breasthook, transom knee, harpin, and half-section patterns for each of the frames, transom, and cockpit seat top. Includes instructions, Bill of Materials, and Fastening Schedule.

If you enjoy all the comforts of houseboating, yet still want fast action on the water, then **GYPSY** may be the boat you've been waiting for. Above the gunwale she's all houseboat, but below the rail she's all speedboat. **GYPSY** has a modern vee bottom monohedron runabout hull, capable of speeds to 30 mph. With a generous flare forward and a spacious cockpit overhang, you'll be assured of a dry ride. Of course, she's just as comfortable with moderate power for leisurely cruising. Obviously, a boat of this type is safest when operated in protected waters.

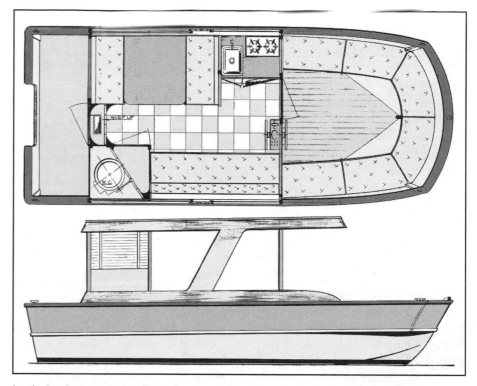

Let's look at some of the features that make **GYPSY** unique. First, observe that spacious cockpit; lots of room for sunbathing or fishing, and she even has provisions for an outside helm. Inside that bright and airy cabin, you'll find an amazing amount of room, with full headroom plus. She sleeps four adults and even has a private enclosed toilet room. The galley has room for the latest marine galley equipment and storage for cooking gear. What's more, you can use the cabin top for a sun deck. With all of these features, **GYPSY** is still easily trailered to your favorite cruising waters and can serve as a "camper" on the way.

AVAILABLE FOR THIS DESIGN:
- **Study Plans**
- **Plans & Patterns**
- **Bronze Fastening Kit**
- **Fiberglass Kit**
See Price List

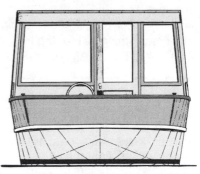

HUCK FINN & SUPER HUCK

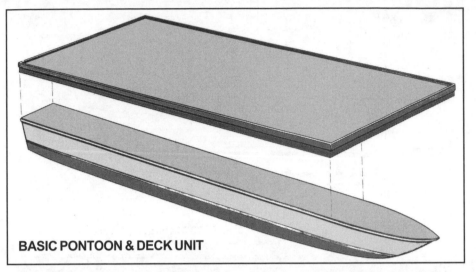

BASIC PONTOON & DECK UNIT

Our **HUCK FINN** and **SUPER HUCK** are versatile, modular concept, pontoon boats which can be built in several different lengths. Just about anyone can build their own, even if the most woodworking experience they've had is chopping wood for the fireplace. We provide the easy-to-use PLANS and FULL SIZE PATTERNS for the pontoons, plus details for the deck unit. You get the pleasure of deciding what to put on top. The possibilities are endless!

Build your own deck boat for the lake using our SPORTS CRAFT "cabin", make a swimming raft for the kids, or select one of our CABIN PLANS for a

real houseboat. These plans are very adaptable and allow you to build a boat to suit your needs to a tee. Use the **HUCK FINN** plans for 12' to 28' lengths with 8' beam if your carrying requirements are modest. For greater loads and more space, select the **SUPER HUCK** plans for extra capacity pontoons from 24' to 32' and beams from 8' to 10'.

Except for the 12' **HUCK FINN**, all units come with flaring bowed pontoons with sharp entry stems for least resistance. Stern sections are rockered to reduce power requirements and make handling easier. All units are stable as a rock. But don't try to

play Kon-Tiki, they are meant for use only in protected waters such as rivers and lakes. These boats are not meant for high speeds; leisurely speeds with low power and economy is the name of the game with either the **HUCK FINN** or the **SUPER HUCK**. All 8' models can be trailered using our special pontoon TRAILER PLANS. Deck units and the pontoons are detachable from each other so that storage need not be a problem.

NOTE: The HUCK FINN and SUPER HUCK PLANS & PATTERNS do not include the plans for the SPORTSCRAFT or HUCK FINN CABINS. These units must be ordered separately.

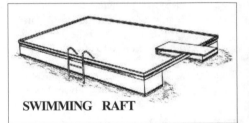

SWIMMING RAFT

COMPLETE PLANS include FULL SIZE PATTERNS for the stem, bow spreader, bow spreader gusset, and half-section patterns for each of the bulkhead/frames and transom. Includes instructions, Bill of Materials, and Fastening Schedule.

CHARACTERISTICS	12'	HUCK FINN VERSIONS				SUPER HUCK VERSIONS					
		16'	20'	24'	28'	24'x8'	24'x10'	28'x8'	28'x10'	32'x8'	32'x10'
Length overall	12'-0"	15'9"	19'-9"	23'-9"	27'-9"	23'-9"	23'-9"	27'-9"	27'-9"	31'-9"	31'-9"
Length of deck (max.)	12'-0"	12'-0"	16'-0"	20'-0"	24'-0"	20'-0"	20'-0"	24'-0"	24'-0"	28'-0"	28'-0"
Pontoon wt. lbs. ea. (approx.)	110	145	180	240	280	545	545	630	630	720	720
Deck unit wt. lbs. (approx.)	255	255	340	420	510	635	870	730	1045	890	1215
Total weight lbs. (approx.)	475	545	700	900	1070	1725	1960	1990	2305	2330	2655
Load capacity lbs. (max.)	1200	1050	1450	1850	2250	3385	3155	4085	3805	4780	4455
Horsepower recommended	--	5-20	5-35	5-45	10-55	15-55	15-55	15-60	15-60	20-75	20-75
Beam (nominal)	8'	8'	8'	8'	8'	8' max	10' max	8' max	10' max	8' max	10' max
Pontoon size (nominal)	All **HUCK FINN** - 18" wide x 19" deep					All **SUPER HUCK** - 24" wide x 24" deep					
Draft at load capacity	All **HUCK FINN** - 9" (plus skeg when used)					All **SUPER HUCK** - 12" (plus skeg when used)					

Hull type: Twin pontoons with deck unit. Developed for sheet plywood planking.
    HUCK FINN: 1/4" and 3/8"planking, 5/8" for deck. All members framed in solid wood.
    SUPER HUCK: 1/2" planking, 3/4" for deck. All members framed in solid wood.
Power: Most practical with single outboard centrally mounted. Anti-cavitation deflector to be installed under deck unit forward of motors (details for construction provided). Horsepower should not exceed recommendations. Twin outboards may be used, preferably with outboard transom mounting brackets aft of each pontoon, with sufficient bracing provided on the transom (details not included). Long shaft motors recommended.
Trailer: Designed for use with GLEN-L SERIES HUCK FINN or SUPER HUCK boat trailer plans.

PONTOON CABIN PLANS

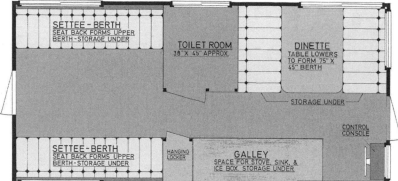

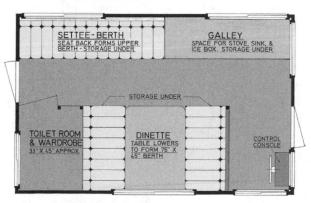

CHARACTERISTICS

	8' Cabin	12' Cabin	16' Cabin
Cabin length	8'-0"	12'-0"	16'-0"
Cabin width	8'-0"	8'-0"	8'-0"
Roof length	12'-0"	16'-0"	20'-0"
Area on deck	64 sq. ft	96 sq. ft.	128 sq. ft.
Height above deck	6'-6"	6'-6"	6'-6"
Sleeping capacity	2	4	6
Weight of structure (approx.)	500 lbs	700 lbs.	900 lbs.

Construction: Lightweight plywood panel interior with 2" stud wall construction and cambered roof over three full length cabin beams. Exterior covered with light gauge aluminum siding.

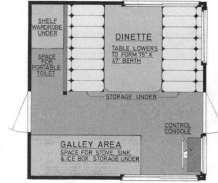

The **HUCK FINN CABIN PLANS** come in three sizes and are specifically designed for use with our **HUCK FINN** or **SUPER HUCK** pontoons. The construction methods used in these **CABIN PLANS** assure you of the lightest weight cabin consistent with strength and simplicity of building. The **8' CABIN** can be used on any version from 20' on up. The **12' CABIN** can be used on any model from 24' on up. The spacious **16' CABIN** can be used on any model from 28' on up.

Whichever **cabin plan** you select, you'll get a comfortable cabin arrangement which offers full headroom up to 6'-5" plus lots of light and ventilation. Each **CABIN PLAN** features a full 3' roof overhang at the front as well as a 4' "porch" both fromt and rear as a minimum. The SUPER HUCK versions built to 10' beam, have a 12" wide side deck each side. Every arrangement

has a control console and facilities for a galley as well.

The construction of the cabin is basic. The simple framework uses ordinary materials and fastenings to cut costs. The **CABIN PLANS** provide all the details for the windows, framing, and outside covering. Also provided are dimensions for all cabinets, settees, and partitions, *plus* printed procedural instructions complete with Bill of Materials.

While the arrangements shown are recommended, the manner in which

you equip your **HUCK FINN CABIN** is up to your desires and requirements. However, remember that the HUCK FINN and SUPER HUCK pontoons are not ocean-going freighters, so keep materials and equipment as light in weight as possible. Note that the weight of the cabin structure, plus everything aboard, must *not* exceed the load capacity listed for the particular pontoon version you are building. Be sure to check carefully the size of **CABIN PLANS** you want before ordering.

NOTE: These CABIN PLANS do not include the plans and patterns required to build the basic HUCK FINN or SUPER HUCK pontoons and deck unit. These must be purchased separately.

SPORTS CRAFT

NOTE: *This PLAN SET does not include plans or patterns required to build the basic HUCK FINN or SUPER HUCK pontoons and deck unit. These must be purchased separately.*

A **SPORTS CRAFT** on your HUCK FINN or SUPER HUCK (with 8' beam maximum), is perfect for fishing, picknicking, or leisurely day cruising. You can build the **SPORTS CRAFT** in either a 12' model for HUCK FINN pontoons 16' and 20' overall, or a 16' model for HUCK FINN pontoons 20' and 24' overall, or for SUPER HUCK in the 24' version with 8' beam. In all cases, one **SPORTS CRAFT** plan set does the job and provides all the details.

The **SPORTS CRAFT** provides plenty of seating plus a centrally located control console for the pilot. The PLANS detail this control console that has a special folding seat which can be folded out of the way so the helmsman can stand or sit in comfort. Boarding gates on each side allow easy entrance and exit, plus there is 6'-3" headroom under the beams.

The seats allow plenty of storage space below. All details for the simple construction are clearly shown, with instructions to supplement the drawings. The material listing specifies standard materials. Because of length variations plus options in materials and equipment, weight of the structure will add approximately 300 to 600 lbs. to the pontoons and must be deducted from the load capacity noted in order to determine weight available for passengers and gear.

MARK TWAIN

**28', 32', 36', & 40'
PONTOON HOUSEBOATS**

The **MARK TWAIN SERIES** features four separate lengths of pontoon houseboats from 28' to 40' long. All models feature a lightweight, stable catamaran hull design with fine bows that glide through the water. The simple construction consists of hulls made of sturdy bulkhead frames and sheet plywood planking with a minimum of bending required. There's no rust or noisy expansion and contraction as with steel drum-type pontoons. When fiberglass covered using our FIBERGLASS COVERING KIT, maintenance requirements are minimal.

The deckhouse on each **MARK TWAIN** is independent of the hull. This means you can change or even omit the deckhouse if you desire, as long as the load does not exceed that recommended. The deckhouse utilizes ordinary lumber, plywood panels, and aluminum sheeting outside. We include all the details necessary for

CHARACTERISTICS	28'	32'	36'	40'
Length overall	27'-8"	31'-8"	35'-8"	39'-8"
Beam	10'-2"	10'-2"	12'-2"	12'-2"
Draft (with skeg)	1'-4"	1'-4"	1'-4"	1'-4"
Freeboard to deck	2'-0"	2'-0"	2'-0"	2'-0"
Hull depth	3'-0"	3'-0"	3'-0"	3'-0"
Height overall	13'-4"	13'-4"	13'-4"	13'-4"
Displacement (lbs.)	6913	8163	9413	10663
Hull weight (approx. lbs.)	2100	2400	3000	3300
Deckhouse weight (approx. lbs.)	1200	1400	1600	1800
Load capacity (cabin, crew, etc.-lbs.)	4813	5763	6413	7363
Deck length	20'-0"	24'-0"	28'-0"	32'-0"
Deck area	200 sq. ft.	240 sq. ft.	336 sq. ft.	384 sq. ft.
Deckhouse length	14'-0"	18'-0"	20'-0"	24'-0"
Deckhouse width	9'-0"	9'-0"	9'-0"	9'-0"
Headroom (min./max.)	ALL VERSIONS - 6'-4" to 6'-10"			
Fuel capacity (gals.)	50	65	80	100
Water capacity (gals.)	50	65	80	100
Sleeping capacity	4	6	6	8
Horsepower capacity (total max.)	70 HP	80 HP	90 HP	100 HP

Hull type: Developed for sheet plywood planking. Hull form: rectangular section, except forward ends taper to pointed bows with flaring topsides. Bow and stern bottoms rockered for economical powering and ease of beaching. Intended for use in protected waters.

Power: Twin outboard motors, or I/O powerplant, mounted at the stern of each pontoon. Engines should not exceed 350 lbs. each.

building your own **MARK TWAIN**, from framing members to the interior cabinetry. Each set of plans includes instructions, a Bill of Materials, and Fastening Schedule, plus, FULL SIZE PATTERNS for all the hull framing members.

COMPLETE PLANS include **FULL SIZE PATTERNS** for the stems, breasthooks, bulkhead-frames, and transoms. Includes instructions with Bill of Materials and Fastening Schedule.

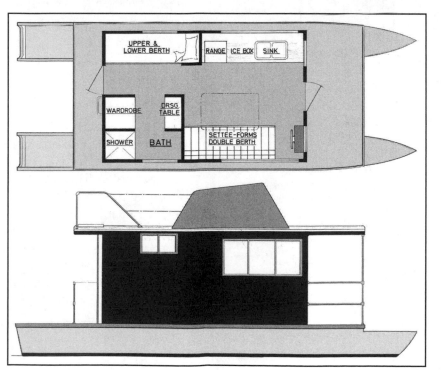

28' This compact version can sleep two couples in complete privacy. The bath area is a split arrangement with separate bath and dressing areas. The galley is the same size as our larger 32' version, as is the deckhouse area. There's plenty of room outside, both under the roof on the bow porch, and up on the cabin roof sun deck complete with flying bridge and twin controls, optional.

Continued on next page...

MARK TWAIN (continued)

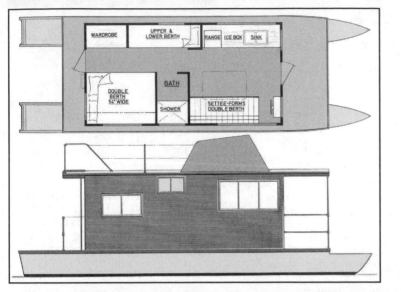

32' You can sleep six in this version. The bath is centrally located and there's a huge wardrobe. The deckhouse is airy and spacious and includes a galley with all the provisions of a modern vacation home. Twin controls can be included by using the sun deck, flying bridge, and inside helm. The bow porch makes a nice shady retreat.

AVAILABLE FOR THIS DESIGN:
- **Study Plans**
- **Plans & Patterns**
- **Bronze Fastening Kit**
- **Fiberglass Kit**
See Price List

36' Walkaround side decks, huge bow porch, and roomy sundeck offer comfort and convenience for a family of six. The galley-deckhouse living area is equal in size and features to our largest **MARK TWAIN**. The separate Owner's Stateroom has a roomy wardrobe and is adjacent to the bath area, and there's plenty of storage space which makes extended cruising a pleasure.

40' For large families where privacy and roominess are important, the **MARK TWAIN 40'** is the ticket. This model sleeps four couples in three cabins, and has a spacious bath complete with lavy and shower. There's plenty of room for everyone with a spacious galley/deckhouse living area, bow porch, huge sun deck with flying bridge, and convenient walkaround decks.

QUEST

A 23' TRAILERABLE HOUSEBOAT

BUILD IN PLYWOOD

CHARACTERISTICS

Length overall	23'-4"
Length waterline	20'-9"
Beam	7'-11"
Hull draft (with skeg)	13"
Freeboard forward	3'-8"
Freeboard aft	3'-3"
Hull depth	4'-5"
Height overall	8'-0"
Displacement	4630 lbs.
Fuel capacity	80 gals. max.
Fresh water capacity	40 gals. max.
Headroom	6' to 6'-6"
Sleeping capacity	5
Cockpit size (approx.)	5' x 7'
Cockpit depth	2'-3"

Hull type: Vee bottom, hard chine, planing hull developed for sheet plywood planking.

Power: Single or twin outboard motors, or single inboard/outboard drive. Maximum engine and drive weight combined not to exceed 600 lbs.

Trailer: Designed for use with GLEN-L SERIES 5000/6000 boat trailer plans with 6000 lbs. capacity option.

COMPLETE PLANS include FULL SIZE PATTERNS for the stem, breasthook, harpin, and half-section patterns for each of the frames, transom, and cockpit sole members. Includes instructions, Bill of Materials, and Fastening Schedule.

Our trailerable **QUEST** houseboat is equally at home poking around your favorite inlet or pulling skiers. Like the GYPSY, the **QUEST** is an ideal camping boat, either on the river or lake. Moor in a quiet spot for your base camp and use your dinghy to explore the shoreline or walk the edge of the river with your fishing pole.

There are sleeping accommodations for five, a roomy toilet room with a shower, a complete galley, big "front porch" forward cockpit, and the entire cabin top is a sun deck. Power can be provided by outboards or sterndrive inboards. With 100 HP you should expect speeds of 24 MPH. Beaching the boat is easy. This is a boat that gives total self-containment possibili-

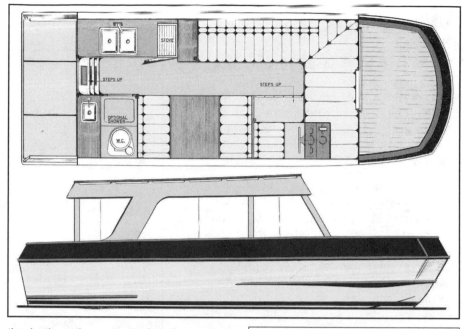

ties both on the water and on the road. Construction is easy, even for the amateur.

The **QUEST** is more than a boat you will be proud to say you built; it is your ticket to a new vacation lifestyle.

AVAILABLE FOR THIS DESIGN:
- Study Plans
- Plans & Patterns
- Bronze Fastening Kit
- Fiberglass Kit

See Price List

WATER LODGE &
WATER LODGE TOO

While not meant for anything fast, foul, or furious, they make a perfect retreat for anchoring a spell in your favorite backwater cove, or for moseying along protected waters in search of game, fish, sights, or solitude.

No special skills are required to build. Anyone who can drill a hole, drive a screw, and saw a board can do the job. In fact, if you can't build this boat, you probably can't build any boat. There's not a curved line anywhere other than the cabin top crown. Hence no lofting is required, and even full size patterns are unnecessary as a result. But plans do include instructions, material lists, plywood utilization layouts, and all the details to carry through at a minimum of effort and expense.

All plywood is standard 4' x 8' exterior grade (marine optional), while hull lumber is mostly 2" nominal stock found in just about any lumberyard. Equipment such as appliances and windows can be like those used on recreational vehicles, or typical residential items rather than costlier marine-types. We do suggest you have access to a table or radial arm saw to ease making long cuts on the 2" stock.

Both models sleep 4 with full headroom, and have similar amenities but with more room on WATER LODGE TOO. These include a settee with seat back that raises to form upper and lower berths, a dinette that converts to a double berth, fully-equipped galley, and enclosed head with shower. There's plenty of tank capacity for fuel, water, or waste. Other features include inside control station, front and back "porches" (decks), and sundeck on the house top.

You can tow on a trailer made from our plans which will basically be made as a "flatbed" type without special bunks or supports due to the flat bottom hull.

AVAILABLE FOR THIS DESIGN:
- **Plans & Patterns**
- **Fiberglass Kit**

See Price List

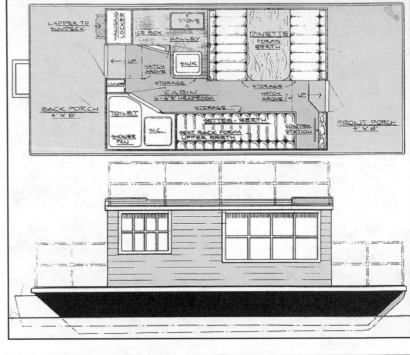

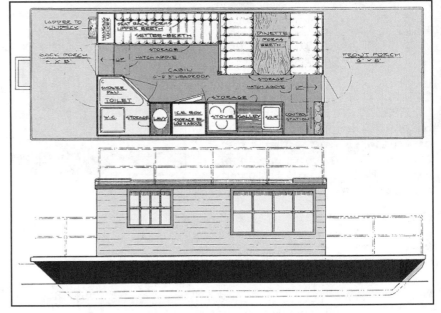

CHARACTERISTICS	Waterlodge	Waterlodge Too
Length overall (hull)	20'2"	24'0"
Beam	8'2"	8'2"
Draft (w/skegs)	11"	11"
Boat height	7'3"	7'3"
Displacement	4000 lbs.	5000 lbs.
Boat weight approx.	2000 lbs.	2400 lbs.
Tankage	110 gals.	110 gals.
Horsepower	25-50	30-70
Headroom	6' to 6'2"	6' to 6'2"
Trailer:	Designed for use with GLEN-L SERIES 5000/6000 boat trailer plans.	

DELTA Q

A 25' TRAILERABLE HOUSEBOAT

BUILD IN PLYWOOD

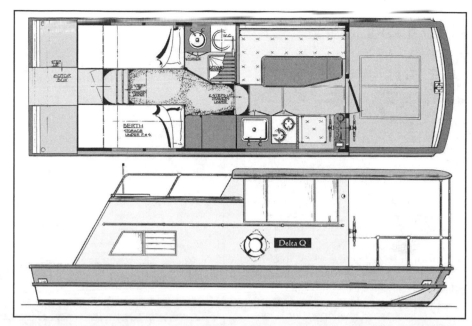

CHARACTERISTICS

Length overall	24'-11"
Length waterline	22'-8"
Beam	8'-0"
Draft (with skeg)	13"
Displacement	5860 lbs.
Height overall	8'-9"
Headroom	6'-1" to 6'-5"
Freeboard	2'-2"
Fuel capacity	90 gals.
Water capacity	85 gals.
Sleeping capacity	4

Hull type: Garvey-type with vee section forward, developed for sheet plywood planking.

Power: Single or twin outboard motors or stern mounted engine with outdrive not to exceed 800 lbs.

Trailer: Designed for use with GLEN-L SERIES 7000/10000 boat trailer plans.

COMPLETE PLANS include FULL SIZE PATTERNS for the stem, breasthook, forward chine and sheer members, and half-section patterns for the frame/bulkheads, transom, and bowpiece. Includes instructions, Bill of Materials, and Fastening Schedule.

The **DELTA Q** is unique in her size for her accommodations, versatility, space, comfort, and safety. The construction is made easy for the amateur builder by the use of rugged sheet plywood.

She provides sleeping comfort for four adults in full width, full length berths in two separate cabins. Six foot plus headroom has been provided throughout as well as a roomy enclosed toilet room and optional shower. In the deckhouse, there is a comfortable L-shaped dinette that will seat four or five for dining, and convert to sleep two at night. There is room for the latest built-in's in the compact galley and an abundance of storage space. Forward of the galley, the control station provides the helmsman with full circle visibility.

An outside helm is ideal when the weather's balmy. An exclusive feature is the hinged catwalks that permit full walk-around accessibility when underway and is legally trailerable when in the down position.

The hull design for the **DELTA Q** provides good rough water ability with considerable vee forward and yet allows her to be beached without damage. The sundeck offers ample room for sunbathing. The arrangement of the **DELTA Q** provides a complete vacation cottage on the water.

> **AVAILABLE FOR THIS DESIGN:**
> - **Study Plans**
> - **Plans & Patterns**
> - **Bronze Fastening Kit**
> - **Fiberglass Kit**
> **See Price List**

223

JUBILEE

A 29' HOUSEBOAT

BUILD IN PLYWOOD

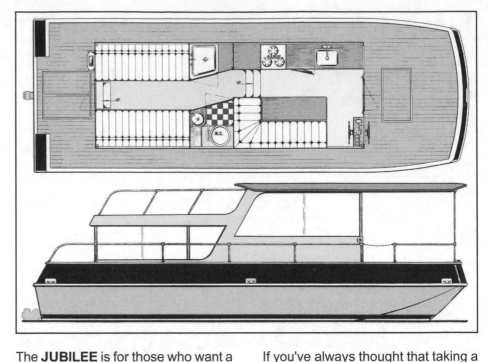

CHARACTERISTICS

Length overall .... 29'-0"
Length waterline .... 26'-3"
Beam .... 10'-2"
Hull draft (with skeg) .... 14"
Freeboard .... 3'-6"
Height overall .... 10'-10"
Displacement .... 7310 lbs.
Fuel capacity .... 100 gals.
Fresh water capacity .... 50 gals.
Headroom .... 6'-3" to 6'-7"
Sleeping accommodations 6
Hull type: Full vee bottom hull with con-
siderable dead-rise in forward
sections. Developed for sheet
plywood planking.
Power: Single or twin outboard motors
with a minimum weight of 250
lbs. Optional single or twin in-
board/outboard drive.
Maximum engine and drive
weight combined not to exceed
850 lbs.

**COMPLETE PLANS include FULL
SIZE PATTERNS for sawn chine
members, bowpiece, sheer harpins,
plywood bow harpin, stem, inter-
mediate stems, and half-section
patterns for the transom, interme-
diate frame, and bulkhead/frames.
Includes instructions, Bill of Materials, and Fastening Schedule.**

The **JUBILEE** is for those who want a compact houseboat, yet with accommodations equal to boats several feet longer. Her modern appearance and smooth lines will please even the most discriminating individual. The galley is sure to please the cook. With a countertop almost 9' long, there is plenty of room for all the shoreside appliances and a wealth of drawer and locker space left over.

If you've always thought that taking a shower during a cruise was impossible, the **JUBILEE** will change your mind. Not only is the shower compartment completely separate from the toilet room, it even has a seat . By day the plush deckhouse settee makes a great place to relax and watch the scenery go by as you sip a cool one at the dinette table. At night the table lowers and the seat backs unsnap to form a double berth. In the aft cabin, those settees make equally great lounging pads by day and berths at night. The seat backs lift to form roomy upper berths.

You'll never get a stuffy feeling on the **JUBILEE**. Plenty of windows let in light and fresh air and let you keep an eye on outside activity. And if you want sun, just climb a couple of steps to the sundeck. There is room under the generous roof overhang for reading or watching the scenery from the shade. It is easy to find your own favorite place on this versatile "pleasure palace" on the water.

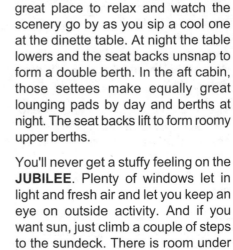

AVAILABLE FOR THIS DESIGN:
- **Study Plans**
- **Plans & Patterns**
- **Bronze Fastening Kit**
- **Fiberglass Kit**
See Price List

DELTA KING
A 33' HOUSEBOAT

CHARACTERISTICS

Length overall .... 33'-0"
Length waterline .... 29'-7"
Beam .... 12'-0"
Hull draft (with skeg) .... 16"
Freeboard .... 3'-5"
Height overall .... 10'-2"
Displacement .... 10,540 lbs.
Fuel capacity .... 160 gals.
Fresh water capacity .... 120 gals.
Headroom .... 6'-2" to 6'-6"
Sleeping accommodations 6
Hull type: Garvey-type with vee section forward, developed for sheet plywood.
Power: Single or twin outboard motors or single or twin inboard/outboard drives.

COMPLETE PLANS include FULL SIZE PATTERNS for stem, breasthook, forward chine, and half-section patterns for each of the bulkhead/frames, transom, and bowpiece. Includes instructions, Bill of Materials, and Fastening Schedule.

One look at her arrangement plan will show that the **DELTA KING** provides all the comforts of a modern apartment with private sleeping quarters for three couples. A full width double berth and an abundance of storage space has been provided in the aft stateroom, while located up forward is a comfortable double stateroom with ample locker and shelf space. A truly spacious galley was designed to take advantage of the latest marine or mobile home-type built-in appliances of the largest sizes available, while the fully enclosed toilet room provides a separate shower. A serving bar between the galley and salon allows meals to be easily served to the adjustable dinette table which, along with the comfortable settee, converts to form a wide double berth.

The control station is a helmsman's delight, providing 360 degree visibility and sliding doors to port and starboard. An exterior steering station is provided in the large covered forward cockpit as well as a full width lounge seat. A truly unique feature is the wide full length walk around decks and bulwark with safety rail. A lounge seat has also been provided in the roomy aft cockpit, and the spacious sun deck allows plenty of room for sunbathing or to carry a small dinghy.

AVAILABLE FOR THIS DESIGN:
- **Study Plans**
- **Plans & Patterns**
- **Bronze Fastening Kit**
- **Fiberglass Kit**
See Price List

BON VOYAGE A 45' HOUSEBOAT

BUILD IN PLYWOOD, FIBERGLASS, OR STEEL

CHARACTERISTICS

Length overall .... 44'-9"
Length waterline .... 40'-0"
Beam .... 14'-0"
Hull draft (with skeg) .... 18"
Hull depth .... 4'-9"
Freeboard forward .... 3'-7"
Freeboard aft.............................. 3'-3"
Height overall .... 15'-3"
Displacement (Plywood) ... 19,255 lbs.
Displacement (Fiberglass)21,155 lbs.
Displacement (Steel) .... 22,125 lbs.
Steel hull components .... 9,000 lbs.
Fuel capacity .... 300 gals.
Fresh water capacity .... 220 gals.
Waste holding capacity .... 250 gals.
Headroom .... 6'-3" to 6'-7"
Sleeping accommodations 8
Hull type: Full length vee bottom hull with considerable deadrise and flare forward.
PLYWOOD Version: Developable double diagonal plywood bottom and sheet plywood on sides.
FIBERGLASS Version: Sandwich core one-off male mold.
STEEL Version: Welded steel.
Power: Twin outboard or twin inboard/ outboard drive. Drive systems should have "power trim" capabilities. Single outboard or inboard optional if boat primarily intended for stationary use.

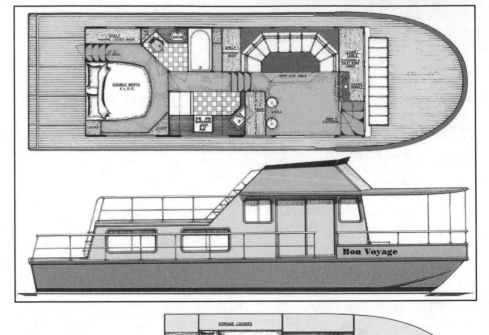

COMPLETE PLANS for the PLY-WOOD version include FULL SIZE PATTERNS for the stem contour, breasthook, deck and cabin cambers, and half-section patterns for station forms and transom plus instructions, Bill of Materials, and Fastening Schedule. The FIBER-GLASS version also includes fiberglass instruction supplement, Fiberglass Manual, and plans supplement. The STEEL version includes Steel Boatbuilding Guide, steel material listing, and steel plans supplement.

Our **BON VOYAGE** offers lavish accommodations with extended cruising capabilities seldom found even in the finest production craft of this size. Separate cabins are available for four couples with each having private access to a toilet room without having to cross through another's cabin. The deckhouse features a 10' long dinette which forms a double berth, an inside control station, and a bar. The galley is a full kitchen open to the deckhouse and adjacent to the bar. Generous window areas assure ample light and ventilation, and storage areas abound.

The **BON VOYAGE** is equally lavish with outdoor areas. In addition to full walkaround decks and aft deck, there's a covered bow porch with lounge seat, plus a huge sun deck and flying bridge control station with back-to-back seats. Ample fuel, water, and even waste holding capacities mean you'll be independent of marina facilities.

Power for your **BON VOYAGE** can be either twin I/O's or outboards. If you don't plan to move the boat too often, a single engine of either type can be used. Even though the hull is intended primarily for protected waters, a vee-form with long skeg assures good handling when the weather kicks up, while the topsides feature a good flare that combines with the forward bulwark to knock down spray for a dry ride.

You can build the hull of your **BON VOYAGE** in plywood, fiberglass, or steel. With plywood, a double diagonal format is used on the bottom, while topsides are standard sheets. With fiberglass, the sandwich core "one-off" male mold method is specified, and with steel, mild welded sheet steel is used. Cabin construction is simple double wall wood-frame plywood in all cases. Instructions, materials listing, and Full Size Patterns make the job as simple as possible.

AVAILABLE FOR THIS DESIGN:
- **Study Plans**
- **Plans & Patterns**
- **Bronze Fastening Kit**
- **Fiberglass Kit**
See Price List

226

OVERNITER
A 10' MINI-CRUISER

BUILD IN PLYWOOD

CHARACTERISTICS

Length overall	15'-11"
Beam	6'-10"
Hull depth	3'-6"
Hull weight (approx.)	650 lbs.
Headroom (nominal)	3'-0"
Sleeping capacity	2

Hull type: Vee bottom, hard chine hull, developed for sheet plywood planking.

Power: Outboard motor to 100 HP.

Trailer: Designed for use with GLEN-L SERIES 750/1000 boat trailer plans.

COMPLETE PLANS include FULL SIZE PATTERNS for stem, breasthook, and half-section patterns for the frames and transom. Includes instructions, Bill of Materials, and Fastening Schedule.

OVERNITER is an ideal combination of cruiser and runabout.

The high freeboard forward with raised deck makes for a very roomy boat. The extra wide beam offers more space with a generous flare in the forward sections. This makes a dry boat that is comfortable and safe for the entire family.

The large flat cockpit area offers a great deal of room for fishing or carrying passengers. When powered with the larger outboards, she will make an ideal ski boat. For just plain boating fun, few boats provide such a wide variety of boating potentials.

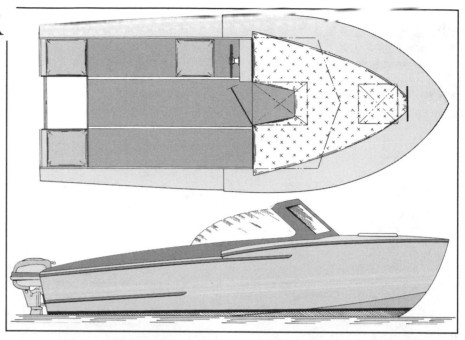

Many variations are possible. The bulkhead and cabin berths may be eliminated, leaving the windshield and plenty of storage area under the foredeck. The resulting 9' cockpit can be rigged with a convertible top from the windshield to provide protection from sun or a sudden rain squall.

OVERNITER will be most appreciated when there are small children on board. The high sides keep them in the boat and the berth area is a great place for laying down or playing games while mom and dad fish or just enjoy the peace and quiet of a day on the water.

AVAILABLE FOR THIS DESIGN:
- **Plans & Patterns**
- **Bronze Fastening Kit**
- **Fiberglass Kit**
See Price List

227

JACKKNIFE
A 14 1/2' DEEP VEE CRUISER

BUILD IN PLYWOOD

CHARACTERISTICS

Length overall .... 14'-6"
Beam .... 6'-9"
Draft .... 9"
Hull depth .... 36"
Hull weight (approx.) .... 600 lbs.
Height overall .... 4'-5"
Headroom (nominal) .... 33"
Sleeping capacity 2
Cockpit size .... 6'-3"x 5'-6"
Hull type: Full length deep vee with lift strakes, radiused keel at transom, and bulbous forefoot, approx. 16° deadrise at transom. Developed for sheet plywood planking.
Power: Single longshaft (20") outboard to 75 HP. Minimum 20 HP.
Trailer: Designed for use with GLEN-L SERIES 750/1000 boat trailer plans.

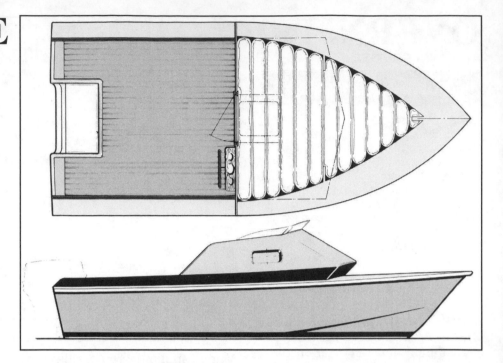

Our **JACKKNIFE** is a brawny boat not to be confused with lesser "feather weight" craft in this compact size. This boat was designed for the person who does not want to sacrifice strength, durability, and riding comfort for light weight and small size. The hull features performance and handling characteristics usually associated only with craft much larger and heavier.

The **JACKKNIFE** features a true full length deep vee hull with a radiused keel section and minimum 16° vee at the stern for as smooth a ride as possible in a boat this length. Critically located lift strakes deflect spray at the chine and lift the hull quickly onto a plane with minimal power. Wide beam and full length flaring topsides assure a stable, dry ride. Yet this is a nimble boat ideal for all sorts of watersports including fishing, diving, and water skiing.

Often referred to as a "pocket cruiser", **JACKKNIFE** includes a cuddy cabin with sitting headroom, two berths, space for a compact portable head, and a deep, safe, cockpit. Power comes from a single outboard (20 HP recommended minimum). Plans include instructions well suited to the first time builder. Although complete details are provided for the cabin, the use of our full size CABIN PATTERNS makes this part of the project even easier. Standard 4' x 8' plywood sheets can be used throughout, and no difficult wood working operations are required.

COMPLETE PLANS include **FULL SIZE PATTERNS** for **stem, breasthook, transom knee, deck beams, and half-section patterns for the frames and transom. Includes instructions, Bill of Materials, and Fastening Schedule.**

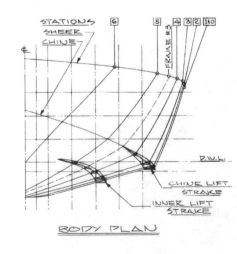

BODY PLAN

AVAILABLE FOR THIS DESIGN:
• **Plans & Patterns**
• **CabinPatterns**
• **Bronze Fastening Kit**
• **Fiberglass Kit**
See Price List

CRUISETTE

A 15' MINI-CRUISER

BUILD IN PLYWOOD

CHARACTERISTICS

Length overall .... 15'-0"
Beam .... 6'-0"
Hull depth .... 33"
Headroom .... 3'-4"
Hull weight (approx.).............. 450 lbs.
Sleeping capacity 2
Hull type: Vee bottom, hard chine hull, developed for sheet plywood planking.
Power: Outboard motor to 60 HP.
Trailer: Designed for use with GLEN-L SERIES 1200/1800 boat trailer plans.

CRUISETTE is a minature cruiser, capable of filling many needs. She has built-in berths for camping or overnight cruising. She has cockpit space for the fisherman, and yet cabin protection from the unexpected squall. And, she has the ability to be a good ski boat as well. The hull is both fast and smooth. You'll appreciate the dry, level ride, and the generous beam gives exceptional safety and load-carrying ability.

The construction of the **sturdy CRUISETTE** is simple for the amateur. And because of the compact size, you can trailer the boat easily to any body of water.

COMPLETE PLANS include **FULL SIZE PATTERNS** for stem, breasthook, transom knee, and half-section patterns for the frames and transom. Includes instructions, Bill of Materials, and Fastening Schedule.

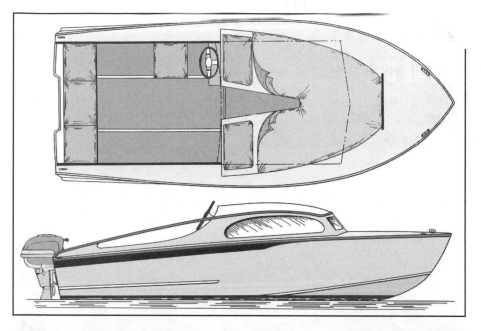

AVAILABLE FOR THIS DESIGN:
• Plans & Patterns
• Bronze Fastening Kit
• Fiberglass Kit
See Price List

229

SHERWOOD QUEEN

A 15 1/2' MINI TUG

BUILD IN PLYWOOD

CHARACTERISTICS

Length overall .... 15'-6"
Beam .... 7'-4"
Hull depth .... 3'-11"
Height overall .... 7'-4"
Hull weight (approx.).............. 600 lbs.
Average passengers 1-4
Hull type: Vee bottom, hard chine hull, developed for sheet plywood planking.
Power: Single inboard or outboard motor to 10 HP.
Trailer: Designed for use with GLEN-L SERIES 1200/1800 boat trailer plans.

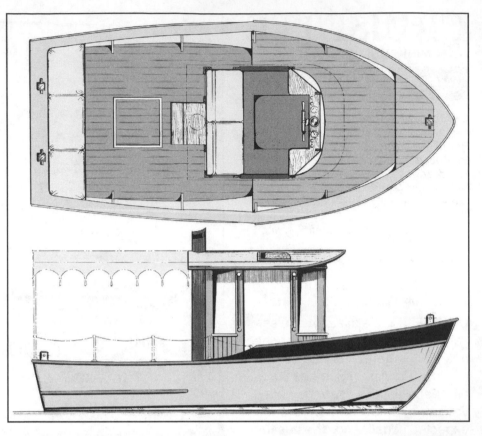

The **SHERWOOD QUEEN** is an attention getter. Use her for a multitude of purposes around the yacht club, harbor, or landing. The small pilothouse has room for the helmsman and a passenger or two. Decks are recessed below the gunnel for walk-around access. Intended for slower speeds, the **SHERWOOD QUEEN** scoots along with minimal power for incredible economy. A small outboard can be mounted on the transom, or in a well within the boat completely concealing the motor. With either, the motor can still kick-up if necessary, or you can use a small inboard centrally located with a straight shaft set-up. Double towing bits aft plus one forward add to the practicality of this mini workboat.

With all her queenly attributes, the **SHERWOOD QUEEN** is not difficult to build. The plans are prepared for the amateur builder with limited experience, providing step-by-step building procedures.

COMPLETE PLANS include **FULL SIZE PATTERNS** for stem, breasthook, forward cabin contour and cabin beam, and half-section patterns for the frames and transom. Includes instructions, Bill of Materials, and Fastening Schedule.

AVAILABLE FOR THIS DESIGN:
- **Plans & Patterns**
- **Bronze Fastening Kit**
- **Fiberglass Kit**
See Price List

CABIN SKIFF
A 16' 3" TABLOID CRUISER

BUILD IN *FAST-G* STITCH-N-GLUE

CHARACTERISTICS

Length overall .... 16'-3"
Beam .... 6'-9"
Hull depth .... 30"
Height overall .... 5'-9"
Headroom under hardtop .... 5'-0"
Hull weight (approx.) .... 500 lbs.
Sleeping capacity 2
Average passengers 1-3
Hull type: Sheet plywood hull developed for *FAST-G* Stitch-N-Glue construction.
Power: Outboard motor to 40 HP
Trailer: Designed for use with GLEN-L SERIES 1200/1800 boat trailer plans.

COMPLETE PLANS include FULL SIZE PATTERNS for forward side/ bottom planking, side planking, butt blocks, form, transom, knee, two breasthooks, motorwell sides, aft bulkhead, sole, berth flat, cabin bulkhead, forward and aft knees, foredeck, sidedeck, bulwark planking, plywood layouts, dimensional cabin drawings. Includes instructions, Bill of Materials, Fastening Schedule, and Stitch-N-Glue Manual.

CABIN PATTERNS are available as an adjunct to the above Plan & Pattern package. Patterns for the cabin side and front, entry beam, centerpost, centerpost knee, windshield, and bridge beam are included.

> **AVAILABLE FOR THIS DESIGN:**
> * Plans & Patterns
> * Cabin Patterns
> * Stitch & Glue Kit
> * Fiberglass Kit
> See Price List

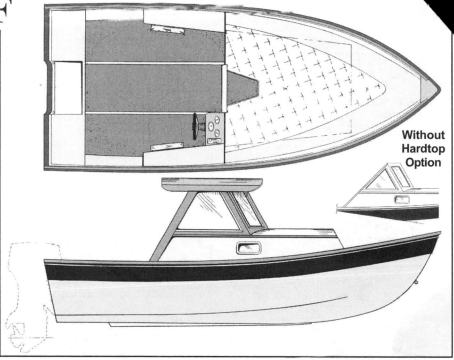

Without Hardtop Option

A compact tabloid cruiser has features usually found only in much larger craft. A full walk-around deck... trunk cabin with berths for two... hardtop shelter... and you can build it by the Stitch-N-Glue *FAST-G* method as described in more detail in the forward section of this catalog.

This is one of the *most completely* patterned boats of its size. *More than 100 square feet* of patterns provide a contour for virtually *every* non-rectangular part. Yes, including *all* planking, decking, floorboards, transom, breasthook, etc. ... a complete PATTERN package to eliminate complex dimensional layouts. Only standard 4' x 8' plywood panels are used. Cabin layouts are furnished in the plans but, as an optional extra, FULL SIZE PATTERNS for the cabin are available. In addition, you receive *complete* material listings with fastening schedules for *both* hull and cabin. Complete scaled drawings with step-by-step written text carry you through all phases of building. First-time builders will appreciate the attention to detail provided, but *most* of all, building with *FAST-G* makes boatbuilding easy.

KNIGHT
R

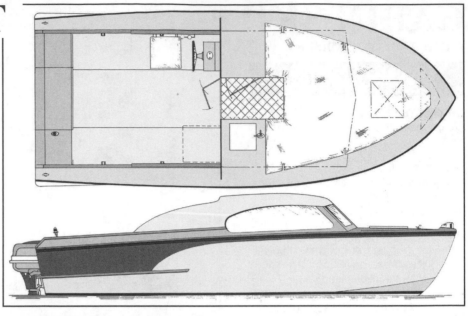

CHARACTERISTICS

Length overall	17'-0"
Beam	7'-2"
Hull depth	3'-2"
Hull weight (approx.)	700 lbs.
Headroom (nominal)	4'-7"
Height overall	5'-0"
Cockpit size	6'x 5'-4"
Sleeping capacity	2

Hull type: Vee bottom, hard chine hull, developed for sheet plywood planking.

Power: Single or twin outboard motors to 100 HP total.

Trailer: Designed for use with GLEN-L SERIES 2300/2800 boat trailer plans.

COMPLETE PLANS include FULL SIZE PATTERNS for stem, breasthook, transom knee, chine blocking, and half-section patterns for the frames and transom. Includes instructions, Bill of Materials, and Fastening Schedule.

The **SEA KNIGHT** has full accommodations for cruising; head, berths, and cooking facilities. The extra large cockpit provides sleeping bag space for additional sleepers. In the cabin, a convenient cabinet converts to a semi-enclosed toilet room. On the opposite side of the cabin is the galley with sink and stove space. In the bulkhead is a pass-through opening that provides service to the galley area. All in all, the **SEA KNIGHT** has all the features of the king sized outboard cruiser, and yet is an ideal length for easy trailering.

The **SEA KNIGHT** requires very little power for acceptable performance, and larger motors can be used if you want to tow skiers. The motor well design is such that the motor is virtually concealed from view and yet readily accessible. The **SEA KNIGHT** makes a nice boat for all water sport activities, including fishing, diving, and water skiing.

AVAILABLE FOR THIS DESIGN:
- **Plans & Patterns**
- **Bronze Fastening Kit**
- **Fiberglass Kit**
See Price List

CARIOCA

A 17' DEEP VEE CRUISER

BUILD IN PLYWOOD

CHARACTERISTICS

Length overall .... 17'-0"
Beam .... 7'-6"
Draft .... 11"
Hull depth .... 3'-4"
Hull weight (approx.)............... 750 lbs.
Headroom (nominal) .... 3'-10"
Height overall .... 5'-9"
Cockpit size .... 6'x 6'-6"
Sleeping capacity 2

Hull type: Full length deep vee with lift strakes, developed for sheet plywood planking.

Power: Single or twin outboard motors to 135 HP. Single stern mounted inboard motor to 500 lbs., connected to an outdrive.

Trailer: Designed for use with GLEN-L SERIES 2300/2800 boat trailer plans.

COMPLETE PLANS include FULL SIZE PATTERNS for stem, breasthook, and half-section patterns for the frames and transom. Includes instructions, Bill of Materials, and Fastening Schedule.

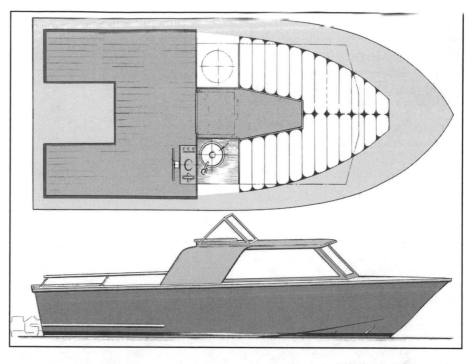

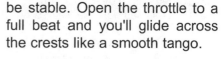

Dance over the waves to the tune of the **CARIOCA**. The full 18° deep vee cushions the chop and makes cruising the local waters a waltz. Although deep vee, the lift strakes stabilize the hull so even at a slow tempo, the hull will be stable. Open the throttle to a full beat and you'll glide across the crests like a smooth tango.

The **CARIOCA** has all of the required facilities for cruising: Two wide, roomy, full length vee berths, a galley area, and space for a head. The ballroom size cockpit provides plenty of extra room for any type of water sport whether it be fishing, scuba diving, or just plain fun on the water. With the proper power, she makes an excellent ski boat in addition to her fine cruising abilities. Why don't you stop shuffling... pick up those feet and swing into the construction of the **CARIOCA, a** wonderful hobby project, both to build and to use.

AVAILABLE FOR THIS DESIGN:
- **Plans & Patterns**
- **Bronze Fastening Kit**
- **Fiberglass Kit**
See Price List

TUG ALONG
A 16' OR 18' OUTBOARD CABIN CRUISER

BUILD IN STITCH-N-GLUE PLYWOOD

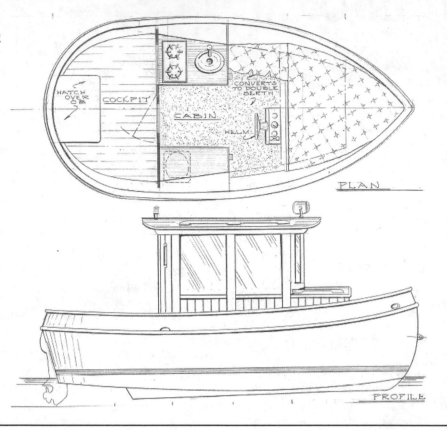

PLAN

PROFILE

CHARACTERISTICS

	16'	18'
Length overall	15'10"	18'0"
Beam	7'9"	7'9"
Hull depth mid	41"	41"
Hull wt-approx	450	525
Overall height	7'7"	7'7"
Cabin headroom	6'6"	6'6"
Water capacity	6 gals.	6 gals.
Holding tank (gray water)	6 gals.	6 gals.
Fuel capacity	11 gals.	11 gals.

Hull type: Flat bottom, developed for sheet plywood with rounded stern. For standard sized plywood assembled by the Stitch and Glue construction method.

Power: Outboard motors to 15 hp.

Trailer: Designed for use with Glen-L Series 1200/1800 boat trailer plans.

COMPLETE PLANS and FULL SIZE PATTERNS include large scale plans with numerous enlarged details, sequential Instructions that include a Bill of Materials, Fastening and Laminate Schedule. Full size patterns are given for the side planking, stern arc planking, tunnel sides, forward, mid and aft bulwarks, front cabin crown, dash beam crown, five bulwark forms, and bulkhead crown. Also included is a half section of the building form and dimensional layout of the bottom.

A palatial, 50 MPH super yacht with deep carpets, marble countertops, and gold faucets is not the TUG ALONG. It is a simple, utilitarian, practical, miniature, affordable yacht that will turn heads whether on the water or perched on the trailer. And, it's easy to build; the flat bottom sheet plywood hull is built by the practical Stitch-N-Glue method with multiple patterns to put the construction within the range of most everyone.

TUG ALONG is small, not quite 16', but with a 7' 9" beam seems much larger. The main cabin has 6' 6" headroom and with all the windows, seems huge. There is room on one side for a small galley with stove and sink while the starboard side has space for a portable head (toilet), storage, and a nice helm station.

The rounded stern is distinctive and the outboard motor (if short shaft) is concealed underdecks and runs in a partial tunnel. Yet the rounded stern is not difficult to build with the furnished patterns.

Sleeping accommodations are spacious for such a diminutive craft. The vee-berth is lengthened by filler cushions that store under the side decks when not in use. When converted, the berth provides a maximum width of 5' 6" and a length of about 6' 3". Yet when not expanded for use, there is space for a roomy helm station and passenger area.

The simple flat bottom hull provides excellent stability but combined with the high windowed cabin is not intended for open sea use. This is a boat to enjoy in quiet water bays, lakes or rivers. You are floating on the water supported by a large (comparative) flat surface that won't rock from side to side when someone moves. A boat for the practical economy minded sailor and one that the entire family can enjoy.

AVAILABLE FOR THIS DESIGN:
- **Plans & Patterns**
- **Stitch & Glue Kit**
- **Fiberglass Kit**
See Price List

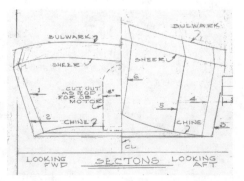

SECTIONS

NOMAD

AN 18' DAY CRUISER

BUILD IN PLYWOOD

CHARACTERISTICS

Length overall .... 18'-0"
Beam .... 7'-9"
Hull depth .... 3'-6"
Hull weight (approx.) .... 800 lbs.
Headroom (nominal) .... 4'-7"
Height overall .... 5'-6"
Cockpit size .... 6'x 6'-6"
Sleeping capacity 2
Hull type: Vee bottom, hard chine hull, developed for sheet plywood planking.
Power: Single or twin outboard motors to 135 HP.
Trailer: Designed for use with GLEN-L SERIES 2300/2800 boat trailer plans.

COMPLETE PLANS include FULL SIZE PATTERNS for stem, breasthook, transom knee, chine blocking, harpin and half-section patterns for the frames and transom. Includes instructions, Bill of Materials, and Fastening Schedule.

The **NOMAD** features an indoor helm with an optional helm outside. The cabin is open in the back to the cockpit for full visability, with sliding windows for an airy interior. Heavy canvas curtains are used to close the back of the cabin in foul weather or for sleeping privacy. The backs of the helmsman and passenger seats are used to convert the seats into two 6'-6" berths up forward. A hinged counter conceals a head, while opposite there's another cabinet for a galley.

The open cabin makes this a good touring or cruising boat, having easy communication with the cockpit area. Some builders have extended the cabin shell aft and increased seating to accommodate more passengers under cover. It is also possible to omit the cabin entirely to make one huge cockpit.

The hull features 3/8" sheet plywood planking for a sturdy yet light-

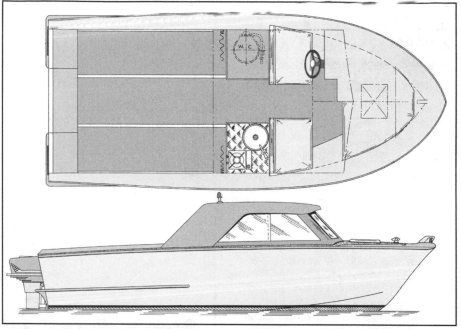

weight hull. The vee forward and flat bottom aft provides a soft ride and quick acceleration. With ad-

equate power, the **NOMAD** is fully capable of pulling skiers.

AVAILABLE FOR THIS DESIGN:
- **Plans & Patterns**
- **Bronze Fastening Kit**
- **Fiberglass Kit**
See Price List

BO-JEST
AN 18' POCKET CRUISER

CHARACTERISTICS

Length overall .... 17'-10"
Waterline length .... 17'-0"
Beam .... 7'-11"
Draft (Inboard version) .... 21"
Draft (Outboard version) .... 14"
Freeboard forward .... 3'-9"
Freeboard aft .... 2'-1"
Hull depth .... 4'-10"
Hull weight (approx.) .... 800 lbs.
Height overall (Inboard version) .. 8'-4"
Height overall (Outboard version) 7'-8"
Cockpit size (approx.) .... 6'x 4'-6"
Headroom (Pilothouse) ... 6'-1" to 6'-4"
Headroom (Trunk cabin) ..4'-1" to 4'-4"
Sleeping capacity 2
Fuel capacity .... 26 gals.
Fresh water capacity .... 20 gals.
Hull type: Hard chine, semi-displacement, vee bottom with skeg, developed for sheet plywood planking.
Power: Single inboard (gasoline or diesel), or outboard (long or short shaft), 5 to 10 SHP for speeds of 5 to 8 knots.
Trailer: Designed for use with GLEN-L SERIES 2300/2800 boat trailer plans.

COMPLETE PLANS include FULL SIZE PATTERNS for stem, breasthook, and half-section patterns for the frames and transom. Includes instructions, Bill of Materials, and Fastening Schedule.

While our **BO-JEST** design is a real charmer, it's much more than just another character boat. You'll find this pocket cruiser packed with pleasant surprises beyond its attractive traditional workboat facade. For example, there's a cozy pilothouse with full standing headroom and virtual full-circle visibility, walk-around decks, self-draining cockpit of ample size, incredible economy, and long range; all features one would expect on larger boats, but are surprising to find on a boat of these modest proportions.

While compact in size, **BO-JEST** has been carefully planned so the cruising couple won't get claustrophobic. Dining, sleeping, and lounging takes place in the trunk cabin on a 7' berth that becomes 6' wide when the table is lowered and pivoted to form a filler. Space for a head is located under the berth, and a curtain can be rigged

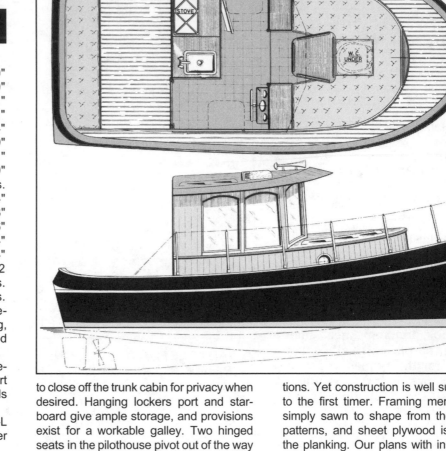

to close off the trunk cabin for privacy when desired. Hanging lockers port and starboard give ample storage, and provisions exist for a workable galley. Two hinged seats in the pilothouse pivot out of the way when not necessary.

The semi-displacement vee bottom hull on **BO-JEST** is both easily driven and maneuverable, being more capable than most boats this size. Freeboard is ample and a skeg assures directional stability for positive control even in tough conditions. Yet construction is well suited even to the first timer. Framing members are simply sawn to shape from the full size patterns, and sheet plywood is used for the planking. Our plans with instructions, material listing, and fastening schedule show how it's all done. Best of all, **BO-JEST** is easy to trail anywhere you wish, expanding your cruising waters considerably.

SWEET 16
A 16' AUTHENTIC TUG MINI-CRUISER

CHARACTERISTICS

Length overall .... 16'2"
Beam .... 7'2"
Draft .... 2'6"
Displacement .... 3300 lbs.
Suggested power range 5-20HP
Speed within HP range .... 5.5 kts.
Fuel capacity .... 30 gals.
Trailer: Designed for use with GLEN-L
SERIES 2900/3800 boat trailer plans.

While this is our smallest Mini-Tug, it has one big feature fit for a queen! That is, the double berth in the cabin is actually 5' wide, the same width as a queen-size bed ashore. A hinged panel at the forward end drops down to form an overall berth length of 6' 2". And since you'll sleep with your head toward the bow there's generous headroom above the berth where it's needed.

There's space below the helm area/ foredeck for a portable head, along with lots of storage here as well as below the berth, which shares space with the engine. Cabin access doors are on both sides and aft, as well as lots of windows for light and ventilation. All this makes a boat that's practical for overnighting by a couple, and a great day boat for seeing the sights at a leisurely pace.

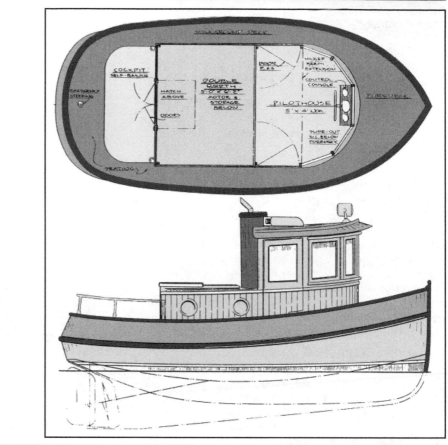

AVAILABLE FOR THESE TUGS:
- **Study Plans**
- **Plans & Patterns**
- **Fiberglass Kit**
See Price List

GOLIATH
AN 18' AUTHENTIC TUG CRUISER

CHARACTERISTICS

Length overall .... 18'6"
Beam .... 7'2"
Draft .... 2'6"
Displacement .... 3300 lbs.
Suggested power range 5-20HP
Speed within HP range .... 5.5 kts.
Fuel capacity .... 30 gals
Trailer:. Designed for use with GLEN-L
SERIES 2900/3800 boat trailer plans.

This Mini-Tug is a step up in size with the result being more space in the cabin and cockpit. The deckhouse shows a seat or galley cabinet partially concealing the motor, but is only a suggestion. You can lay out the area to suit. Or if you wish, you can extend the deckhouse a foot or two for even more interior space, if at some decrease in cockpit length. It's an easy alteration most can carry out so the details are not a part of the plans.

A private double stateroom is located forward. The berths are 6' 3" long with sitting headroom above the berth tops and space below forward for a portable head. Plenty of windows, ports, and a trunk cabin hatch assure generous ventilation and light. Storage is below the berths as well as along the house sides below the side decks, and in any cabinets you might provide in the deckhouse.

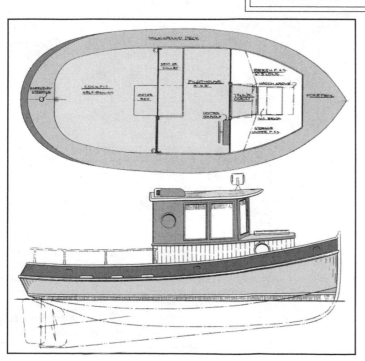

TITAN A 20' OR 21' AUTHENTIC TUG CRUISER

CHARACTERISTICS

Length overall .... 20'2"(*)
Beam .... 8'2"
Draft .... 2'9"
Displacement .... 5850 lbs.
Suggested power range 15-40HP
Speed within HP range .... 6.5 kts.
Fuel capacity .... 45 gals
Trailer: . Designed for use with GLEN-L SERIES 7000/10,000 boat trailer plans. (*)21'6" optional

Titan is similar in arrangement and hull shape to our Goliath design, but longer and with different superstructure styling. The plans include two length options. The deckhouse contains a seat or galley cabinet as in Goliath, but these are not mandatory. A builder could also extend the house aft up to several feet for more interior space, and rearrange the layout to suit. Such alterations are simple enough so that extra details are unnecessary.

Two berths in the private double stateroom forward are 6' 6" long with sitting headroom above the berth tops, with space below forward for a portable head. Ample windows, ports, and a trunk cabin hatch assure generous ventilation and light. Storage is below the berths as well as along the house sides below the side decks, and in any cabinets you might provide in the deckhouse.

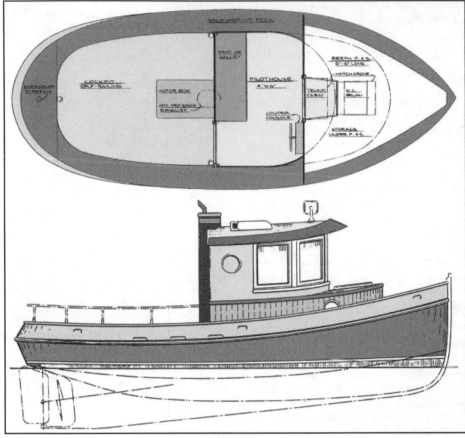

FRED MURPHY
A 26' TO 29' AUTHENTIC TUG CRUISER

CHARACTERISTICS

Length overall .... 26'2"(**)
Beam .... 9'8"
Draft .... 3'0"
Displacement .... 8350 lbs.
Suggested power range 20-50HP
Speed within HP range .... 7 kts.
Fuel capacity .... 60 gals.
(*)21'6" optional
(**)28'10" opt.

It's probably not fair to class our Fred Murphy as a "mini-tug" since it's capable of serious cruising whether for work or play. The deep draft displacement hull has the seakindliness and feel of a little ship whether you build the short or longer option, both of which use the same plan set.

The spacious forward cabin includes two 6' 6" berths with space for a head below and with hanging lockers aft both sides. Additional storage is below the berths and whatever one arranges in the deckhouse, which can be outfitted with additional accommodations, galley, and helm station as desired. You can even lengthen the house a couple of feet for more enclosed space if you wish.

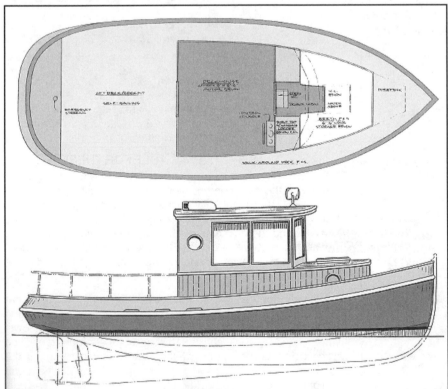

REBEL TUG HIGH PERFORMANCE TUG

CHARACTERISTICS

Length overall	19'3"
Beam	8'6"
Draft (hull w/skeg)	1'6"
Displacement	3800 lbs.
Fuel capacity	80 gals.
Sleeping capacity	2

Trailer:. Designed for use with GLEN-L SERIES 2900/3800 boat trailer plans.

Amaze your friends, family, and open-mouthed on-lookers as your "little ole tug" rises to the surface and blasts past at ski-boat speeds. It's possible because these trailerable designs look like authentic tugs above the waterline. But below, they're modern out-and-out planing boats capable of high speeds with either I/O or outboard power. And they're dry and smooth riding too. Their variable v-bottom hulls include a wave-flattening 45° bow entry leading to a semi-deep-v 13° stern. A full-length integral chine flat deflects spray and assures stability.

Other features include roomy self-bailing cockpit, side decks with raised bulwarks, 6'3"+ pilothouse headroom, 2 berths in the trunk cabin with sitting headroom above, and space for a head and galley. Construction is aimed at the do-it-yourselfer in either plywood or aluminum. Frame and backbone member contours are given as FULL SIZE PATTERNS, while plans include sequential instructions with material lists.

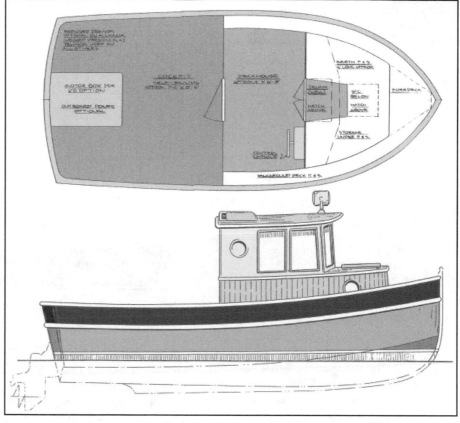

VANDAL HIGH PERFORMANCE TUG

CHARACTERISTICS

Length overall	22'3"
Beam	8'6"
Draft (hull w/skeg)	1'6"
Headroom (pilothouse)	6'3"+
Displacement	4400 lbs.
Fuel capacity	85 gals.
Sleeping capacity	2

Trailer:. Designed for use with GLEN-L SERIES 5000/6000 boat trailer plans.

AVAILABLE FOR THESE TUGS:
- **Study Plans**
- **Plans & Patterns**
- **Fiberglass Kit**

See Price List

CS-20

A 20' OUTBOARD CABIN CRUISER

BUILD IN STITCH-N-GLUE PLYWOOD

CHARACTERISTIC

Length overall .... 19'-10"
Beam .... 8'-4"
Hull depth .... 3'-0"
Hull weight (approx.) .... 650 lbs.
Height overall .... 7'-6"
Cabin headroom .... 4'-6"
Hedroom under hardtop .... 6'-2"
Cockpit size .... 6'-4" x 6'-6"
Berth length .... 6'-5"
Sleeping accommodations 2
Hull type: Vee bottom, developed for sheet plywood, intended for Stitch-n Glue construction.
Power: Outboard motors to 175 HP maximum. Minimum to plane 40 HP. Practical all purpose 80 HP.
Trailer: For use with Glen L Series 2900/3800.

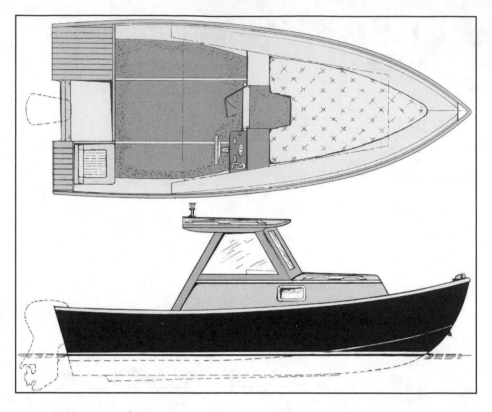

The CS-20 is a takeoff from the original Glen-L "Cabin Skiff", a design proven by many builders as an excellent durable performer. The enlarged version CS-20 is a little larger overall and we've tweaked a few things for even better performance. The vee has been made a little deeper but not enough so the boat won't still be stable. The bridge headroom has been increased to full standing status. But, the popular recessed deck has been retained. You asked for it. Here it is.

The CS-20, like her predecessor, is built by our Stitch-N-Glue method. Just cut out the planking from dimensional layouts and use the patterns to duplicate the other

necessary parts for the hull. Lay them in the specially detailed and patterned cradle and stitch together with short lengths of copper wire. No traditional building form is required: the hull is formed around a permanent bulkhead that acts as a mold to form the hull contour. Glue and tape the seams and the hull becomes a reality. Of course there are numerous interior longitudinals and other members that reinforce the structure.

The hull is very rigid and features a double layered bottom totaling 5/8" in thickness. The entire boat is built from standard 4' x 8' ply-

wood sheets. No complicated building procedures are used. There are no difficult bends that require steaming of the wood. This is a boat that most average handyman can build. But it won't build itself. Get off the couch, get a set of Plans and Patterns and start building. It's fun!

COMPLETE PLANS plus FULL SIZE PATTERNS include large scale plans with numerous enlarged details, sequential Instructions that include a Laminate Schedule, Bill of Materials, and Fastening Schedule. Also included are full dimensional layouts for both the side and bottom plywood. Full size patterns are given for the Knee, Cabin Arc, Bridge Crown, Breasthook and half section patterns for the Transom, and Bulkhead/Building Form. Special plan details and patterns are also furnished for the building cradle to form and support the hull during construction.

AVAILABLE FOR THIS DESIGN:
- **Plans & Patterns**
- **Stitch & Glue Kit**
- **Fiberglass Kit**
See Price List

TWO PLUS

A 19' CRUISER

BUILD IN PLYWOOD

CHARACTERISTICS

Length overall	18'-6"
Beam	7'-9"
Hull depth	4'-0"
Hull weight (approx.)	985 lbs.
Headroom (nominal)	4'-7"
Height overall	6'-3"
Cockpit size	5'-9"x 6'-6"
Sleeping capacity	2-4

Hull type:Vee bottom, hard chine hull, developed for sheet plywood planking.

Power: Single or twin outboard motors to 135 HP.

Trailer: Designed for use with GLEN-L SERIES 2300/2800 boat trailer plans.

COMPLETE PLANS include FULL SIZE PATTERNS for stem, breasthook, transom knee, and half-section patterns for the frames and transom. Includes instructions, Bill of Materials, and Fastening Schedule.

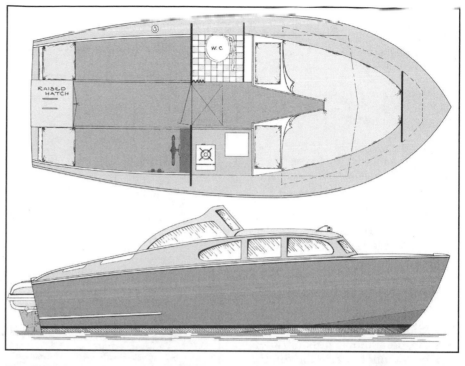

The **TWO PLUS** is designed in a traditional style that harkens back to the heyday of mahogany cruisers. She features complete cruising accommodations for *two, plus* an optional fold out canvas berth for the kids. Her roomy vee berths are a full 6'-6" in length. The efficiently organized cabin makes this boat an ideal camping boat. The head area is enclosed for privacy, unusual on a boat this size. A compact galley area has room for a sink, stove, and ice box.There's hanging space and plenty of storage areas. The cockpit has room for fishing or sitting while sightseeing, and in warm weather has room for sleeping bags for sleeping under the stars.

The hull is designed for lightweight, allowing her to get up on a plane quickly with minimal power. With larger motors, the **TWO PLUS** can easily pull skiers. The broad flare at the bow keeps the boat dry running, and the bridge windshield keeps the bugs out of your teeth underway.

Like most cabin cruisers, it is possible to change the cabin configuration. One builder eliminated the cabin completely to make a roomy touring boat for taking visiting relatives on sight seeing tours up his local river. Whatever your need, take a good look at the **TWO PLUS**, she's a boat full of possibilities.

AVAILABLE FOR THIS DESIGN:
- **Plans & Patterns**
- **Bronze Fastening Kit**
- **Fiberglass Kit**
See Price List

WANDERLUST
A 19' UTILITY CRUISER

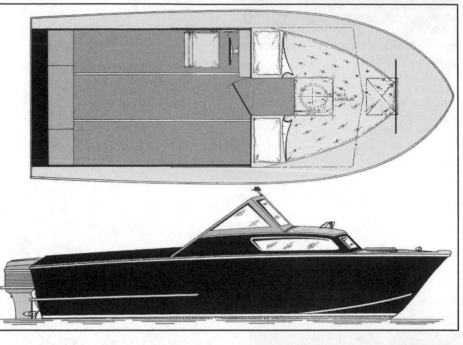

CHARACTERISTICS

Length overall	19'-0"
Beam	7'-10"
Hull depth	3'-7"
Hull weight (approx.)	950 lbs.
Headroom (nominal)	4'-6"
Height overall	6'-3"
Cockpit size	6'-2" x 8'-0"
Sleeping capacity	2

Hull type: Vee bottom, hard chine hull, developed for sheet plywood planking.

Power: Single or twin outboard motors to 150 HP total. Optional stern mounted inboard motor to 700 lbs. connected to an outdrive.

Trailer: Designed for use with GLEN-L SERIES 2300/2800 boat trailer plans.

PLANS include FULL SIZE PATTERNS for stem, breasthook, transom knee, and half-section patterns for the frames and transom. Includes instructions, Bill of Materials, and Fastening Schedule.

The **WANDERLUST** was designed to maximize work space. Scuba divers and fisherman will appreciate the huge 6'-2" x 8' cockpit where you have lots of elbow room for fishing or putting on your gear. The cabin offers a snug place to get in out of the weather, and sleeps two in generous 6'-6" vee berths. The cockpit can be utilized for sleeping by guests with sleeping bags. There is space to stow a portable toilet under the berths.

The hull is made from 3/8" sheet plywood with sawn frames, making her both rugged and lightweight. At the bow the planking forms a generous vee to give a softer ride. The bottom flattens out aft to reduce resistance to allow the boat to plane quickly. The bottom shape also gives a stable platform for fishing, and plenty of hull depth makes this a safe boat for the entire family. Power can be supplied by either an outboard or an inboard with an outdrive. With sufficient power, the **WANDERLUST** can easily pull skiers.

Because of the current interest in classic runabouts and cruisers, the **WANDERLUST** is frequently finished with natural finishes on the deck and cabin, and with shiny chrome hardware, to make her into a real show stopper.

AVAILABLE FOR THIS DESIGN:
- **Plans & Patterns**
- **Bronze Fastening Kit**
- **Fiberglass Kit**
- **See Price List**

CHINOOK

A 19' OR 20' PILOTHOUSE SPORTFISH CRUISER

CHARACTERISTICS

Length overall .... 19'0"(*)
Beam .... 8'2"
Draft (hull) .... 13"
Hull depth (max) .... 4'7"
Displacement .... 3100 lbs.
Hull weight (approx.)............. 1200 lbs.
Fuel capacity .... 55 gals.
Headroom (pilothouse) .... 6'3"
Sleeping capacity 2
Horsepower (max.) 200
Trailer:. Designed for use with GLEN-L SERIES 2900/3800 boat trailer plans.
(*) 20'6" option also in plans.

For reasons that escape us, there are few production boats like our CHINOOK. But if you're like us, there are times when you want to get out of the sun or rain or wind or cold, yet still be on the water. Hence for the fisherman, diver, or cruiser wanting such luxury - along with decent accommodations in a compact hull that really performs - then this is the boat for you.

Besides a private cabin with sitting headroom that sleeps two and has space for a portable head, there's also an enclosed pilothouse with full standing headroom, spacious seating, a hanging locker, drop-leaf table, and lots of shelves. Cockpit space will surprise you - 7' wide x 6-1/2' long - not to mention generous fuel capacity.

Yet CHINOOK acts like a much bigger boat. Using our full-planing "WIDE-TRACK" chine design, the deep-v (45° bow deadrise) gives an easy ride, but with the stability and economy of semi-vee hulls (13° transom deadrise). Integral chine flats and flaring topsides knock down spray while providing easy sidedeck access.

Power can be single outboard or I/O's to 700 lbs. (900 lbs. with 20'6" length). Build in sheet plywood (1/2" total bottom, 3/8" sides) over sawn frames, or welded aluminum (3/16" bottom, 1/8" sides).

Plans include FULL SIZE PATTERNS for frame members, instructions especially for do-it-yourselfers, material listings, plus a fastening schedule on the wood version.

AVAILABLE FOR THIS DESIGN:
- **Study Plans**
- **Plans & Patterns**
- **Bronze Fastening Kit**
- **Fiberglass Kit**

See Price List

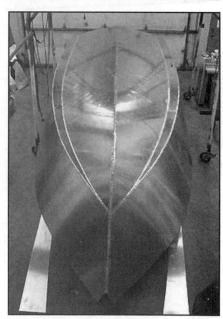

MACKINAW A 20' I/O OR OUTBOARD SPORTFISHER

CHARACTERISTICS

Length overall	20'6"(*)
Beam	8'2"
Draft (hull)	13"
Hull depth (max)	4'7"
Displacement	3500 lbs.
Hull weight (approx)	1400 lbs.
Fuel capacity	70 gals.
Horsepower (max)	200
Sleeping capacity	2
Cockpit size (nom)	11'3" x 7'
Trailer:	Designed for use with GLEN-LSERIES 2900/3800 boat trailer plans.

(*) 19'0" Optional

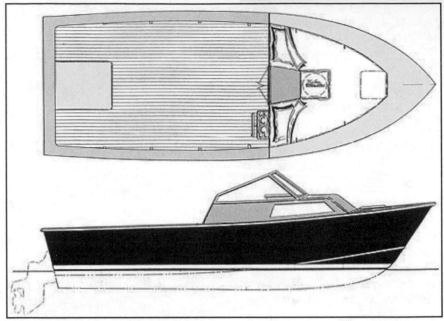

Our MACKINAW express cruiser features a 2-berth cabin with portable head so you can lay over while enjoying fishing, diving, or other watersports. A roomy cockpit provides plenty of space. And there's plenty of fuel capacity for long runs - no need to rush home after a day's fun as with less-commodious boats. Based on our "WIDE-TRACK" hull, outdoorsmen will appreciate this beamy, fast, and stable design. The deep-v (45° bow deadrise) forefoot blending into a semi-v (13° transom deadrise) aft provides an easy ride. Flaring topsides with integral chine flats knock down spray. Power can be single outboard or I/O's to 900 lbs. (700 lbs. with 19' length).

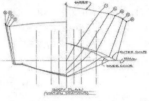

With construction aimed at do-it-yourself builders, (even first-timers!), you can build from sheet plywood (1/2" bottom, 3/8" sides) over sawn frames, or welded aluminum (3/16" bottom, 1/8" sides). Plans include FULL SIZE PATTERNS for frame members, instructions, material listings, plus a fastening schedule on the wood version.

OLYMPIAN 23

A 23' TRAILERABLE ENCLOSED CABIN SPORTFISHER

CHARACTERISTICS

Length overall	23'2" (*)
Length waterline	19'6"
Beam	8'6"
Draft (hull)	15"
Hull depth (max.)	5'0"
Height overall	7'9"
Displacement	5000 lbs.
Hull weight (approx.)	1400 lbs.
Fuel capacity	120 gals.
Headroom	6'3"
Sleeping capacity	3-4
Cockpit size	7' x 7'
Trailer:	Designed for use with GLEN-L SERIES 5000/6000 boat trailer plans.

(*) 21'2" to 24'8" optional

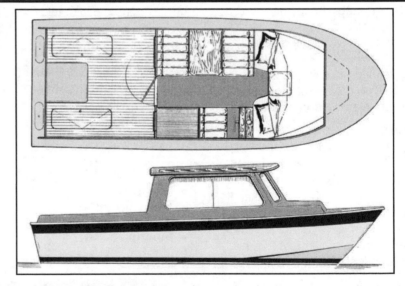

For those fishing and cruising where seas can get windy, wet, rough, and cold, our OLYMPIAN 23 is especially for you. You'll appreciate the protection of an enclosed helm station and cozy cabin with all the amenities. These include a 3' wide dinette that forms a 6'+ berth, a 6'3" v-berth with portable toilet below, galley space, and a helm seat that allows for sitting, standing, or extra galley space depending on position.

More important to anglers is a spacious and deep (28" min.) self-bailing cockpit (a second helm station can be provided here optionally). And if a longer cockpit is desired, you can increase boat length or shorten the cabin. Plans detail a simple way to vary boat length between about 21' and 25'.

Whatever your choice, this trailerable hull can take the elements. Capable of high planing speeds, the full-length hard-chine deep-vee bottom (18-1/2° at the stern) features lift strakes and chine flats to deflect spray and pop you up on plane without fuss. Plans detail

inboard (I/O or jet to 1200 lbs.) or single or twin outboards (20" or 25" shaft lengths).

Build in plywood (1/2" bottom; 3/8" sides) or welded aluminum (3/16" bottom, 1/8" sides). Full size patterns are used to form hull backbone members (i.e., frames, stem, transom) - no lofting required. Hulls are built upside down over this framework. After longitudinals are sprung around, hull panels are positioned, marked to shape, cut, and fastened or welded to these to complete the hull. Plans also include instructions and material listings to assure professional results.

ALBERT E

A 21' *CLASSIC* INBOARD CRUISER

BUILD IN PLYWOOD

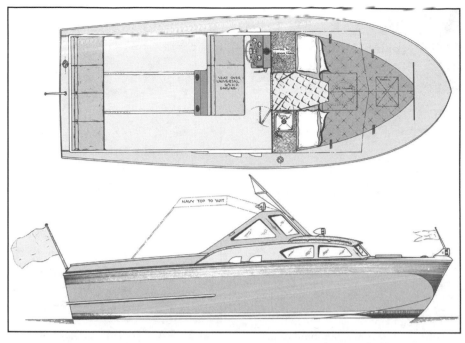

CHARACTERISTICS

Length overall	20'-7"
Length waterline	18'-0"
Beam	7'-10"
Draft	14"
Hull depth	3'-9"
Displacement	3100 lbs.
Hull weight (approx.)	990 lbs.
Freeboard forward	2'-11"
Freeboard aft	2'-4"
Headroom	4'-8"
Height overall	6'-8"
Cockpit size	6'x 10'-3"
Sleeping capacity	2

Hull type: Vee bottom, hard chine hull with bulbous keel and reverse curve at the chine. Bottom designed for double diagonal planking, sides developed for sheet plywood planking.

Power: Single centrally located inboard motor to 850 lbs.

Trailer: Designed for use with GLEN-L SERIES 5000/6000 boat trailer plans.

The **ALBERT E** was designed for one of our favorite fisherman for quick runs to the fishing grounds. Of course, she is not limited to fishing and has all the facilities for limited cruising. Her big cockpit is suitable for a wide variety of water sports. The cabin features two large berths with space for a limited galley and locker facilities. A head can be located under the vee berth. Forward is a rope locker with a deck hatch for ease of handling the anchor lines, and a great spot for small spectators.

Seating is provided for the helmsman at the control console with additional seating for companions. Here they are able to sit protected and comfortable, making long stretches at the wheel much more pleasant.

Using a centrally located engine like bigger yachts, the **ALBERT E** will prove to be a reliable and comfortable craft. The hull design features a double curvature bottom for an easy and exceptionally dry ride. Best of all, you can moor your **ALBERT E** on its own trailer.

COMPLETE PLANS include FULL SIZE PATTERNS for stem, breasthook, and half-section patterns for the frames and transom. Includes instructions, Bill of Materials, and Fastening Schedule.

AVAILABLE FOR THIS DESIGN:
- **Plans & Patterns**
- **Bronze Fastening Kit**
- **Fiberglass Kit**
See Price List

VERA CRUISE
A 21' OUTBOARD CRUISER

BUILD IN PLYWOOD

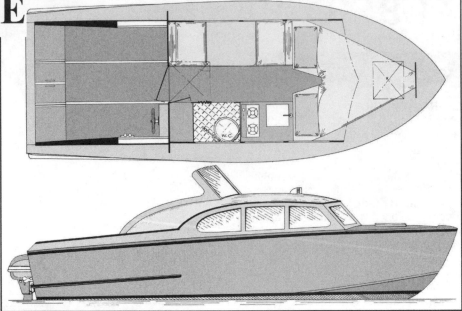

CHARACTERISTICS

Length overall .... 21'-0"
Length waterline .... 18'-0"
Beam .... 7'-10"
Draft .... 10"
Hull depth .... 4'-3"
Hull weight (approx.)............. 1200 lbs.
Headroom (nominal) .... 5'-4"
Freeboard forward .... 3'-5"
Freeboard aft................................ 2'-5"
Height overall .... 7'-3"
Cockpit size .... 6'x 5'
Sleeping capacity 3
Hull type: Vee bottom, hard chine hull, developed for sheet plywood planking.
Power: Single or twin outboard motors. Optional stern mounted inboard motor to 700 lbs. connected to outdrive.
Trailer: Designed for use with GLEN-L SERIES 2900/3800 boat trailer plans.

COMPLETE PLANS include FULL SIZE PATTERNS for stem, breasthook, transom knee, and half-section patterns for the frames and transom. Includes instructions, Bill of Materials, and Fastening Schedule.

The **VERA CRUISE** is a complete cruiser that can sleep three adults. Her bright, airy cabin has a dinette, galley, and even an enclosed head and hanging locker. The galley provides space for a sink, stove, and ice box. A hatch in the foredeck next to the rope locker simplifies handling the lines during docking, increases air circulation and will quickly become a favorite observation post. The cockpit provides plenty of room for diving, fishing, or just plain lounging; all this in just 21'.

For simplicity of construction, her hull was designed for sheet plywood with the bottom flowing from a generous vee forward to a slight vee at the transom. Power can be provided by single or twin outboards, or an optional inboard with stern drive. Although **VERA CRUISE** looks like her

larger sisters, her small size makes it practical to trailer her almost anywhere. Whether cruising or camping, the **VERA CRUISE** is an ideal boat for getting the family together on the water.

AVAILABLE FOR THIS DESIGN:
- **Study Plans**
- **Plans & Patterns**
- **Bronze Fastening Kit**
- **Fiberglass Kit**
See Price List

LAZY DAZE
A 23' SEDAN CRUISER

BUILD IN PLYWOOD

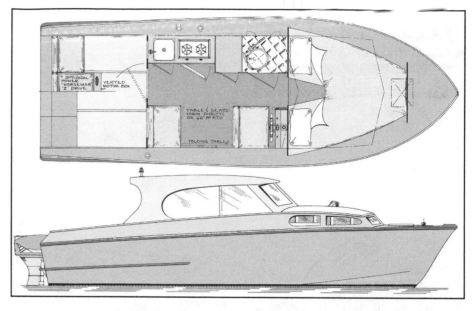

CHARACTERISTICS
Length overall	22'-9"
Length waterline	20'-0"
Beam	7'-11"
Draft	12"
Hull depth	4'-4"
Displacment	3573 lbs.
Hull weight (approx.)	1500 lbs.
Headroom (deckhouse)	6'-1"
Headroom (trunk cabin)	4'-8"
Freeboard forward	3'-3"
Freeboard aft	2'-3"
Height overall	6'-11"
Cockpit size	5'x 6'
Sleeping capacity	2-4
Fresh water capacity	15 gals.

Hull type: Vee bottom hard chine hull, developed for sheet plywood planking.

Power: Single or twin outboard motors. Optional stern mounted inboard motor to 600 lbs. connected to outdrive or vee drive.

Trailer: Designed for use with GLEN-L SERIES 5000/6000 boat trailer plans.

The deckhouse on the **LAZY DAZE** features full headroom and berths are a generous 6'-6" in length. The head is fully enclosed and there's a roomy hanging locker. The galley offers provisions for total self-containment. The helmsman seat reverses to form a dining area in conjunction with the aft seat. Optionally, the builder could install upper and lower berths here in lieu of the single berth formed by the dinette. The cabin has a light and spacious feeling due to the large window area.

The hull has plenty of depth, and features a vee entry that flattens out aft for economy and stability. Power can be outboard or stern drive inboard.

COMPLETE PLANS include **FULL SIZE PATTERNS** for stem, breasthook, transom knee, and half-section patterns for the frames and transom. Includes instructions, Bill of Materials, and Fastening Schedule.

AVAILABLE FOR THIS DESIGN:
- **Study Plans**
- **Plans & Patterns**
- **Bronze Fastening Kit**
- **Fiberglass Kit**

See Price List

MONSOON

A 22' EXPRESS CRUISER

BUILD IN PLYWOOD

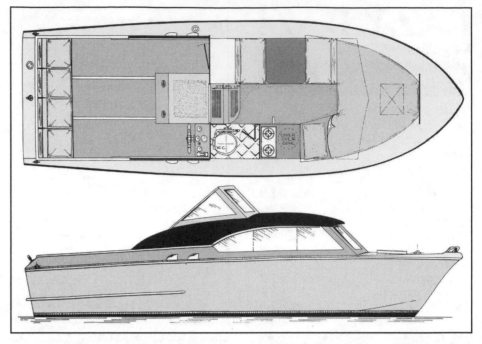

CHARACTERISTICS

Length overall	22'-3"
Length waterline	19'-4"
Beam	7'-11"
Draft	15"
Hull depth	4'-0"
Displacment	3970 lbs.
Hull weight (approx.)	1400 lbs.
Headroom	5'-6"
Freeboard forward	2'-10"
Freeboard aft	2'-3"
Height overall	7'-9"
Cockpit size	6'X 8'
Sleeping capacity	2-3
Fresh water capacity	20 gals.
Fuel capacity	50 gals.

Hull type: Vee bottom hard chine hull, double diagonal plywood bottom, sheet plywood planking on sides.

Power: Single inboard centrally located.

Trailer: Designed for use with GLEN-L SERIES 5000/6000 boat trailer plans.

COMPLETE PLANS include FULL SIZE PATTERNS for stem, breasthook, harpin, and half-section patterns for the frames and transom. Includes instructions, Bill of Materials, and Fastening Schedule.

The **MONSOON** is a spacious, but compact cruiser featuring a reliable centrally located inboard engine. The roomy, airy cabin has fore and aft sliding windows as well as a ventilating access hatch on the foredeck. There is a fully enclosed head on the starboard side of the cabin, with a hanging locker opposite that conveniently opens into the cockpit. The locker top provides an excellent shelf for a ship-to-shore radio near the dinette. The galley has room for a stove and sink with storage below that extends under the forward berths. The dinette converts to form a part of the generous vee berths.

Power can vary considerably as the motor is located over the cen-

ter of bouyancy so that different weights do not affect the trim of the boat. Speeds of 20 knots are possible with 75 SHP; 100 SHP, 23 knots; 180 SHP, 31 knots.

The hull has a double curvature bottom just like our larger boats for a strong hull that rides well and is dry running. The hull construction is designed to be as simple as possible, keeping the amateur builder in mind.

AVAILABLE FOR THIS DESIGN:
- Study Plans
- Plans & Patterns
- Bronze Fastening Kit
- Fiberglass Kit

See Price List

ESCORT
A 22' FLY BRIDGE CRUISER

BUILD IN PLYWOOD

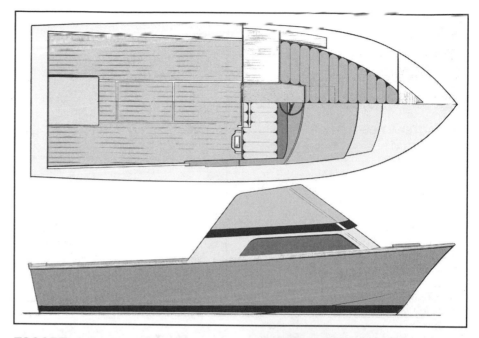

CHARACTERISTICS
Length overall .... 22'-2"
Length waterline .... 18'-4"
Beam .... 8'-0"
Draft .... 12 1/2"
Hull depth .... 4'-6"
Displacment .... 3600 lbs.
Hull weight (approx.)............ 1200 lbs.
Headroom .... 6' max.
Freeboard forward .... 3'-5"
Freeboard aft................................ 2'-2"
Height overall .... 7'-9"
Cockpit size .... 10'-6"x 6'-6"
Sleeping capacity 2
Fuel capacity .... 40 gals.
Hull type: Full length deep vee with 16°
      min. deadrise. Hard chine hull,
      developed for sheet plywood
      planking.
Power: Single or twin outboard motors,
      or stern mounted inboard mo-
      tor to 800 lbs. connected to an
      outdrive or vee drive.
Trailer: Designed for use with GLEN-L
      SERIES 5000/6000 boat trailer
      plans.

COMPLETE PLANS include FULL SIZE PATTERNS for stem, breasthook, and half-section patterns for the frames and transom. Includes instructions, Bill of Materials, and Fastening Schedule.

The **ESCORT** is just the boat for the fishing and diving enthusiast. A compact flying bridge offers visability all around to enable the pilot to be aware of all the activities of the crew members. The full length deep vee hull provides a smooth ride even when speeding to those far away fishing or diving areas. An 8' beam and lightweight hull allows **ESCORT** to be trailered anywhere, thus avoiding mooring fees and letting you take faster and shorter overland routes to far away or inaccessible fishing areas. With the cockpit forming over half of the boat, there is plenty of room for fisherman or divers and their gear. The cabin features a surprising 6' headroom in the galley area where there is plenty of room for an ice box, sink, stove, and related equipment. The 6'-2" vee berths have a space for a head under the center portion.

ESCORT can be powered with a single inboard stern mounted motor driving through a stern drive (I/O) or vee drive. Optionally, single or twin outboard motors can be used. The lightweight, sturdy plywood hull makes a good turn of speed possible. Sheet plywood makes the hull easy to build, and the bulkhead framing method goes together quickly using the FULL SIZE PATTERNS.

AVAILABLE FOR THIS DESIGN:
- **Plans & Patterns**
- **Bronze Fastening Kit**
- **Fiberglass Kit**
See Price List

MAI TAI
A 23' DEEP VEE EXPRESS CRUISER

BUILD IN PLYWOOD

CHARACTERISTICS

Length overall .... 23'-2"
Length waterline .... 19'-4"
Beam .... 8'-0"
Draft .... 13"
Hull depth .... 4'-6"
Displacment .... 3900 lbs.
Hull weight (approx.)............. 1200 lbs.
Freeboard forward .... 3'-5"
Freeboard aft................................. 2'-2"
Height overall .... 7'-4"
Headroom .... 4'-10"
Cockpit size (approx.) .... 11'x 6'-6"
Sleeping accommodations 2
Fuel capacity .... 45 gals.
Fresh water capacity .... 10 gals.
Hull type: Full length deep vee with 16°
minimum deadrise. Hard chine
hull, developed for sheet plywood planking.
Power: Single or twin outboard motors,
or stern mounted inboard motor to 800 lbs. connected to an
outdrive or vee drive.
Trailer: Designed for use with GLEN-L
SERIES 5000/6000 boat trailer
plans.

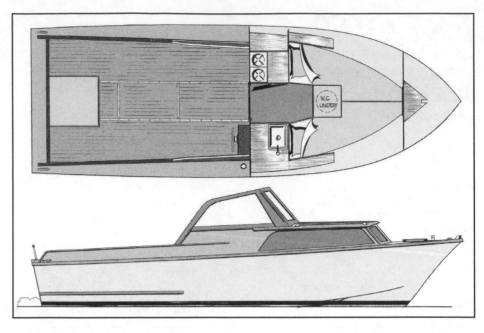

The **MAI TAI** is a versatile blue water sportfishing and recreation boat with exceptional speed potential when the going gets rough. The boat has a full length deep vee hull that makes the ride smooth and dry even in choppy conditions. The keynote of the design is the large cockpit. Imagine a cockpit over 6' in width and nearly 11' long. This size affords plenty of room for recreation, fishing, or scuba diving, with room for all the gear. The range is ample due to generous fuel and water capacities.

The forward cabin has berths for two plus a galley and space for a head below the berths. The helm position is well protected by the windshield and side wings, and the entire cockpit could be used for extra sleeping if desired. A folding top can be used to protect the cockpit area.

The bulkhead type of construction used on the **MAI TAI** is very sturdy and yet easy for the amateur to build. You can build your own **MAI TAI** at a fraction of the cost of factory built boats *and* your **MAI TAI** will be every bit as good or better than one you might buy.

AVAILABLE FOR THIS DESIGN:
• **Plans & Patterns**
• **Bronze Fastening Kit**
• **Fiberglass Kit**
See Price List

COMPLETE PLANS include FULL SIZE PATTERNS for stem, breasthook, and half-section patterns for the frames and transom. Includes instructions, Bill of Materials, and Fastening Schedule.

RAVEN
A 23' DEEP VEE SEDAN CRUISER

BUILD IN PLYWOOD

CHARACTERISTICS

Length overall .... 23'-0"
Length waterline .... 19'-4"
Beam .... 8'-0"
Draft .... 13"
Hull depth .... 4'-6"
Displacment .... 4000 lbs.
Hull weight (approx.)............ 1500 lbs.
Headroom (deckhouse) .... 6'-4"
Headroom (trunk cabin) .... 4'-7"
Freeboard forward .... 3'-5"
Freeboard aft................................ 2'-2"
Height overall .... 7'-4"
Cockpit size (approx.) .... 4' x 7'
Deckhouse size (approx.) .... 6' x 7'
Sleeping capacity 3-4
Fuel capacity .... 50 gals.
Fresh water capacity .... 40 gals.
Hull type:Full length deep vee with 16°
      min. deadrise. Hard chine hull,
      developed for sheet plywood
      planking.
Power: Single or twin outboard motors.
      Optional stern mounted in-
      board motor to 600 lbs.
      connected to an outdrive.
Trailer: Designed for use with GLEN-L
      SERIES 5000/6000 boat trailer
      plans.

COMPLETE PLANS include FULL SIZE PATTERNS for stem, breasthook, and half-section patterns for the frames and transom. Includes instructions, Bill of Materials, and Fastening Schedule.

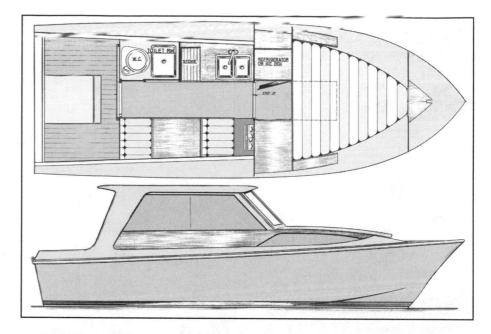

The **RAVEN** is a genuine cruiser in the truest sense. From a distance, her lines will deceive you; she has the appearance of a 35 footer! And yet, this is a boat you can trailer legally to your favorite port of call. With a full length deep vee hull and a fuel capacity of 50 gallons, you can call any cruising area your home without fear of getting caught out when a chop kicks up. Her 40 gallon fresh water capacity means there is plenty of water to supply that optional shower you'll find so pleasurable on extended cruises.

It's rare to have two cabin privacy on a boat this size, but **RAVEN** will provide it for you. The trunk cabin has a large full width vee berth that will spaciously sleep two adults, and can even sleep three in a pinch. There's a large hanging locker here, plus plenty of shelf and storage space for all the gear you'll need. You can install a large ice box or refrigerator and the galley area is still roomy enough for a double bowl sink, several drawers, a stove, and lockers. The full standing headroom in the well lit deckhouse makes cooking a joy.

The toilet room is fully enclosed and provides space for a self-contained head as well as optional shower. The dinette has a unique reversible seat which provides a helmsman seat in the forward position and a dinette seat when facing aft. The dinette also converts to form a full length, full width berth with lots of extra storage space under as well.

```
AVAILABLE FOR THIS DESIGN:
• Plans & Patterns
• Bronze Fastening Kit
• Fiberglass Kit
See Price List
```

SHANGRI LA

A 23' DEEP VEE DOUBLE CABIN CRUISER

BUILD IN PLYWOOD

CHARACTERISTICS

Length overall .... 23'-2"
Length waterline .... 19'-4"
Beam .... 8'-0"
Draft .... 14"
Hull depth .... 4'-6"
Displacment .... 4500 lbs.
Hull weight (approx.)............. 1200 lbs.
Freeboard forward .... 3'-4"
Freeboard aft................................ 2'-1"
Height overall .... 7'-5"
Headroom (aft cabin) .... 4'-2"
Headroom (forward cabin) .... 4'-10"
Headroom (cockpit) .... 6'-2"
Cockpit size (approx.) .... 4' x 6'
Sleeping capacity 4
Fuel capacity .... 45 gals.
Fresh water capacity.............. 10 gals.
Hull type:Full length deep vee with 16°
     min. deadrise. Hard chine hull,
     developed for sheet plywood
     planking.
Power: Single stern mounted inboard
     motor to 800 lbs. connected to
     an outdrive.
Trailer: Designed for use with GLEN-L
     SERIES 5000/6000 boat trailer
     plans.

SHANGRI LA... an all weather cruising boat with private accommodations for two couples. Yet, the boat can be easily trailered to distant areas.

The hull shape is our deep vee type that provides a soft ride and level planing. Intended for inboard power coupled to an outdrive, the hull is fast, able, and maneuverable.

The spacious layout features a central helm and cockpit area, weather protected, with two companion seats. The aft cabin roof will accommodate the sun worshipers while the forward cabin features twin vee berths. The galley provides full headroom with the hatch open. Space is provided for a sink, two burner stove, 4.5 cu. ft. ice box, cutlery drawer, and

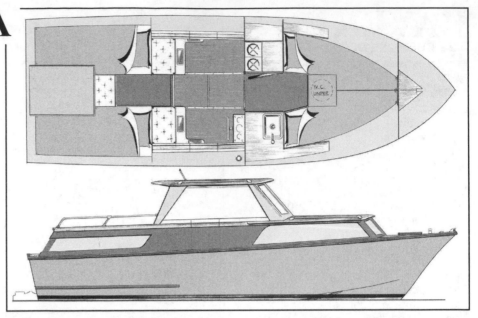

dish and food lockers. Additional storage space is provided under all of the berths, shelves up forward, and two hanging lockers in the aft cabin. A concealed marine head may be located in the forward cabin, while the motor box aft doubles as a table top.

The construction features a bulkhead system that imparts great strength with light weight.

AVAILABLE FOR THIS DESIGN:
- **Plans & Patterns**
- **Bronze Fastening Kit**
- **Fiberglass Kit**
See Price List

COMPLETE PLANS include **FULL SIZE PATTERNS** for stem, breasthook, and half-section patterns for the frames and transom. Includes instructions, Bill of Materials, and Fastening Schedule.

252

HARBORMASTER

STRIP PLANKED, COLD-MOLDED, OR FIBERGLASS

CHARACTERISTICS

Length overall .... 23'-2"
Length at waterline .... 20'-0"
Beam .... 7'-3"
Displacement .... 3160 lbs.
Draft .... 1'-9"
Freeboard forward .... 3'-0"
Freeboard aft .... 2'-0"
Hull depth .... 4'-9"
Height overall .... 8'-9"
Cockpit size (approx.) .... 14'x6'
Cockpit depth .... 2'-3" to 3'-0"
Headroom (min.) .... 6'-3"
Fuel capacity .... 20 gals.

Hull type: Round bilge displacement hull of traditional power launch form with tumblehome topsides aft and deep skeg.

Construction: Hull can be built in wood using conventional strip planking or cold-molded epoxy strip planking with double laminated outer wood veneers. Alternately, hull may be built in "one-off" fiberglass, using fiberglass planking or PVC foam or end-grain balsa sandwich construction.

Power: Single, centrally located, in-line shaft, gasoline, diesel, steam, or electric inboard, 5 to 10 horsepower for speeds to approximately 6 knots.

Trailer: Designed for use with GLEN-L SERIES 5000/6000 boat trailer plans.

WOOD VERSION

COMPLETE PLANS include FULL SIZE PATTERNS for all contoured hull forming members, instructions, Table of Offsets, and hull material listing (both wood methods).

FIBERGLASS VERSION

COMPLETE PLANS include FULL SIZE PATTERNS for all contoured male mold hull forming members, instructions, fiberglass manual, Table of Offsets, and hull material listing (both fiberglass methods).

STUDY PLAN AVAILABLE

AVAILABLE FOR THIS DESIGN:
- **Study Plans**
- **Plans & Patterns**

See Price List

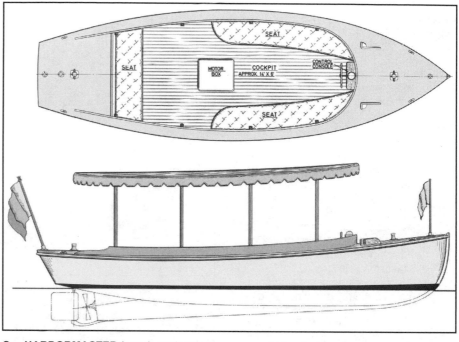

Our **HARBORMASTER** launch conjures up images of more elegant times; of warm summer days, lingering twilight sunsets, and picnic baskets filled with fine cheese, seasonal fruit, and vintage wines. Imagine gentleman in white straw hats accompanied by pretty girls in flowered dresses, laughing and trailing their hands in the water as the **HARBORMASTER** glides along with nary a ripple.

Whether motoring around the harbor, crossing a mountain lake to a vacation cottage, drifting down a lazy river, or viewing the yacht club regatta, our **HARBORMASTER** is *the* boat to be seen in. This replica of a traditional steam launch, common in the early part of the century, will be noticed by all who appreciate beauty and elegance in watercraft. Be prepared for waving hands from those on passing boats and shouts asking what this boat is and where you got her. Imagine the pride you'll have in this showpiece of your craftsmanship, all fitted out with gleaming brass fittings and natural wood trimmed decks.

New materials and modern construction methods make building the **HARBORMASTER** well suited to the amateur, and result in a stronger, lighter, more durable boat that's much easier and cheaper to maintain than those built in the past. Construction of the shapely,

round-bilge hull can be done in wood using conventional strip planking or epoxy strip planking with a double outer layer of wood veneers. Either method requires only a minimum of internal framing and no steam bending. Or you can build in "one-off" fiberglass using C-FLEX fiberglass planking or sandwich core methods with either PVC foam or end-grain balsa.

Whichever method you select, your **HARBORMASTER** is incredibly economical to operate. The slim, low-resistance hull slips through the water, requiring only a few horsepower to reach hull speed. A full length deep skeg with a large rudder and propeller makes it easy to handle in tight corners. After a day's run, just pull the boat onto its trailer and head home, avoiding costly slip fees.

Plans for the **HARBORMASTER** include full size patterns so no lofting is required, although a Table of Offsets is provided for those gluttons who wish to do it themselves. The instructions cover all aspects of the project, plus hull material listing. For a shorter version, the plans give the option of reducing the length by 10% maximum, however, lengthening the boat is not recommended.

LUCKY PIERRE

A ST. PIERRE DORY

CHARACTERISTICS

Length overall ....25'-11"
Beam ....7'-11 1/2"
Hull depth (max.)...........................5'-6"
Hull depth (amidship) ....2'-9"
Bottom width (max.) ....4'-0"
Hull weight (approx.)............. 1000 lbs.
Height overall ....5'-9"
Cockpit depth ....30" to 39"
Cockpit size (max.) ....10'x 7'
Sleeping capacity 2
Cabin headroom (max.) ....5'-0"
Fuel capacity .... 20 gals.
Hull type: Flat bottom St. Pierre type dory hull with flaring topsides, developed for sheet plywood planking; two layers of 1/2"on the bottom, one 3/8" or 1/2" layer on topsides.

Power: Single well-mounted outboard, conventional gasoline or diesel powered inboard, or traditional dory-type haul-up shaft inboard power with retractable shaft and propeller. Recommended horsepower from 5 to 30 depending on engine type. Approx. operating speeds 6 to 10 knots, depending on loading, weight, power, and propeller used.

Trailer: Designed for use with GLEN-L SERIES 5000/6000 boat trailer plans.

COMPLETE PLANS include FULL SIZE PATTERNS for stem, forward deck beam, transom knee, and half-section patterns for the frames, bulkheads, deck beams, and transom. Includes instructions, Bill of Materials, and Fastening Schedule.

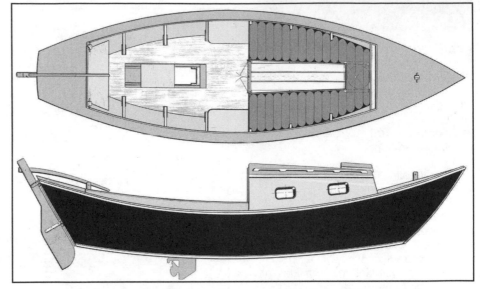

Evolution is sometimes responsible for the most versatile and respected boats, and the Grand Banks dory as exemplified by the famous St. Pierre type is a perfect example. For over 100 years these seaworthy craft have been carrying their crews of two or three fishermen to the fishing grounds off Newfoundland with incredible reliability, safety, and economy. Returning with a ton or two of fish in any sea condition is nothing unusual. While the first craft used sails, most switched to power generations ago. In the event of a power failure, the boats could be rowed home. Because of limited mooring facilities, the fishermen pulled the boats up on shore, made easy by the flat bottom. To make this practical with an engine, however, a haul-up shaft and propeller arrangement was incorporated which has become a traditional arrangement.

Our **LUCKY PIERRE** carries the evolution of the St. Pierre dory several steps further. Not only is the traditional haul-up shaft version detailed on the plans, but also a well-mounted outboard version that can be tilted up free of the bottom for easy beaching and shoal draft operation. Or for those who want a conventional diesel or gasoline inboard, this version is included too.

Most important with our **LUCKY PIERRE** is the greatly simplified form of construction. Traditional St. Pierre dories are not really suitable for most amateurs, but we've changed all that. The flat bottom and straight flaring topsides readily adapt to simple and economical sheet plywood construction. By careful design including the use of full size patterns, framing up for the **LUCKY PIERRE** is quick and easy, even for the rank amateur. No difficult joints or steam bending is required. To hold down costs, there's a minimum of outfitting required because of such things as built-in mooring bitts and steering provided by a simple, reliable tiller connected to a retractable transom-mounted rudder.

The excellent qualities of the St. Pierre dory should not be restricted to the Grand Banks, and that's why we kept the beam of our **LUCKY PIERRE** under 8'. You can trailer the boat anywhere, launching wherever there's a place to slide the craft into the water. A cabin with full sitting headroom and long settee-berths plus optional head means that two can lay over if need be. Of course, for those who do not want the cabin, it can be omitted for even more room. All in all, the **LUCKY PIERRE** is hard to beat where a really low cost, seaworthy, simple powerboat is required. Our easy-to-follow plans and instructions will show you how to have your own for less work and money than you might think.

> ### AVAILABLE FOR THIS DESIGN:
> - **Study Plans**
> - **Plans & Patterns**
> - **Bronze Fastening Kit**
> - **Fiberglass Kit**
>
> **See Price List**

JEAN PIERRE

A 27' ST. PIERRE DORY WITH SAIL OPTION

CHARACTERISTICS

Length overall	26'11"
Length waterline	22'0"
Beam	9'6"
Bottom width (max)	5'10"
Draft (Power Version)	2'6"
Draft (Sail Version max)	3'6"
Displacement (@ DWL)	5460 lbs.
Ballast (Sail Version)	1650 lbs.
Sail area (Sail Version)	293 sq. ft.
Fuel capacity	60 gals.

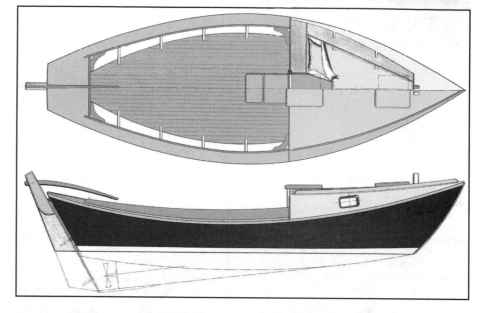

Jean Pierre was originally done as a custom design for a series of fishing craft to be used off the coast of Darwin, Australia. The plan set was later expanded to include both Sail and Power versions. Due to the wide hull and fixed ballast fin keel of NACA-foil section (either cast lead or iron can be used), the boat can carry generous sail with good windward ability. Easily built wood spars are detailed, but aluminum extruded types are optional.

There are several motor options on the Power version. The standard engine is a straight prop-and-shaft in-line unit passing through a long skeg that supports the rudder to protect the underwater gear. Another power option shows the once-traditional "haul-up" shaft and prop, but without the skeg which allows for easy beaching. There is also an option for a thru-hull "saildrive" type motor without skeg. Or for those who prefer outboards, you can use a well-mounted 20" to 25" long shaft motor.

On the sail version, the cabin door is offset to one side to clear the mast. Power can be a thru-hull "saildrive" type motor or straight shaft inboard with the shaft supported by a strut; a skeg is not used. In all cases, 10 to 20 horsepower is all you need regardless of motor type.

There is full-sitting headroom above the full-length v-berth with space for a head below. Construction is sheet plywood planking over straight-contoured frames of ordinary lumber, with little additional fairing required. Plans include instructions, material lists, and fastening schedules plus FULL SIZE PATTERNS so no lofting is required.

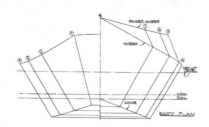

HERCULES

A 24' TRAILERABLE CRUISING YACHT

BUILD IN PLYWOOD

CHARACTERISTICS

Length overall .... 24'-1"
Length waterline .... 22'-0"
Beam .... 7'-11 1/2"
Draft.. 24"
Hull weight (approx.)..................... 1600 lbs.
Displacement................................. 5532 lbs.
Freeboard forward .... 5'-0"
Freeboard Aft .... 3'-2"
Hull depth .... 6'-9"
Height overall .... 10'-10"
Fuel capacity .... 80 gals.
Fresh water capacity..................... 40 gals.
Cockpit size...................................... 6'x 4'-3"
Cockpit depth (nominal) .... 32"
Headroom .... 6' to 6'-6"
Sleeping capacity .... 2 adults, 2 children
Hull type: Semi-displacement, hard chine hull
with practical cruising speed of
7 knots, and a maximum hull speed
of approx. 9 knots. Bottom design features bulbous forefoot
with a reverse curve at the chine.
Double diagonally planked to a
total thickness of 1/2". Topsides
planked with sheet plywood to a
total thickness of 3/8". Carvel
planking or other conventional
types are optional but not detailed
in the plans.
Power: Single centrally mounted diesel
or gasoline inboard; 10 SHP for 7
knot cruising speed, 25 SHP for
maximum 9 knots intermittently.
Reduction gear may be required.
Engines rated over 35 SHP not
recommended. Stern mounted
motor driving through outdrive,
optional. Total engine and gear
max. 600 lbs.
Trailer: Designed for use with GLEN-L
SERIES 7000/10000 boat trailer
plans.

COMPLETE PLANS include FULL SIZE PATTERNS for stem, breasthook, and half-section patterns for the frames and transom. Includes instructions, Bill of Materials, Table of Offsets and Fastening Schedule.

HERCULES has the traditional character of larger blue water cruising yachts including economy of operation and extended range, in a size that's trailerable anywhere free of low bridges! You can cruise over 600 miles on one filling of diesel fuel, and when the voyage is over, just moor your **HERCULES** in your own backyard! No slip fees necessary! This is a perfect cruiser for the young family or retired couple on a budget. While not intended for worldwide ocean cruising, **HERCULES** makes a great island hopper, perfect for your yearly vacations.

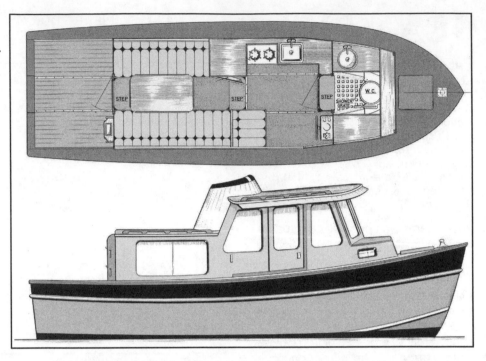

We've planned **HERCULES** for comfortable cruising, with full standing headroom through-out, even in the head! The forward toilet room even has a shower, not to mention a lavy and roomy hanging locker, located for privacy. For safety and convenience, all line and anchor handling forward can be done from inside through the forward hatch. No need to stand on a pitching foredeck. There's a real pilot-house with helmsman's seat, "salty" control console, and sliding door for safety and convenience.

Designed for economical cruising, the **HERCULES** is no speedboat, so don't at-tempt to cram in more power than you need. With a high freeboard and deep forefoot, you'll cruise along with an easy ride, but at a lei-surely pace. By using the FULL SIZE PAT-TERNS, the lofting process is not required, but a Table of Offsets is included if you wish the "fun" of lofting your own frames. If you've built a boat before, or have some woodwork-ing experience, the **HERCULES** will be a re-warding project for you.

While **HERCULES** is a compact craft, she packs in a lot of accommodations. The gal-ley can be outfitted for complete self-con-tainment. The settees in the salon area are perfect for dining or loafing, and make up two full size berths for the skipper and his mate, plus two shorty berths for the crew. The cockpit is deep and self-draining for safety, plus there's a transom door for going to shore. The cabin top can be reached by ladder and makes a perfect place for sunbathing.

AVAILABLE FOR THIS DESIGN:
- **Study Plans**
- **Plans & Patterns**
- **Bronze Fastening Kit**
- **Fiberglass Kit**
See Price List

COASTAL CRUISER

A 25' TRAILERABLE MOTORYACHT

BUILD IN PLYWOOD, STEEL or ALUMINUM

CHARACTERISTICS

Length overall	25'0" (*)
Length waterline	23'0" (*)
Beam	8'6"
Draft (hull)	1'4"
Displacement	5150 lbs.
Hull Depth (max)	6'1"
Height overall	9'9"
Fuel capacity	60 gals.
Water capacity	40 gals.
Headroom	6'-3"/5'-7"
Sleeping capacity	4
Trailer:	Designed for use with GLEN-L SERIES 5000/6000 boat trailer plans.

(*) 23' or 27' options given on plans

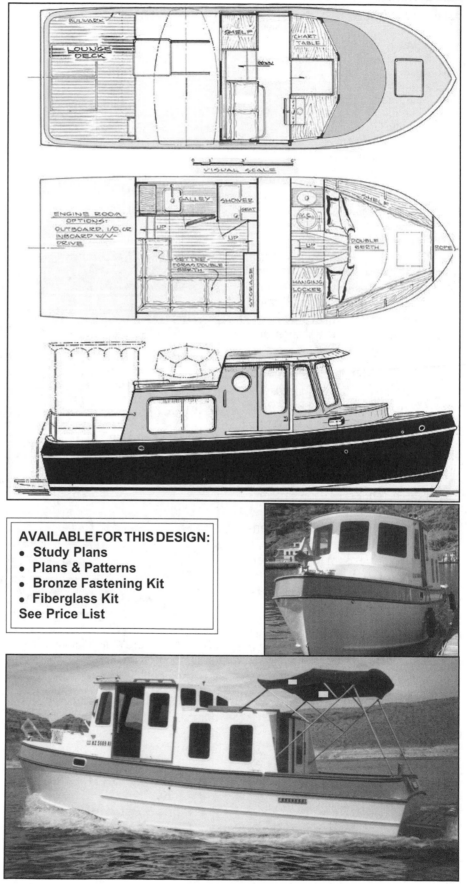

With accommodations and amenities much like larger vessels, it's surprising that this popular design is readily trailerable. There's a private double stateroom forward with head, lavatory, and hanging locker. The pilothouse has ready access both sides, seats two, and plenty of room for charts and electronics. A unique feature is the separate shower with seat, while the galley can be fully self-contained. A roomy L-shaped settee converts to a double berth. Both pilothouse and main cabin have full-standing headroom, with 5'7" in the stateroom when the hatch is closed.

You can cruise at 10-12 knots with 45-60 SHP - about twice the speed of sailboats this length. Or hit speeds in the 18-20 MPH range with I/O motors in the 150-160 HP range. For easy service and simplicity, plans detail stern-located outboard, I/O, or inboard V-drive power options, all located below a spacious raised deck. You can carry an 8' dinghy on the house top.

Low-cost, easy, but husky construction is ideal for do-it-yourselfers, even first-timers. Wood hulls use sheet plywood throughout rather than more time-consuming double diagonal or "cold mold" methods. Or you can optionally build in welded all-aluminum, or in steel for the hull (wood superstructure) - see study plans for more details. FULL SIZE PATTERNS give frame member contours in all cases - no lofting required. Instructions include material listings and fastening schedule (wood hulls).

AVAILABLE FOR THIS DESIGN:
- **Study Plans**
- **Plans & Patterns**
- **Bronze Fastening Kit**
- **Fiberglass Kit**

See Price List

TRUE-GRIT
A 25' TRAILERABLE SPORTFISH UTILITY/CRUISER

CHARACTERISTICS

Length overall .... 25'0"(*)
Length waterline .... 23'0"
Beam .... 8'6"
Draft (hull) .... 1'4"
Displacement .... 5150 lbs.
Hull depth (max.)........................ 6'1"
Height overall .... 9'1"
Fuel capacity .... 80 gals.
Trunk cabin headroom .... 5'7"
Shelter/deckhouse headroom ...... 6'6"
Sleeping capacity 2-4
Trailer: . Designed for use with GLEN-L
SERIES 5000/6000 boat trailer plans.
(*) 23' to 27' optional

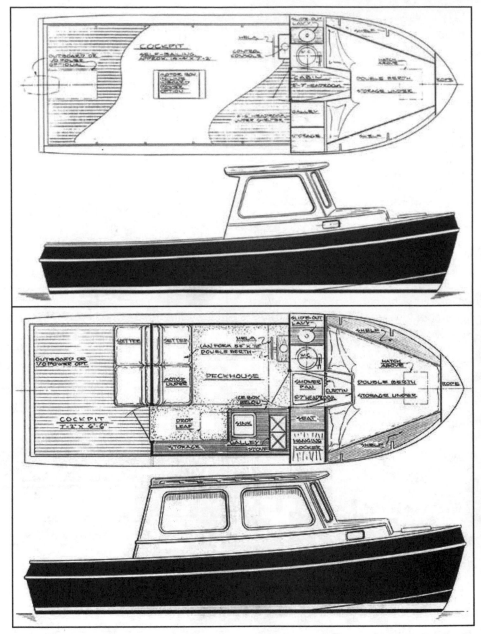

Options and features are many on this rugged, practical trailerable design. Low-cost construction is fast and easy in sheet plywood, steel, or aluminum. FULL SIZE PATTERNS for all frame member contours mean no lofting. Instructions include material listings and include options for 23' and 27' lengths.

Power options detailed include outboard, I/O, or direct drive inboard, gas or diesel. It only takes 45-60 SHP for 10-12 knot speeds. Or kick power up to the 150-160 HP range for speeds in the 18-20 MPH category. There's plenty of fuel in any case.

Inspired by cient Ken Tyson's modification, we've added a Sedan Cruiser Version option. This features an enclosed deckhouse, sleeping for four, a larger galley, and room for a shower, with settees inside and out (inboard motor below), and a nice cockpit that's easily covered if desired.

Otherwise, the Utility Version sleeps 2, has space for a head, and room for a hanging locker or galley, and a huge cockpit for all sorts of watersport or workboat activities. On both versions, cockpits are self-bailing and at least 30" deep. There's also full headroom under the house tops, and nearly so in the trunk cabins.

NOTE: Steel hull plans include aluminum version plans with list of scantling changes for steel. Steel hulls weigh approximately 2000 lbs more than aluminum and draw 2" to 3" more than listed; speeds will also be less with similar power. Steel option also includes plywood and wood superstructure details.

AVAILABLE FOR THIS DESIGN:
- **Study Plans**
- **Plans & Patterns**
- **Bronze Fastening Kit**
- **Fiberglass Kit**
See Price List

KONA KAI
A 25' DEEP VEE FLY BRIDGE CRUISER

BUILD IN PLYWOOD

CHARACTERISTICS

Length overall	24'-6"
Length waterline	20'-0"
Beam	7'-10"
Draft	15"
Hull depth	4'-6"
Displacment	5110 lbs.
Hull weight (approx.)	1200 lbs.
Headroom	6'-1"
Freeboard forward	3'-3"
Freeboard aft	2'-4"
Height overall	9'-4"
Cockpit size (approx.)	7'-6"x 7'-6"
Sleeping capacity	3-4
Fuel capacity	80 gals.
Fresh water capacity	20 gals.

Hull type: Full length deep vee with 18° min. deadrise, bulbous keel section, and lift strakes. Hard chine hull, developed for sheet plywood planking.

Power: Single or twin outboard motors or stern mounted inboard motor connected to an outdrive or vee drive. Maximum motor weight with outdrive: 800 lbs; with vee drive: 900 lbs. Reduction gear may be required, depending on engine.

Trailer: Designed for use with GLEN-L SERIES 7000/10000 boat trailer plans with 6000 lbs. capacity option.

COMPLETE PLANS include FULL SIZE PATTERNS for stem, breasthook, and half-section patterns for the frames and transom. Includes instructions, Bill of Materials, and Fastening Schedule.

The **KONA KAI** is a real sportfisher *and* it's trailerable! No need for expensive moorings and limited fishing grounds. Just hitch up to the family auto and go where the big ones are biting. The **KONA KAI** has all the capability of sport fishing boats much larger. First, the flying bridge makes handling and fish finding easy. Second, the large self-draining cockpit is flush; no tripping around engine boxes here. Third, the hull is a real full length deep-vee with a minimum 18° deadrise right at the transom and has lift strakes to get up on a plane quickly, cut resis-

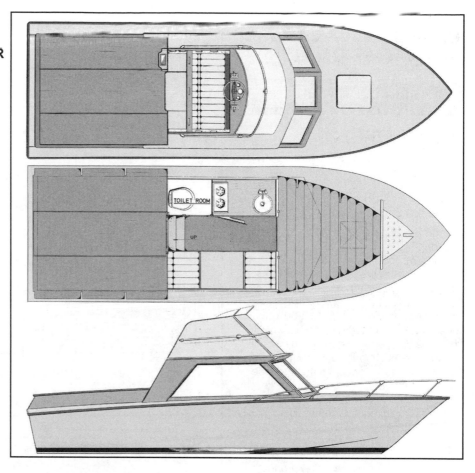

tance, and keep spray down. To compliment these features, there's 80 gallons of fuel and 20 gallons of fresh water which makes the **KONA KAI** truly a long range craft capable of going out where the action is. So you won't have to worry about coming back the same day, there's a truly livable cabin. It sleeps three people honestly (four in a pinch!) and has a fully enclosed head. The galley is complete with lots of storage space.

The **KONA KAI** is easy to build and recommended for the experienced amateur. This is a boat you'll be proud of, *and* you'll save a bundle by doing it yourself.

AVAILABLE FOR THIS DESIGN:
- Study Plans
- Plans & Patterns
- Bronze Fastening Kit
- Fiberglass Kit

See Price List

ESCAPADE

A 26' FLY BRIDGE CRUISER

BUILD IN PLYWOOD

CHARACTERISTICS

Length overall .... 26'-2"
Length waterline .... 22'-0"
Beam .... 10'-0"
Displacement .... 6050 lbs.
Draft .... 19"
Freeboard forward .... 3'-11"
Freeboard aft .... 3'-0"
Hull depth .... 5'-2"
Headroom (nominal) .... 6'-3"
Cockpit size (approx.) ...... 8'-0" x 10'-3"
Hull weight (approx.) .... 1400 lbs.
Fuel capacity .... 100 gals.
Water capacity .... 30 gals.
Sleeping accommodations 4
Hull type: High speed planing hull of full
    length modified deep vee de-
    sign. Bottom of compound type
    with bulbous section at keel
    and reverse curve at chine.
    Designed for double diagonal
    planking on bottom and sheet
    plywood planking on sides.
Power: Inboard marine engine, gaso-
    line or diesel with appropriate
    reduction gears, usually 1 1/2:
    1 or 2:1. Engine may be cen-
    trally located with conventional
    drive or stern mounted with ei-
    ther vee drive or outdrive unit.
    Engine weight should not ex-
    ceed 1100 lbs. for stern
    mounted units. Twin screws
    may be used centrally mounted
    with the addition of motor boxes
    in the cockpit.

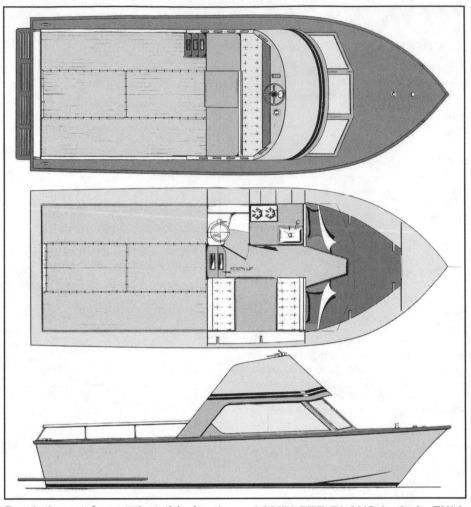

The **ESCAPADE** has all the best features of a typical deep vee hull such as soft entry, easy ride, and high speed potential. But, unlike some deep vees, the **ESCAPADE** won't make like a rocking chair when the crew walks from one side of the boat to the other. The reverse curvature at the chine not only makes for a stable fishing platform, but deflects all that spray without the use of power wasting appendages. You get up on a plane at lower speeds and with less power than most of the extreme vee jobs.

But let's not forget that this boat was designed with the sports fisherman in mind. Take a look at that flying bridge. It's not only spacious, but comfortable too, and with full circle visibility for easy docking and fish finding. Check that cockpit! There's room for a chartered party and all their gear. What's more, it's self-draining and never need be covered, you won't trip over any motor boxes because it's flush. You'll be able to sleep four in full length berths too. The galley is complete with sink, stove, and ice box or refrigerator, plus lots of storage space. The head is completely enclosed and has a roomy hanging locker.

COMPLETE PLANS include FULL SIZE PATTERNS for the stem, breasthook, and half-section patterns for the frames and transom. Includes instructions, Bill of Materials, and Fastening Schedule.

AVAILABLE FOR THIS DESIGN:
- **Study Plans**
- **Plans & Patterns**
- **Bronze Fastening Kit**
- **Fiberglass Kit**
See Price List

CORONADO
A 26' TRAILERABLE CONVERTIBLE FLYING BRIDGE CRUISER

CHARACTERISTICS

Length overall	25'8" (*)
Length waterline	21'3"
Beam	8'6"
Draft (hull)	15-1/2"
Hull depth (max.)	5'1"
Height overall	9'7"
Displacement	5900 lbs.
Hull weight (approx.)	1500 lbs.
Fuel capacity	120 gals.
Headroom	6'2"
Sleeping capacity	4

Trailer: Designed for use with GLEN-L SERIES 5000/6000 boat trailer plans.
(*) 23'1" to 28'3" optional

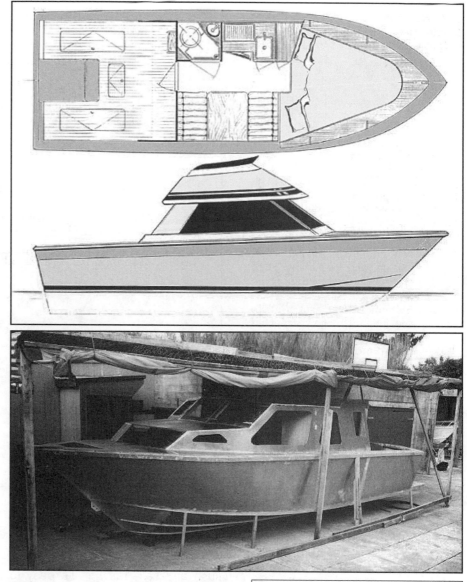

This stylish craft serves equally well for sportfishing or family cruising. Accommodations include an oversize v-berth forward, complete galley, hanging locker, a dinette that forms a 6'3" double berth, and enclosed head with lavy and space for a shower. Controls are on the flying bridge, and a roomy self-bailing cockpit nearly 9' long is aft.

A modern deep-v hull softens the ride with a 40+° vee forefoot, while the 18-1/2° vee at the transom adds stability and performance in conjunction with wide chine flats and two lift strakes per side. Power comes from I/O units to 1300 lbs., or single or twin outboards (25" shaft length for singles; 20" or 25" for twins).

Building your own is not difficult nor expensive. The plywood planked hull has a 1/2" total bottom and sides, over sawn frames and longitudinal stiffeners. Or build in welded aluminum with 3/16" bottom and 1/8" sides.

Plans include FULL SIZE PATTERNS for the seven frame contours, stem, and transom, along with our instructions and material listings, plus fastening schedule on wood version.

AVAILABLE FOR THIS DESIGN:
- Study Plans
- Plans & Patterns
- Bronze Fastening Kit
- Fiberglass Kit
See Price List

CATALINA EXPRESS

A 27' TRAILERABLE CRUISER

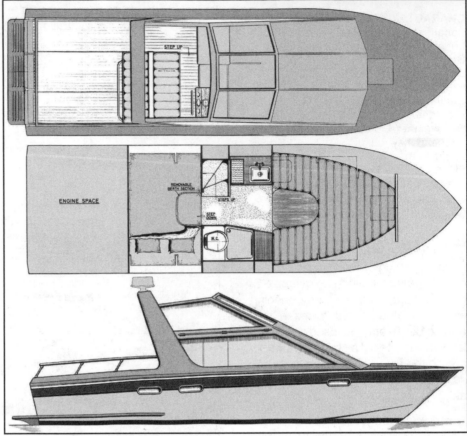

CHARACTERISTICS

Length overall	27'-1/2"
Length waterline	22'-6"
Beam	7'-10"
Draft	15"
Hull depth	4'-6"
Displacment	6015 lbs.
Hull weight (approx.)	1300 lbs.
Headroom	6' to 6'-3"
Freeboard forward	3'-3"
Freeboard aft	2'-4"
Height overall	9'-8"
Cockpit size (approx.)	10'-9"x 6'-6"
Sleeping capacity	4-5
Fuel capacity	90 gals.
Fresh water capacity	35 gals.

Hull type: Full length deep vee with 18° min. deadrise, bulbous keel section, and lift strakes. Hard chine hull, developed for sheet plywood planking.

Power: Stern mounted diesel or gasoline inboard motor connected to an outdrive or vee drive. Maximum motor weight with outdrive: 850 lbs; with vee drive: 950 lbs. Reduction gear may be required, depending on engine. "Sea Drive" power plants are also suitable.

Trailer: Designed for use with GLEN-L SERIES 7000/10000 boat trailer plans.

Here's one way to beat the high cost of boating. Build your own stylish trailerable **CATALINA EXPRESS** and say goodbye to slip rental fees. Our FULL SIZE PATTERNS make the job easier than you might think. Plans include instructions, material listings, and fastening schedule specially intended for amateurs. The sheet plywood hull is easy and cheap to build, resulting in a quality boat with exceptional strength and light weight. This latter quality is especially important for economical cruising and easy trailering.

The hull design is an easily driven, easy riding, full length deep vee. The hard-chine hull with lift strakes is exceptionally dry running even in the sloppiest of conditions. Either an I/O or v-drive inboard can be used for power, gasoline or diesel. The engine sets under the cockpit sole which is flush and self-draining. It's easy to cover the cockpit with a convertible top from the radar bar. The stylish radar bar is functional too, making an ideal mounting location for a radar unit for those who want this feature.

The flying bridge control station is located over the aft cabin which features a 54" wide double berth, sitting headroom, and remarkable privacy for a boat this size. A dual-width seat is provided for the helmsman which is backed up by a lounge seat facing aft. Stepping down the spiral stairs, one enters a cabin featuring 6'+ headroom, even in the fully enclosed toilet room.

Here there's space for a shower, with a hanging locker located forward. A fully equipped galley is opposite, with a drop-leaf for additional counter top space. The lounge-dinette forward seats 4 and forms a full width berth 7'-9" long for 2 or 3. All in all, the **CATALINA EXPRESS** offers accommodations and features seldom associated with a trailerable boat.

COMPLETE PLANS include **FULL SIZE PATTERNS** for stem, breasthook, and half-section patterns for the frames and transom. Includes instructions, Bill of Materials, and Fastening Schedule.

AVAILABLE FOR THIS DESIGN:
- **Study Plans**
- **Plans & Patterns**
- **Bronze Fastening Kit**
- **Fiberglass Kit**

See Price List

PHANTOM

A 27' TRAILERABLE CRUISER

BUILD IN PLYWOOD

CHARACTERISTICS

Length overall	27'-1/2"
Length waterline	22'-6"
Beam	7'-10"
Draft	15"
Displacement	6015 lbs.
Freeboard forward	3'-3"
Freeboard aft	2'-4'
Hull depth	4'-6"
Hull weight (approx.)	1300 lbs.
Headroom	6'-1" to 6'-3"
Cockpit size (approx.)	7'-6" x 6'-0"
Fuel capacity	90 gals.
Water capacity	35 gals.
Height overall	9'-5"
Sleeping capacity	4-5

Hull type: Full length deep vee with 18° min. deadrise, bulbous keel section, and lift strakes. Hard chine hull developed for sheet plywood planking.

Power: Stern mounted inboard gasoline or diesel engine driving through an outdrive or v-drive. Maximum engine and drive weight with I/O option 850 lbs. Maximum engine and gear weight with vee drive option 950 lbs. Reduction gear to suit.

Trailer: Designed for use with GLEN-L SERIES 7000/10000 boat trailer plans.

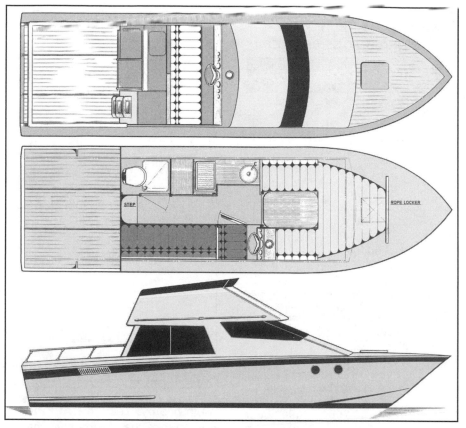

It's unbelievable that our **PHANTOM** is only 27' long. Bold European styling gives her the look of a 40 footer. What's even more unbelievable is that the **PHANTOM** can be legally trailered anywhere! Say goodbye forever to expensive, inconvenient moorings and slip rental fees. You can build *and* moor this rakish beauty in your own backyard! Your cruising waters are limited only by the highways that will carry you and your family to your favorite launching ramp.

The **PHANTOM** is more than just another tag-along boat; this is a real yacht! Just look at these big boat features: Full length soft riding, dry running, deep-vee hull... I/O or vee drive inboard power for high speeds... Dual control stations with a roomy flying bridge... Enclosed toilet room with shower... Spacious dinette seats 4... Fully equipped galley... Comfortable settee... Sleeping for 4 or 5 adults (or more if some are kids)... Big self-bailing flush decked cockpit... Full headroom... Extensive fuel and water capacities... Storage space equal to larger boats. Truly the *ultimate* trailerable cruiser!

You can build your own **PHANTOM** for far less money and effort than you might imagine. The comprehensive plans with procedural instructions show you how. Our FULL SIZE PATTERNS minimize errors and speed construction. Sheet plywood planking throughout is not only simple and inexpensive, but makes for an incredibly light, but sturdy vessel capable of taking anything that can be expected of a boat this size. So if you've been wondering how to beat the high costs of bigger boats with accompanying high mooring and maintenance costs, take a second look at our trailerable **PHANTOM** cruiser.

> ### AVAILABLE FOR THIS DESIGN:
> - **Study Plans**
> - **Plans & Patterns**
> - **Bronze Fastening Kit**
> - **Fiberglass Kit**
>
> **See Price List**

COMPLETE PLANS include **FULL SIZE PATTERNS** for the stem, breasthook, and half-section patterns for each of the frames and transom. Includes instructions, Bill of Materials, and Fastening Schedule.

CALYPSO

A 27' FLYING BRIDGE CRUISER

BUILD IN PLYWOOD

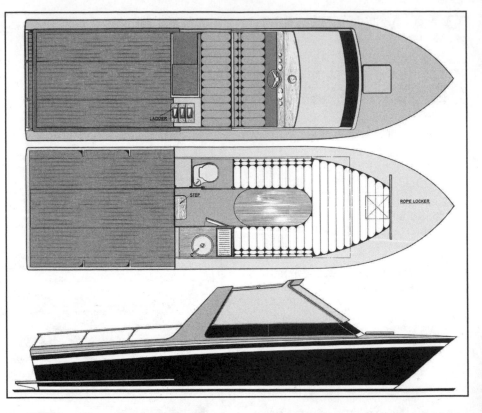

CHARACTERISTICS

Length overall .... 27'-1/2"
Length waterline .... 22'-6"
Beam .... 7'-10"
Displacement .... 6015 lbs.
Draft .... 15"
Freeboard forward .... 3'-3"
Freeboard aft .... 2'-4"
Hull depth .... 4'-6"
Headroom (maximum) .... 6'-0"
Cockpit size (approx.) .... 7'-6"x 9'
Hull weight (approx.) .... 1300 lbs.
Fuel capacity .... 140 gals.
Water capacity .... 35 gals.
Sleeping accommodations 4-5
Hull type: Deep vee 18° minimum deadrise for sheet plywood planking.
Power: Stern mounted inboard with vee drive (1600 lbs. max.) or outdrive unit (1200 lbs. max.).
Trailer: Designed for use with GLEN-L SERIES 7000/10000 boat trailer plans.

COMPLETE PLANS include FULL SIZE PATTERNS for the stem, breasthook, and half-section patterns for the frames and transom. Includes instructions, Bill of Materials, and Fastening Schedule.

Could our **CALYPSO** be the ultimate boat for the water sports buff? Well, just check out these features and decide for yourself. For openers, there's a large 7 1/2' x 9' cockpit so you won't be elbow to elbow with your fishing or diving buddies. There's no motor box to bust your shins on because the motor is below the cockpit. It's self-draining and watertight as well. Any water that comes aboard drains aft and overboard, which makes clean-up a breeze. Next, look at the flying bridge. It'll seat three or four, plus there's a sunbathing lounge/seat that is perfect for watching the action in the cockpit.

But the best feature of our **CALYPSO** is that it can be trailered anywhere without special wide load permits. You get the big boat feel of a 27' craft, but with the ability to do your fishing or diving anywhere there's a launching ramp nearby. Yet, the **CALYPSO** is built to take the rough stuff. The full length deep vee hull makes high speeds possible even in choppy conditions. That large fuel capacity means that you can run out to where the action is. If you want to lay over, most of the cabin has 6' headroom where four or five people can cook, eat, and sleep, complete with the privacy of an enclosed head.

You can power your **CALYPSO** with an inboard gasoline or diesel motor, using either a vee drive or an outdrive for exhilarating high speed planing performance. Sheet plywood planking, together with our detailed plans and instructions, makes construction easy and inexpensive. Your finished **CALYPSO** will be a performer that you will be proud of.

AVAILABLE FOR THIS DESIGN:
- **Plans & Patterns**
- **Bronze Fastening Kit**
- **Fiberglass Kit**
See Price List

VARIANT
A 29' FLY BRIDGE SEDAN CRUISER

BUILD IN PLYWOOD

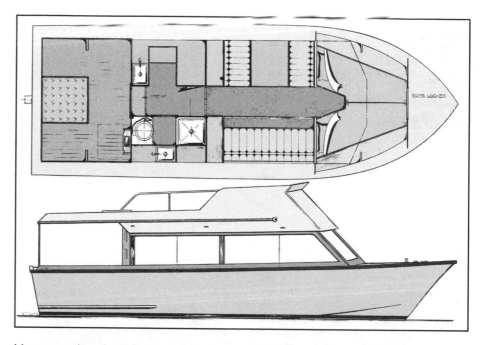

CHARACTERISTICS

Length overall .... 28'-10"
Length waterline .... 24'-8"
Beam .... 10'-1"
Displacement .... 7637 lbs.
Draft .... 16"
Freeboard forward .... 3'-10"
Freeboard aft .... 2'-11"
Hull depth .... 5'-2"
Height overall .... 10'-6"
Headroom .... 6'-3"min.-6'-6"
Cockpit size (approx.) .... 6'-0" x 8'-0'
Hull weight (approx.) .... 1800 lbs.
Fuel capacity .... 110 gals.
Water capacity .... 30 gals.
Sleeping accommodations 6
Hull type: Full length modified deep vee design (9° at the transom) with bulbous section at the keel and reverse curve at the chine. Designed for double diagonal planking on bottom and sheet plywood planking on sides.
Power: Inboard marine engine, gasoline or diesel, with appropriate reduction gears, usually 1 1/2: 1 or 2:1. Engine to be stern mounted with either vee drive or outdrive unit. Twin screws may be used by using compact power plants.

Vary your boating pleasure with the **VARIANT.** A deep vee cruiser with houseboat accommodations, packaged in a hull designed for high speed, rough water use. You can have these spacious accommodations in one of two versions. If you like the comfort of a sheltered cockpit for those hot summer days or to keep out the wet, build her as shown. If you're one of the sportfishing set, leave the cockpit cover off and use the roomy 6' x 8' cockpit for fishing. The **VARIANT** can be powered by either an I/O or a vee drive installation mounted under the flush cockpit. Both versions are fully detailed in the plans and covered by the instructions. In either version, you get the same cabin layout designed to sleep up to six full size adults, plus an extra large flying bridge deck where the crew can bask in the sun.

Storage areas are in abundance, with a large hanging locker located amidship on either side of the boat, plus lots of space under all berth areas. The hanging locker on the port side also acts as a serving counter for the galley. Rarely will you see a galley like this on a 29' boat. Space is provided for a large ice box, a large stove with oven, sink and abundant locker and drawer space. The U-shaped layout allows the chef to work out of the way of in and out traffic. The toilet room has a shower in addition to the sink and toilet, plus plenty of storage space here too. Choose the **VARIANT** if you are looking for maximum accommodations and elbow room in a boat under 30'.

AVAILABLE FOR THIS DESIGN:
- **Plans & Patterns**
- **Bronze Fastening Kit**
- **Fiberglass Kit**
See Price List

COMPLETE PLANS include FULL SIZE PATTERNS for the stem, breasthook, and half-section patterns for the frames and transom. Includes with instructions, Bill of Materials, and Fastening Schedule.

ISLANDER
A 25' CLASSIC EXPRESS CRUISER

BUILD IN PLYWOOD

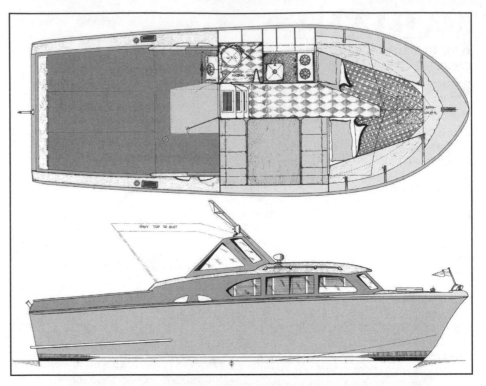

CHARACTERISTICS

Length overall	24'-11"
Length waterline	21'-7"
Beam	9'-8"
Displacement	5355 lbs.
Draft	17"
Freeboard forward	3'-7"
Freeboard aft	2'-8"
Hull depth	4'-11"
Headroom	6'-1/2"
Cockpit size (approx.)	7'x 10'
Hull weight (approx.)	1500 lbs.
Fuel capacity	56 gals.
Water capacity	25 gals.
Sleeping accommodations	4

Hull type: Vee bottom hard chine hull with bulbous section at keel and reverse curve at chine. Designed for double diagonal planking on bottom and sheet plywood planking on sides.

Power: Single centrally located inboard motor. Reduction gear may be required.

COMPLETE PLANS include FULL SIZE PATTERNS for the stem, breasthook, harpin, and half-section patterns for the frames and transom. Includes instructions, Fastening Schedule, and Bill of Materials.

The **ISLANDER** has the classic look that has become so popular in recent years. There's no need to drool over that expensive classic moored at the marina. You can make your own and not have to worry about the potential problems of a forty year old boat.

The **ISLANDER** is both a reliable and economical boat to own. The centrally located inboard uses the time proven straight shaft set-up. Virtually any automotive conversion can be used depending on desired speed. The hull features our seaworthy double curvature vee entry forward that flattens out aft for economical running with stability. The beamy hull allows a large cabin with a roomy dinette, enclosed head, galley, and vee berth arrangement for tall and "shorty" crew members. The large cockpit has plenty of area for fishing, diving, and dockside

use, plus a convertible top can be used over the bridge in conjunction with the windshield for inclement weather.

When finished with plenty of bright work and chrome fittings, the **ISLANDER** becomes an instant classic. An ideal boat for the builder who enjoys putting extra care and detail in his projects.

AVAILABLE FOR THIS DESIGN:
- Study Plans
- Plans & Patterns
- Bronze Fastening Kit
- Fiberglass Kit

See Price List

266

GUNG HO

A 28' *CLASSIC* EXPRESS CRUISER

BUILD IN PLYWOOD

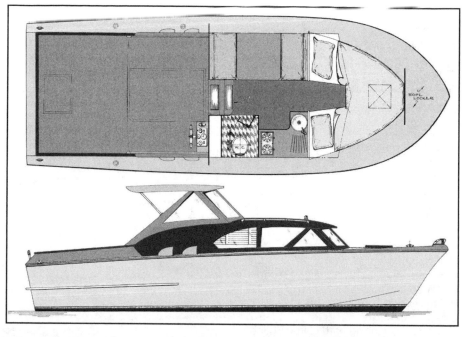

CHARACTERISTICS

Length overall .... 28'-0"
Length waterline .... 24'-2"
Beam .... 10'-4"
Displacement .... 7550 lbs.
Draft .... 19"
Freeboard forward .... 4'-0"
Freeboard aft.............................. 2'-11"
Hull depth .... 5'-4"
Headroom (cabin) .... 6'-3"
Headroom (cockpit) .... 6'-6"
Cockpit size (approx.) .... 8'-0'x 11'-3"
Hull weight (approx.) .... 2000 lbs.
Fuel capacity .... 100 gals.
Water capacity .... 30 gals.
Sleeping accommodations 4
Hull type: Vee bottom hard chine hull with bulbous section at keel and reverse curve at chine. Designed for double diagonal planking on bottom and sheet plywood planking on sides.
Power: Single or twin centrally mounted inboard motors.

COMPLETE PLANS include FULL SIZE PATTERNS for the stem, breasthook, harpin, and half-section patterns for the frames and transom. Includes instructions and Bill of Materials.

Like the ISLANDER, the **GUNG HO** is a boat for the person looking for traditional styling; an instant classic. This is one of those boats that draws the attention from passers-by at the marina or yacht club. When properly finished with natural mahoghany and chrome fittings, she has the look of those classic cruisers often seen in the yachting magazines.

And she's not just a pretty face. The **GUNG HO** is spacious with full 6'-3" headroom in the cabin and accommodations that make extended cruising practical. One

builder logged over 18,000 hours on his before building one of our larger designs. The cabin has an enclosed head, L-shaped galley, vee berths, and a convertible dinette, all with full headroom both in the cabin and under the shelter top (which can be omitted if desired). As with many of our larger high speed cruisers, the **GUNG HO** features our bulbous keel and reverse curve at the chine for excellent rough water ability.

AVAILABLE FOR THIS DESIGN:
- **Study Plans**
- **Plans & Patterns**
- **Bronze Fastening Kit**
- **Fiberglass Kit**
See Price List

TEMPEST

A 27' DEEP VEE CRUISER

BUILD IN COLD-MOLDED WOOD OR FIBERGLASS

CHARACTERISTICS

Length overall	27'-0"
Length waterline	22'-8"
Beam	9'-11"
Draft	16"
Displacement	6800 lbs
Freeboard forward	4'-10"
Freeboard aft	4'-6"
Hull depth	6'-2"
Headroom	6'-3"
Cockpit size	9'x 6'
Hull weight (approx.)	2000 lbs
Fuel capacity	115 gals
Water capacity	40 gals
Height overall	9'-8"
Sleeping capacity	5-7

Hull type: Full planing hard chine. Bottom has full length deep vee with 18° minimum deadrise, bulbous keel section, and lift strakes. Sides have reverse curve flaring sections forward and canted raised topsides above sheerline. Wood hulls are triple diagonal planked to 3/4" on bottom; sides are double diagonal planked to 1/2". Fiberglass hulls are built using "one-off" male mold methods, either fiberglass planking or PVC foam sandwich construction.

Power: Single or twin stern mounted engines driving through outdrives or vee drives. Engine weight range: I/0 - 750 to 1600 lbs. Vee drive - 850 to 2000 lbs. Other stern mounted drive systems optional but not shown on plans. Diesel or gasoline powered engine acceptable.

COMPLETE PLANS include FULL SIZE PATTERNS for the stem, breasthooks, deck beams, transom and station (frame) contours. Includes with instructions, Bill of Materials, Fastening Schedule, and cabin construction details. *FIBERGLASS version includes FIBERGLASS MANUAL.*

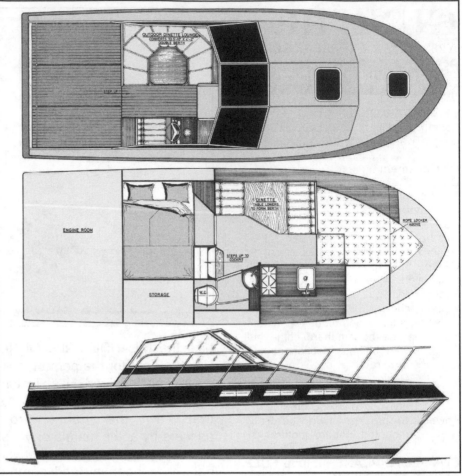

We invite you to compare the accommodations of our **TEMPEST** design with those of boats much larger. For example, virtually half the boat is devoted to outdoor activities yet the cabin is truly spacious. There's a private owner's stateroom aft with hanging locker, fully enclosed toilet room with shower, an inside dinette-convertible berth that supplements the outdoor dining lounge, a complete galley opposite, and another double berth forward that can be curtained off for privacy. Storage and shelf spaces abound, yet the cabin has an open, airy, appearance.

Moving aft and topside on the **TEMPEST** brings you to what's best described as the outdoor living area. Here's an outdoor dining lounge that also converts to a double berth for sleeping under the stars. There's space for a bar that can be fitted out with an ice maker or refrigerator. The cockpit is large and deep (32" min.) and self-draining making it suitable for fishing, diving, or lounging about. The control station is situated so the helmsman can join in on all the fun, yet still offers full circle visibility. In fact, this is a boat that's even practical for water skiing if the urge strikes.

TEMPEST can really perform, too. The hull is a full length 18° minimum deep vee with stabilizing, spray-deflecting lift strakes and a ride softening bulbous keel section. Hull depth is comparable to much larger boats for security. The attractive topsides flare outward in broad reverse curves. This shape results in ample reserve bouyancy forward that prevents plunging in headseas and helps keep spray off the deck.

Building your own **TEMPEST** is not as difficult as you might think. Since our designers are amateur boatbuilding specialists, the method and materials have been adapted to the abilities of the do-it-yourselfer whether choosing to build in wood or fiberglass. WOOD versions are cold-mold planked using strips of plywood or solid wood veneers, applied diagonally in layers over sawn frame members, reinforced by longitudinal battens inside. No difficult woodworking operations, such as steam bending are required.

For FIBERGLASS hulls, the proven one-off male mold methods are used, either fiberglass planking (C-FLEX) or PVC foam sandwich. Either method uses internal reinforcing longitudinal and transverse members for a strong but lightweight hull. Cabin construction in all versions uses simple wood and plywood materials, with exterior surfaces sheathed in fiberglass.

AVAILABLE FOR THIS DESIGN:
- **Study Plans**
- **Plans & Patterns**
- **Bronze Fastening Kit**
- **Fiberglass Kit**
- **See Price List**

SEA ANGLER

**A 35' CONVERTIBLE
SPORTFISHER-CRUISER**

BUILD IN COLD-MOLDED WOOD OR FIBERGLASS

CHARACTERISTICS

Length overall	35'-3"
Length waterline	30'-0"
Beam	13'-8"
Displacement	18,000 lbs.
Draft	2'-6"
Freeboard forward	5'-4 1/2"
Freeboard aft	3'-1"
Hull depth	7'-10 1/2"
Height overall	14'-9"
Headroom	6'-3" to 6'-9"
Cockpit size (approx.)	9'-6"x 10'-9"
Deckhouse size	8'-4"x 10'-9"
Fuel capacity	360 gals.
Water capacity	100 gals.
Sleeping accommodations	6

Hull type: Hard chine hull form with convex bulbous deep vee entry and flaring topsides forward, and modified vee aft with flatter sections for stability and lower power requirements. Tri-mode hull form allows practical operation at displacement, semi-displacement, or full planing speeds. Hull intended for cold-molded, multi-diagonal wood or plywood planking (thickness of 3/4" on sides, 1" on bottom), or "one-off" fiberglass construction.

Power: Twin inboard in-line engines, either gasoline or diesel powered. Single engine optional but not detailed. Recommended practical speed range is 14-17 knots, although speeds to approximately 27 knots are posssible.

COMPLETE PLANS include FULL SIZE PATTERNS for the stem, breasthook, and transom and station (frame) contours. Include instructions, Bill of Materials, Fastening Schedule, and cabin construction details. *FIBERGLASS version includes FIBERGLASS MANUAL.*

Our **SEA ANGLER** design is often referred to as a convertible; that is, a boat suitable for *both* cruising and sport fishing. For the sportfisherman, look at all these features: Huge self-draining cockpit close to the water for easy landing of the catch, made more handy with an optional transom door, and flush coamings with optional thigh padding; space for one or two fighting chairs, including a bait prep area with sink and top-loading freezer, plus a large fish box; spacious flying bridge with the helmsman in full view of cockpit activity, comfortable lounge seat for passengers,

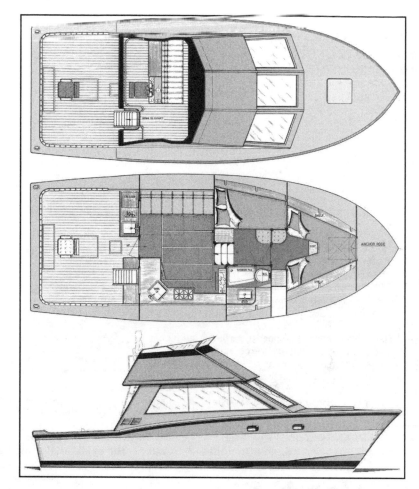

and plenty of room for the latest in electronics gear.

For cruising, **SEA ANGLER** sleeps six in three cabins with generous headroom throughout. The two staterooms each feature a hanging locker, shelves, and seat for easy dressing. The light and airy deckhouse includes an optional inside control station, fully equipped galley, and settee which converts to a double berth. Tables which hinge out of the way are used for dining, while the area above the aft stateroom makes a huge chart table/navigation station. The fully equipped toilet room includes a shower and plenty of storage space, while the engine room is directly below the deckhouse through hatches in the sole.

SEA ANGLER features an efficient tri-mode hull design practical for use in the three speed ranges of displacement (as during trolling), semi-displacement (for economy with speed), or full-planing operation when one needs to get to the fishing grounds in a hurry or to outrun foul weather. Normal speed range is 14 to 17 knots, with speeds up to about 27 knots possible with sufficient horsepower. Generous tank capacities allow extended cruising range, and there's space for a good-sized generator so you can have all the luxuries of shoreside living aboard. Twin gasoline or diesel in-line engines assure reliability and nimble handling, while a long, deep skeg provides positive directional stability in difficult sea conditions.

SEA ANGLER features a hard-chine hull form

with spray strakes, raised sheer, high freeboard, and flaring topsides forward for dry running and added lift in rough seas. The bulbous convexed deep vee bottom forward cushions the ride, while the modified vee at the transom and flatter sections aft provide a rock-stable platform so desirable for fishing, crew comfort, and fuel economy.

Building **SEA ANGLER** is straight forward for the more advanced do-it-yourselfer using either wood or fiberglass for the hull construction. Wood methods consist of multi-layered diagonal cold-molded wood veneers or plywood strips laid over a framework of longitudinal members and sawn transverse frames spaced several feet apart. No steam bending or difficult woodworking operations are required. Fiberglass methods include the "one-off" systems using sandwich core materials or the fiberglass planking method. Either wood or fiberglass hulls result in strong structures that are light in weight for economical operation with reduced maintenance. Cabin construction in all cases is of wood/plywood composite for simplicity, strength, light weight, and low cost.

AVAILABLE FOR THIS DESIGN:
- **Study Plans**
- **Plans & Patterns**
- **Bronze Fastening Kit**
- **Fiberglass Kit**
See Price List

ALLEGRO A 33' EXPRESS CRUISER

CHARACTERISTICS

Length overall .... 33'-3"
Length waterline .... 29'-2"
Beam .... 14'-1"
Displacement .... 14,000 lbs.
Draft .... 24"
Freeboard forward .... 4'-10"
Freeboard aft................................ 3'-6"
Hull depth .... 5'-7"
Headroom .... 6'-3"
Cockpit size (approx.) ..... 13'-0"x 11'-0"
Fuel capacity .... 200 gals.
Water capacity .... 50 gals.
Sleeping accommodations 6
Hull type: Full planing hull with double diagonal planking on the bottom, and sheet plywood on the sides.
Power: Single or twin inboard motors, centrally located.

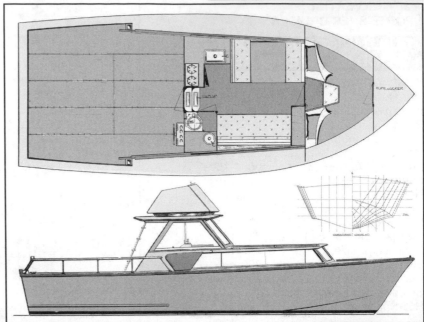

The **ALLEGRO** is a beamy, high speed flying bridge cruiser with plenty of room in the cabin *and* the cockpit. The cabin sleeps 6, has a complete toilet room, and a self-contained galley. There are dual control stations and the self-draining cockpit does not need a cover in foul weather. The hull of the **ALLEGRO** has a ride-cushioning bulbous keel section and spray reducing reverse curved chine all on a modified deep vee hull. Speed is only limited by the single or twin power installed, and the hull is built for strength and ease of construction.

COMPLETE PLANS include **FULL SIZE PATTERNS** for the stem, breasthook, and half-section patterns for the frames and transom. Includes instructions, Bill of Materials, and Fastening Schedule.

SORRENTO

36' SEDAN CRUISER

CHARACTERISTICS

Length overall .... 36'-0"
Length waterline .... 31'-8"
Beam .... 14'-1"
Displacement .... 15,600 lbs.
Draft .... 24"
Freeboard forward .... 4'-10"
Freeboard aft................................ 3'-6"
Hull depth .... 5'-7"
Headroom forward cabin (min.)... 6'-3"
Headroom deckhouse (min.) ...... 6'-4"
Cockpit size (approx.) .... 6'3"x 10'-6"
Deckhouse size .... 9'-6"x 10'-0"
Fuel capacity .... 200 gals.
Water capacity .... 100 gals.
Sleeping accommodations 4-6
Hull type: Full planing hull with double diagonal planking on the bottom, and sheet plywood on the sides.
Power: Single or twin inboard motors, centrally located with proper reduction gear.

COMPLETE PLANS include **FULL SIZE PATTERNS** for the stem, breasthook, and half-section patterns for the frames and transom. Includes instructions, Bill of Materials, and Fastening Schedule.

SORRENTO has a spacious deckhouse with aft cockpit and will handle three couples. There's a complete galley and spacious dinette, plus the convenience of a toilet room *and* separate shower room all adjacent to the owner's stateroom. The helmsman has full circle visibility in the deckhouse. The beamy **SORRENTO** hull features our proven bulbous entry with reverse curve at the chine for a smooth, dry ride. Optionally, the boat can be built as an express cruiser, with or without the flying bridge.

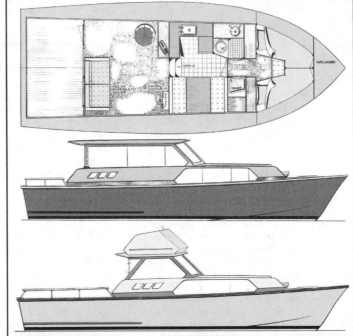

NORDCOASTER A 27' MOTORYACHT

CHARACTERISTICS

Length overall	27'0"(*)
Length waterline	24'0"
Beam	9'11"
Draft w/skeg	1'7" (I/O)
	2'8" (Inbd)
Freeboard fore/aft	5'0"/2'11"
Displacement	6900 lbs.
Hull weight (approx)	2200 lbs.
Fuel capacity	100 gals.
Water capacity	50 gals.
Sleeping capacity	4
Headroom (nom)	6'0"-6'4"
Motor weight (lbs/max)	650 (I/O)
	900 (Inbd)

(*) With Radiused Transom; 26'0" or 28'0" opt.

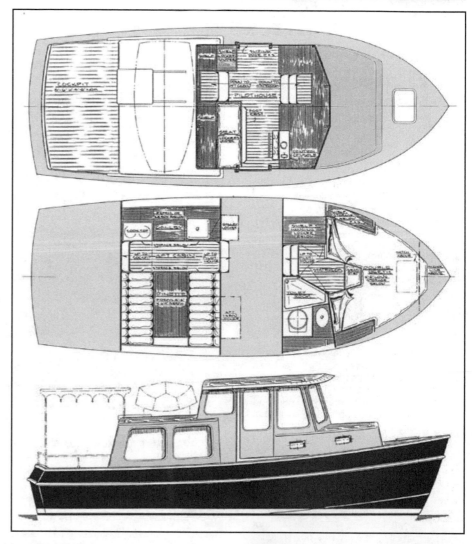

Why pay a 6-figure ransom for production tug yachts when you can build our NORDCOASTER for a fraction of the cost? Compare features: Double stateroom, enclosed head and shower, roomy pilothouse with side deck access both sides, self-contained galley, wide convertible dinette, lots of tankage, roomy cockpit, dinghy boatdeck, plenty of storage, and more!

Construction in plywood or welded aluminum is well suited to do-it-yourselfers. Plywood hulls with straight transom use a double diagonally planked bottom (3/4" total thickness) and 1/2" sheet plywood sides. Aluminum hulls use straight or radiused transom, with .160" sides and .188" thick bottom.

Power options include single centrally-located inboard or stern-mounted I/O. Speeds from 6 to 18 knots are possible, within a power range of 25 to 155 HP. And assuming a wide load permit with a suitable tow vehicle, trailering NORDCOASTER is an option that can save slip fees and broaden your choice of cruising grounds (I/O option recommended for trailering).

The easily-driven semi-planing hull features a deep-V forefoot and ample freeboard forward for an easy, dry ride. Bottom lines transition to a modified V aft for economy and stability. Keel options include a long, deep skeg (recommended where ultimate top speed is not critical), or an abbreviated shallower skeg where optimum speeds or I/O motor are desired.

FULL SIZE PATTERNS are provided for all frame member contours. Plans include instructions and hull material listings, and fastening schedule for wood hulls.

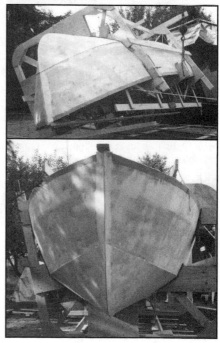

AVAILABLE FOR THIS DESIGN:
- Study Plans
- Plans & Patterns
- Bronze Fastening Kit
- Fiberglass Kit
See Price List

JOLLY ROGER

A 28' CRUISING YACHT

BUILD IN PLYWOOD OR FIBERGLASS

CHARACTERISTICS

Length overall .... 27'-9"
Length waterline .... 25'-0"
Beam .... 10'-10"
Draft .... 2'-9"
Displacement .... 10,433 lbs.
Freeboard forward .... 5'-6"
Freeboard aft .... 2'-10"
Hull depth .... 8'-3"
Height overall .... 12'-2"
Headroom .... 6'-1" to 6'-5"
Cockpit size (approx.) .... 5'-0"x 9'-6"
Cockpit depth (nominal) .... 31"
Fuel capacity .... 190 gals.
Water capacity .... 120 gals.
Cruising range (approx.) .... 1000 miles
Sleeping accommodations 4

Hull type: Semi-displacement hard chine hull with practical cruising speed of 7 1/2 knots. Build in plywood or "one-off" fiberglass. Bottom features deep bulbous forefoot with reverse curve at the chine. Plywood version: double diagonal plywood planking on the bottom to a total thickness of 3/4", sheet plywood sides to 1/2". Topsides feature broad flare with raised deck forward. Fiberglass version utilizes fiberglass planking or PVC foam or balsa core sandwich construction.

Power: Single diesel engine recommended of approximately 25 continuous shaft horsepower for 7 1/2 knot cruising speed. This power figure includes a 50% reserve to offset adverse wind and sea conditions. Engine weight should range between 500 and 700 lbs. Gasoline power is optional.

The **JOLLY ROGER** has all the character and capabilities of the larger traditionally styled cruising yachts, but in a more compact and economical size. The seaworthy semi-displacement hull of hard chine form is easily driven, requiring only about 25 shaft horsepower for a cruising speed of 7 1/2 knots. At this speed,

the **JOLLY ROGER** has the incredible ability to cruise approximately 1000 miles on one loading of fuel when using economical diesel power.

The **JOLLY ROGER** features a flush raised deck forward which gives high freeboard and a lot of space below in the forward stateroom. The aft hull areas feature full walkaround decks with full height rails and protective bulwark, so that access is possible to both sides of the pilothouse. This pilothouse has a seat for two plus a good sized chart table and shelf space for electronics gear. Adjacent to the stateroom forward is a complete toilet room with shower. There's a dressing table and hanging locker plus generous shelf and storage areas in the stateroom.

The aft cabin sleeps two on the convertible settee. If desired, the builder could provide a standard type dinette in lieu of the settee. Dining is accomplished by using the hinged table which folds up out of the way against the bulkhead when not in use. Warmth in the cabin for year round cruising can be provided by a marine-type fireplace. The galley

is self-contained, having a sink, stove, and ice box or refrigerator.

COMPLETE PLANS include **FULL SIZE PATTERNS** for the stem, breasthook, and transom and station (frame) contours. Includes instructions, Bill of Materials, Fastening Schedule, and cabin construction details, *FIBERGLASS version includes FIBERGLASS MANUAL.*

AVAILABLE FOR THIS DESIGN:
- **Study Plans**
- **Plans & Patterns**
- **Bronze Fastening Kit**
- **Fiberglass Kit**

See Price List

JACK TAR

A 31' CRUISING YACHT

BUILD IN PLYWOOD OR FIBERGLASS

CHARACTERISTICS

Length overall	31'-1"
Length waterline	27'-6"
Beam	10'-11"
Draft	3'-0"
Displacement	11,476 lbs.
Freeboard forward	5'-8"
Freeboard aft	2'-11"
Height overall	14'-0"
Headroom (at centerline)	6'-3" min.
Cockpit size (approx.)	3'-8"x 7'-4"
Deckhouse size	7'-4"x 9'-2"
Fuel capacity	310 gals.
Water capacity	200 gals.
Cruising range (approx.)	1000+ miles
Sleeping accommodations	5

Hull type: Semi-displacement hard chine hull with deep bulbous forefoot and reverse curvature forward. Build in plywood or "one-off" fiberglass. Plywood version: double diagonal plywood planking on the bottom to a total thickness of 3/4", sheet plywood sides to 1/2". Topsides feature broad flare with raised deck forward. Fiberglass version: plans detail fiberglass planking and sandwich core construction.

Power: Single diesel engine recommended of approximately 68 continuous shaft horsepower for 9 knot cruising speed. This power figure includes a 50% reserve to offset adverse wind and sea conditions. Gasoline power is optional.

COMPLETE PLANS include FULL SIZE PATTERNS for the stem, breasthook, and transom and station (frame) contours. Includes instructions, Bill of Materials, Fastening Schedule, and cabin construction details, *FIBERGLASS version includes FIBERGLASS MANUAL.*

Our **JACK TAR** looks, performs, and has features like long range cruising yachts much larger in displacement and length. Imagine cruising over 1,000 miles on a single filling of fuel using a modest sized diesel of about 45 SHP. That's economy! At just a hair over 31', you'll appreciate the compact size when it comes time to pay the slip rental fee. But just because this boat's short, don't sell it short!

The **JACK TAR** is a real triple cabin yacht that will easily accommodate a family of five in comfort and privacy. The aft cabin is the owner's haven, having a double berth and complete toilet room adjacent, including a shower and roomy hanging locker. An additional upper berth could be worked in above

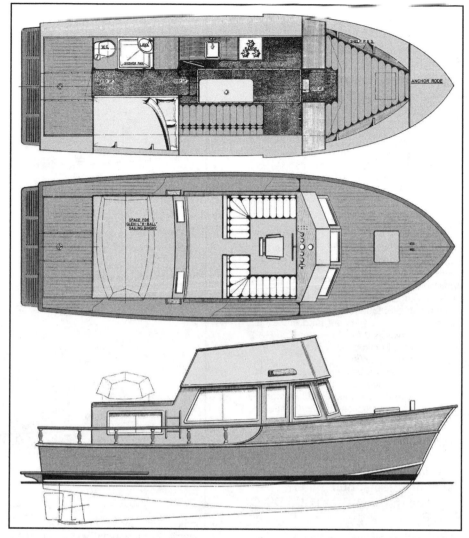

the double berth if needed. The deckhouse has a complete galley, plus a settee berth (which could be made into a convertible double if desired). The dining table is removable and stows against the overhead when not needed. There's a chart table to port and an inside helm to starboard for use in inclement weather. Sliding doors are located port and starboard for safe, easy handling of the vessel. Another double cabin is located forward, with berths flanked outboard with shelves and two hanging lockers aft. With the added berths noted, you could sleep up to seven if everyone is friendly!

JACK TAR also has big yacht features outside too. There's a good sized aft cockpit with a handy optional transom gate and transom step for easy and safe boarding. A boat deck readily accommodates a dinghy up to 8' long, and the flying bridge has another control sta-

tion plus lounging seats for the entire crew. Wide side decks and an uncluttered foredeck assure easy and safe handling at dockside, anchoring, or mooring.

Our **JACK TAR** can be built in plywood and wood using sheet plywood for the topside planking and double diagonal planking on the bottom. Or you can build the hull using our "one-off" fiberglass materials and methods. With either version, the hull design is meant for long range blue water cruising in just about any weather. There's plenty of tankage for fuel and water, and plenty of room below for gear and equipment necessary for long cruises. The single engine, with large diameter propeller and ample rudder combined with a full length skeg, assures positive handling under all conditions. If you'd like more information before building your own **JACK TAR**, order our STUDY PLAN brochure.

AVAILABLE FOR THIS DESIGN:
- **Study Plans**
- **Plans & Patterns**
- **Bronze Fastening Kit**
- **Fiberglass Kit**
See Price List

UNION JACK

A 31' SEMI-DISPLACEMENT CRUISING YACHT

BUILD IN STEEL

CHARACTERISTICS

Length overall	30'-11"
Length waterline	28'-0"
Beam	11'-6"
Draft	3'-4 1/2"
Displacement	17,100 lbs.
Weight of steel hull components (est.)	7,000 lbs.
Freeboard forward	5'-6"
Freeboard aft	3'-0"
Height overall (w/stack)	12'-7 1/2"
Headroom	6'-2" to 6'-8"
Fuel capacity	350 gals.
Water capacity	250 gals.
Cruising range (@ 7 knots)	1000+ miles
Sleeping accommodations	5

Hull type: Semi-displacement hard chine hull developed for sheet steel (10 GA.) construction with practical speeds to 8 1/2 knots.

Power: Single diesel engine of 40 to 70 continuous shaft horsepower for 7 to 8 1/2 knot speed using appropriate reduction gear and propeller.

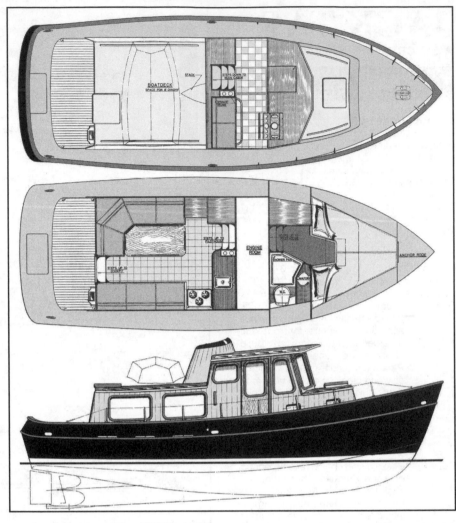

COMPLETE PLANS include FULL SIZE PATTERNS for station (frame) contours, beam cambers, stem contour. Includes Steel Detail Sheets, Table of Offsets, hull material listing, and STEEL BOATBUILDING GUIDE.

Our **UNION JACK** offers a high degree of seagoing ability, comfort, and economy all with the security and safety of steel hull and deck construction. The low resistance semi-displacement hard-chine hull requires only minimal power for exceptional cruising range at operating speeds from 7 to 8-1/2 knots. Full walkaround decks include the security of a raised protective bulwark all around, forming a convenient full width cockpit seat aft. The rudder, propeller, and shaft are all protected from damage by a deep 1/2" thick solid steel skeg. Flaring topsides plus a deep convex forefoot deflect waves and cushion the ride when the going gets tough. The plans give options for either the curved cruiser stern, or the more basic transom stern.

Accommodations aboard the **UNION JACK** are especially complete and well suited to the cruising couple or family. The forward stateroom contains luxurious accommodations for two isolated from the rest of the boat for privacy. The head is complete with lavatory and shower, while the stateroom has plenty of storage including a big hanging locker. The pilothouse features full circle visibility, a seat for two, space for working on charts, and sliding doors port and starboard for quick and easy access so handy when operating with a minimum crew. The main cabin aft features a complete galley with large ice box or refrigerator, a range with oven, sink, and spacious worktop. The L-shaped dinette is raised so that crew members can see out while seated, and also forms a berth for sleeping. The settee to starboard also converts to an upper and lower berth so that total sleeping capacity is five adults. For ship-to-shore use, you can carry an 8' dinghy on the housetop. Emergency steering provisions are accessible through the aft hatch, along with additional storage facilities. A watertight collision bulkhead separates the chain locker from the cabin area forward.

Construction of **UNION JACK** is aimed at the abilities of the amateur builder who has welding skills. Full size patterns provided make the lofting process unnecessary; however, a Table of Offsets is provided for those who wish to loft the lines. Hull lines are such that the sheet steel conforms to the framework without the necessity of heating or forming the plates. Hull, decks, and bulwarks are all welded steel construction, while the cabin superstructure and interior are conventional wood and plywood construction with exterior plywood surfaces sheathed in fiberglass. The plans cover all phases of the project and are supplemented with numerous standard detail sheets as well as an instruction manual. Hull building costs can be estimated beforehand by multiplying the weight of steel hull components by the cost per pound of steel in the local area. Study plans are available.

AVAILABLE FOR THIS DESIGN:
- **Study Plans**
- **Plans & Patterns**

See Price List

YUKON
A 36' CRUISING YACHT

BUILD IN PLYWOOD OR FIBERGLASS

CHARACTERISTICS

Length overall .... 35'-8"
Length waterline .... 31'-3"
Beam .... 13'-9"
Draft .... 3'-3"
Displacement .... 17,400 lbs.
Freeboard forward .... 6'-6"
Freeboard aft .... 4'-6"
Height overall (less mast) .... 15'-1"
Headroom (nominal) .... 6'-3"
Cockpit size (approx.) .... 4'x 11'
Deckhouse size .... 9'-6"x 10'-3"
Flying bridge size .... 10'x 10'
Fuel capacity .... 470 gals.
Water capacity .... 230 gals.
Cruising range (approx.) .... 1100 miles
Sleeping accommodations 6

Hull type: Semi-displacement hard chine hull with efficient speed range to 10 knots. Build in plywood or "one-off" fiberglass. Bottom features deep bulbous forefoot with reverse curve at the chine. Plywood version: double diagonal plywood or solid wood planking on the bottom to a total thickness of 1", sheet plywood, double diagonal wood or plywood, or batten seam carvel planked sides to 3/4". Fiberglass version utilizes fiberglass planking or PVC foam sandwich construction. Balsa core can be used but not detailed in plans.

Power: Single diesel engine recommended of approximately 100 SHP range with suitable reduction gear. Twin motors may be used but not preferred. Gasoline power is optional.

COMPLETE PLANS include FULL SIZE PATTERNS for the stem, breasthook, transom and station (frame) contours. Includes instructions and Bill of Materials. *FIBERGLASS version includes FIBERGLASS MANUAL.*

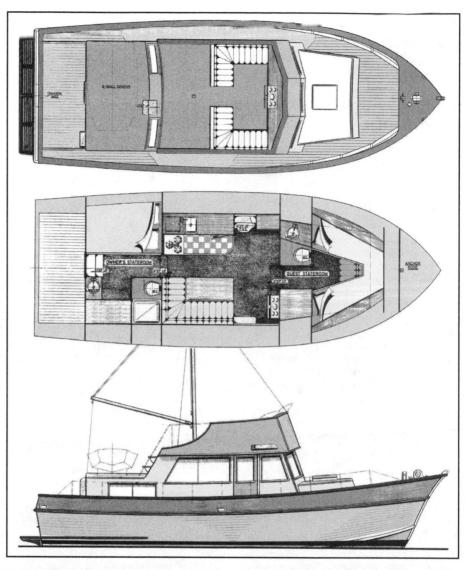

In the **YUKON,** "trawler yacht" means a seaworthy, comfortable, and economical craft. Based on a previous successful hull design, her semi-displacement form achieves speeds up to 10 knots with incredible economy and range in just about any sea condition. Imagine all this with just a single modest sized engine! Twin engines are optional, but handling, responsiveness, and directional stability are everything that the experienced helmsman could ask for when using the standard single engine.

Convenience and safety features include full walkaround decks with cabin access on either side, dual control stations, mast and boom for dinghy launching, a boat deck for a good sized dinghy, and a spacious flying bridge. The wide beam and spacious accommodations make the **YUKON** seem much larger than she is. The tri-cabin layout offers exceptional privacy for three couples. Each stateroom has its own toilet room and commodious storage spaces. The deckhouse is perfect for socializing and entertaining as it also contains the fully equipped galley.

The **YUKON** is the type of design that will always be in style, so plan on having yours for a long while. This is the type of boat that the owner will find endearing, especially so when it is owner-built. Our plans show how the experienced builder can build his own, using either plywood and lumber methods or "one-off" fiberglass materials for the hull structure. Order our STUDY PLANS if you need further information.

AVAILABLE FOR THIS DESIGN:
- **Study Plans**
- **Plans & Patterns**
- **Fiberglass Kit**

See Price List

ODYSSEA

A 36' CRUISING YACHT

BUILD IN PLYWOOD OR FIBERGLASS

CHARACTERISTICS

Length overall	35'-8"
Length waterline	31'-3"
Beam	13'-9"
Draft	3'-3"
Displacement	17,400 lbs.
Freeboard forward	6'-6"
Freeboard aft	3'-3"
Height overall (less mast)	14'-10"
Headroom (minimum)	6'-3'
Cockpit size (approx.)	4'x 11'
Deckhouse size	8'x 10'
Boat deck size	13'x 15'
Aft cockpit size	6'x 12'
Fuel capacity	240 gals. (470 optional)
Water capacity	220 gals.
Cruising range (approx.)	1050 miles
Sleeping accommodations	6

Hull type: Semi-displacement hard chine hull with efficient speed range to 10 knots. Build in plywood or "one-off" fiberglass. Bottom features deep bulbous forefoot with reverse curve at the chine. Plywood version: double diagonal plywood or solid wood planking on the bottom to a total thickness of 1", sheet plywood, double diagonal wood or plywood, or batten seam carvel planked sides to 3/4". Fiberglass version utilizes fiberglass planking or PVC foam sandwich construction. Balsa core can be used but not detailed in plans.

Power: Single diesel engine recommended of approximately 100 SHP range with suitable reduction gear. Twin motors may be used but not preferred. Gasoline power is optional.

COMPLETE PLANS include FULL SIZE PATTERNS for the stem, breasthook, transom and station (frame) contours. Includes instructions, Table of Offsets, and Bill of Materials. *FIBERGLASS version includes FIBERGLASS MANUAL.*

The timeless character of the **ODYSSEA** has made it one of our most popular designs in this size range. Numerous vessels have been built in many parts of the world by sensible skippers who appreciate the features necessary to make a blue water all-weather cruising yacht. Her semi-displacement hull makes sense in this day and age, requiring only a modest single engine to maintain cruising speeds in the 10 knot range with exceptional economy. Directional stability and handling are superb, with many owners commenting on their surprise at finding the **ODYSSEA** more responsive than their previous boats equipped with wasteful twin engines.

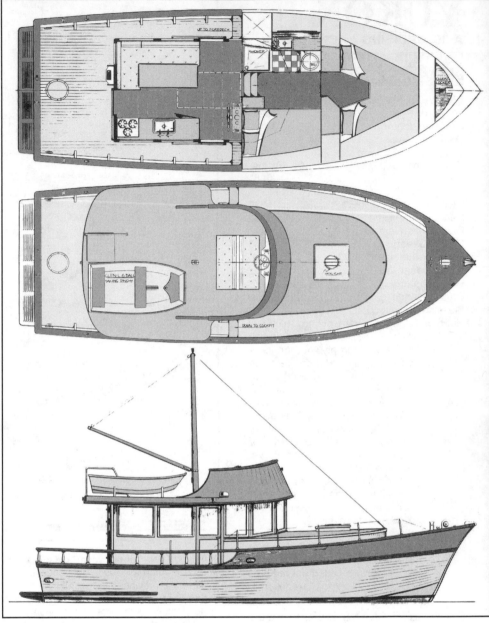

Seaworthy features include high freeboard and generous flare forward, wide walk-around decks with bulwarks and rails, a self-bailing cockpit with transom gate and boarding platform, two control stations plus emergency steering provisions, a spacious boatdeck with mast and boom for easy dinghy handling, and convenient waist level ground tackle handling. Accommodations are provided for three couples in three cabins, and include a roomy toilet room with apartment size enclosed shower. The galley is in the light and airy deckhouse for convenient serving and entertaining.

While a challenging undertaking by the experienced builder, the **ODYSSEA** is a prized possession that will be admired in any port. Construction plans are available for both plywood and "one-off" fiberglass materials, depending on the builder's desires for the basic hull material. Specifications describe the complete construction procedure. Study plans are available for more detailed information.

AVAILABLE FOR THIS DESIGN:
- **Study Plans**
- **Plans & Patterns**
- **Fiberglass Kit**

See Price List

CORINTHIAN

A 42' SEMI-DISPLACEMENT CRUISING YACHT

BUILD IN PLYWOOD OR FIBERGLASS

CHARACTERISTICS

Length overall	42'-0"
Length waterline	38'-4"
Beam	15'-3"
Draft	3'-10"
Displacement	27,900 lbs.
Freeboard forward	7'-6"
Freeboard aft	5'-0"
Height overall (approx. less mast)	17'-2"
Fuel capacity	700 gals.
Fresh water capacity	290 gals.
Deck house size	12'x 10'
Aft cabin size	8 1/2'x 10'
Flying bridge size	10'x 11'
Cockpit size	10'-6"x 3'-6"
Boat deck size	10'-6"x 6'-6"
Headroom	6'-2" - 6'-8"
Sleeping accommodations	6-7

Hull type: Semi-displacement, hard chine hull with bulbous bow and reverse curve at chine forward. Practical speed range of 10 to 12 knots. Triple diagonal cold-molded plywood or solid wood on bottom to 1 1/8" thick, and double diagonal plywood or wood on sides to 3/4" thick, fiberglass or comparably sheathed. Fiberglass hull construction optional.

Power: Single diesel motor of approximately 145 continuous shaft horsepower with suitable reduction gear. Twin motors may be used, but are not as practical or economical, and hence not recommended.

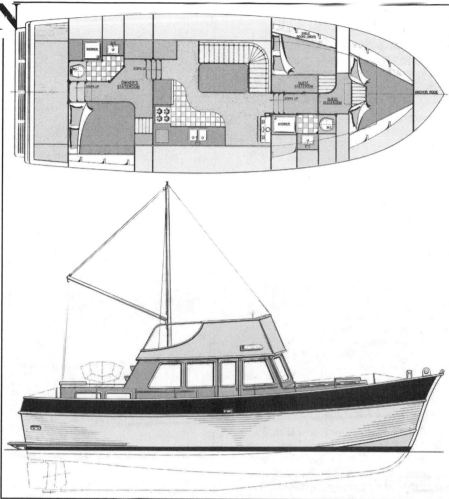

Our **CORINTHIAN** design features surprising accommodations equal to much larger trawler yachts. The beamy hull encompasses three double staterooms, two complete toilet rooms each with their own separate enclosed stall showers with built-in seats, a huge deckhouse complete with apartment-like galley, dual control stations, a spacious flying bridge, a boat deck for carrying a dinghy, lots of storage space, an aft cockpit with boarding gate and transom step, and full width walkaround decks.

The **CORINTHIAN** features economical single diesel power of about 145 SHP for speeds in the 10 to 12 knot range. With 700 gallons of fuel, a cruising range of 1,000+ miles is possible and practical. Full flaring topsides combined with a raised bulwark plus a bulbous forefoot and long skeg make a vessel that handles with ease, and stays dry even when conditions are rough. Standby power can be provided by a generator power take-off in lieu of going to twin engines more vulnerable to damage, not to mention being more expensive.

You can build your **CORINTHIAN** in either wood or fiberglass for the hull, using wood and plywood for the superstructure and decks, surfaced with fiberglass sheathing. Wood construction plans use plywood or solid wood, cold-molded over sturdy sawn frames and husky longitudinals. Or, if you prefer a fiberglass hull, details are provided for the "one-off" materials, either the fiberglass planking method or foam sandwich core with balsa optional.

Either set of plans for the **CORINTHIAN** includes complete instructions plus hull material listings. Although a Table of Offsets is provided, the FULL SIZE PATTERNS available make this tedious process unnecessary. If you desire more information on this economical and practical design, STUDY PLANS are available.

COMPLETE PLANS include FULL SIZE PATTERNS for frames (station contours), stem, transom, and transom knee. Includes builder's specifications, Table of Offsets, and Bill of Materials. *FIBERGLASS version includes FIBERGLASS MANUAL.*

AVAILABLE FOR THIS DESIGN:
- **Study Plans**
- **Plans & Patterns**
- **Fiberglass Kit**
See Price List

ANDANTE

A 38' SEMI-DISPLACEMENT CRUISING YACHT

BUILD IN STEEL

CHARACTERISTICS

Length overall	38'-5"
Length overall (w/transom step)	39'-9"
Length waterline	36'-0"
Beam	14'-4"
Draft	4'-2"
Displacement	29,200 lbs.
Wt. of steel hull components	12,000 lbs.
Freeboard forward	6'-4"
Freeboard aft	3'-9"
Height overall	15'-9"
Fuel capacity	400 gals.
Fresh water capacity	300 gals.
Cruising range (approx. @ 8 knots)	700 miles
Headroom	6'-4" - 6'-6"
Sleeping accommodations	6

Hull type: Semi-displacement, hard chine hull developed for sheet steel construction (10 Ga. sides, 3/16" bottom).

Power: Single diesel motor of 65 to 140 continuous shaft horsepower for 8 to 10 knot speeds respectively, with suitable reduction gear.

COMPLETE PLANS include FULL SIZE PATTERNS for the station forms, beam cambers, and stem contour, including steel detail sheets, STEEL BOATBUILDING GUIDE, and Table of Offsets.

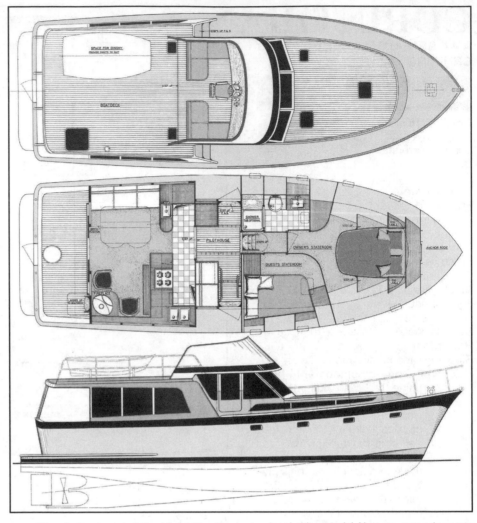

Our **ANDANTE** design proves that you don't have to give up shoreside comforts *or* cruising capabilities *or* economy to have a true luxury live-aboard boat. Just look at the features our designers have incorporated into this modest sized vessel. The list of galley equipment alone reads like a residential brochure, including a large refrigerator, separate freezer adjacent to the pantry/bar, built-in washer and dryer, a trash compactor, double bowled sink, range and oven, microwave oven, and even a dishwasher! The spacious deckhouse includes a long settee which converts to a double berth, a big drop leaf table for dining along with two occasional chairs, plenty of window area, and a fireplace with fuel storage below. For indoor-outdoor living, sliding doors open up onto a large covered cockpit area having direct access through a transom gate to the transom swim step as well as to the ladder leading to the boat deck.

Up forward, **ANDANTE** provides private accommodations for two couples. The Owner's stateroom forward is truly sumptuous, including a full size double berth complete with end tables each side, a huge hanging locker, and direct access to the toilet room. The Guest's stateroom to starboard also features a big double berth, plus dressing table, and a large hanging locker. The toilet room to port includes a separate compartment that can be fitted out as a tub or shower with a built-in

seat. The pilothouse runs full cabin width with massive expanses of windows, and has a large area for charts and navigation equipment, as well as a good sized observation seat. Doors port and starboard give quick access to the side decks as well as to the ladders each side for access to the boatdeck and flying bridge control station.

But what about cruising capabilities, you say? **ANDANTE** has generous tankage by virtue of integral dual tanks each for fuel and water, plus a 215 gallon waste holding tank for a generous cruising range. Power is provided by a modest sized single diesel engine driving a large propeller for efficiency and economy. The underwater gear is protected by a long, deep skeg that supports the rudder as well. A large capacity generator can be used for all electrical requirements, and when connected to a power take-off, provides emergency power in the unlikely event of engine failure. Emergency steering provisions are also available in the event of a steering failure making either one of the helms unusable. For ship-to-shore use, an 8' dinghy can be carried on the boat deck.

For safety at sea, **ANDANTE** features all-welded steel hull construction. A watertight collision bulkhead separates the chain locker from the cabin area, and all windows are glazed in polycarbonate plastic, a virtually

unbreakable material. Numerous opening ports and hatches, together with cabin doors, assure a positive flow of ventilation throughout the living spaces. Decks and cabin sides are also of steel, while cabin tops are plywood covered with teak or fiberglass sheathing overlays. The hard-chine hull features generous flaring topsides and a built-in spray rail forward for a dry, buoyant ride. The bottom lines flatten out aft into a long run made possible by the transom step extension for a good turn of speed with exceptional economy. Directional stability is assured because of the long skeg, however, close quarter handling is much like twin-screw boats since the forefoot is relieved and the rudder area is generous. Construction plans include a Table of Offsets, however, the FULL SIZE PATTERNS provided eliminate the lofting process. The hull lines have been specifically developed for sheet steel material so that plating is simplified.

ARGOSY
A 42' CRUISING YACHT

BUILD IN PLYWOOD OR FIBERGLASS

CHARACTERISTICS

Length overall	42'-0"
Length waterline	38'-4"
Beam	15'-3"
Draft	3'-9"
Displacement	27,868 lbs.
Freeboard forward	7'-6"
Freeboard aft	3'-10"
Height overall (less mast)	16'-9"
Fuel capacity	670 gals.
Fresh water capacity	220 gals.
Cruising range (approx.)	
	1300 statute miles @ 10 knots
Deck house size	13'x 10'-3"
Pilothouse size	11'x 10'
Cockpit size	13'x 6'-6"
Boat deck size	14'x 13'
Headroom	6'-3"to 6'-6"
Cockpit depth	3' nominal
Hull depth	9'-9"
Sleeping accommodations	4-7

Hull type: Semi-displacement, hard chine hull with bulbous bow and reverse curve at chine forward. Practical speed range of 10 to 12 knots. Triple diagonal cold-molded plywood or solid wood on bottom to 1 1/8" thick, and double diagonal plywood or wood on sides to 3/4" thick, fiberglass or comparably sheathed. Topsides feature broad flare fore and aft with bulwark protecting walkaround decks. Fiberglass hull construction optional.

Power: Single diesel motor of approximately 145 continuous shaft horsepower maximum for 10 to 12 knot cruising speed with suitable reduction gear. Twin motors may be used, but are not as practical or economical, and hence not recommended.

COMPLETE PLANS include FULL SIZE PATTERNS for frames (station contours), stem, transom, and transom knee. Includes builder's specifications, Table of Offsets, and Bill of Materials. *FIBERGLASS version includes FIBERGLASS MANUAL.*

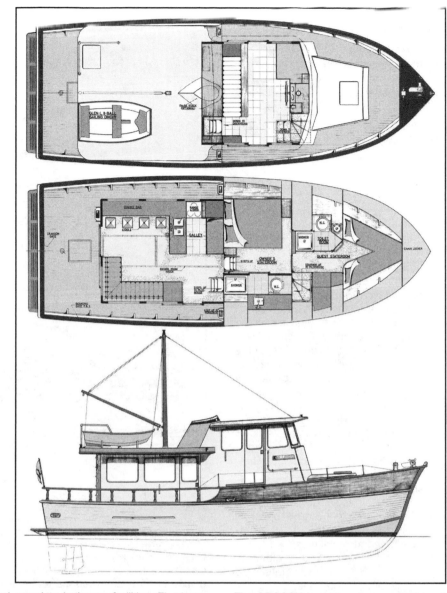

It is difficult to fully describe a vessel the size of the **ARGOSY** in a single page. For this reason, a STUDY PLAN brochure is available. A brief description, though, is possible. As can be seen, the **ARGOSY** is a traditionally styled yacht capable of extensive cruising in comfort. Her range and sea-keeping ability will appeal to the cruising skipper, while her simple, straightforward, but rugged construction will appeal to the amateur builder who wants more for his money.

The design features two cabin total privacy for the skipper and guest parties. Each double cabin features separate access, big berths, and complete bathroom facilities. The huge beam of the **ARGOSY** allows an abundance of locker, shelf, and storage space not found on most yachts this size. The pilothouse is equal to that on a 60 footer and comes with a centerline helm for full circle visibility, access to either side of the vessel, a large flat chart table, a settee-berth, and plenty of storage space for navigation equipment, charts, and foul weather gear.

The spacious deckhouse has large glass areas sheltered by the boat deck overhang. The U-shaped galley is a model of convenience and efficiency. The freezer is located for outside access to ease loading, while the refrigerator is countertop mounted in an area wasted in most designs. The "chef" can mingle with the rest of the crew and yet be out of the traffic lane.

The dining bar allows everyone to view the scenery while eating, and avoids those ordinary convertible dinettes and folding tables found on other boats. A comfortable L-shaped settee coupled with a stereo cabinet makes deckhouse entertaining a pleasure.

The **ARGOSY** is a stay-at-sea vessel in all respects. Aft of the deckhouse is a roomy cockpit with provisions for an emergency tiller. Access forward is by way of wide walkaround decks. A ladder leads to a spacious boat deck complete with a mast and boom for easy dinghy and light cargo handling.

The construction is aimed at the abilities of the accomplished amateur or small custom yard. The **ARGOSY** can be built to any stage for later completion by the owner. The Specifications are of a type used by professional boatbuilders and can form the basis of a builder's contract. Materials used are rugged, but of standard sizes and types.

AVAILABLE FOR THIS DESIGN:
- **Study Plans**
- **Plans & Patterns**
- **Fiberglass Kit**

See Price List

MIRAGE
A 44' AFT CABIN MOTOR YACHT

BUILD IN PLYWOOD OR FIBERGLASS

CHARACTERISTICS

Length overall ....43'-11"
Length waterline ....39'-0"
Beam ....15'-2"
Draft ....3'-0"
Displacement ....30,600 lbs.
Freeboard forward ....6'-1"
Freeboard aft.............................6'-1"
Height overall ....16'-0"
Fuel capacity ....450 gals.
Fresh water capacity............200 gals.
Headroom ....6'-3" - 6'-7"
Hull depth ....9'-1"
Sleeping accommodations...........4-6
Hull type:Hard chine hull with built-in spray deflector/hull stabilizer, convex bulbous deep vee entrance and flaring topsides forward, and modified vee aft with flatter sections for stability and lower power requirements. Hull intended for cold-molded multi-diagonal wood or plywood planking (thickness of 1 1/4" on bottom, 1" on sides), or "one-off" fiberglass hull construction.

Power: Twin inboard in-line engines, either gasoline or diesel powered. Single engine optional, but not detailed. Recommended practical speed range is 15 to 22 knots, although speeds to approximately 28 knots are possible.

COMPLETE PLANS include FULL SIZE PATTERNS for transom and frame contours, stem, breasthook, and beam camber. Includes instructions, illustrated manual, Bill of Materials, and Fastening Schedule. *FIBERGLASS version includes FIBERGLASS MANUAL.*

Why not build your own luxury "love boat"? Our **MIRAGE** is the perfect candidate. This floating home away from home offers accommodations for six in elegance and styling comparable to any production boat in this size range, at a fraction of the cost because you build her yourself.

You and your guests will revel in the luxury and privacy of two staterooms, each with queen sized double berths. Two additional guests can sleep on the huge deckhouse settee. Each of the two heads includes a roomy shower with built-in seat. So you'll be independent of shoreside facilities, there's space for a stackable washer-dryer. Storage space in the form of lockers, drawers, bins,

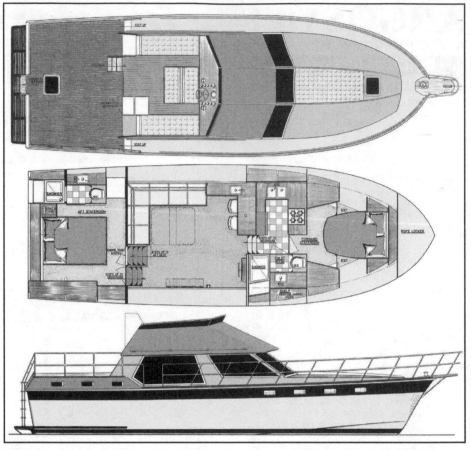

and hampers abounds.

The huge deckhouse appears even more spacious and airy because of generous window areas. A wet bar includes space for a built-in ice maker, and there's a control station to starboard in case of foul weather. The large U- shaped galley, fit for a gourmet chef, is integrated with the deckhouse, yet out of view and out of traffic. There's space for a domestic-sized refrigerator-freezer, range, double sink, and microwave, with abundant shelf, countertop, and storage space remaining.

On deck you'll find wide open spaces suitable for just about any social activity. The huge aft sundeck has a ladder to the transom step for easy, safe boarding of the ship-to-shore dinghy. Wide walkaround decks allow safe access forward where two can soak up the rays on the double sun lounge. A convenient anchor pulpit makes handling ground tackle a snap. In fair weather, why not mix business with pleasure on the roomy flying bridge? With an unobstructed view, this is the ideal place to control the vessel while socializing with guests.

The **MIRAGE** offers more than deluxe accommodations. The bottom design includes a bulbous deep vee entrance to cushion rough seas, but flattens out aft for economy. A built-in full length chine deflector casts the bow wave down and out for a dryer ride while enhancing lift and adding stability. A long skeg aids tracking and improves handling in difficult wind and sea conditions. The beauty of full

flaring topsides also provides reserve buoyancy and helps keep spray off deck.

While construction is aimed at the abilities of the amateur, this vessel is tough whether the hull is built in wood or fiberglass. Husky members reinforce all hull areas and are oversized where they support the engines and tanks. WOOD hulls are planked with plywood strips or wood veneers in double diagonal format with a fiberglass sheathing recommended on the exterior. FIBERGLASS hulls can be built with our proven "one-off" methods using fiberglass planking or PVC foam core sandwich. Fiberglass covered wood and plywood are used for the deck and cabin in all cases.

Power can be provided for the full planing hull by twin in-line diesel or gasoline powered engines. The engine room has space for a high-capacity generator, and access is from the aft cabin or forward passageway step, or through the deckhouse sole for major work. Generous fuel and water capacities assure adequate cruising range. Doesn't this sound like the boat you've been dreaming about? Why not start living that dream now!

AVAILABLE FOR THIS DESIGN:
- **Study Plans**
- **Plans & Patterns**
- **Bronze Fastening Kit**
- **Fiberglass Kit**

See Price List

280

MARAUDER

A 44' SPORT FISHERMAN

BUILD IN PLYWOOD OR FIBERGLASS

CHARACTERISTICS

Length overall .... 43'-9"
Length waterline .... 39'-0"
Beam .... 15'-2"
Draft .... 3'-0"
Displacement .... 30,600 lbs.
Freeboard forward .... 6'-1"
Freeboard aft .... 3'-9"
Hull depth .... 9'-1"
Height overall .... 16'-0"
Fuel capacity .... 450 gals.
Fresh water capacity .... 200 gals.
Headroom .... 6'-3" - 6'-7"
Cockpit size .... 10'x 12'
Sleeping accommodations 4-6

Hull type: Hard chine hull with built-in spray deflector/hull stabilizer, convex bulbous deep vee entrance and flaring topsides forward, and modified vee aft with flatter sections for stability and lower power requirements. Hull intended for cold-molded multi-diagonal wood or plywood planking (thickness of 1 1/4" on bottom, 1" on sides), or "one-off" fiberglass hull construction.

Power: Twin inboard in-line engines, either gasoline or diesel powered. Single engine optional, but not detailed. Recommended practical speed range is 15 to 22 knots, although speeds to approximately 28 knots are possible.

COMPLETE PLANS include **FULL SIZE PATTERNS for transom and frame contours, stem, breasthook, and beam camber. Includes instructions, illustrated manual, Bill of Materials, and Fastening Schedule.** *FIBERGLASS version includes FIBERGLASS MANUAL.*

Our **MARAUDER** can be built in wood or fiberglass using methods especially suited to the amateur builder. Construction is husky, yet light in weight for high speeds with economy. WOOD versions are built with the proven cold molded multi-diagonal format using plywood strips or solid wood veneers over transverse frames and full length longitudinals, all covered with fiberglass outside. FIBERGLASS versions are built using proven one-off methods with fiberglass planking or PVC foam sandwich core construction. With all versions, decks and superstructure are straightforward wood and plywood covered with fiberglass.

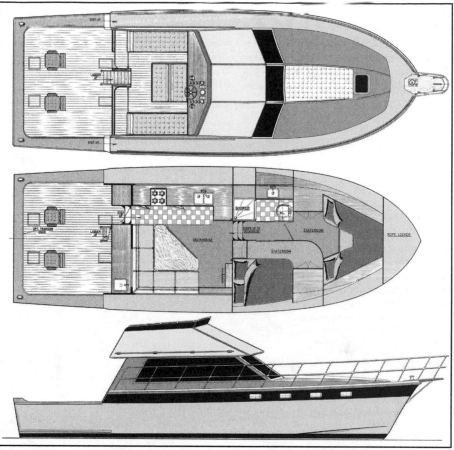

Hull form on the **MARAUDER** is state of the art, carefully designed to fulfill the boat's function. The bottom design includes a bulbous deep-vee entrance for smooth going in headseas, flattening out in a long run aft to reduce fuel consumption at speed, and to provide a stable fishing platform at rest. A long, deep skeg assures instant helm response, while a built-in full length chine deflector knocks water down and away from the deck while adding lift. Topsides are full flaring reverse curves forward for beauty and added reserve buoyancy.

Driven by twin in-line diesel or gasoline powered engines, the full planing hull can also operate efficiently at lower speeds. The midship engine room has space for a good sized generator and ample fuel tankage port and starboard at the center of buoyancy to assure proper hull balance at all tank loadings. Total capacity is more than sufficient for even extended fishing expeditions.

Yet the heart of any sportfishing boat is the cockpit, and this is where the **MARAUDER**

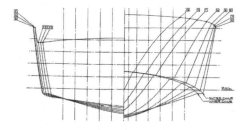

shines. While near to the water, it's still self-bailing and HUGE! There's an optional transom gate shown for landing the big ones, plus a high area for bait prep, gear storage, bait well, fish box, etc. A roomy flying bridge is just up the ladder, while there's a double sun lounge on the foredeck and a handy anchor pulpit at the bow, all readily accessible via wide sidedecks.

Your **MARAUDER** is equally suited to extensive cruising whether with a family or a gang of anglers. Forward, there are twin private double staterooms with hanging lockers, shelves, and plenty of storage space in each. A spacious centrally located toilet room comes complete with separate stall shower and seat. The deckhouse includes a fully equipped galley, monstrous 7' x 7' settee-dining area, and enclosed control station to starboard when weather conditions are foul. Generous window areas all around provide light, ventilation, and a view, even while seated. In summary, the **MARAUDER** offers you the ultimate fishing machine/cruiser equal or superior to anything you could buy.

AVAILABLE FOR THIS DESIGN:
- **Study Plans**
- **Plans & Patterns**
- **Bronze Fastening Kit**
- **Fiberglass Kit**
See Price List

KLONDIKE
A 49' CRUISING YACHT

BUILD IN PLYWOOD OR FIBERGLASS

CHARACTERISTICS

Length overall .... 49'-0"
Length waterline .... 44'-0"
Beam .... 15'-6"
Draft .... 4'-2"
Displacement .... 33,948 lbs.
Freeboard forward .... 7'-11"
Freeboard aft .... 4'-10"
Height overall (approx. no mast) ..... 16'-11"
Fuel capacity .... 840 gals.
Fresh water capacity .... 315 gals.
Cruising range (approx.) 1300 statute miles
@ 12 knots
Deck house size .... 10'-3" x 16'-3"
Pilot house size .... 10'-3" x 12'-6"
Cockpit size .... 6' x 13'-6"
Boat deck size .... 14' x 16'-3"
Headroom .... 6'-3" to 6'-9"
Cockpit depth .... 36" nom.
Hull depth .... 12'-1"
Sleeping accommodations 8-9

Hull type: Semi-displacement, hard chine hull
with practical cruising speed of
12 knots continuous and up to 14
knots intermittently. Bottom design
features deep bulbous forefoot
with reverse curve at chine. Triple
diagonal cold-molded plywood to
1 1/8" net bottom thickness.
Topsides feature broad flare fore
and aft with full bulwark protecting walk around deck areas.
Double diagonal cold-molded plywood to 3/4" net side thickness.
Fiberglass hull construction optional.

Power: Single diesel motor of approximately 150 continuous shaft
horsepower for speeds of 12 knots
or 230 continuous shaft horsepower if speeds up to 14 knots are
desired. Appropriate reduction gear
is required, usually a ratio of 2:1.
Compact twin motors may be used,
but are not as practical or economical, and hence not recommended.
Gasoline powered engines should
not be used for a vessel of this
size and type.

**COMPLETE PLANS include FULL SIZE
PATTERNS for frames (station contours), stem, transom, and transom
knee. Includes builder's specifications,
Table of Offsets, and Bill of Materials.
*FIBERGLASS version includes FIBER-
GLASS MANUAL. Plywood version
includes Boatbuilding with Plywood
book***

The **KLONDIKE** was designed to meet the
demand for a larger version of our successful
ARGOSY model. Here again it is virtually impossible to describe the myriad features of a
vessel this large, so we have prepared a
special STUDY PLAN.

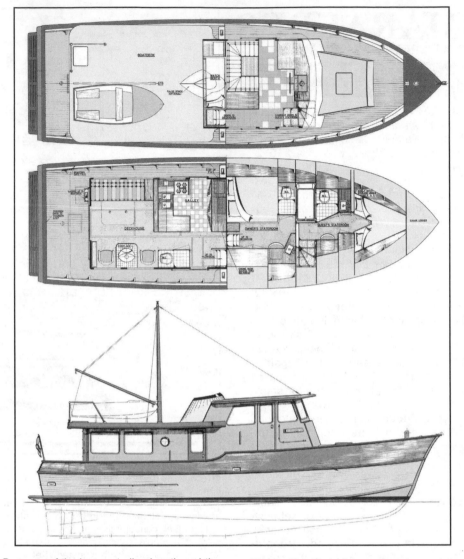

Because of the long waterline length and the
easily driven, semi-displacement hull, the
KLONDIKE can cruise 1300 miles on 840 gallons of fuel at a respectable 12 knots, with
intermittent speeds of 14 knots possible. We
have included the proven bulbous forefoot
with reverse curve at the chine for easy
entrance, plus flaring topsides to keep spray
down and to prevent plunging. The bulwark
goes entirely around the deck at full height to
protect the full walkaround decks.

The accommodations of the **KLONDIKE** are
equal to or better than boats half again her
length. Her pilothouse is huge, the chart table
is large and flat, and there's a watch berth as
well. A pass-through to the galley makes the
pilothouse dinette really practical. There's quick
access to all areas, not to mention full circle
visibility. Sensible skippers will appreciate our
concern for privacy. Both staterooms feature
private access and have private toilet rooms.
In the Owner's Stateroom, the lavatory is conveniently located in the dressing area, separate from the head. As is our custom, no
space has gone to waste. There are lockers,
both large and small, plus drawers and shelf
space just about everywhere. All berths are
more than full size; in fact the Owner's double
is 66" wide. Up to 9 adults can sleep aboard.

The deckhouse is living room size and has
access port, starboard, and aft. The galley
work area is U-shaped for efficiency and the
buffet houses a tremendous refrigeration capacity below. A folding table allows formal
dining in the deckhouse, and there's space
for a marine-type fireplace to take off the
winter's chill. The deckhouse toilet room makes
it convenient for the on-watch as well as for
dockside use of guests and swimmers.

As with our other designs of this type, the
construction is uncomplicated, but sturdy.
Standard material types and sizes are specified. Construction is possible for the accomplished amateur or custom yard to any stage
of completion. The Specifications and Equipment Listing are especially comprehensive
and can be used by the professional yard to
form a contract.

AVAILABLE FOR THIS DESIGN:
- **Study Plans**
- **Plans & Patterns**
- **Fiberglass Kit**
See Price List

ORDERING INFORMATION

4 WAYS TO ORDER

1 ONLINE

www.BoatDesigns.com
24 hours a day, order through our secure online shopping cart using your Mastercard, Visa, Discover, American Express or PayPal. Our web site includes all of our designs with additional color photos and information not included in this catalog.

2 PHONE

Using your credit card
Monday through Friday, 8:30 am to 5:00 pm, Pacific Time. Have your Mastercard, Visa, Discover or American Express ready. You will need the card number and expiration date. Have the name or item number ready to give our friendly sales staff.

Call toll free: 888-700-5007

3 MAIL

Send through the mail

1. Use our printed order form or any plain piece of paper to place your order.

2. Print your name, address and phone number clearly and legibly.

3. List the item numbers (shown on blue price list), item name, price and quantity you are ordering.

4. Call us toll free at 888-700-5007 for shipping costs to add to your order.

5. Enclose payment in the form of money order or check. You can also use a credit card--be sure and include the card number and expiration date.

NOTE: All Canadian orders and orders outside the US must be made payable in US funds, drawn on a US bank.

6. Send your order to the address at the right.

4 FAX

24 hours a day. Transmit your credit card number and expiration date along with your order and shipping address to:

FAX: 562-630-6280

Glen-L Marine
9152 Rosecrans Ave.
Bellflower, CA 90706
USA

Designing for the Home Builder Since 1953

GLEN-L 100% MONEY BACK GUARANTEE

We want you to be fully satisfied with your Glen-L purchase. If you are not happy with your product, return it to us within 30 days of receipt and we will refund your money. We just ask that the product be returned in the condition that it was received and that you pre-pay the return postage. You don't have to give us a reason for the return, but we would sure like to know so we can improve our products and/or service. We value our clients and strive to be the best we can be.

Remember that we are available by phone or email to help you decide which boat to build so you can make the right choice for your needs. Also, we have study plans available for many designs to order prior to purchasing the full plans and patterns.

You CAN Build a Boat Like These Folks did...

FIFE built by Bret Bordner of Bellevue, WA. Bret built this for his mom's 80th Birthday--that's one lucky lady!

AUDEEN built by Bob Aubry of Port St. Lucie, FL

Glen-L 25 Duet built by David Sauer of Sun Prairie, WI. David comments: "The boat sails very well and is so well balanced I can let go of the tiller for 5-10 minutes and it stays on course."

LA PAZ built by Fabio & Paolo Licenza in Italy.

BARRELBACK (background) and SQUIRT (foreground) built by Greg Roy in New Zealand--this is 2 of 4 Glen-L boats in his family!

TORNADO built by Dennis Goodenough of Janesville, WI. This boat was featured in the 1976 issue of Powerboat Magazine.

SEA KNIGHT built by Bob Maskel of Apple Valley, MN. Bob is a regular at the Annual Glen-L Gathering of Boatbuilders in Alabama.

TAHOE 23 built by Butch Barto in Crestview, FL. Butch has won many boat show awards with this beauty...

SQUIRT--another build by Bret Bordner with the help of sons Jack & Ryan. They loved the Squirt so much, they built two!